PERSPECTIVES
IN MARKETING THEORY

Edited by

Jerome B. Kernan
University of Cincinnati

and

Montrose S. Sommers
University of Toronto

*PERSPECTIVES
IN MARKETING THEORY*

New York

APPLETON-CENTURY-CROFTS

Division of Meredith Corporation

648-1

Library of Congress Card Number: 68-19476

PRINTED IN THE UNITED STATES OF AMERICA

E 50500

For Betty and Helen

Preface

As a recognized academic subject, marketing theory is comparatively new. Marketing, as an area of inquiry, has grown rather like Topsy. Accordingly, its students have been preoccupied with keeping abreast of the latest in managerial strategies, institutional change, and so forth. Only in the past few years have scholars made a concerted effort to *explain* marketing; that is, to step aside from considerations of what, where, when, and how, to address the fundamental question of the "why" of marketing.

This movement toward explicating the why of marketing is, of course, the movement which seeks to fashion marketing theory. And if it is not always a harmonious effort (My theory's better than yours!), it is becoming a widespread one. Theory is not the exclusive property of the academic recluse. Practitioners are becoming increasingly aware of its practicality, especially as a guide to the increasingly greater investments required to attain and maintain market position.

Because we believe theory to be the mainspring of marketing knowledge, we have compiled this collection of papers. Our position is a very blunt one: if you want to learn about marketing, theory is where to start. Accordingly, we consider this book suitable fare for *any* marketing course, graduate or undergraduate. With a wide, potentially diverse audience in mind, we have included papers that are comprehensible to the intelligent, yet relatively unsophisticated, student. An effort has been made to include readings that are "meaty" but not so esoteric as to be forbidding.

Two points bear mentioning regarding the readings in this volume. First, we do not pretend that, as a set, this collection is comprehensive. It is not all the marketing theory to be found in the literature. We have made an effort, however, to present the reader with a representative sample of the literature. Second, the papers are reproduced in their original form. We have not "doctored" them in order to make them consistent or to make them conform to any particular pattern. Thus, the reader should not be surprised to find two or more authors in dispute over some theoretical notion. In fact, this is more the rule than the exception. If this bothers the reader, we can suggest only that such is the current state of development in marketing theory. Moreover, such diverse perspectives are sound pedagogically; they force the student to assess each position and take one of his own.

We have arranged the readings into five convenient (if not altogether mutually exclusive) parts. Part I, MARKETING THEORY AND MARKETING SCIENCE, contains six readings, chronologically ordered, which serve to introduce the student to marketing as a formal body of knowledge and to assess its current level of development. The critical issue addressed in this part is not whether marketing is a science, but rather what constitutes a "science." As the papers make clear, this issue remains unresolved. The student must take his own position on this point.

In Part II, GENERAL MARKETING THEORY, there are three papers which deal with marketing theory at a global (macroscopic) level. As these readings indicate, there are essentially two approaches to general marketing theory: that of the functionalists, whose leading exponent was the late Wroe Alderson, and that of the institutionalists, best reflected in the writings of Professor Revzan. Whether these two approaches are complementary or at odds is a question the student should resolve.

Part III, CONSUMER THEORY, comprises four papers that deal with a topic utterly central to marketing theory: how and why consumers act. From among the legion of papers available on this subject we have included those that, in our judgment, present useful and relatively comprehensive statements regarding consumer behavior. That there are different approaches to this aspect of marketing theory is clearly evidenced by the four papers.

Part IV, MARKETING THEORY AND MARKETING MANAGEMENT, is the largest part of the book. This proportioning was quite deliberate on our part. Our motive is simple: we wish to convince the student by illustrations that theory is indeed "practical." Accordingly, papers in this part are grouped under five subheadings, corresponding to well-accepted areas of managerial endeavor. The first of these, "Managerial Processes," includes five papers. They deal with major managerial functions such as planning, organizing, and controlling. Also, there is a paper dealing with the role of information in decision making (Green's), as well as a philosophical statement construing marketing theory as marketing management (Churchman's). Collectively, the papers in this section afford an essential rationale for the management of marketing effort.

The remaining four sections in Part IV are devoted to the familiar decision areas of marketing management. There are two papers each dealing with product, price, distribution, and promotion decisions. These are not "how to" sections. Rather, the readings should serve to afford the student a *foundation* upon which to build decision-making acumen.

Part V. MODEL BUILDING AND MARKETING THEORY, consists of four papers whose collective purpose is to encourage students to focus on how marketing theory can be improved and extended. The papers in this part are arranged in a natural progression, beginning with an overview of why marketing theorists have turned to models (Lipson's), through a discussion of models, per se (Lazer's and Kuehn's), to a consideration of what ultimate use to make of them (Halbert's).

A book such as this is not possible without the help and consideration of many people. We are pleased to acknowledge the courtesies extended us by the authors whose papers appear here. Their publishers, by granting reprint permissions, literally make this book possible. We have benefited greatly from the encouragement given us by Professor James U. McNeal of Texas A & M University. For cheerfully handling the essential typing and clerical chores we wish to thank Nancy Heleman, Trudy Jones, Sheryl Kohutek, Karen McAnulty, and Karen Smith. Considering all this support, this volume should contain no errors. If it does, Kernan blames Sommers and Sommers blames Kernan.

J.B.K.
M.S.S.

Contributors

WROE ALDERSON
University of Pennsylvania

ROBERT BARTELS
The Ohio State University

WILLIAM J. BAUMOL
Princeton University

LOUIS P. BUCKLIN
University of California, Berkeley

ROBERT D. BUZZELL
Harvard University

C. WEST CHURCHMAN
University of California, Berkeley

NORMAN R. COLLINS
University of California, Berkeley

JOHN DOUGLAS
University of Kentucky

PAUL E. GREEN
University of Pennsylvania

MICHAEL H. HALBERT
Marketing Science Institute

EDWARD R. HAWKINS
University of California, Berkeley

JOHN A. HOWARD
Columbia University

KENNETH D. HUTCHINSON
Boston University

JEROME B. KERNAN
University of Cincinnati

PHILIP KOTLER
Northwestern University

ALFRED A. KUEHN
Carnegie-Mellon University

WILLIAM LAZER
Michigan State University

HAROLD J. LEAVITT
Stanford University

PRESTON P. LE BRETON
University of Washington

SIDNEY J. LEVY
Northwestern University

HARRY A. LIPSON
University of Alabama

MILES W. MARTIN
University of Pennsylvania

GORDON E. MIRACLE
Michigan State University

FRANCESCO M. NICOSIA
University of California, Berkeley

LEE E. PRESTON
University of California, Berkeley

DAVID A. REVZAN
University of California, Berkeley

WILBUR SCHRAMM
Stanford University

JAGDISH N. SHETH
Columbia University

MONTROSE S. SOMMERS
University of Toronto

WELDON J. TAYLOR
Brigham Young University

W. T. TUCKER
The University of Texas

Contents

Preface   vii

Contributors   xi

**I.   MARKETING THEORY AND MARKETING
           SCIENCE**   1

  1. Can Marketing Be a Science?   *Robert Bartels*   3
  2. Marketing As a Science: An Appraisal   17
      Kenneth D. Hutchinson
  3. On the Role of Marketing Theory   27
      W. J. Baumol
  4. Is Marketing a Science?   *Robert D. Buzzell*   36
  5. "Is Marketing a Science?" Revisited   49
      Weldon J. Taylor
  6. Marketing Theory and Marketing Science   58
      Michael H. Halbert

II. GENERAL MARKETING THEORY   67

  7. The Analytic Framework for Marketing   69
      Wroe Alderson
  8. Marketing and Alderson's Functionalism   83
      F. M. Nicosia
  9. The Holistic-Institutional Approach to Marketing   97
      David A. Revzan

III. CONSUMER THEORY   137

  10. Toward a Model of Consumer Decision Making   139
       Francesco M. Nicosia
  11. Summary of the Theory of Buyer Behavior   154
       John A. Howard and Jagdish N. Sheth
  12. Behavioral Models for Analyzing Buyers   174
       Philip Kotler
  13. A Time for Propositions   *W. T. Tucker*   191

IV. **MARKETING THEORY AND MARKETING MANAGEMENT**

A. Managerial Processes

14. Marketing Theory as Marketing Management   205
C. West Churchman

15. Development of a Framework for a Theory of   214
Marketing Planning   *Preston P. LeBreton*

16. Uncertainty, Information, and Marketing Decisions   227
Paul E. Green

17. A Comparison of Management Theory Y With   251
the Marketing Concept   *John Douglas*

18. The Analysis of Market Efficiency   265
Lee E. Preston and Norman R. Collins

B. Product Decisions

19. Symbolism and Life Style   *Sidney J. Levy*   283

20. Product Characteristics and Marketing Strategy   293
Gordon E. Miracle

C. Price Decisions

21. Price Policies and Theory   *Edward R. Hawkins*   305

22. A Note on Some Experimental Findings About the   319
Meanings of Price   *Harold J. Leavitt*

D. Distribution Decisions

23. Postponement, Speculation and the Structure of   327
Distribution Channels   *Louis P. Bucklin*

24. Toward a Formal Theory of Transactions and   340
Transvections   *Wroe Alderson and
Miles W. Martin*

E. Promotion Decisions

25. How Communication Works   *Wilbur Schramm*   361

26. Meaning, Value, and the Theory of Promotion   386
Jerome B. Kernan and Montrose S. Sommers

V.   MODEL BUILDING AND MARKETING THEORY   409

27. Formal Reasoning and Marketing Strategy   411
Harry A. Lipson

28. The Role of Models in Marketing   *William Lazer*   420

29. Mathematical Models and Marketing Theory   429
Alfred A. Kuehn

30. The Requirements for Theory in Marketing   441
Michael H. Halbert

I

MARKETING THEORY
AND MARKETING SCIENCE

1

Can Marketing Be a Science?

ROBERT BARTELS

Scattered interests in marketing theory have in recent years become sufficiently coherent that professional discussions and published writings have dealt with the subject. There yet prevail, however, diverse opinions concerning not only the content of such a theory but also concerning the meaning of the terms "theory" and "science" as they pertain to marketing. The language of science and philosophy has varied connotations even to seasoned students, and, as a consequence, it is not uncommon to find informed thinkers expressing opposing views as to the prospects of science or theory in marketing. It is more common, in fact, to find that many students of marketing have not formulated an opinion concerning the matter.

That marketing is not more generally characterized as a science is the result of two factors. First, the objectives of science are not always achieved in marketing study. Second, while the goal of marketing inquiry has usually been to study marketing phenomena scientifically, it has not always been the intent of marketing men to evolve a science of marketing. At the present time, therefore, many students of marketing are considering the methodology of science and the body of marketing knowledge for a resolution of questions concerning their relationship. It is to the consideration of some of the problems involved in the development of marketing science and theory that this article is devoted.

The Objectives of Science in Marketing

The presumption that marketing is, or ever could become, a science is one which is questioned by some critics, partly on the grounds of doubts con-

Reprinted with permission from the *Journal of Marketing,* national quarterly publication of the American Marketing Association, Vol. 15 (January, 1951), pp. 319-328.

cerning the scientific status of the social studies in general and partly on the grounds that marketing is too narrow a field of investigation to be regarded as a science. This criticism opens for reconsideration an old question of whether the development of science is contingent primarily upon the nature of the subject studied, upon the method of analysis employed, or upon the definitive nature of the generalizations derived.

It is generally recognized that the object of scientific inquiry is the derivation of laws or principles[1] which may serve as a basis for prediction, decision, and action. Prediction in any field of study, however, is possible only because of and to the extent of the uniformity of the phenomena studied. Because the conditions and events of physical nature are found to have a relatively high degree of uniformity, predictions concerning them are regarded as comparatively reliable, and the methods by which such phenomena have been studied have become the standard for scientific research. On the other hand, social phenomena, of which marketing activities are a part, are regarded as not possessing such a high degree of uniformity and, therefore, when studied by the so-called "objective" methods of the natural sciences, as not providing the highly reliable generalizations with which science has been identified. This claim, of course, is founded largely upon the belief that human behavior cannot be *predicted* because people independently "determine" their actions through reason and impulse. While this is true to some extent in individual cases, the stability of the behavior of *groups* and the tendency of individuals to conform to the group pattern constitute a uniformity sufficient for making valid and reliable predictions.

The laws of science upon which prediction is based are generally recognized to be of two types, distinguished by the methods by which they are derived: namely, empirical[2] laws and theoretical[3] laws. The former

---

[1] According to *Webster's Unabridged Dictionary,* law and principle are defined as follows:

Law—"A statement of an order or relation of phenomena which, so far as known, is invariable under the given conditions; as, the *law* of falling bodies; a *law* of heredity."

Principle—"A fundamental truth; a comprehensive law or doctrine, from which others are derived, or on which others are founded; a general truth; an elementary proposition or fundamental assumption; a maxim; an axiom; a postulate. . . . A settled rule of action; a governing law of conduct, ... Principle emphasizes the idea of fundamental truth or general application; Rule, that of more specific direction or regulation."

[2] *Empirical*—"Depending on experience or observation alone, without due regard to science or theory. . . . Pertaining to, or founded upon, experiment or experience."

Empirical law—"A generalization from experience; specif., a law arrived at by observation of cases."

[3] *Theoretical*—"Pertaining to theory; depending on, or confined to, theory or speculation; speculative; terminating in theory or speculation."

have been commonly associated with "pure" science and with the application of the scientific method as it is used in the natural sciences. Theoretical laws, on the other hand, have been the more closely associated with the social sciences.

Empirical laws are generalizations derived from an accumulated mass of evidence. Synthetic universal propositions—which are often stated in a mathematical expression or in a simple, positivistic form of law—when stated in a high order of generalization, they are regarded as voidable by a single negative instance.[4] Such generalizations are supposed to possess "objective validity" and to be of the highest order of generality. Being the outgrowth of the logic of scientific procedure, they are regarded as "strict," physical, or causal laws.

Theoretical laws, on the other hand, are in contrast to empirical laws in several respects. In the first place, they are essentially interpretations based upon presupposed notions and not upon tangible, measurable evidence. Theoretical laws are rules of inference on the basis of which probability and prediction are *warranted*. In other words, the theoretical scheme of interpretation warrants or implies a relationship among phenomena which experience may not always confirm but which, if the theory is well framed, will generally be found to be plausible. The existence of a negative or contrary instance does not nullify or invalidate a theoretical law, for the law in the first place was not predicated upon any supposedly completely uniform aspect of the phenomena. Such a law is frequently taken as a standard of behavior or as a norm, rather than as an absolute explanation of behavior.

Because both types of laws serve for predicting, it is conceivable that a science could consist of either or both types. That is generally the case. The natural sciences have been mainly empirical, but in recent years they have come to embrace also a number of theoretical laws.[5] Contrariwise,

---

[4] Examples of prominent empirical laws of natural science are such as the following:

Law of Gravitation: That the force of gravitation is proportional to the product of the masses of two bodies, and inversely proportional to the square of the distance between them.

Law of Partial Pressures: That in a mixture of gases each gas exerts the same pressure that it would exert if it alone occupied the space.

Law of Superposition: (Geology) That where there has been no subsequent disturbance, sedimentary strata were deposited in ascending order, younger beds successively overlying older beds.

Snell's Law: (Optics) That the ratio of the sines of the angles of incidence and refraction is constant for all incidences in any given pair of media for waves of a definite frequency.

[5] An example of a theoretical law in physics is the proposition presented by Einstein that mass times the square of the velocity of light equals energy. This has been confirmed, but the generalization is described as theoretical because the explanation of the origin of heat in the sun is theoretical—speculative.

generalizations[6] in the social sciences have been typically theoretical, although with added evidence and refined methods generalizations of a more empirical nature are being made. By reason of the nature of generalizations which may be drawn concerning it, therefore, marketing is no less qualified for recognition as a science than are other areas of social study. Granting, moreover, that theoretical as well as empirical laws constitute a science, social sciences have as much claim to the name as have the physical sciences.

A science is judged, however, not only by the nature of its generalizations but by its subject matter and by the methods of investigation which it employs. Involving as marketing does many subjective influences determining overt behavior, both its material and its methods are at times questioned. Some critics believe that scientific inquiry must be confined to objective facts and that subjective factors do not yield objective knowledge. Another group holds an opposite viewpoint, contending that subjective factors can be reduced to scientific statement in law. The latter viewpoint, obviously, is the only one tenable if progress toward social science is expected, and it is in accord with a statement by Aristotle to the effect that every science assumes its subject matter and does not give account of it. Subjective factors as well as physical phenomena may be the subject of science.

It is a reasonable presumption, nevertheless, to expect the methods

---

[6] Although throughout this article the term "law" is applied to social generalizations in the social sciences rather than "principle" or "rule," this is done mainly to preserve consistency of the concept of generalization that is being developed. In marketing, so-called "theoretical laws" are commonly regarded as principles and rules of action, although the term law is in a few instances applied. Such marketing generalizations as the following may be cited:

That as income increases the percentage of income spent for food decreases; for rent, fuel, and light remains the same; for clothing remains the same; and for sundries increases (Engel's Law).

"That two cities attract retail trade from an intermediate city or town in the vicinity of the breaking point (the 50 per cent point), approximately in direct proportion to the populations of the two cities and in inverse proportion to the square of the distance from these two cities to the intermediate town" (Reilly's Law of Retail Gravitation).

Obviously, although these may be sound "laws" in that they generalize phenomena usefully, they are not like physical laws in that a single negative or contrary instance would destroy the reliability and validity of the generalization, as would be the case for laws such as those cited in Footnote 4.

Still other examples of types of marketing generalizations may be cited, the first illustrating a "principle" and the other two "rules of action":

That door-to-door selling by manufacturers' salesmen is most likely to be successful when either (1) the product is of high unit-value or (2) a variety of products is offered to the customer.

That the most valuable space in a retail store should be allocated to those departments with the highest sales possibilities.

That layout must combine utility with eye appeal.

of a science to be adequate for dealing with its subject matter. Some of the methods of the physical sciences have not proved equally useful in the social sciences, but the latter are not the less scientific because of that. The effort of social scientists to plumb the depths of subjectivity and to understand other aspects of social behavior has led to the development of new methods, which, combined with older techniques adapted to the new needs, are gradually placing the study of marketing on a more scientific basis.

The Meaning of "Science"

The object of inquiry into the meaning of "science" is to test the possible breadth of marketing thought, thereby to invalidate the belief that marketing is solely a technique, or to sustain the content that it has broad scientific and philosophic characteristics. Whatever it may be is not readily apparent in the mere evidence of marketing facts. Neither is it manifest in the common usage of scientific terms, for their several possible definitions are equivocal.

Something of the breadth of marketing thought can be determined by measuring marketing against such concepts as science, discipline, philosophy, and art, to ascertain whether marketing corresponds to any one or a combination of these classifications. According to definitions given in *Webster's Unabridged Dictionary,*

Science is "any branch or department of systematized knowledge considered as a distinct field of investigation or object of study, . . . A branch of study which is concerned with observation and classification of facts, especially with the establishment of verifiable general laws, chiefly by induction and hypotheses; . . . Specifically, accumulated and accepted knowledge which has been systematized and formulated with reference to the discovery of general truths or the operation of general laws; knowledge classified and made available in work, life, or the search for truth;

Philosophy is "the science which investigates the most general facts and principles of reality and of human nature and conduct; . . . The body of principles or general conceptions underlying a given branch of learning, or major discipline, a religious system, a human activity, or the like, and the application of it; as, the *philosophy* of history, Christianity, or of business";

A *Discipline* is "that which is taught to pupils: teachings; learnings; doctrine. . . . A subject that is taught; a branch of knowledge; also, a course of study";

Art is "a branch of learning; a science; especially, a science such as grammar, logic, or mathematics, serving chiefly as a discipline or as an instrument of knowledge; . . . . The general principles of any branch of learning or of any developed craft; a system of rules or of organized modes of operation serving to facilitate the performance of certain actions; . . . . Systematic application of knowledge or skill in effecting a desired result."

In the light of these definitions, marketing may be a science, discipline, or art. It is rarely regarded as a philosophy because it is not of the order of generality of philosophy; nevertheless, the expression "a philosophy of marketing" is sometimes heard, signifying usually a theory colored by a particular viewpoint.

To regard marketing as an art emphasizes the *doing* rather than the *knowing*. The art of marketing is the technical, professional, applicative aspect of the subject. Of the several concepts, it is the narrowest and least suggestive of the scientific character of marketing.

The conception of marketing as a discipline emphasizes the academic side of the subject. A discipline embraces less than a science, for science is the generic name for a number of disciplines. Moreover, as a discipline, marketing like any "subject that is taught," may be taught in a variety of ways with widely differing emphasis and integration.

As a science, marketing consists of the body of knowledge of distribution, with its methodological concomitants of theories, laws, principles, and concepts.

If marketing is to be so regarded as a science, the study of it both in form and content must correspond to the standards of science in the social realm. First, the objective of observation and investigation must be the establishment of *general* laws or *broad* principles, not merely settled rules of action or operating procedures. Second, prediction made possible through the development of laws should be of social import and not merely institutional application. Third, theory and hypotheses employed in prediction and in the drawing of further inferences should be useful for the extension of knowledge as well as for guiding administrative means toward profitable ends. Fourth, abstractions as well as concrete facts should be used in the explanation of marketing phenomena.

The fact that marketing is held not yet to have attained the status of a science raises a question of whether this is attributable to the relative newness of the study or to inherent characteristics of the subject matter. The progress which has been made in understanding marketing gives hope that continued scientific research would ultimately result in the development of a science. Such confidence is confirmed by the statement made by Karl Pearson that the unity of all science lies not in its materials but in its methods. Nevertheless, some characteristics of marketing need further consideration relative to this point.

Unlike other areas of the social sciences, marketing is in some respects not the "distinct field of investigation" which is by definition requisite for a science. It is true that the technical aspects of marketing are now a distinct field of study and application, but the scope of such technical knowledge is more characteristic of a trade or profession than of a science. On the other hand, when the broader aspects of marketing are considered, from which general principles, theory, and perhaps laws may be formulated, it is seen that marketing is in reality a combination of parts of a number of other disciplines and sciences. Marketing is particularly a phase of economic activity; its motives and means being economic, it is an integral part of the general science of economics. Marketing knowledge, however, is also derived from psychology, sociology, accounting, law, production, engineering, and political science, in addition to being drawn from experience in the institutional and functional aspects of marketing. The scientific student or practitioner of marketing on a broad scale must know the fundamental principles of all of those areas of thought. The principles or laws of marketing must express the interrelationships of those areas.

Because of this amorphous nature of marketing, some students believe that the only scientific aspects of marketing are those broad aspects which, they claim, are indistinguishable from economics. Perhaps the same may also be said of monetary and labor theory and of other branches of economics as well. If that were the case, laws and principles of marketing would be essentially and only laws of economics. Notwithstanding this limiting view, when proper recognition is given to the prominent economic function performed in distribution and to the unique position, among the various branches of economic theory, which marketing holds in relation to other social disciplines, marketing may reasonably be regarded at least as a child in the family of social sciences.

This regard, however, is warranted only insofar as the knowledge of marketing becomes systematized and formulated with reference to the discovery of general truths of the operation of general laws. Like all sciences, its raison d'etre should be not for the sake of knowledge alone, but that through the interrelated principles, laws, and theories of the system prediction, direction, and control of social import will be made possible.

Science in Marketing Literature

If it is admitted that the subject of marketing lends itself to scientific statement, one may reasonably inquire to what extent the marketing literature now presents the subject as a science. It will be remembered that the formal study of marketing is only about fifty years old and that during the past half century all that is known objectively as marketing has been evolved—on the one hand, from extensive observation of marketing phenomena, and on the other hand, from a small number of economic deductions concerning trade activity. The literature published during this period has expanded from a handful of books in two or three fields to a library of volumes in the institutional, functional, and policy aspects of marketing.

In any field of scientific study, it is obviously impossible for the entire body of scientific knowledge to be presented in any one volume or even in a set of volumes. Many of the newest scientific contributions are not quickly reduced to writing, and the rate of current reporting is so swift that many studies could at best be but briefly mentioned. Some areas of investigation are the subject of specialized literature. On the other hand, the fullest, and at the same time the most concise, statements of a science are usually found in the general texts in the subject. If they are well written, such works serve not only to acquaint the reader with the scope and general structure of the subject, but they present the essential laws and principles of the subject. Consequently, while no one book and perhaps no one part of the total literature may present an entire science, or even all of the important individual contributions, in the general works on the subject one may expect to find the best evidence of the scientific status of the study.

So in the field of marketing one may expect to find in the general writings the best evidence of the over-all development of the subject as a science, notwithstanding the fact that many important individual contributions are not represented therein. Rarely is the work of any single individual indispensable to the whole field of a science. On the other hand, if the systematized body of knowledge has not been brought together in a general statement, that in itself is symptomatic of the stage of development of the study.

Throughout the marketing literature one may observe evidences both of the scientific methodology which has characterized the study and of the generalizations formulated through the study. There are numerous evidences of observation, definition of terms, classification of data, experimentation, and scientific analysis, all of which are essential to the development of science.

The marketing literature indicates that there has been very wide observation in the study of the subject. In fact, some of the earliest studies of marketing were based upon observation, for pioneer teachers in the field were insufficiently acquainted with distributive activities without resort to first-hand observation to speak or write intelligently of it. They actually accompanied commodities to the market in order to observe what became of them and how and by whom they were handled. They talked with merchants and observed the behavior of consumers as well as of distributors. Much-repeated practices became regarded as behavior patterns, and from such patterns of activity generalizations were made. So prevalent, in fact, has been research by observation in marketing studies that one might almost think that investigators looked for empirical laws of market behavior.

Along with observation, research in marketing has also been characterized by conscious definition of terms and concepts. Choice of the term "marketing," identification and definition of functions, institutions, channels, and the like have been methodological problems to which much attention has been given by writers, both individually and collectively.

Classification of data, too, has been an important methodological function in the study of marketing. Among the numerous phenomena classified have been the following: types of consumers, markets, wholesale and retail establishments, marketing functions, buying motives, commodities and services, channels of distribution, policies, and practices. If the sorting of experiences by types and classes is an essential step in the formulation of scientific laws, the study of marketing has been properly distinguished by this activity.

Experimentation, as a method of scientific discovery, has also characterized the study of marketing, although the social nature of the subject does not lend itself to experimentation as a means of verifying definitively assumed hypotheses or of demonstrating with great exactitude the terms of marketing law. Social behavior does not lend itself well to experimentation, because the numerous variables cannot be closely controlled and social situations cannot be duplicated. Nevertheless, experimentation has had increasing application in some phases of marketing research.

There is little reason to doubt, therefore, that scientific methods have been employed in the formal and informal study of marketing. On the other hand, the employment of such methods does not necessarily evolve a science, although it may yield a body of operating principles. Judged from the character of generalizations produced—their narrowness, their simplicity of statement, and their variability—marketing study can scarcely be said to have attained scientific status, at least as it is shown in the more general works in the field.

One criticism which may be made of marketing thought expressed in the general writings is that it is more descriptive than theoretical or even analytical. That is inevitable in the early stage of scientific investigation, for many facts and repeated narratives are necessary for establishing the uniformity of market behavior. Facts are always important, but theories or theoretical laws (explanations) are indispensable to the development of science. Inductive, experimental study may yield satisfying generalizations, but without theoretical speculation there is no answer to the question of science "Why?" nor is there a basis for prediction.

Theorizing has not been entirely absent from the marketing writings, but it has been subordinated to descriptive material. Undoubtedly this relative emphasis on facts betrays a lingering preoccupation among marketing writers with technical aspects of marketing and a neglect by them of its broader reaches. On the other hand, merely to aggregate unrelated theories does not advance a science, for the essence of science is system, order, and coherence in the body of knowledge.

The objective, and the inevitable result, of much of the past inquiry into marketing has been the development of rules of action rather than broad generalizations. The bulk of the marketing literature is of a technical nature dealing with retailing, wholesaling, advertising, credit, marketing research, and the like. Examination of books in any such field reveals traditional frameworks overlaid with a descriptive veneer designed to tell "how it is done and how it can be done better." Craftsmen rather than general marketing theorists are trained with such works. Functions and institutions are sometimes introduced in their socio-economic position, but the treatment of that aspect of the subject is usually brief.

General texts do not go so far in stating rules of action; they concern themselves usually with the statement of "principles." The statement of marketing principles has long been an objective of basic marketing inquiry. When general works on marketing were in their early years of development about 1920, the term "principles" found its way into text titles and it has prominently remained there ever since. In recent years, even those who have professed to write of marketing principles have been reappraising the concept, for it is recognized that what have passed for principles have often been but rules of action. In very few instances, however, were the so-called principles set forth even as boldly as the few in economics texts have been. Consequently, even this degree of scientific generalization has been more often implied than expressed.

There is little wonder that the concept of laws in marketing should be practically non-existent. It is true that the dignity of "law" has been associated with a few generalizations, such as those concerning retail trade gravitation, but they only serve to illustrate the fact that marketing scientists' concept of law relates it to the fact-gathering type of research which in the physical sciences has led to the statement of empirical laws. By reason of the nature of marketing phenomena, accumulated evidence can yield at best only very tentative generalizations. Inasmuch as real theorizing has been generally neglected by students of marketing, generalizations worthy of recognition as marketing laws are extremely rare in either the general or specialized marketing literature.

A Science of Marketing

Interest in the development of a broader science of marketing is in part the result of the appearance of marketing problems which the present body of knowledge is incapable of solving. The present body of knowledge and known principles have served useful purposes and will continue to do so. But their usefulness has been primarily institutional, for the solution of private problems. Such problems continue to exist and require perhaps even better information than has theretofore been available. However, with the elevation of marketing practice above a level of strictly competitive interests, and with the emergence of social interests in marketing beyond its technical application, old principles no longer furnish the guidance needed in new situations. Consequently, for prediction and guidance on a broader scale, perhaps even in public policy determination, laws of such scope and integration are called for as would comprise a science of marketing.

What such a body of information would be like is not easy to foretell. Yet by analogy to existing sciences and by analysis of the subject matter of marketing itself, something of its constitution may be known. Possessing the characteristics of a science, it would be a systematized body of knowledge, broad and general in scope yet adaptable to the solution of varied problems. Possessing, however, as it does, the unique characteristics of a field overlapping the areas of other social sciences, a science of marketing would necessarily appropriate some of their pertinent laws. Arising out of empirical evidence as well as proceeding from theoretical assumptions, it would provide generalizations of both inductive and deductive origin and of both general and technical scope. The laws of marketing would be mainly theoretical rather than empirical, because of the difficulty of duplicating social conditions experimentally or of reaching such conclusions that no negative instance would violate without destroying the usefulness of the law.

Every science has what may be regarded as its core and its periphery —in other words, the essential subject matter of its inquiry and the scope of its extension in different but related directions. For example:

Physics is the science of the world of inanimate matter, especially motion; it comprises the related sciences of mechanics, heat, electricity, light and sound, radiation, and atomic structure;.

Chemistry is the science of the composition of substances and the transformations which they undergo; it comprises the fields of physical, organic, inorganic, analytical, biological, physiological, electro, pharmaceutical, and industrial chemistry;

Geology is the science of the earth; it comprises the sciences and disciplines of paleontology, petrology, physiography, and stratigraphy, as well as historical, physical, economic, glacial, structural, and dynamic geology;

Sociology is the science of the origin and evolution of society, or of the forms, institutions, and functions of human groups;

Economics is the science that investigates conditions and laws affecting the production, distribution, and consumption of wealth, or the material means of satisfying human desires.

Technically, marketing bears to economics a relation similar to that of mechanics to physics. Marketing is that field of study which investigates the conditions and laws affecting the distribution[7] of commodities and services. It is the institutionalized function of providing consumers with goods for their use. Its core or focal point lies in the area of its institutional framework and of its more or less technical aspects, including types of institutions, comparative competitive advantages, costs, pricing practices, functions, policies, channels, and the like. Its perimeter, however, embraces portions of such related sciences and disciplines as the following:

Economics: price theory, institutional influences, income distribution, theories of scale of operation, monopoly, competition, monetary factors, finance facilities;

Psychology: rationale of choice in purchasing, individual behavior, prejudices, motives, incentives, utility, and satisfaction;

Sociology: group behavior, expenditure patterns and habits, population and its shifts, group mores;

Law: legislative history, theory, and philosophy, fairness, competition, legal procedure;

Political science: forms of government as means to ends, administrative agencies, government intervention, taxation;

Production and engineering: materials, processes, and types of production;

Accounting: theories and techniques of accounting.

The science of marketing, accordingly, may comprise any number of theories,[8] each treating the explanation of some aspect of the science.

---

[7] Distribution is here used to mean the movement of goods and services from producers to consumers and not the apportionment of the fruits of production among the contributors thereto, as that term is employed in economic theory.

[8] *Theory*—"The result of contemplation; hence, an analysis or explanation; . . . The general or abstract principles of any body of facts real or assumed; . . . A general principle, formula, or ideal construction, offered to explain phenomena and rendered more or less plausible by evidence in the facts or by the exactness and relevancy of the reasoning; . . . A plan or scheme theoretically constructed. A hypothesis offered as a basis of thought on a given subject; loosely, any idea, guess, etc., put forward to be accepted or rejected in seeking the explanation of some condition, occurrence, or the like. . . . In scientific usage, a *hypothesis* is a provisional conjecture regarding the causes or relations of certain phenomena; a *theory* is a hypothesis which has undergone verification, and which is applicable to a large number of related phenomena."

Some theories may be narrow and simple, dealing with perhaps a technical phase of the subject. Others would be more comprehensive, relating to topics of broader scope and more general import. As theory, however, such expositions would possess a conceptual framework and be not merely a compilation of classified observations described as self-evident facts. Mental perception of related attributes of marketing phenomena precedes the classification and definition of evidence. To students of such thought, the classifications or conceptions are likely to appear obvious and tangible and be taken for granted. For example, "channels" of distribution, "convenience" goods, "agent" middlemen, "rational" buying motives, price "schedules," and the like originally were—and still are—conceptions,[9] ideas, and not material facts.

By relating pertinent aspects of several concepts one may arrive at a statement of marketing principles. Again for example, a principle of channel determination may be suggested as follows: the channel of distribution tends to be relatively longer for goods of low unit value, small size, general consumption, and staple nature, which are bought frequently and habitually by large numbers of people. Also: the distance which goods tend to travel to market is a direct function of the difference between price differentials in two markets and the costs of transportation between them. Study of any aspect of marketing proceeding from conceptual premises and generalized in the form of basic principles, if carried to a stage of sufficient development would constitute a theory. The consistent integration of broad theories would constitute, in turn, the science of marketing.

The evolution of marketing science must be the joint contribution of men working not only in marketing itself but in the related social sciences. Those who are most intimately associated with marketing facts will formulate generalizations based upon their experiences; students of other social and economic conditions will in their own fields do likewise and will reach conclusions pertinent to marketing which marketing specialists may refute, challenge, or incorporate into their own thinking and body of knowledge. Marketing theorists, in contrast to marketing technicians, will endeavor to integrate and to balance in a systematic body the knowledge stemming from observation and investigation, on the one hand, and from theoretical deductions, on the other.

When such a development of thought takes place in the study of marketing, it may be expected to appear in writings as general works on

---

[9] *Conception*—"The act or process of forming the schematized idea or notion of a thing, or the idea or notion formed. . . . Any idea or notion, or thought-formation, whether accompanied with belief in the reality of its object or not. . . ."("Conception is the act of grasping together two or more attributes into the unity of thought which we call a single concept." Bowen)

marketing. Their difference from existing general texts on the subject would lie mainly in viewpoint and approach. The viewpoint would be characterized by interest in application of the knowledge mainly to problems of broader than technical or institutional scope. The approach would be admittedly from sound theory as well as from tested facts. The product would be an integrated statement of principles and laws which, while not incontrovertible as natural empirical laws are, would be sufficiently stable to explain marketing conditions and activities in a broad and long-run scale.

2

Marketing As a Science: An Appraisal

KENNETH D. HUTCHINSON

During the past few years one of the ways in which the increased interest in marketing subjects has expressed itself is in the rather intense exploration of the field with a view to determining the exact significance of its subject matter. More explicitly, several scholars have either attempted to demonstrate that marketing should be admitted into the category of a science, or have discussed the subject as though it already were included. Interest in the project first became apparent through the appearance of an exploratory survey made by P. D. Converse in *The Journal of Marketing.*[1] However, since this particular essay had the merit of not attempting any demonstration of the thesis that marketing is a science, one can not be sure that the article really served as the foundation of future discussions on the problem.

At the time that Professor Converse wrote, regard for the application of scientific methodology to marketing problems was an increasing force, and the momentum of this interest carries on today. Three years later, Lyndon O. Brown discussed the need for the development of professional standards among marketing men in an essay which tended in the main not to regard the subject as a science, except possibly in one cloudy passage.[2] The question of the status of marketing appeared to be developing some urgency in the minds of numerous marketing scholars because in

---

Reprinted with permission from the *Journal of Marketing,* national quarterly publication of the American Marketing Association, Vol. 16 (January, 1952), pp. 286-293.

[1] P. D. Converse, "The Development of a Science of Marketing," *Journal of Marketing,* Vol. X, No. 1, July, 1945, p. 14.

[2] Lyndon O. Brown, "Toward a Profession of Marketing," *Journal of Marketing,* Vol. XIII, No. 1, July, 1948, p. 27. Brown states that there is a need for "precise raw materials which are the foundation of any science, and in turn the art of the practitioner in any field."

the next issue of the *Journal* there appeared a very thoughtful and searching article exploring the notion of developing a theory of marketing.[3] The authors were quite circumspect in writing this essay, omitting any direct reference to marketing as a science. Little doubt was left in the minds of the readers, however, that the authors considered marketing to be a unified body of thought; and from this one can infer that they suspect that it is a science.

At least one marketing scholar received this impression from that essay for, in the *Journal* the following spring, Roland S. Vaile wrote a communication[4] commenting on that point of view. If anyone held illusions as to the character of marketing, Professor Vaile's article should have removed them; but marketing men apparently have great tenacity and refuse to give up easily. Although the conclusion of this essay was that marketing did not have the earmarks of a science, the question of whether this was true was to be raised again on later occasions. In 1951 a new essay was presented on the question by Robert Bartels,[5] who concluded that marketing was indeed a science and entitled to respect as such.

It would be misleading to consider this latter essay as an isolated instance; the ferment which had been started in the minds of students of marketing was working steadily and other evidences of this conclusion (that marketing is a science) can be found. The Cox and Alderson article, to which reference has been made, led to a book of essays on marketing theory;[6] in some of these are further references to the science of marketing.[7] This compilation of essays affords a rather varied fare for the scholar seeking enlightenment on the true nature of marketing. Points of view differed and there were some who indicated their conviction that there was no such thing as a theory of marketing, and hence also, no science of marketing.[8]

---

[3] W. Alderson and R. Cox, "Towards a Theory of Marketing," *Journal of Marketing,* Vol. XIII, No. 2, October, 1948, p. 137.

[4] Roland S. Vaile, "Toward a Theory of Marketing—A Comment," *Journal of Marketing,* Vol. XIII, No. 4, April, 1949, p. 520.

[5] Robert Bartels, "Can Marketing Be A Science?," *Journal of Marketing,* Vol. XV, No. 3, January, 1951, p. 319.

[6] R. Cox and W. Alderson, editors, *Theory in Marketing* (Chicago, Richard D. Irwin, Inc., 1950).

[7] In *Theory in Marketing,* C. West Churchman, in the essay "Basic Research in Marketing," discusses market research as though the field were a science. W. Alderson, in "Survival and Adjustment in Organized Behavior," refers to "the science of marketing." E. R. Hawkins, "Vertical Price Relationships," after making some penetrating analyses of economic theory, leaves the impression that marketing is a part of the science of ecnomics.

[8] In the same work, G. L. Mehren, in the essay "The Theory of the Firm and Marketing," says that "there is no theory of marketing." E. T. Grether, in "A Theoretical Approach to the Analysis of Marketing," takes a cautious view of theorizing in the field, as does Oswald Knauth, in "Marketing and Managerial Enterprise."

Reasons for Confusion

This disagreement, or confusion, in the minds of marketing students over the nature of their field arises in no small part from the comprehensive character and variety of activities embraced by the term marketing. Three distinct types of activity are discernible. First, there is a group of activities which center around the day-to-day distribution of goods and services. Second, there are those activities which center around the interpretation of the subject in schools and colleges. Third, there is a group of activities which arises out of the explorations by market research men working on specific problems, some of which have rather broad implications. With these three different approaches to the field there would naturally arise some differences in viewpoints.

Of the first group, those whose job it is to distribute goods, almost no one would contend seriously that they are engaged in some form of scientific endeavor; wholesalers and retailers hardly fit the mold of scientists. Neither the second group, the teachers, nor the third group, the market research men, are so easily disposed of, particularly since some of them are concerned with systematizing the subject. All are interested in employing scientific methodology in the field. Members of these two groups have pressed the case most earnestly for the inclusion of marketing among the fields of science. We have seen, however, that there has been no unanimity of opinion among them. Their work with the scientific method has induced many of them to broaden their scopes, and it is to those who have attempted to demonstrate that marketing is a science that this essay is directed.

In appraising the progress which has been made in developing a science of marketing, one is tempted to make allowances for the relatively short period of time in which the issues have been under discussion. But after making whatever allowances are called for, one is likely to be somewhat disappointed over the lack of progress to date. One should expect far more in the way of results if the venture is to prove successful, and the dearth of progress to date lends the suspicion that the project is ill-advised. There seems to be little evidence to support the claim that all that is needed is time and patience until there will emerge the new and shining science of marketing.

Two Approaches to Demonstrating That Marketing Is a Science

In attempting to demonstrate that marketing is a science, two lines of approach to the problem are discernible. The first of these might pass under the name of the semantic approach according to which the various essay-ists wrestle with dictionary meanings, warping them and twisting them, until at last marketing is seen to have fulfilled many, though not all, of the requisite characteristics of a science. The pseudo-precision of this method may be highly admirable even though it lacks some perspective. A somewhat fairer interpretation of such semantic exercises might rea-sonably lead to the conclusion merely that marketing has now become a field for human study. Since there are many fields of study, and since not all of them are sciences, such a conclusion should not be looked upon as any great step forward.[9]

To be more explicit, a homely example might be drawn; the field of carpentry could conceivably turn out to be such a field of study. There are books written on the subject; it is taught in schools; and it concerns itself with human experience. Furthermore it has empirical laws of a sort (those of gravity and leverage, for example) and perhaps some theoretical ones (whether screws or nails are preferable in certain jobs). Now all this pedantry does not create a science out of the trade of car-pentry; but it illustrates how pseudo-scientific word juggling might be used to convert many humble human activities into recognized sciences. Something of this sort is now appearing in marketing literature. The func-tion of business, however, is the economic production and marketing of goods and services; if we insist, therefore, that marketing is a science, we must be prepared to admit manufacturing and finance. Unless one wants to broaden his conception of science so as to include nearly all human activity, he is not likely to achieve success in making marketing a science through this process of distorting the meaning of words.

The second approach to the task of demonstrating the scientific character of marketing might be called the economic. Students of mar-keting interested in "practical" as well as academic matters seem to find the time-worn theories of neo-classical economics to be unsatisfying or downright inapplicable. This has led to a wholesale onslaught on many of the time honored concepts in which, curiously enough, they find many economists sympathetic. For some years economists themselves have been trying to free their subject from the fetters placed there by the static as-sumptions inherited from the classical school traditions. Some progress is being made in modernizing economic doctrines but there still remain numerous concepts which lack realism. It has been this factor which has

---

[9] Dr. Bartels recognizes this widespread characteristic of marketing in the article referred to above. After discussing the characteristics of an art, a discipline, and a science, he concludes that there is much in favor of accepting the subject of market-ing as a science.

encouraged students of marketing to pursue further the task of clarification; in fact—such work was essential.[10]

The result of such interest in economic theory is that considerable study by marketing theorists has been devoted to developing more refreshing viewpoints and more workable concepts. A review of progress to date indicates that much of it has stemmed from the practice of holding economic theories up to a critical light for re-examination. One might naturally wonder whether all this analysis is serving only to enrich current economic doctrines rather than to further the development of an independent set of marketing theories. From the standpoint of over-all human understanding, such efforts of marketing men are probably not in vain. In the long run it may well turn out that theoretical economists have derived benefits from having their concepts held up to this different type of scrutiny. Marketing students will also benefit through the possession of a better tool of analysis which this criticism may produce.

In looking over the work of marketing theorists it appears that considerable effort has been expended in attacking the generally accepted, or "orthodox," if you will, doctrines which relate to price setting. It is apparently true that much of this body of thought has been erected upon a foundation which contains some rather unrealistic assumptions, and certainly some which appear foreign to a marketer. Thus far, however, the contributions of marketing theorists to economic theory of pricing remain restricted to the field of criticism. If one were to seek evidence of constructive scholarship along these lines he would discover that no notable body of new theory has been brought forth to replace the seemingly discredited notions. An even harsher observation could be made: the probing of marketers into economic theory has tended more to becloud than to clarify the issues. In casting the light of realism upon this field such a result may well have been unavoidable. It should be interesting to inspect a few of the concepts which have had their clarity dimmed.

To the neo-classical economist the concept of price was reasonably clear, whereas to the new marketing theorists there is no great certainty as to what is meant by the term. To them price represents a wide composite of characteristics which are subject to notable variances which can conceivably differ with each transaction. Another concept which

---

[10] Evidence of this concern for clarification and modification of economic theory can be found in Cox and Alderson, *Theory in Marketing,* cited above. Essays which are chiefly critiques of economic doctrines are: R. G. Gettell, "Pluralistic Competition"; E. T. Grether, "A Theoretical Approach to the Analysis of Marketing"; G. L. Mehren, "The Theory of the Firm and Marketing"; R. S. Vaile, "Economic Theory and Marketing"; E. R. Hawkins, "Vertical Price Relationships"; R. Cassady, Jr., "The Time Element and Demand Analysis"; A. G. Abramson, "Public Policy and the Theory of Competition"; R. Cox, "Quantity Limits and the Theory of Economic Opportunity"; and J. Dean, "Market Competition under Uniform F.O.B. Pricing."

seemed to give the economist little trouble was that of a commodity. Under the new scrutiny, this also turns out to possess less clarity, varying to some extent from transaction to transaction, a fact which accounts for the varying prices. Although some attention has been directed by marketing theorists to such other concepts as competition, monopoly, market controls, and freedom of entry, it can be said with fair reliability that human comprehension of these subjects has been very little advanced. Whether one is inclined to agree with these immediate conclusions is of no great importance; what does seem to be important is the fact that marketing scholars can never expect to develop their own body of theory merely by critical appraisal of the shortcomings of another one. In time, some positive contributions must be forthcoming if the desired goal is to be achieved.

Marketing Not a Science

There is a real reason, however, why the field of marketing has been slow to develop an unique body of theory. It is a simple one: marketing is not a science. It is rather an art or a practice, and as such much more closely resembles engineering, medicine, and architecture than it does physics, chemistry, or biology. The medical profession sets us an excellent example, if we would but follow it; its members are called "practitioners" and not scientists. It is the work of physicians, as it is of any practitioner, to apply the findings of many sciences to the solution of problems. Among the sciences which the medical man employs are biology, physiology, chemistry, physics, psychology, and many more. Engineers and architects are also practitioners who make use of chemistry, physics, psychology and other sciences. It is a characteristic of a practice that the solution of each problem faced calls for a different and distinct combination of techniques and approaches. The fact that each problem is different, however, does not deter practitioners from approaching them in the scientific manner and spirit.[11]

What constitutes a science is a question which has been settled in general for centuries, but from time to time the issues arise again as new subjects are held up for scrutiny. Within modern times the areas of social study, the socio-economic fields, have caused considerable debate over the character of science itself. The trouble with attacking this problem from a semantic point of view is that words have multiple meanings and one is enabled to prove almost anything, and almost nothing, by careful selection of the definition which seems to fit his case. Since we are using

---

[11] This point of view was expressed somewhat differently by R. S. Vaile in *The Journal of Marketing* article cited above.

words in this essay, we are in danger of falling into the same trap in trying to show that marketing is *not* a science that others have fallen into by trying to show that it *is* one, particularly when their demonstration has depended heavily upon the twist of word meanings. A much sounder approach to the problem would seem to be upon the ground of human experience, contrasting the place of science in human affairs with that of the arts.

Science is a word we apply to a multitude of varying activities carried on by man in his effort to understand his environment. For centuries man has attempted to comprehend the planetary processes which are all parts of the great universe of knowledge. It should be unnecessary in this age and with this group of readers to labor this particular concept; it might be more profitable to return to it after we have discussed the field of the arts.

The arts is also a comprehensive term covering human activities of a wide scope. To satisfy his wants, mankind has engaged in various practices over the centuries; as time has gone on, these practices have tended to become more complex. The various arts are those related to obtaining food, preparing clothing, and obtaining shelter, along with others which are related to aesthetic satisfactions. Man found early that he could thrive much better if he did not attempt to produce all of his commodities but instead would exchange some of his output with a neighbor who had a surplus of some other product. Early barter and later market transactions are the true predecessors of modern marketing. The forbears of modern marketing men were great merchants, not great scientists. It is the drollest travesty to relate the scientist's search for knowledge to the market research man's seeking after customers.

Relationship Between Marketing and the Sciences

What then is the relationship existing between the sciences and marketing if indeed there be one? The answer to this query has already been indicated but perhaps should be restated. Men of science have come to develop a systematic approach to their problems which is known as the scientific method. Hypotheses are developed, facts are gathered to support or confute the hypotheses, and then tests are conducted to see if hypotheses are sound. In actual research work, the techniques employed vary with the problem at hand but the spirit of careful analysis and testing is not relaxed. Engineers and physicians are trained to approach their problems in this spirit of scientific inquiry; marketing men are learning rapidly to follow their examples. What must be realized is that the method is open for all to use and that the employment of it does not necessarily make the user a scientist nor his subject a science. A physician who studies all of his patient's symptoms before prescribing, and who keeps checking up on the progress of his treatments, is still a practitioner and not a scientist.

Such a conclusion must be inevitable or else the gates will be opened to include almost all types of human activity under the heading of sciences. Dry cleaners often approach a problem in a scientific manner but dry cleaning is not a science, nor are road building, paint mixing, poultry raising and countless other human arts. The processes which culminate in getting goods from mines, fields, and factories into the hands of consumers with the least expenditure of time, effort and money are not those that will fit into the mold of a science. That many marketing problems call for extensive computations and calculations can not be denied nor can the fact that the best approach to them is through some variant of the scientific method of investigation, trial and test. In actual practice, however, many, and probably most, of the decisions in the field resemble the scientific method hardly any more closely than what is involved in reading a road map or a time table. If one remains unconvinced, he must be prepared to admit into the brotherhood of new sciences the fields of retailing, wholesaling and presumably salesmanship.

The arts and practices seem to differ from the sciences in still another respect. When problems present themselves to practitioners there is almost without exception rather serious urgency to have them solved. An engineering project must be put through immediately; a sick patient must be helped now; and a sales manager wants his analysis of the market from his research man as soon as (and usually sooner than) is possible. Any market research man who is working on a problem the answer to which may not be found for another generation, or perhaps a century, would be an exception whereas such a circumstance tends to be rather commonplace among the sciences where immediacy tends more to be the exception. At best this point of difference between the arts and the sciences is probably only a symptomatic effect rather than an underlying force separating the two.

Thinking along these lines has become confused in the minds of some individuals because of the tendency of scientists to desert their fields of research to attack some current practical problem. When a scientist leaves his field of scientific investigation to solve a difficult problem, he drops the role of a scientist seeking to expand man's grasp over the universe; he is no longer engaged in pushing out the frontiers of knowledge. At that point he becomes a practitioner in a role similar to the engineer, the physician and the architect. A physicist who leaves his pursuit of science to construct a machine (except one to further an experiment) becomes an engineer, even though one with a superior training in physics. The point being made here is not a new one, having been well settled in other fields of learning; but the truth of it seems to have been overlooked by numerous marketing men.

We do not intend to deny here that scientists should turn their attention to the solution of human problems, nor are we attempting to indicate that scientific endeavor should lack applicability. No claim is being presented here for the advantages of pure research, that form of activity which seems to do little more than satisfy the curiosity of some investigator. Science has a purpose; its function is to help mankind to understand his universe. Whether men will use the knowledge or will even misuse it is not the particular concern of the scientist. At present writing the problem of cancer is one of great concern to several fields of science and each one is developing an attack upon it. Some investigators are approaching the problem from the standpoint of the effect of behavior patterns upon its cause. Others study the structure of human cells, still others the effects of drugs, and still others the effects of radiation, and so on. This is a practical problem which science is trying to solve; but how any given patient suffering from the disease is to be treated is a problem for the practitioner.

The real dilemma of the marketing research man is that his own field of learning is inadequate to permit proper diagnoses and prescriptions, but that the other fields upon which he should be able to lean are themselves still in somewhat beginning stages. It may seem unfair to a one hundred seventy-five year old science such as economics to classify it as "beginning," but one has only to examine the protests of marketing men over many economic concepts to learn the tenuous nature of economic principles. Sociology and psychology are also just beginning to build up a body of reliable doctrine and are far from complete tools for analysis. The market research man needs knowledge of population trends, consumer preferences, price trends, and purchasing power, merely to name a few of the concepts on which exact information is lacking. It happens to be unfortunate that marketing research has to depend upon the numerous and inexact social sciences.[12]

While we are examining the place of marketing among the various fields of learning and activity, one further point should be made. Marketing men not infrequently contribute to one of the several sciences upon which they depend. In trying to find information to solve his immediate problem he may strike upon some principle which actually enlarges the science involved. Market problems vary widely in scope. Some are of almost no social consequence, being chiefly competitive in nature; others are broader in character and depend for solution upon a

---

[12] We are accepting for present purposes, the idea that economics and sociology are sciences, being fully aware that controversies exist over this point.

wide understanding of social forces and of human behavior. It is in the pursuit of these solutions that contributions to the fields of science result. Such additions to the universal body of knowledge must be looked upon as by-products of market research, and not its chief purpose.

Beyond such small contributions, however, there is an area in which marketing scholars can produce profound results in the sciences. There is evidence that already some of this work is being done. By focusing the attention of scientists upon those concepts which are inadequately developed, the inquiring minds of marketing men can do much to give useful direction to scientific investigation. Already students of economics, sociology, and psychology are feeling the impact of this curiosity and are tending to advance knowledge along the lines demanded. Engineers and physicians have in their turn exerted powerful influences over the direction which scientific research should take. This aspect should not be overlooked in our quest for progress in the field.

Conclusion

An examination of the factors involved indicates that marketing is not a science, since it does not conform to the basic characteristics of a science. A much more realistic view shows it to be an art, in the practice of which reliance must be placed upon the findings of many sciences. Marketing research men, like engineers and physicians, have to adopt a scientific approach to their problems, but their relation to the fields of science are even closer than this. Although at times they may make a contribution to some field of science, their chief contribution should be that of directing the course of scientific investigation along the lines most needed.

3

On the Role of Marketing Theory [1]

W. J. BAUMOL

Nature of Theory

The completion of a comprehensive work on marketing theory by Wroe Alderson[2] seems an appropriate occasion to review the aspirations and promise of a theoretical approach to marketing. There seems to be much misunderstanding about the nature of theory in general and that of marketing theory in particular, and this paper seeks to shed some light on these matters.

"Theory" in Popular Language

Words mean different things to different people and there is little point in arguing definitions. But meaningful discussion is only possible if the connotation of a word is the same to all who employ it. This has not been the case in the use of the word "theory," which means one thing to the layman and something entirely different to the theorist. As a result, the public has a distorted view of the goals and methods of theoretical research.

In common parlance "theoretical" is taken to be a contradictory either of "factual" or of "practical." "A theory" is the term often used to denote an allegation of fact for which no evidence has been presented.

Reprinted with permission from the *Journal of Marketing,* national quarterly publication of the American Marketing Association, Vol. 21 (April, 1957), pp. 413-418.

[1] This paper has its origins in a talk delivered before the Marketing Theory Seminar at Burlington, Vermont, which was held during the week of August 27, 1956.

[2] Wroe Alderson, *Marketing Behavior and Executive Action* (Homewood, Illinois: Richard D. Irwin, Inc., 1957).

Unverified statements about the chemical composition of some compound, or about the behavior of some group of Australian aborigines, or about the nature of the so-called "canals" on Mars are all likely to be labeled theories. However, in the literature of scientific method, the statement, "the canals on Mars contain water," has nothing to do with astronomical or biological or any other theory. Rather, such an assertion would be re- ferred to as an "unverified hypothesis."

The distinction is no mere quibble. A hypothesis is a pure question of fact while theory, to the theorist, is concerned with explanation. The Martian canal hypothesis is either true or false and its validity can be settled one way or another by the first space ship to return from Mars, should one ever succeed in making the trip. Final disposition of the question on the Australians may be even simpler and may be contingent only on the financing of an anthropological expedition by one of the foundations. With theory, as we shall indicate presently, the question of verification is not so simple.

There is also a second common use of the term "theory," character- ized by the frequently encountered statement: "That may all be very well in theory, but when we get down to practical matters. . . ." Of course, most theorists prefer to believe that their work can be immensely helpful to the practical man. Whether this is likely frequently to be the case, the reader must judge for himself from the sequel. At this point we only recall the rather hackneyed illustrations which are usually employed to show that in some cases at least theory can have enormous practical implica- tions. We have often been reminded that the well-publicized developments in electronics and atomic energy would not now be possible without the work of the theoretical physicists. Even Edison's work, which itself was totally devoid of theory, depended heavily on earlier theoretical results which by his time had become part of the standard equipment of the tech- nician.

"Theory" as Used by the Theorist

Roughly, the theorist uses the word "theory" to mean "systematic expla- nation." A theory is a structure which describes the workings and inter- relations of the various aspects of some phenomenon. Philosophers tell us that the word "explanation" has a great variety of meanings, but this need not concern us here. We can avoid this expository difficulty by describing in some detail what the theorist seeks to do.

Essentially, his procedure involves the examination of some aspect of reality and the construction of a simplified small-scale model which be- haves in at least some ways like the phenomena under observation. The analyst can understand and trace out the workings of his model while reality is far too complicated and chaotic for this to be possible. In practice a particular day's demand for refrigerators may be conditioned by a family quarrel in Abilene, a case of mumps in South Bend, and the statement of a tea-leaf-reading gypsy to one of her clients in Jersey City. It is hopeless to seek to take all of these considerations into account in an investigation of the appliance market. Instead, one deals with a simplified make-believe market in which consumer demand is conditioned by income, advertising expenditure, and a few other variables.

This method is well established in the natural sciences. The physicist cannot predict just what path will be followed by a real automobile left free to roll down a real hill or the time a real chestnut will take to pop in a real fire. He can only tell us what will happen in the artificial circumstances described by a controlled experiment, where the elements carefully held constant in the laboratory are the aspects of reality from which his simplified model abstracts. Once he steps out of the laboratory, his conclusions must be treated with extreme caution. That is why the salaries of test pilots are high!

Basically, the need for theory arises because facts unfortunately do not speak for themselves. An inflationary movement in prices or a fall in the sales volume of a shoe manufacturer is compatible with a variety of hypotheses. Facts supply us with correlations, not with structural relationships. At times all of us are prepared to reject conclusions which appear to be implied by the facts because these conclusions conflict with the rudimentary theoretical structures which we implicitly accept. For example, no one ever treated seriously, as an explanation of prosperity and depression, the statistics which showed that at least for a time there was a high correlation between the level of national income and the height of feminine skirt hems. None of the theories of the business cycle to which we more or less unconsciously adhere allows for dictation of the level of America's industrial activity by Christian Dior.

Perhaps a better example is the relationship between interest rates and industrial construction. Statistics show that they tend to go up and down together and apparently imply that a rise in interest rates encourages the appearance of new factories and equipment. But economic theory usually denies this violently and argues plausibly that a rise in the cost of borrowing increases the businessman's construction costs and serves to deter this type of investment. The economist then accounts for the observed fact by pointing out that a third variable enters in and confuses matters. When national income is high, construction is profitable and the demand for funds to finance it raises interest rates. Which version of the facts is correct, we may never be sure, but the recent reaction of businessmen to Federal Reserve tight-money policies lends credence to the view that high interest costs are no stimulus to the creation of industrial capital goods.

We see then that since the facts themselves are silent, theory must be invented to describe their workings. If we desire to understand the structure of reality, we desire theory in the sense the theorist employs the terms. This does not mean that nontheoretical research is undesirable or even less desirable than the work of the theorist. Their purposes are different—one supplies the data; the other, the explanations.

Illustration: An Empirical and a Theoretical "Law"

As an example of an empirical result in marketing, let us consider "Reilly's law." As originally formulated, this states that "Two cities attract retail trade from any intermediate city or town in the vicinity of the breaking point, approximately in direct proportion to the populations of the two cities and in inverse proportion to the square of the distances from these two cities to the intermediate town."[3]

When Reilly presented this result, he marshaled an impressive array of market data in its support but made no attempt at systematic explanation. The assertion was nevertheless useful and illuminating to marketing men.

Let us compare this with a somewhat related theoretical result which we owe to Fetter.[4] Consider two manufacturing centers *A* and *B* which produce a similar product at different unit costs. If they both pay the same cost of transportation per mile, what is the borderline between the territories that will be served by *A* and *B*? The answer is that if goods are sold at cost plus the same percentage markup, and customers buy from the man who sells most cheaply, the borderline will be a hyperbola whose formula is easily written down by a freshmen mathematics student. For at every point, *X*, of equal price (cost), the difference between the distance of *X* to *A* and that of *X* to *B* will just make up for the different in manufacturing cost at the two centers. In other words, there will be a constant difference between the distance of a point on the borderline to *A* and the distance from the point to *B*. But in analytic geometry, a hyperbola is defined as the locus of all points the difference in whose distances to two fixed points is a constant, and Fetter's conclusion follows at once.

Let us now see what the theoretical result does and what it does not

---

[3] William J. Reilly, *The Law of Retail Gravitation* (New York: Pilsbury Publishers, 1931), p. 9.

[4] Frank A. Fetter, "The Economic Law of Market Areas," *Quarterly Journal of Economics,* vol. XXXVIII, May 1924.

do. Because we understand its workings we can easily see how the conclusion is affected by changes in the circumstances. If transportation cost is not strictly proportioned to the distance a cargo is carried, or if the pattern of pricing is not simply cost plus, or if in some other way the situation is known to differ from that postulated in the derivation of the original theorem, it may not be difficult to modify the analysis to take this into account. Should there be a proposed change in railroad rate structure, we could in advance examine the nature of its effects on competitive market areas with the aid of this theoretical analysis. Here, an empirical generalization would be of very little help because this can only tell us how things stand. Since it offers no clues as to how things work, it cannot tell us what will happen under changed conditions until after the change occurs and its results are observed. This, then, is a major advantage of the theoretical construct. It can help us in this way because it permits us to understand the *structure* of the situation.

On the other hand, the empirical law is—as a result of the way in which it is derived—virtually certain to be in closer agreement with the facts. The empirical law *states* the facts. The theoretical law describes not the facts, but a simplified model which at best only approximates them fairly well. We have said that a distinguishing feature of a factual hypothesis is that it is either right or wrong. By contrast, we may assert that a theoretical construct is sure to be more or less wrong in that it oversimplifies and hence distorts or omits some aspects of the circumstances under investigation.

Characteristics of "Good" Theory

Though all theory is in this sense wrong, it is not all of one quality. One piece of theoretic work is considered more successful than another. To account for this difference, we may list some of the desiderata of a theoretical model:

1. The model should be a sufficiently simple version of the facts to permit systematic manipulation and analysis. This means that a more realistic model may often be a poorer model. It is, of course, always desirable to make a model more realistic if this can be done without seriously complicating the investigation.

2. On the other hand, the model must be a sufficiently close approximation to the relevant facts to be usable. How close an approximation is necessary and which facts are relevant depend, of course, on the problem under investigation. It follows, and this cannot be overemphasized, that a model which is appropriate for the examination of one problem arising out of a given set of circumstances may be totally useless and even mis-

leading for the investigation of another problem arising out of these same circumstances.

How difficult it is to find a theoretical model which acceptably meets these two criteria is partly a matter of luck. Some problems may just be so complicated that any model which is sufficiently simple to be analytically useful must be too gross a misrepresentation of the situation which it seeks to describe. This observation is sometimes advanced as a partial explanation of the less than spectacular progress that has characterized the social sciences.

It is worth mentioning one more feature to be desired of a theory:

3. Its conclusions should be relatively insensitive to changes in its assumptions. An example which comes to mind is a pricing recommendation which was made to a client on the basis of an operations research analysis. The relevant cost data were not unambiguously indicated by the accounting records, so a wide variety of cost assumptions was investigated. It was shown that these had little effect on the computed optimum price—and the recommended price structure could consequently be regarded with considerably greater confidence. The basic point is that the assumptions of a model are never more than approximately valid, and if the structure of a model is such as seriously to magnify errors, this inaccuracy in the premises is likely to be translated into thoroughly undependable conclusions.

Is There a Place for Marketing Theory?

Even when it is granted that theoretical work can play a useful role, questions are sometimes raised about the possibility of a distinctive marketing theory. It is pointed out that the problems of marketing now fall under the purview of various fields, including psychology, sociology, and economics, each of which already has developed a considerable body of theory. This is true, but it is not entirely relevant. Pursued to its limits, this argument might have economics and sociology as branches of psychology; the latter, in turn, might be labeled a field in biology; and all the sciences might end up reclassified as physics. It seems to me that economics and psychology may more usefully be taken to provide some bricks for the construction of marketing theory rather than constituting its sum and substance. The difference between two disciplines often lies in the point of view with which they view the same subject. Clinical pathology which makes up so much of the psychologist's subject matter is of little interest to the marketing man whose attention is focused more on the behavior of groups than of the individuals which constitute them and on behavior which is in some sense normal. The appropriate choice of theory is, as I have emphasized, a matter of the problem in which the investigator is interested. It must surely be admitted that marketing has its special problems and may, therefore, well find it useful to develop further its own body of theory.

The Functionalist Approach to Marketing Theory

The application of some of these criteria for theory is exemplified in the recent book by Wroe Alderson, which bears the subtitle "The Functionalist Approach to Marketing Theory." While it is rich in insights drawn from experience, it cannot be characterized as a description of marketing processes and institutions. It does not pretend to create a comprehensive new model for the marketing mechanism. Attainment of such a goal would be too much to expect of a pathbreaking work in any young discipline. But the book succeeds entirely in its more modest purpose: the provision of perspectives for model building directed either toward general interpretation of marketing or the solution of individual problems.

The fundamental theme of the book is problem solving in marketing, regarded as a function of organized behavior systems. The behavior system is said to function as if it were pursuing inherent goals of survival and growth, although it is recognized that the vital urge apparent in the system rests on the expectations of the individuals who participate in its activities in the effort to realize their own objectives.

The author describes his viewpoint as "functionalism" because he begins with an examination of the way in which organized groups function in continuous adjustment to an operating environment. The focal point of interest, however, is in the problems of adjustment which arise to threaten the security of the system and which must be solved to maintain or enhance its efficiency. The problem which faces the executive responsible for making a decision on behalf of any system lies in the uncertainty of success of any course of action which he chooses to adopt. Problem solving is the attempt to reduce uncertainty to tolerable limits so that action can be taken.

The author points out that uncertainty in marketing springs in part from the radical heterogeneity on both the demand side and the supply side of the market and from the stream of innovations which produce heterogeneity over time. The market mechanism undertakes to match each segment of demand with the appropriate segment of supply. Matching is difficult since the parties to be brought together are separated by distance and by lack of knowledge and contact. From the viewpoint of the agencies engaged in marketing functions, this may be described as the matching of opportunity with effort. Each segment of demand is potential opportunity for some supplier and all supply can be regarded as production and marketing effort expended to satisfy demand.

The matching of supply and demand is carried on through the shaping, fitting, and sorting of goods and services. Sorting in its various forms is held to be the essential marketing process and is taken to include allocation or the breaking down of supplies and assorting or the building up of assortments. Efficiency in production requires the development of marketing intermediaries to deal with sorting and related functions. Efficiency in marketing requires routinization of transactions and the development of specialized marketing channels.

The book reminds us that the structure of marketing agencies is constantly changing in response to changes in the scale and character of the marketing job to be done. The dynamics of this process arise from the economics of differential advantage. Every vigorous competitor is constantly engaged in trying to gain an edge over his rivals. One way to gain a differential advantage in the performance of a marketing function is to be better organized to perform it. Freedom to compete includes freedom to organize the market. The most crucial function of all is the creation of structure through which to function. A marketing executive is not only concerned with action but with capacity for action. He follows the power principle in making decisions, which means that he acts in such a way as to promote the power to act.

The book also illuminatingly pictures consumers as coming into the market to solve problems and reduce uncertainty as to the realization of their anticipations. Household commodity inventory assortments are created to meet future occasions of use, taking account of both the relative importance of these occasions and the probability of their occurrence. The housewife, too, makes executive decisions in her capacity as purchasing agent for the household. In a sense, her task is more complicated than that of the business executive since the family, which is her operating environment, is the principal setting for the congenial (inherently pleasant) behavior which is presumed to be the end and aim of all instrumental behavior including shopping. The seller can solve his problems only by helping buyers to solve their problems. The recognition of the consumer buyer as a problem solver is perhaps the most novel and characteristic aspect of this view.

Marketing theory in this version accepts the basic assumption of rational behavior posited in classical economics. It attempts to place rational problem solving in a broader theory of behavior derived from psychology and sociology. In addition to distinguishing between instrumental and congenial behavior, this theory recognizes a third category of symptomatic behavior springing from maladjustment. Yet, rational problem solving remains the central concept insofar as the book is truly theoretical. To the extent that it permits deductions about market behavior, they must rest on this concept. Since conscious and deliberate problem solving does not presumably occupy a large part of the time of either executives or housewives, a book with this emphasis can scarcely be regarded as realistic description. To justify its claim as a beginning step in marketing theory, it does not have to mirror reality in all its complexity. The test will be whether it can fulfill its promise as a means of interpreting "market behavior and executive action" and for giving direction to further research.

4

Is Marketing a Science?

ROBERT D. BUZZELL

If you ask the average business executive what the most important agent of progress is in contemporary society, the odds are good that he will answer, "Science." There is a general respect, even awe, for the accomplishments of science. The satellites in orbit, polio vaccine, and television are tangible pieces of evidence that science conquers all.

To be against science is as heretical as to be against motherhood. Yet when executives are asked to consider the social and economic process of marketing as a science or prospective science, most confess to extreme skepticism. Is marketing a science? If not, can it ever become one? If so, what does this imply for management?

These questions are hardly new ones, but they have a special interest in light of several recent developments:

Perhaps the most noteworthy of these is the formation, in mid-1962, of the Marketing Science Institute, an organization supported by some 29 large corporations and devoted to "fundamental research" in the field of marketing.

At the same time, the American Marketing Association, a professional group dedicated to "the advancement of science in marketing," has re-examined its own goals and taken stock of its accomplishments to date.

Finally, the issue of science in marketing—and especially the use of science or of its results by executives responsible for marketing decisions—also has received considerable attention in several recently published books.

Thus, it seems appropriate at this point to pause and consider the status of science in marketing, to sift out the claims and counter-claims, and to ask whether any basic changes are needed in management's approach to marketing problems.

Reprinted with permission from the *Harvard Business Review,* Vol. 41 (January-February, 1963), pp. 32 ff.

What Is Marketing Science?

The Marketing Science Institute is headed by Dr. Wendell R. Smith, formerly Staff Vice President for Marketing Development at the Radio Corporation of America, and before that a university teacher. Smith stated in an address delivered to the Kansas City Chapter of the American Marketing Association on July 10, 1962, that the goals of the MSI were:

1. To contribute to the emergence of a more definitive science of marketing

2. To stimulate increased application of scientific techniques to the understanding and solving of marketing problems.

It is useful to keep these two points separate. First, we can consider whether or not there is such a thing as a science *of* marketing, comparable in some sense to the sciences of physics, biology, and so on. Secondly, there is still remaining the question of how and to what extent scientific techniques can be applied *to* marketing—whether or not it is, or may be, a science in itself.

Of the two goals set forth by the MSI, certainly the first is the more ambitious. In order to qualify as a distinct science in its own right, marketing will have to meet some rather stringent requirements. For example, it is generally agreed that a science is

. . . a classified and systematized body of knowledge,

. . . organized around one or more central theories and a number of general principles,

. . . usually expressed in quantitative terms,

. . . knowledge which permits the prediction and, under some circumstances, the control of future events.

Few believe that marketing now meets these criteria. True, there is a substantial body of classified knowledge about marketing, but there certainly is no central theory; furthermore, there are few accepted principles, and our ability to predict is limited indeed. One reason for this state of affairs is that, for most of the 50 years since the beginnings of concerted efforts to study marketing, our emphasis has been predominantly on fact-gathering.

The story of attempts to describe and understand marketing phenomena, beginning in the early 1900's, is chronicled by Robert Bartels of Ohio State University in his new book, *The Development of Marketing Thought*.[1] Bartels sees the early study of marketing as an offshoot of eco-

AUTHOR'S NOTE: I gratefully acknowledge the assistance of Michael Halbert, who read the original version of this article and made many useful suggestions on it.

[1] Robert Bartels, *The Development of Marketing Thought* (Homewood, Illinois, Richard D. Irwin, Inc., 1962).

nomics, brought about by changes in economic conditions in the late nineteenth century. These changes produced a "growing disparity between facts and assumptions underlying prevailing [economic] theory," and one of the primary missions of the pioneer marketing students was to reconcile this disparity.

In particular, Bartels notes that while traditional economic theory assumed that producers could (and would) adjust to the market, by 1900 they increasingly sought to adjust the market to their own needs instead. Similarly, orthodox theory had little place for middlemen, and provided no key to understanding the growing size and diversity of such organizations as department stores and mail-order houses. In short, prevailing economic theory did not explain the observed facts about marketing, much less provide any basis for intelligent management.

Believing that economic theory was inadequate as a basis for understanding the marketing system, early students of marketing set out to describe existing institutions and practices and to discover, if possible, the rationale underlying them. Consequently, a spirit of thoroughgoing empiricism pervaded their efforts. For example, Bartels describes a project undertaken in the 1920's by the New York University School of Retailing in cooperation with a group of New York City department stores. This project culminated in the publication of the so-called "Retailing Series," which described the best contemporary practices in merchandising, retail credit, and so on.[2]

This empiricism of academic investigators was strongly reinforced by the philosophy of most business executives. Recently there have been indications that some executives are becoming more receptive to the notion of "theory." The willingness of its sponsors to support MSI provides an outstanding example of this. But most managers who are responsible for day-to-day decisions are still typically inclined to distrust generalizations. Charles Ramond of the Advertising Research Foundation pointed out in a paper, "Theories of Choice in Business," delivered at the Annual Convention of the American Psychological Association in St. Louis on September 5, 1962:

> The businessman's practical wisdom is of a completely different character than scientific knowledge. While it does not ignore generalities, it recognizes the low probability that given combinations of phenomena can or will be repeated. . . . In place of scientific knowledge, then, the businessman collects lore.

---

[2] This series included more than a dozen titles by various authors, such as James L. Fri, *Retail Merchandising, Planning, and Control* (New York, Prentice-Hall, Inc., 1925) and Norris A. Brisco and John W. Wingate, *Retail Buying* (New York, Prentice-Hall, Inc., 1925).

Both academicians and practitioners have concentrated on the accumulation of facts about marketing. To some extent, these facts have been systematized through a process of definition, classification, and analysis. But it must be admitted that few real principles have emerged. Bartels lists a number of generalizations drawn from the literature of marketing; but some of these are actually derived from traditional economic theory, while others are merely tautologies. As an example of the first type, we are told that sellers, under pure competition, will expand output until marginal cost equals marginal revenue. An illustration of a tautology is the assertion that "when conditions demand modification in the existing marketing structure, the change will be made."

Related Sciences

While marketing does not yet appear to qualify as a science in its own right, high hopes have been placed on the applications of findings and methods from other fields which are, presumably, further along the evolutionary trail. This optimism is reflected in several articles among those reprinted in a new revision of *Managerial Marketing: Perspectives and Viewpoints—A Source Book,* edited by William Lazer and Eugene Kelley.[3] First among these articles is one by Joseph W. Newman, originally appearing in HRB,[4] which asserts:

As marketers have become increasingly aware of how much they have to learn about the nature of buying and consumption, they have turned for assistance to the behavioral sciences, which have made great progress in recent times. Much can be gained from this move.

Some of the potential benefits of adopting and applying the results of scientific inquiry in psychology, sociology, and other fields are outlined by Lazer and Kelley in another of the papers in their collection, under the formidable title of "Interdisciplinary Contributions to Marketing Management." These authors distinguish between "discovery disciplines" (i.e., those concerned with discovering regularities in specified aspects of nature) and "application disciplines" (i.e., those oriented to specific types of problems).

In these terms, marketing would appear to be primarily an area for application of findings *from* the sciences (especially behavioral sciences),

---

[3] William Lazer and Eugene Kelley, editors, *Managerial Marketing: Perspectives and Viewpoints—A Source Book* (Homewood, Illinois, Richard D. Irwin, Inc., 1962).

[4] Joseph W. Newman, "New Insight, New Progress, for Marketing," HBR November-December 1957, p. 95.

and not a science in itself. Should the attempt to make it a science, then, be abandoned as a wild-goose chase?

No, it should be continued, W. J. Baumol argues in "On the Role of Marketing Theory," another article included in the Lazer and Kelley book. Baumol points out that while the problems of marketing do, in fact, fall within the spheres of such fields as economics, sociology, and psychology, it is also possible to argue that economics is merely a branch of psychology, and so on. He concludes that "marketing has its special problems and may, therefore, well find it useful to develop further its own body of theory."

But what form should this theory take? Baumol warns that it is too much to expect that theory will permit *exact* predictions of the future. Theory, of necessity, involves abstraction from, and simplification of, reality. Thus, the theorist's task includes:

> . . . examination of some aspect of reality and construction of a simplified small-scale model which behaves in at least some ways like the phenomena under observation. The analyst can understand and trace out the workings of his model while reality is far too complicated and chaotic for this to be possible. . . . The method is well established in the natural sciences. The physicist cannot predict just what path will be followed by a real automobile left free to roll down a real hill. . . . He can only tell us what will happen in the artificial circumstances described by a controlled experiment, where the elements carefully held constant in the laboratory are the aspects of reality from which his simplified model abstracts.

Has any useful theory in this sense been developed in marketing? One interesting attempt is described by Leo Aspinwall in "The Characteristics of Goods Theory" in the same book. Aspinwall's theory is designed "to predict with a high degree of reliability how a product will be distributed," that is, to predict the marketing channels that will be used to reach ultimate consumers or other end users. Five characteristics or "distinguishing qualities" are defined:

1. Replacement rate—the rate at which a good is purchased and consumed.
2. Gross margin—the total cost of moving a product from point of origin to final consumer.
3. "Adjustment"—the extent of services which must be "applied to goods in order to meet the exact needs of the consumer."
4. Time of consumption—durability of the product.
5. Searching time required to procure the product.

Aspinwall argues that these five characteristics are interrelated—in particular, replacement rate is inversely related to the other four, which in turn are directly related to each other. Hence, it is possible to combine the characteristics and derive a threefold classification of goods, arbitrarily designated as "red," "orange," and "yellow." Red goods, with a high replacement rate, low gross margin, low degree of adjustment, short consumption time, and low searching time, will be characterized by "broadcast distribution" and relatively long marketing channels. Yellow goods, with the opposite characteristics, will be distributed direct, while orange goods occupy an intermediate position.

Now, it is possible to criticize the Aspinwall theory on several counts. First, if it is true that replacement rate is invariably related to the other four characteristics, then the whole theory could be built on this single factor; the others are redundant. In the physical sciences, the principle of "parsimony" is well established. William of Ockham, a fourteenth century English scholastic, laid down the rule that theories should be as simple as possible, and the reasons for this seem as compelling in marketing as anywhere else.

A second criticism of the characteristics-of-goods theory is that, to some extent, it seems circular. It can be argued that the total gross margin required to distribute a product and the searching time required to obtain it are *results* of the marketing channels used, not underlying causes. Finally, there is some ambiguity as to whether Aspinwall is trying to explain how goods *are* distributed or how they *should be* distributed. If the implication is that these are one and the same, then there is a hidden premise in the theory.

But the point is not whether or not Aspinwall's theory is correct. In either case it may well be *useful,* because it provides a way of *organizing* facts about marketing. Lazer believes that this is the ultimate value of theory. In "Philosophic Aspects of the Marketing Discipline," another selection included in the book, he argues:

> Marketing thought should not proceed merely by the accumulation of observations which are unregulated by theory. It is generally accepted that fruitful observations cannot be made, nor their results arranged and correlated, without the use of hypotheses which go beyond the existing state of knowledge.

Marketing Science and Managers

At this point, the executive may well ask: "What has all this to do with me?" Many feel that the whole debate about science in marketing is strictly an academic red herring, and that the quest for science is really a roundabout form of academic status-seeking. Indeed, there is a certain unintentional irony in the plaint by Lazer and Kelley that "as a discipline, marketing is often assigned a relatively low status in the academic spectrum."

But there is more at stake than the vanities of professors. Some very "practical" men feel that even the modest progress to date toward science in marketing calls for a new approach by management. On this score, Donald R. Longman, President of the American Marketing Association, said in a message to members of the association in September 1962:

The concept of science in marketing and the idea of objective and thorough study of issues, acquisition and evaluation of relevant facts, are no longer the exclusive province in business of the researcher. The scientific approach has spread, permeating all senior levels of decision making. . . . This is a new thing—the marketing staff manager and decision maker as a researcher concerned with the science of marketing.

This viewpoint is strongly advocated by Edward C. Bursk in his new book, *Text and Cases in Marketing: A Scientific Approach.*[5] Bursk states flatly that "old-fashioned judgmental decision making must be supplanted by a more scientific approach."

What does such an approach entail? Bursk sets forth three requirements:

1. The use of scientific theories, and techniques based on them, wherever available.

2. Increased use of experimentation.

3. The use of analysis to decide on action in a "systematic, planned way."

Perhaps even more important than these prescriptions is the concept of *integration* between decision making and research activities which pervades this entire book. While many executives have long recognized the need for information on which to base intelligent decisions, and have spent substantial sums on research to get such information, all too often research is not really used effectively.

Joseph W. Newman, in another HBR article,[6] has noted:

Only in a relatively small number of companies has marketing research become a regular part of the making of important policy and operating decisions.

In companies with marketing research units, a wide gap typically separates research personnel and management personnel.

What typically happens, Newman observes, is that the role of marketing "research" is seen purely as one of fact gathering. The manager recognizes the need for information on market shares, advertising recall, extent of distribution, and the like. But the relationships between these things and a firm's marketing policies are seldom analyzed. When they are, in some

---

[5] Edward C. Bursk, *Text and Cases in Marketing: A Scientific Approach* (Englewood Cliffs, New Jersey, Prentice-Hall, Inc., 1962).

[6] Joseph W. Newman, "Put Research Into Marketing Decisions," HBR March-April 1962, p. 105.

massive "one-shot" study, the results are usually disappointing, and the atmosphere becomes antagonistic to further investigation for several years.

Executives who distrust research per se take these failings as justification of their attitude. (Ha! You see? Even with all their formulas, they couldn't predict what would happen in Moline! What we need here is experienced judgment, not a lot of harebrained theories!)

It is probably unfortunate that the term "research" ever came to be used to describe the activities of most marketing research staff units. A much better designation would be "marketing intelligence," since the purpose of these activities is directly analogous to those of a G-2 unit in the Army. Military intelligence personnel are not expected to develop a science of warfare. Their mission, instead, is to obtain complete, accurate, and current information.

Such concentration on detailed, particularized data is, in fact, inconsistent with real scientific inquiry. For the same reason, it is probably hopeless to expect much progress in the development of science in marketing as a result of simply stockpiling more and more current facts. This does not mean that facts are unimportant. But they should be looked on as the raw materials of research, not its end results.

All of this suggests that what is needed is a very different kind of research, together with a very different approach to it by management. This approach will require, among other things, that research specialists and management "generalists" know more about each others' jobs. Beyond this, Newman advocates the use of "research generalists" who would serve as middlemen between executives and research technicians. A similar proposal has also been made by Marion Harper, Jr.[7] Finally, progress in marketing science will require a view of research as a continuous, cumulative process, with constant interaction between investigators and the decision-makers who utilize their findings.

Development Problems

Granted for the moment that the goal of science in marketing is a desirable one, why does the task appear to be so difficult? There are essentially three schools of thought on this point.

1. That science in marketing can be achieved by continued application of the same methods used in other fields, but that results are harder to achieve because the phenomena being studied are more complex.

2. That marketing phenomena (and human behavior in general) differ

---

[7] "A New Profession to Aid Marketing Management," *Journal of Marketing,* January 1961, pp. 1-6.

in *kind* from those of the physical sicences, so that *different methods* will have to be employed in studying them.

3. That marketing (and, again, human behavior in general) can never become a science because of its inherent elusiveness. Thus, the search for science is well intentioned but doomed to failure.

Bursk subscribes to the first of these beliefs, asserting that "the material is so intricate and intangible that hitherto it has not been tackled consciously and formally." His reasons for believing as he does are based on these facts:

Buying and selling involve a "subtle, fluid interaction," with actions on each side affecting actions on the other.

The number of possible combinations of actions by a seller is very large.

General economic conditions are continually changing, and this clouds the effects of a firm's marketing programs.

The actions of competitors also influence marketing results.[8]

In brief, these reasons boil down to the idea that since observed behavior in marketing is influenced by *many variables,* it is very difficult to isolate the effect of any one or any small combination of variables. But is this not also true in the physical sciences? The behavior of a missile, for example, is subject to the influences of numerous factors, including some which are only dimly perceived.

In the speech referred to earlier, Charles Ramond suggested that the events studied by physical scientists are easier to understand and predict because physical systems are basically simpler than human behavior systems. First, physical systems are "loosely coupled." While many variables affect an event, it is possible to study one or a few as if they were, in fact, isolated. A statistician would term this a "low degree of interaction"; for example, while both temperature and atmospheric pressure may affect some event, it is possible to hold one of these constant and measure the effects of the other, and get good predictive results. In contrast, variables affecting human behavior interact to such an extent that the familiar "other-things-being-equal" assumption can lead to mistaken conclusions.

Further, according to Ramond, physical scientists have generally been able to represent real systems by *linear equations,* i.e., by relatively simple models which can readily be manipulated. But such simple models have not been found adequate to describe human behavior. For example, forecasts of sales, population growth, and so forth based on linear regression models have usually been very inaccurate.

And finally, while relationships among physical phenomena are char-

---

[8] Bursk, op. cit., pp. 6-7.

acteristically *stable* over extended time periods, marketing is thought to be highly *dynamic.* Thus, relationships which seem to describe a system at one time may not hold at some future time.

Because marketing deals with events which are, in Ramond's phrase, "tightly coupled, nonlinear, and dynamic," the progress of science is slow and painful at best. An excellent illustration of the difficulties encountered in the "scientific approach" is afforded by Alfred R. Oxenfeldt in "Diary of a Research Project in the Television Set Industry."[9] Oxenfeldt describes, blow by blow, his efforts over a five-year period to explain changes in the market shares of TV set manufacturers.

He postulated that these changes resulted from differences in product quality, prices, dealer margins, and advertising efforts. To test this hypothesis, it was first necessary to get reasonably complete information on the "independent variables" as well as on market-share results. But Oxenfeldt found that only partial information on any of the variables could be obtained; for instance, quality ratings by product-testing agencies were based on only one or two of the 15 or 25 models offered by a manufacturer. Worse still, many of the terms used in the industry (such as "margin") ". . . cannot be defined rigorously or even in a manner that would insure substantial uniformity of usage." Finally, it was discovered that no records at all were kept of some of the most important actions taken by manufacturers.

Further investigation led Oxenfeldt to the conclusion that it would probably be impossible to discover any meaningful regularities in the TV set market as a whole. He felt that in the end, each local market was a separate case, that each manufacturer was different from all the others, and that conditions changed significantly from one time period to the next. This, in effect, supports the notion that marketing systems are *unstable;* and this, in turn, implies that conclusions reached from the study of the past have only limited applicability to the future.

Note that the assumption of stability underlies much of what is known in the physical sciences. For example, it has been found that certain substances undergo radioactive disintegration at a constant rate relative to time. This provides the basis for the "dating" methods used in geology and archaeology. Suppose, however, that radioactive disintegration were *not* a stable process; indeed, there is no way to prove that it is. If the rate of disintegration does change, then all of the dates applied to various epochs in the earth's history are, in fact, wrong.

Thus, there is a serious question about the belief, expressed by Harlan D. Mills in "Brand A Versus Brand B—A Mathematical Approach," that

---

[9] Presented as a case in Bursk, op. cit., pp. 31-44 (adapted from "Scientific Marketing: Ideal and Ordeal," HBR March-April 1961, p. 51).

"marketing 'laws' can be derived in the same manner as the laws of physics [so that] the way is open for marketing to become, more and more, a science."[10]

If the concepts and methods of the physical sciences cannot be lifted bodily over to the study of marketing, what then? As noted earlier, one of the missions of the Marketing Science Institute is to promote the use of scientific *techniques* in marketing. Presumably this includes the development of new, special-purpose techniques. It is not possible to foresee just what form these new techniques may take.

It seems likely, however, that some of them will be based on the technology of the computer. Already some operations researchers have found that complex models of market behavior are best "solved" by simulation—that is, by generating artificial experience and testing the effects of changes by simulated experimentation. Since field experiments in marketing are so costly—and sometimes downright impossible—simulation may play an increasing role in the future.

Even if a new scientific tool kit can be developed, there are some who think marketing can never be a science. E. B. Weiss, the Madison Avenue iconoclast, espouses this extreme viewpoint.[11] Weiss argues, first, that attempts to discover scientific principles over the past 40 years have been unsuccessful, and that many of them have really been hoaxes. More important, he notes that even honest efforts involve the use of such concepts as "average behavior," i.e., the use of probability theory and statistical analysis. Weiss claims that there is "no such thing as an 'average mind' or 'average behavior.' "

If this argument is meant to imply that knowledge expressed in terms of probabilities is essentially unscientific, then much of modern physics is also unscientific. The phenomenon of radioactive disintegration mentioned earlier, in fact, rests squarely on probability theory. The rate of disintegration used in dating objects is an *average* rate, and the only justification for using it is that the number of objects (atoms) involved is so large that individual deviations become unimportant.

To the extent that marketing deals with the behavior of large groups of people, the same reasoning applies to it. Certainly the notion of "average behavior" has been used effectively by insurance companies. Conclusions based on the probabilities of certain kinds of behavior among large groups cannot, of course, legitimately be applied to individuals; but predictions of individual responses may not be necessary for scientific marketing.

---

[10] Presented as a case in Bursk, op. cit., pp. 23-30 (adapted from "Marketing as a Science," HBR September-October 1961, p. 137).

[11] E. B. Weiss, "Will Marketing Ever Become a Science?" *Advertising Age,* August 20, 1962, pp. 64-65.

Art of Using Science

Let us suppose for a moment that the millenium does arrive, and marketing does, indeed, become a full-fledged science. What then? Will marketing decisions become routine, with computers grinding out solutions in response to the proper inputs? Not so, is the view of Theodore Levitt, as expressed in his book, *Innovation in Marketing.*[12] Levitt points out that "management has always sought formulas and prescriptions for easier decision making." As a result, management has become susceptible to the "seductions of science," and has fallen easy prey to the exaggerated claims of some researchers. Further, he believes that the root of the problem is that "all too often neither the researchers nor the corporate bosses really know what it is they are trying to do." This is another way of saying that marketing science—even in its relatively crude present state—is concerned with means, not ends. This is equally true of the most advanced branches of knowledge. Scientists can (presumably) tell us how to get a man to the moon, but do we really *want* a man on the moon? The main theme of *Innovation in Marketing* is the need for management to define just where it is trying to go. This need will remain regardless of how much progress may be made in developing marketing as a science.

For a long time to come, it seems clear that marketing science will not advance to a stage in which the element of risk is eliminated from decisions. Bursk says that risk is an integral part of marketing management. Levitt goes even further: "That is what management is all about—taking risks." While increased knowledge can help in *identifying* the risks involved in decisions, and in some cases provide *measures* of their magnitudes, it can never eliminate them altogether.

Because science is concerned with means, it does not offer any answers to the basic questions of *values* underlying marketing management. It is a commonplace that the results of science can be used rightly or wrongly. Consequently, no matter how scientific marketing may become, managers must still govern their actions, in part, by considerations of their ultimate effects on customers, employees, and society at large.

Indeed, advancements in marketing science will put ethical issues into even bolder relief than at present. To some extent, science usually implies *control.* A vision of "the hidden persuaders," only this time equipped with true scientific knowledge rather than just the dubious baggage of depth interviewing, is disturbing to many observers. It can only be hoped that along with increased knowledge will come increased competence to use it wisely.

---

[12] Theodore Levitt, *Innovation in Marketing* (New York, McGraw-Hill Book Company, Inc., 1962).

In any case, at least for a long time to come, it will remain the responsibility of the manager to evaluate the worth of alleged advances in marketing science, and to decide whether and how new knowledge is to be used in administration. As Levitt phrases it:

The highest form of achievement is always art, never science. . . . Business leadership *is* an art worthy of [the manager's] own respect and the public's plaudits.

5

"Is Marketing a Science?" Revisited

WELDON J. TAYLOR

The science of the postmodern world will put the "Is Marketing a Science?" debate in a new perspective. The change should relieve some of the tension of the "schizophrenia" resulting from the two opposing views.

Tomorrow's science will maximize the advantage of the marketing concept as an approach to the study of marketing. It will forsake for the moment the hope that the universe can be described into predictable patterns. It will embrace the reality of a dynamic world which can be explained in terms of science only provisionally.

History of "Is Marketing a Science?"

In 1948 Lyndon O. Brown, in support of the emphasis given for many years by the American Marketing Association, published an article entitled "Toward a Profession of Marketing."[1] He made no claims for marketing as a science; but he urged the accumulation of a body of knowledge, the development of an analytical approach, and the sharpening of research as a basic tool for management. Nonetheless, his paper ignited the embers of the "Is Marketing a Science?" debate.[2]

Reprinted with permission from the *Journal of Marketing,* national quarterly publication of the American Marketing Association, Vol. 29 (July, 1965), pp. 49-53.

[1] Lyndon O. Brown, "Toward a Profession of Marketing," *Journal of Marketing,* Vol. 13 (July, 1948), pp. 27-31.

[2] Articles which appeared as a chain reaction to Brown's were Wroe Alderson and Reavis Cox, "Towards a Theory of Marketing," *Journal of Marketing,* Vol. 13 (October, 1948), pp. 137-151; Roland S. Vaile, "Towards a Theory of Marketing— a Comment," *Journal of Marketing,* Vol. 13 (April, 1949), pp. 520-522; Neal E. Miller, "Social Science and the Art of Advertising," *Journal of Marketing,* Vol. 14 (January, 1950), pp. 579-584; Robert T. Bartels, "Can Marketing Be a Science?" *Journal of Marketing,* Vol. 15 (January, 1951), pp. 319-328; Kenneth D. Hutchinson, "Marketing As a Science: An Appraisal," *Journal of Marketing,* Vol. 16 (January, 1952), pp. 286-293; S. F. Otteson, editor, *Marketing: Current Problems and Theories* (Bloomington: University of Indiana, 1952), pp. 11-18.

Probably the best report on the contemporary score is by Robert D. Buzzell.[3] However, in measuring the achievements in marketing against the standards of a science, he finds much to be desired. One of the contributions in Buzzell's article is a succinct and accurate phrasing of the standards of a science:[4]

. . . a classified and systematized body of knowledge,

. . . organized around one or more central theories and a number of general principles,

. . . usually expressed in quantitative terms,

. . . knowledge which permits the prediction and, under some circumstances, the control of future events.

Yet today there is little if any central core of theory or durable principle in marketing. Quantitative formulas applied to marketing that are part of an enduring theory or generalization are rare. The background in which the process occurs changes too rapidly for a stable philosophy of prediction to emerge.[5]

On the other hand, the scientific forces arrayed to further the scientific objectives of marketing are formidable. During the last decade there has emerged a new attitude toward the meaning of both science and marketing that may provide a new balance to the arguments.

Innovations in the Concept of Science

The change in attitude toward science is described by Huston Smith, Professor of Philosophy at the Massachusetts Institute of Technology.[6] He states that "our generation is playing a crucial part in the radical revolution of thought, the development of the postmodern mind and a new view of reality." He says that this century will ". . . rank with the fourth century which witnessed the triumph of Christianity, and the seventeenth, which

---

[3] Robert D. Buzzell, "Is Marketing a Science?" *Harvard Business Review,* Vol. 41 (January-February, 1963), pp. 32-34, 36, 40, 166, 168, and 170.

[4] Same referenece as footnote 3, at p. 32.

[5] Some of the more recent references, in addition to Buzzell's, treating the subject of marketing as a science are Joseph W. Newman, "New Insights, New Progress for Marketing," *Harvard Business Review,* Vol. 35 (November-December, 1957), pp. 95-102; Alfred R. Oxenfeldt, "Scientific Marketing: Ideal and Ordeal," *Harvard Business Review,* Vol. 39 (March-April, 1961), pp. 51-64; Harlan D. Mills, "Marketing as a Science," *Harvard Business Review,* Vol. 39 (September-October, 1961), pp. 137-141; Edward C. Bursk, *Text and Cases in Marketing: A Scientific Approach* (Englewood Cliffs, New Jersey: Prentice-Hall, Inc., 1962); E. B. Weiss, "Will Marketing Ever Become a Science?" *Advertising Age* (August 20, 1962), pp. 64-65; H. W. Huegy, editor, *The Conceptual Framework for a Science of Marketing* (Urbana, Illinois: University of Illinois, 1963).

[6] Huston Smith, "The Revolution in Western Thought," *Saturday Evening Post* (August 28, 1961), pp. 28-29, and 59-60.

signalled the dawn of human science. . . ."[7] This change, according to him, despairs of the hope that science as presently conceived can bring life and its physical environment into an orderly focus.

Professor Smith asks "how are we to picture an electron traveling two or more different routes through space concurrently or passing from orbit to orbit without traversing the space between them at all? What kind of model can we construct of a space that is finite yet unbounded, or of light which is both wave and particle?"[8]

He quotes P. W. Bridgman of Harvard, who suggests that "we have reached the limit of the vision of the great pioneers of science, the vision, namely, that we live in a sympathetic world in that it is comprehensible by our minds."[9]

Many of the basic theories describing the ultimate nature of the universe have been shot through with conflict and diversity. The cosmic breakthrough shattered the dream of the scientist who hoped that he and his colleagues were making significant progress in cataloging the unknowns of the universe into laws and principles.

Indeed, the scientific millennium, the quest for which began in the seventeenth century, was visualized as a period when the basic questions about the universe and its nature would be settled. Today the scientific millennium is viewed as a period when a maximum number of trained minds exercising scientific skill will achieve greater speed in finding significant and useful relationships in an infinite unknown.

Conant's Contribution

James Bryant Conant, renowned chemist and former President of Harvard University, describes different boundaries of science; and his definition meets the demands of the new cosmic reality: "Science is an interconnected series of concepts and conceptual schemes that has developed as a result of experimentation and observation and are *fruitful* of further experimentation and observations."[10]

He continues. "Science is a *speculative enterprise* [italics added]. The validity of a new idea and the significance of a new experimental finding are to be measured by the consequences—consequences in terms of other ideas and experiments. Thus conceived, science is not a quest for certainty;

---

[7] Same reference as footnote p, at p. 59.

[8] Same reference as footnote 6, at p. 59.

[9] Same reference as footnote 6, at p. 59.

[10] James Bryant Conant, *Science and Common Sense* (New Haven: Yale University Press, 1951), p. 25.

it is rather a quest which is successful only to the degree that it is continuous."[11]

Conant points to the disillusionment that came about in the 1930s, wherein physicists had to forsake their previous belief that experiments could find unchanging principles and reliable answers to many problems. He says, "This episode in itself is for me sufficient justification for treating all *scientific theories and explanations as highly provisional* [italics added]."[12]

Conant's first requirement for a valid science consists of conceptual schemes that are fruitful. Such schemes or plans contribute to the increasing flow of other such schemes or plans. Unlike the general principle, they may become obsolete and be supplanted by those which include or transcend them. Their test as a part of a valid science is in their fruitfulness as a basis for new concepts.

The second criterion for scientific endeavor is that it would tend to ". . . lower the degree of empiricism or to extend the range of theory."[13] In other words, science should make possible the predicting of outcomes.

Conant states that by the application of basic theory the surveyor can describe a variety of areas having no similarity as to boundaries. On the other hand, the recipe of the chef is good for only one dish. If he attempts to discover another tasty dish, he will not have foreknowledge of his findings. He must experiment to determine its quality. If he succeeds, there will be little in his discovery that will apply to additional dishes.

Another example to illustrate the extending of the range of theory is Boyle's Law, relating to the expansion of gases. This law operates in steam, gasoline, diesel, or jet engines. It also applies to firearms and explosives. Unlike the chef's recipe, the predictability possible as a result of the law enables men to extend the range of theory and know results before they happen. This law is one of the conceptual schemes that were fruitful in leading to the discovery of a means for splitting the atom.

This predictability aspect of science is the popular one. By extending the range of theory in light, sound, and chemistry, man has discovered leverage with which he has completely changed the world.

It was thus a natural development that social problems were subjected to this so-called scientific analysis. A typical incident is in the evolution of price determination as a measure of value. Smith, Malthus, Ricardo, Mill, and others were contributors to a man-hour theory of value. Nearly a hundred years later Hungarian economists, supported by Jevons from England, advanced a different view of value based on utility.

In 1890 Alfred Marshall published his *Principles,* which compro-

---

[11] Same reference as footnote 10, at pp. 25-26.
[12] Same reference as footnote 10, at p. 28.
[13] Same reference as footnote 10, at p. 58.

mised the differences and synthesized the opposing views. His example of the two blades of the scissors describing the interaction of demand and supply curves meets Conant's test of science in the social realm. The meeting of the forces of demand with the forces of supply at the market place to set a price is a conceptual scheme that extends the range of theory in the science of economics.

The New Concept of Science and Marketing

According to Conant's proposition, the would-be marketing scientists should not discontinue their search for laws, principles, and central theories. Yet the great returns that will accrue to marketing scientists lie in three overlapping areas.

First is the development of conceptual schemes that will open new frontiers in marketing knowledge and suggest additional avenues for observation and experiment. The results of these developments will be of sufficient merit that they will be recorded, analyzed, and published.

Second, the marketing scientist will draw on the fruitful conceptual schemes and develop others that extend beyond fruitfulness to usefulness. Usefulness consists of a quality which makes the marketing manager better able to predict the outcome of his commitment and more successful in his enterprise than he would have been without such knowledge.

Third, the marketing scientist constantly will be refining the present concepts to greater usefulness and adapting them to the changing patterns and practices of the market place.

This process is well under way. It began when man first described and analyzed market activities and published the results for the benefit of others. From an infinite number of examples of this continuing process, two of contemporary interest and significance will serve as illustrations.

Study by Coffin

The first example comes from a pioneering experiment in assessing advertising effectiveness, in which Thomas E. Coffin includes an example of both the fruitful and the useful conceptual scheme.[14] He states: "It has taken audience researchers some three decades and upwards of a hundred million dollars spent on audience research of all varieties to arrive at a point where *they can produce reasonably accurate answers to the question of how many?* [Italics added.] Isn't it logical to expect the same sequence of events to accrue in determining how hard?"[15]

---

[14] Thomas E. Coffin, "A Pioneering Experiment for Assessing Advertising Effectiveness," *Journal of Marketing,* Vol. 27 (July, 1963), pp. 1-10.

[15] Same reference as footnote 14, at p. 2.

Coffin's statement in the context of "Is Marketing a Science?" says in effect: It has taken researchers three decades and a hundred million dollars in experimenting with conceptual schemes that are fruitful to establish one that is useful. Isn't it logical to expect the same sequence of events in determining a similar yet different objective? Having thus cited a useful example, Coffin introduces one that is fruitful. He reports the results of his experiment wherein a 2-wave panel composed of the same individuals was reinterviewed to determine the comparative impact of television and magazine advertising at two points in time, three months apart; and he is duly modest in claiming his experiment to be fruitful but not yet useful.

Many would disagree with Daniel's Starch's claims that he is able to measure the specific results in sales of a magazine advertisement or a television commercial in his "net-ad-produced-purchases" method.[16] Yet there are few who would deny that his conceptual scheme contains seeds which will sometimes and in some manner influence predictability.

The above-described activities are still "speculative enterprise." Their "fruitfulness" will be measured in terms of the "other ideas and other experiments" they stimulate, and the degree to which they are "continuous."

Study by Oxenfeldt

The second illustrative example is in the area of sales outcome. Alfred R. Oxenfeldt reports an observation that has already proved fruitful in stimulating comment in learned journals and books.[17] He captures a "speculative" and "continuous" tone by presenting his experiment in a diary form which includes his own speculations.

If judged by the law, principle, or central-theory category (the benchmarks of traditional science), his experience was disillusioning. Because of the inadequacy of records available to him and the dynamics of the competitive television industry, whose share-of-market results he was studying, he was unable to discover the information he originally sought. Although he despaired at several levels, there were residual ingredients in his observations. He lists seven generalizations to guide similar and subsequent scientific undertakings. He also lists four conclusions for business executives and four points which describe the nature of executive decisions as they relate to scientific undertakings.

Oxenfeldt delves courageously into that twilight area where marketing decisions grow out of *knowledge* about the problems and practices of business and the analytical or *administrative* skill of the executive. Which of these two ingredients is strategic?

---

[16] Daniel Starch, "How to Relate Readership to Sales," *Printer's Ink,* Vol 287 (May 15, 1964), pp. 25-28.

[17] Oxenfeldt, same reference as footnote 4.

He takes the view that it is not an either-or situation, but rather a combination. One is prompted by his thinking to reason as follows: The rigorous analysis of the available facts and subsequent action by the executive may have three residues: (1) the actual *results* of his course of action; (2) an *improved administrative skill* resulting from his experience; and (3) the *knowledge* gained from putting his plans into action.

For the purpose of this discussion, the last of these is strategic. If this knowledge is analyzed and given a degree of permanence in writing and its validity determined, it may stimulate the development of other useful or fruitful ideas.

The use of electronic data processing will make the recording and analyzing of facts related to everyday business transactions more common. This extensive and intensive examination of transactions will serve as a feedback from actual experience. It could provide a prolific resource for discovering and refining relevant conceptual schemes. Oxenfeldt's project was just such an attempt to measure the effect of marketing transactions on a broad front. Even though he did not discover specific reasons for the change in market shares, it would reveal a lack of imagination not to see in his study a residue of significant knowledge. His contribution included at least the beginning of conceptual schemes that were speculative, fruitful, continuous, and possibly useful.

Scientific Method

The traditional view of scientific method includes agreement among respected scholars as to the meaning of terms, classifying data so that they will achieve a high degree of accurate mobility, and finally testing the validity of hypotheses.

Conant's failure to agree that these points are controlling does not mean that he would neglect them. He would expect such conditions to prevail in any scientific endeavor. Yet he considers them as routines and not the source of the dynamics and vitality of science. His three steps in describing the scientific process are: (1) speculative thinking as a creative act; (2) deductive reasoning; and (3 cut-and-try or empirical experimentations.[18] This describes a process of getting a working hypothesis in mind; eliminating it or improving on it; projecting its potentials by deductive reasoning; and then actually testing it in the field or the laboratory.

The conceptual schemes resulting from this process are often more tenuous, dynamic, and speculative than the reliable, stable, traditional law and principle. Yet they describe the area of science in which most modern scientists are engaged.

---

[18] Same reference as footnote 10, at p. 45.

An Art or a Science?

In answer to the recurring question, "Is marketing an art or a science?" Jevon's word is the simplest: ". . . science is to know, and art is to do. . ."[19]

Knowledge makes it possible to improve the skill in doing; and doing serves as a means of testing and enhancing knowledge. To pinpoint an instance, the act of performing an experiment in the laboratory requires an artistic skill to some degree. Yet the residue of knowledge recorded as a result of the experiment is science. It will serve as a means of improving the effectiveness of the next experiment. Science in marketing will provide guides to more efficient action and a means of sharpening skill.

Marketing men are constantly improving their effectiveness by means of a growing body of conceptual schemes that move from the fruitful into the useful stage. The act of marketing is an art. The practitioner as such is not a scientist. Yet in the course of his work he may publish observations and conduct experiments. To the extent that he does so and contributes to the fund of conceptual schemes that are fruitful and that extend the range of theory in marketing, he functions as a scientist.

The Marketing Concept

Winning the consumer's choice in a highly competitive world at a minimum cost forced the marketing executive to break free from traditional patterns of thinking. The method of science which consisted of dividing and classifying, then redividing and reclassifying, in search of principles or laws did not satisfy the demands of reality in marketing.

In order to see all the forces influencing marketing success in their interrelationships within the whole, the many intangible ingredients of choice had to be included. Synthesis had to complement analysis. The marketing department had to be viewed as a part of the unified whole.

Its success depended on interrelationships among production, product development, packaging, finance, personnel, and public relations. A conceptual view indicated that all of these, as well as controllable areas outside the firm, were in some manner an influence on the customer's choice or on the cost of winning it. The manner in which these activities were coordinated in a dynamic process to achieve the desired impact gave coherence and an integrated unity to the process.

The adoption of the term *marketing concept* reemphasized the consumer's choice as the center of the concentric circle and made it the heart of the marketing universe.

---

[19] See "Science," *Webster's Third New International Dictionary, unabridged.*

Basic to all other conceptual schemes in marketing are those used in the financial statements. The costs and satisfactions resulting from the processes of the firm are converted into expenses and incomes, and summarized to determine profits. They provide a basis for measuring the ultimate effect of all other conceptual schemes.

The concept approach to marketing releases valuable relationships which were "frozen out" of use by traditional compartmentalized treatment. It provides a potential for the development of many such schemes that are yet in their budding stages. The quest is a speculative enterprise, yet fruitful and continuous.

6

Marketing Theory and Marketing Science

MICHAEL H. HALBERT

The marketing process, in some form or other, is a part of any social or cultural system, no matter how far back we look in the history of organized human affairs. In fact, the twin forces of specialization and motivation, which are characteristic of any culture, lead inevitably to the development and maintenance of marketing. Specialization in various skills, as well as specialization in resources and needs, requires that goods and services be exchanged; motivation, both of individuals and of the culture as a whole, requires that at least some aspects of this exchange be mutually rewarding. Exchange for individual profit is, from the anthropological viewpoint, a rather recent development, probably not more than three thousand years old. Earlier exchange was for social, religious, or communicative purposes. For example, it is likely that trade between tribes developed out of the practice of ritualistic exchange as a sign that the tribes were at peace, and only gradually developed into an exchange of surpluses for mutual utilization.

Man of necessity, then, develops marketing. But there is nothing necessary that impels man to develop a *theory* of marketing. To describe man's reasons for developing marketing theory, we must look at the general problem of the relation of theory to practice and the motives that lead to the development of theory in any area of human endeavor. A brief sketch of this type of human activity will set the stage for a better understanding of the present state of marketing theory, its origins and history, and its probable immediate future.

There are two parallel lines of development that usually coalesce to force the development of theory in any particular area. One of these lines is the intensely practical desire to improve the performance of any operation. The ideas and notions developed under this pressure are usually not associated with the name "theory" or "concept" or "natural law," but rather with phrases like "understanding the operation," "knowing how it works," or "developing the skills involved in operating the system." Every practical and practicing marketing executive wishes to perform his task better and more easily. To do this he must have some understanding of how the actions he initiates are related to the phenomena he observes. This for him is the beginning of a marketing theory, and the extent to which he does well or poorly is in part a reflection of how adequately he can theorize, although he probably would resist the implication that he is engaged in anything traditionally thought to be so "impractical" as the development or use of theory.

The other line of development that leads to theory is the one more often associated with the term, and this stems from the intellectual curiosity of the theorizer. There seems to be (in humans at any rate) a more or less pronounced desire to organize the world about them so that it can be discussed, communicated, thought about, and understood—understood with the fewest concepts and rules that can be made sufficient. This is the extreme opposite of the assumption that there is no order in the phenomena and no continuity in the system being managed. Thus, the conventional theorist is impelled by his dislike of chaos rather than by any pragmatic desire for improved performance. However, it has been proved repeatedly, to the embarrassment of both groups, that the practical operator is often theoretical and conceptual, and that the abstract theorizer is often intensely practical. It is time that both groups moved closer together and openly acknowledged their interdependence. The operating executive or manager must recognize his need for theory and conceptualization, and the "pure" theorist must realize that not only to *develop* his theories, but to *prove* and *check* their adequacies, he must immerse himself in the practical operating side of the world in addition to the purely conceptual side.

This has even happened in the higher reaches of pure mathematics, but it is perhaps more readily apparent in the social and behavioral sciences (and for the moment, at least, we can class marketing here). The essential contribution of the marketing scientist is to bring to the level of consciousness the implicit operating theories of marketing managers and executives, and to bring to bear upon these explicated theories the analytic devices of the more formal sciences. Only then can we remove inconsistencies, develop programs for experimentation and refinement of testable hypotheses, and, above all, aid in the gradual development of a body of theory or marketing that will be intellectually satisfying to the formalist, and also be practically meaningful and useful to the operator and executive in the marketing area.

The Meaning of Theory

If for the moment we concern ourselves with only explicit theory, then it is quite obvious that many areas of human activity operate, and operate quite well, without an adequate body of explicit theory. This is true not only in the business or managerial sciences such as marketing, but also in the physical and engineering aspects of human endeavor. Many of the major contributions in the sciences, and almost all of the successful innovations in business, have been made without the benefit of developed theory. When the steam engine was first invented, it was purely pragmatic in its design. The thermodynamic theory of heat transfer had not yet been developed. In fact, steam engines were built and operated successfully for over a hundred years before the theory was developed. At that point in time the design of steam engines underwent a radical change. They were designed from theoretical principles rather than from a history of pragmatic data on how past steam engines had behaved, and their efficiency increased tremendously. This same general history has applied to many areas of human activity. They were arts or techniques or skills when they were first being practiced, but when a sound theoretical basis was developed many problems disappeared and others became much easier to solve. At least operating problems that had concerned the practitioners became easier, but then the harder, more basic problems began to emerge, and attention could be directed toward them for the first time.

Before the development of modern accountancy, financial analysis and the keeping of ordinary business records the executive needed the highest skill, interpretive talent, intuition, and "feel of the business." Now much of this is relegated to machines, but the net result has been to upgrade the position of accountancy in the corporate organization. This is because the implications of the basic problems of accountancy for general corporate policy, for managerial decision making, and for national and international policy became apparent; and the attention of competent accountants is now being directed toward these much more difficult problems. Perhaps in time they also will be explained by new theoretical developments and thus can be relegated to some type of automation (be it human or mechanical). Then the next level of problems which are hidden beyond the limits of present knowledge will become apparent, and accountants can move on to even higher and more difficult tasks. This is what we can expect and hope for in the study of marketing. There are very few, if any, marketing problems today that yield to theoretical analysis well enough that decisions involving them can be safely relegated to machines or to lower-level personnel. Someday, assuming that a science of marketing emerges, many of the problems with which today's marketing management is concerned can be relegated to such levels, but the higher-order problems which are obscured today—the relation of marketing to the total firm, to the industry, to the economy, and to national and international affairs—will become more apparent and more amenable to attack. When that day comes, the common problems of today's marketing management will be viewed much as we view the Roman's difficulties with long division (try XLVIII/XII) from the vantage point of modern positional decimal system (48/12). It was the language, not the problem, that was hard.

Before we proceed much further with this discussion, it is necessary to say a few words about the meaning of theory as it is used in this book. Like all abstractions, the word theory has been used in many different ways, in many different contexts, at times so broadly as to include almost all descriptive statements about a class of phenomena. At other times it is used so narrowly as to exclude everything but a series of terms and their relationships that satisfy certain logical requirements. We shall want to take a somewhat middle position here and say that at the very least a theoretical statement within the framework of marketing must do more than merely describe the phenomena being observed. Even here, though, we must be careful, for to describe implies to have observed, and to have observed implies a choice as to which aspects of the marketing world should be chosen for observations. Also implied in any description are choices of what measurements or classifications were used in the descriptions. All these are decisions which are based ultimately on a theory or a set of theories that explain what it is important to observe and to report about marketing phenomena. Thus, the process of observation or recording or description cannot be divorced from the process of theory construction.

Perhaps more important to our present viewpoint is the notion that we cannot accept the somewhat arbitrary, slightly naïve descriptions of scientific method that start out with observation, then the construction of hypotheses, which in turn leads to theory development, as though theory were the end product of this process rather than an integral and necessary part of each phase of it. This is all by way of emphasizing the distinction between implicit and explicit theory. In the simple recording of a sale of any company's product, a great deal of theory is implicit. The implicit theory must describe not only what a sale is, who the parties to the sale are, and what the price is, but must also include the much more pervasive background concepts that tell us why it is worth using up company resources to record the sale at all. If it is to be recorded, then the method of recording implies what future operations are to be performed on the data, and this in turn implies knowing the information requirements for managerial decisions and ultimately for policy decisions. The often-heard complaint of analysts or executives that "the data weren't recorded in a way that makes such and such an analysis or decision possible" is an illustration of the awkward results of being implicit instead of explicit about the requirements of the information. Therefore, at this point we shall confine our discussion to explicit theory.

It is in this sense that a theory must be more than a mere recording of observations or the results of an analysis performed upon such data; it must also be more than a mere set of definitions and logical operations that can be performed on the definitions. There must be the complete statement of the operational or "semantic" relations between the terms in the definitions and the behaviors in the real world to which the definitions refer. One of the most common definitions of theory is that it is an explanation of a set of phenomena. But explanation involves people —data do not explain themselves. Why would anyone *want* to explain a set of phenomena? Why, to *use* the explanation, of course. To use it in making decisions, perhaps for the most basic research needs, perhaps for the most pressing practical reasons. A theory, then, must include an explanation of its own uses, that is, how one can make decisions with it. Thus, a theory exists for a set of phenomena when all the possible decisions to be made involving those phenomena can be explained. These explanations must fit all possible individuals who make these decisions, and the fitting must be satisfactory to the theorist.

Including the phrase "must be satisfactory to the theorist" leads to rather interesting consequences. The emphasis on the relation of theory to decision making implies that rather than developing theory to explain and understand the physical world, as distinguished from human endeavor and apart from human interests, any adequate notion of theory must include the behavior of people who are operating on the class of phenomena about which the theory is constructed. Thus, if one wishes to find out about the theory of metals, one observes people behaving with metals and asks them to explain the decisions they are making. Those people who can explain most adequately have the best theories of metals, and one usually expects to find them in scientific research laboratories. Following the same line of reasoning, if one wishes to find out abou theories of marketing, one observes people making decisions about marketing phenomena, be they buyers or sellers, executives or manufacturers, business or government policy makers. Here we run into what at first looks like an anomaly, for we do not always find in our universities and academic circles the most adequate explanations for the decisions made about marketing.

The more adequately developed the theory of an area is, the more likely we are to find professional and academic groups concerned with it. In mathematics, astronomy, chemistry, physics, etc., we find that the most competent theorists are associated with high-ranking universities. In most of the business disciplines, and in many of the social and behavioral disciplines, these theorists will be found among the competent practitioners as often as in universities or academic research areas. This is by no means a criticisim of the academic; rather, it reflects the state of theory development in these areas. If marketing is to develop and proceed as a science in future years, we can confidently expect the development and presence of marketing theory in university circles to increase very rapidly and to take its expected and respected place among the other scientific disciplines. That this is not yet the case merely provides us with a challenge for the future. The interest exists; the practice of marketing goes on and provides the resources wherewith to develop a theory. It is up to the scientists to take the initiative and to show that although the task is hard, it is not impossible. In anthropology it has been said that a person understands a culture when he knows enough about it to specify, for any particular situation, what information he needs to select the culturally appropriate response. We can borrow this and say that we will understand marketing when, for any conceivable marketing situation, we can specify what information we need to make the correct decision.

The Need for Theory

The practice of marketing has been going on for many years in this country and abroad. It has developed rapidly and is now one of the major forces in determining the values of civilization and in helping to transmit those values to the members of the culture. Why then all this fuss about theory? If no adequate theory of marketing has developed so far, why is there any need for theory and, even if there is a need, why is this the time to devote so much effort toward filling it? There are really two questions here, and they are answered in turn. First, the need for marketing theory has increased very rapidly in the last two decades, because the complexity of our economic system and the interrelationship of one part of a company with the others and with other companies in the industry has grown so rapidly that the lack of theory has become more burdensome.

The benefits that could be derived from theory have increased as the total competitive picture shifts its emphasis from productive efficiency to marketing adaptability. The advantages of having a theoretical basis for marketing are that decisions can be made more quicky, more correctly, and at less cost. As the scale and cost of operations increase, the commitments that must be made become larger and larger in terms of the available resources and tend to have their impact over a longer period of time. This introduces an inflexibility which means that our commitments of today bind us further into the future, and problems resulting from our commitments of yesterday are harder to solve. Also, as we turn our attention to the nation as a whole and to its place in the world community, we often find marketing being used as an implement of national strategy and of international negotiation. Thus, the costs of not having adequate marketing theory are rising rapidly. We are at the point where marketing is more often the bottleneck in corporate, industrial, and national affairs than are raw materials, production, or finance. When any area becomes a bottleneck in a society, the society devotes its efforts to breaking that bottleneck and to moving forward at a maximum pace. One reason, then, for directing our efforts to the solution of marketing problems through the development of marketing theory is the urgency and magnitude of the problem.

The second kind of answer derives from reasons that are equally powerful. For the first time the techniques and analytic methods for large-scale serious attack on the problems of marketing theory are available. Developments in the other sciences and disciplines, notably in the philosophy of science and in the behavioral sciences, have supplied us with intellectual and analytic tools far beyond those available only twenty or thirty years ago. Computers give us the ability to analyze data and to conduct simulations that would have been impossible in the recent past. They promise for the near future an even greater expansion of these potentialities. The behavioral sciences are developing and have developed very detailed insights into the functioning of human systems and the makeup of human personalities. But perhaps the most encouraging development of all comes from the current temper of philosophic thought. This is true both of its most rigorous applications in logic, as well as in its traditional area of epistemology. This encouragement is due to the inclusion in the problems of methodology of those that arise from the study of human needs and wants and the attempts to satisfy these needs and wants. Problems that had long been thought outside the serious concern of scientists have thus in the last twenty years been attacked from the most fundamental point of view that science has been able to develop in its entire history.

It is by no means certain that a body of science or a set of theories can be constructed as a conscious effort of any group. If one looks at the history of the development of science, there seems to be a natural pace and a cultural setting appropriate for the evolution of scientific thought and of theoretical constructs. One may accept the position that the development of marketing science will not come as the result of a systematically designed research program. Even if it follows the development of the other sciences—a gradual accumulation and amalgamation of bits and pieces of relevant research—an exciting possibility remains. By conscious effort and planned research the speed of this evolutionary process can be increased. Man is no longer at the mercy of natural evolution. If we have consciously developed new breeds and types of plants and animals and have even produced new physical elements, why cannot the same society speed up the production of socal, business, and marketing theories?

II

GENERAL MARKETING THEORY

7

The Analytical Framework for Marketing

WROE ALDERSON

My assignment is to discuss the analytical framework for marketing. Since our general purpose here is to consider the improvement of the marketing curriculum, I assume that the paper I have been asked to present might serve two functions. The first is to present a perspective of marketing which might be the basis of a marketing course at either elementary or advanced levels. The other is to provide some clue as to the foundations in the social sciences upon which an analytical framework for marketing may be built.

Economics has some legitimate claim to being the original science of markets. Received economic theory provides a framework for the analysis of marketing functions which certainly merits the attention of marketing teachers and practitioners. It is of little importance whether the point of view I am about to present is a version of economics, a hybrid of economics and sociology, or the application of a newly emergent general science of human behavior to marketing problems. The analytical framework which I find congenial at least reflects some general knowledge of the social sciences as well as long experience in marketing analysis. In the time available I can do no more than present this view in outline or skeleton form and leave you to determine how to classify it or whether you can use it.

An advantageous place to start for the analytical treatment of marketing is with the radical heterogeneity of markets. Heterogeneity is inherent on both the demand and the supply sides. The homogeneity which the economist assumes for certain purposes is not an antecedent

Reprinted with permission from *Proceedings: Conference of Marketing Teachers from Far Western States,* Delbert J. Duncan, ed. (Berkeley: Schools of Business Administration, University of California, 1958), pp. 15-28.

condition for marketing. Insofar as it is ever realized it emerges out
of the marketing process itself.

The materials which are useful to man occur in nature in heterogeneous mixtures which might be called conglomerations since these
mixtures have only a random relationship to human needs and activities. The collection of goods in the possession of a household or an
individual also consitutes a heterogeneous supply, but it might be called
an assortment since it is related to anticipated patterns of future behavior.
The whole economic process may be described as a series of transformations from meaningless to meaningful heterogeneity. Marketing produces
as much homogeneity as may be needed to facilitate some of the intermediate economic processes but homogeneity has limited significance or
utility for consumer behavior or expectations.

The marketing process matches materials found in nature or goods
fabricated from these materials aganst the needs of households or individuals. Since the consuming unit has a complex pattern of needs, the
matching of these needs creates an assortment of goods in the hands of
the ultimate consumer. Actually the marketing process builds up assortments at many stages along the way, each appropriate to the activities
taking place at that point. Materials or goods are associated in one way
for manufacturing, in another way for wholesale distribution, and in still
another for reail display and selling. In between the various types of
heterogeneous collections relatively homogeneous supplies are accumulated through the processes of grading, refining, chemical reduction and
fabrication.

Marketing brings about the necessary transformations in heterogeneous supplies through a multiphase process of sorting. Matching of every
individual need would be impossible if the consumer had to search out
each item required or the producer had to find the users of a product one
by one. It is only the ingenious use of intermediate sorts which make it
possible for a vast array of diversified products to enter into the ultimate
consumer assortments as needed. Marketing makes mass production possible first by providing the assortment of supplies needed in manufacturing
and then taking over the successive transformations which ultimately
produce the assortments in the hands of consuming units.

To some who have heard this doctrine expounded, the concept of
sorting seems empty, lacking in specific behavioral content, and hence
unsatisfactory as a root idea for marketing. One answer is that sorting
is a more general and embracing concept than allocation which many
economists regard as the root idea of their science. Allocation is only one
of the four basic types of sorting all of which are involved in marketing.
Among these four, allocation is certainly no more significant than assorting, one being the breaking down of a homogeneous supply and the other

the building up of a heterogeneous supply. Assorting, in fact, gives more direct expression to the final aim of marketing but allocation performs a major function along the way.

There are several basic advantages in taking sorting as a central concept. It leads directly to a fundamental explanation of the contribution of marketing to the overall economy of human effort in producing and distributing goods. It provides a key to the unending search for efficiency in the marketing function itself. Finally, sorting as the root idea of marketing is consistent with the assumption that heterogeneity is radically and inherently present on both sides of the market and that the aim of marketing is to cope with the heterogeneity of both needs and resources.

At this stage of the discussion it is the relative emphasis on assorting as contrasted with allocation which distinguishes marketing theory from at least some versions of economic theory. This emphasis arises naturally from the preoccupation of the market analyst with consumer behavior. One of the most fruitful approaches to understanding what the consumer is doing is the idea that she is engaged in building an assortment, in replenishing or extending an inventory of goods for use by herself and her family. As evidence that this paper is not an attempt to set up a theory in opposition to economics it is acknowledged that the germ of this conception of consumer behavior was first presented some eighty years ago by the Austrian economist Boehm-Bawerk.

The present view is distinguished from that of Boehm-Bawerk in its greater emphasis on the probabilistic approach to the study of market behavior. In considering items for inclusion in her assortment the consumer must make judgments concerning the relative probabilities of future occasions for use. A product in the assortment is intended to provide for some aspect of future behavior. Each such occasion for use carries a rating which is a product of two factors, one a judgment as to the probability of its incidence and the other a measure of the urgency of the need in case it should arise. Consumer goods vary with respect to both measures. One extreme might be illustrated by cigarettes with a probability of use approaching certainty but with relatively small urgency or penalty for deprivation on the particular occasion for use. At the other end of the scale would be a home fire extinguisher with low probability but high urgency attaching to the expected occasion of use.

All of this means that the consumer buyer enters the market as a problem-solver. Solving a problem, either on behalf of a household or on behalf of a marketing organization means reaching a decision in the face of uncertainty. The consumer buyer and the marketing executive are opposite numbers in the double search which pervades marketing; one looking for the goods required to complete an assortment, the other looking for the buyers who are uniquely qualified to use his goods. This is not to say that the behavior of either consumers or executives can be completely characterized as rational problem-solvers. The intention rather is to assert that problem-solving on either side of the market involves a probabilistic approach to heterogeneity on the other side. In order to solve his own problems arising from heterogeneous demand, the marketing executive should understand the processes of consumer decisions in coping with heterogeneous supplies.

The viewpoint adopted here with respect to the competition among sellers is essentially that which is associated in economics with such names as Schumpeter, Chamberlin and J. M. Clark and with the emphasis on innovative competition, product differentiation and differential advantage. The basic assumption is that every firm occupies a position which is in some respects unique, being differentiated from all others by characteristics of its products, its services, its geographic location or its specific combination of these features. The survival of a firm requires that for some group of buyers it should enjoy a differential advantage over all other suppliers. The sales of any active marketing organization come from a core market made up of buyers with a preference for this source and a fringe market which finds the source acceptable, at least for occasional purchases.

In the case of the supplier of relatively undifferentiated products or services such as the wheat farmer differential advantage may pertain more to the producing region than to the individual producer. This more diffused type of differential advantage often becomes effective in the market through such agencies as the marketing cooperative. Even the individual producer of raw materials, however, occupies a position in the sense that one market or buyer provides the customary outlet for his product rather than another. The essential point for the present argument is that buyer and seller are not paired at random even in the marketing of relatively homogeneous products but are related to some scale of preference or priority.

Competition for differential advantage implies goals of survival and growth for the marketing organization. The firm is perennially seeking a favorable place to stand and not merely immediate profits from its operations. Differential advantage is subject to change and neutralization by competitors. In dynamic markets differential advantage can only be preserved through continuous innovation. Thus competition presents an analogy to a succession of military campaigns rather than to the pressures and attrition of a single battle. A competitor may gain ground through a successful campaign based on new product features or merchandising ideas. It may lose ground or be forced to fall back on its core position because of the successful campaigns of others. The existence of the core position helps to explain the paradox of survival in the face of the destructive onslaughts of innovative competition.

Buyers and sellers meet in market transactions each side having tentatively identified the other as an answer to its problem. The market transaction consumes much of the time and effort of all buyers and sellers. The market which operates through a network of costless transactions is only a convenient fiction which economists adopt for certain analytical purposes. Potentially the cost of transactions is so high that controlling or reducing this cost is a major objective in market analysis and executive action. Among economists John R. Commons has given the greatest attention to the transaction as the unit of collective action. He drew a basic distinction between strategic and routine transactions which for present purposes may best be paraphrased as fully negotiated and routine transactions.

The fully negotiated transaction is the prototype of all exchange transactions. It represents a matching of supply and demand after canvassing all of the factors which might affect the decision on either side. The routine transaction proceeds under a set of rules and assumptions established by previous negotiation or as the result of techniques of pre-selling which take the place of negotiation. Transactions on commodity and stock exchanges are carried out at high speed and low cost but only because of carefully established rules governing all aspects of trading. The economical routines of self-service in a super market are possible because the individual items on display have been pre-sold. The routine transaction is the end-result of previous marketing effort and ingenious organization of institutions and processes. Negotiation is implicit in all routine transactions. Good routines induce both parties to save time and cost by foregoing explicit negotiation.

The negotiated transaction is the indicated point of departure for the study of exchange values in heterogeneous markets. Many considerations enter into the decision to trade or not to trade on either side of the market. Price is the final balancing or integrating factor which permits the deal to be made. The seller may accept a lower price if relieved from onerous requirements. The buyer may pay a higher price if provided with specified services. The integrating price is one that assures an orderly flow of goods so long as the balance of other considerations remains essentially unchanged. Some economists are uneasy about the role of the negotiated transaction in value determination since bargaining power may be controlling within wide bargaining limits. These limits as analyzed by Commons are set by reference to the best alternatives available to either partner rather than by the automatic control of atomistic competition. This analysis overlooks a major constraint on bargaining in modern markets. Each side has a major stake in a deal that the other side can live with. Only in this way can a stable supply relationship be established so as to achieve the economics of transactional routines. Negotiation is not a zero sum game since the effort to get the best of the other party transaction by transaction may result in a loss to both sides in terms of mounting transactional cost.

In heterogeneous markets price plays an important role in matching a segment of supply with the appropriate segment of demand. The seller frequently has the option of producing a streamlined product at a low price, a deluxe product at a high price or selecting a price-quality combination somewhere in between. There are considerations which exert a strong influence on the seller toward choosing the price line or lines which will yield the greatest dollar volume of sales. Assuming that various classes of consumers have conflicting claims on the productive capacity of the supplier, it might be argued that the price-quality combination which maximized gross revenue represented the most constructive compromise among these claims. There are parallel considerations with respect to the claims of various participants in the firm's activities on its operating revenue. These claimants include labor, management, suppliers of raw materials and stockholders. Assuming a perfectly fluid situation with respect to bargaining among these claimants, the best chance for a satisfactory solution is at the level of maximum gross revenue. The argument becomes more complicated when the claims of stockholders are given priority, but the goal would still be maximum gross revenue as suggested in a recent paper by William J. Baumol. My own intuition and experience lead me to believe that the maximization of gross revenue is a valid goal of marketing management in heterogeneous markets and adherence to this norm appears to be widely prevalent in actual practice.

What has been said so far is doubtless within the scope of economics or perhaps constitutes a sketch of how some aspects of economic theory might be reconstructed on the assumption of heterogeneity rather than homogeneity as the normal and prevailing condition of the market. But there are issues raised by such notions as enterprise survival, expectations, and consumer behavior, which in my opinion cannot be resolved within the present boundaries of economic science. Here marketing must not hesitate to draw upon the concepts and techniques of the social sciences for the enrichment of its perspective and for the advancement of marketing as an empirical science.

The general economist has his own justifications for regarding the exchange process as a smoothly functioning mechanism which operates in actual markets or which should be taken as the norm and standard to be enforced by government regulation. For the marketing man, whether teacher or practitioner, this Olympian view is untenable. Marketing is concerned with those who are obliged to enter the market to solve their problems imperfect as the market may be. The persistent and rational action of these participants is the main hope for eliminating or moderating some of these imperfections so that the operation of the market mechanism may approximate that of the theoretical model.

To understand market behavior the marketing man takes a closer look at the nature of the participants. Thus he is obliged, in my opinion, to come to grips with the organized behavior system. Market behavior is primarily group behavior. Individual action in the market is most characteristically action on behalf of some group in which the individual holds membership. The organized behavior system is related to the going concern of John R. Commons but with a deeper interest in what keeps it going. The organized behavior system is also a much broader concept including the more tightly organized groups acting in the market such as business firms and households and loosely connected systems such as the trade center and the marketing channel.

The marketing man needs some rationale for group behavior, some general explanation for the formation and persistence of organized behavior systems. He finds this explanation in the concept of expectations. Insofar as conscious choice is involved, individuals operate in groups because of their expectations of incremental satisfactions as compared to what they could obtain operating alone. The expected satisfactions are of many kinds, direct and indirect. In a group that is productive activity is held together because of an expected surplus over individual output. Other groups such as households and purely social organizations expect direct satisfactions from group association and activities. They also expect satisfactions from future activities facilitated by the assortment of goods held in common. Whatever the character of the system, its vitality arises from the expectations of the individual members and the vigor of their efforts to achieve them through group action. While the existence of the group is entirely derivative, it is capable of operating as if it had a life of its own and was pursuing goals of survival and growth.

Every organized behavior system exhibits a structure related to the functions it performs. Even in the simplest behavior system there must be some mechanism for decision and coordination of effort if the system is to provide incremental satisfaction. Leadership emerges at an early stage to perform such functions as directing the defense of the group. Also quite early is the recognition of the rationing function by which the leader allocates the available goods or satisfactions among the members of the group.

As groups grow in size and their functions become more complex functional specialization increases. The collection of individuals forming a group with their diversified skills and capabilities is a meaningful heterogeneous ensemble vaguely analogous to the assortment of goods which facilitates the activities of the group. The group, however, is held together directly by the generalized expectations of its members. The assortment is held together by a relatively weak or derivative bond. An item "belongs" to the assortment only so long as it has some probability of satisfying the expectations of those who possess it.

This outline began with an attempt to live within the framework of economics or at least within an economic framework amplified to give fuller recognition to heterogeneity on both sides of the market. We have now plunged into sociology in order to deal more effectively with the organized behavior system. Meanwhile we attempt to preserve the line of communication to our origins by basing the explanations of group behavior on the quasi-economic concept of expectations.

The initial plunge into sociology is only the beginning since the marketing man must go considerably further in examining the functions and structure of organized behavior systems. An operating group has a power structure, a communication structure and an operating structure. At each stage an effort should be made to employ the intellectual strategy which has already been suggested. That is, to relate sociological notions to the groundwork of marketing economics through the medium of such concepts as expectations and the processes of matching and sorting.

All members of an organized behavior system occupy some position or status within its power structure. There is a valid analogy between the status of an individual or operating unit within the system and the market position of the firm as an entity. The individual struggles for status within the system having first attained the goal of membership. For most individuals in an industrial society status in some operating system is a prerequisite for satisfying his expectations. Given the minimal share in the power of the organization inherent in membership, vigorous individuals may aspire to the more ample share of power enjoyed by leadership. Power in the generalized sense referred to here is an underlying objective on which the attainment of all other objectives depends. This aspect of organized behavior has been formulated as the power principle, namely, "The rational individual will act in such a way to promote the power to act." The word "promote" deliberately glosses over an ambivalent attitude toward power, some individuals striving for enhancement and others being content to preserve the power they have.

Any discussion which embraces power as a fundamental concept creates uneasiness for some students on both analytical and ethical grounds. My own answer to the analytical problem is to define it as control over expectations. In these terms it is theoretically possible to measure and evaluate power, perhaps even to set a price on it. Certainly it enters into the network of imputations in a business enterprise. Management allocates or rations status and recognition as well as or in lieu of material rewards. As for the ethical problem, it does not arise unless the power principle is substituted for ethics as with Macchiavelli. Admitting that the power principle is the essence of expediency, the ethical choice of values and objectives is a different issue. Whatever his specific objectives, the rational individual will wish to serve them expediently.

If any of this discussion of power seems remote from marketing let it be remembered that major preoccupation of the marketing executive, as pointed out by Oswald Knauth, is with the creation or the activation of organized behavior systems such as marketing channels and sales organizations. No one can be effective in building or using such systems if he ignores the fundamental nature of the power structure.

The communication structure serves the group in various ways. It promotes the survival of the system by reinforcing the individual's sense of belonging. It transmits instructions and operating commands or signals to facilitate coordinated effort. It is related to expectations through the communication of explicit or implied commitments. Negotiations between suppliers and customers and much that goes on in the internal management of a marketing organization can best be understood as a two-way exchange of commitments. A division sales manager, for example, may commit himself to produce a specified volume of sales. His superior in turn may commit certain company resources to support his efforts and make further commitments as to added rewards as an incentive to outstanding performance.

For some purposes it is useful to regard marketing processes as a flow of goods and a parallel flow of informative and persuasive messages. In these terms the design of communication facilities and channels becomes a major aspect of the creation of marketing systems. Marketing has yet to digest and apply the insights of the rapidly developing field of communication theory which in turn has drawn freely from both engineering and biological and social sciences. One stimulating idea expounded by Norbert Wiener and others is that of the feedback of information in a control system. Marketing and advertising research are only well started on the task of installing adequate feedback circuits for controlling the deployment of marketing effort.

Social psychology is concerned with some problems of communication which are often encountered in marketing systems. For example, there are the characteristic difficulties of vertical communication which might be compared to the transmission of telephone messages along a power line. Subordinates often hesitate to report bad news to their superiors fearing to take the brunt of emotional reactions. Superiors learn to be cautious in any discussion of the subordinate's status for fear that a casual comment will be interpreted as a commitment. There is often a question as to when a subordinate should act and report and when he should refer a matter for decision upstream. Progress in efficiency, which is a major goal in marketing, depends in substantial part on technological improvement in communication facilities and organizational skill in using them.

The third aspect of structure involved in the study of marketing systems is operating structure. Effective specialization within an organization requires that activities which are functionally similar be placed together but properly coordinated with other activities. Billing by wholesaler grocers, for example, has long been routinized in a separate billing department. In more recent years the advances in mechanical equipment have made it possible to coordinate inventory control with billing, using the same set of punch cards for both functions. Designing an operating structure is a special application of sorting. As in the sorting of goods to facilitate handling, there are generally several alternative schemes for classifying activities presenting problems of choice to the market planner.

Functional specialization and the design of appropriate operating structures is a constant problem in the effective use of marketing channels. Some functions can be performed at either of two or more stages. One stage may be the best choice in terms of economy or effectiveness. Decision on the placement of a function may have to be reviewed periodically since channels do not remain static. Similar considerations arise in the choice of channels. Some types of distributors or dealers may be equipped to perform a desired service while others may not. Often two or more channels with somewhat specialized roles are required to move a product to the consumer. The product's sponsor can maintain perspective in balancing out these various facilities by thinking in terms of a total operating system including his own sales organization and the marketing channels employed.

The dynamics of market organization pose basic problems for the marketing student and the marketing executive in a free enterprise economy. Reference has already been made to the competitive pursuit of differential advantage. One way in which a firm can gain differential advantage is by organizing the market in a way that is favorable to its own operations. This is something else than the attainment of a monopolistic position in relation to current or potential competitors. It means creating a pattern for dealing with customers or suppliers which persists because there are advantages on both sides. Offering guarantees against price declines on floor stocks is one example of market organization by the seller. Attempts to systematize the flow of orders may range from various services offered to customers or suppliers all the way to complete vertical integration. Another dynamic factor affecting the structure of markets may be generalized under the term "closure." It frequently happens that some marketing system is incomplete or out of balance in some direction. The act of supplying the missing element constitutes closure, enabling the system to handle a greater output or to operate at a new level of efficiency. The incomplete system in effect cries out for closure. To observe this need is to recognize a form of market opportunity. This is one of the primary ways in which new enterprises develop, since there may be good reasons why the missing service cannot be performed by the existing organizations which need the service. A food broker, for example, can cover a market for several accounts of moderate size in a way that the individual manufacturer would not be able to cover it for himself.

There is a certain compensating effect between closure as performed by new or supplementary marketing enterprises and changes in market organization brought about by the initiative of existing firms in the pursuit of differential advantage. The pursuit of a given form of advantage, in fact, may carry the total marketing economy out of balance in a given direction creating the need and opportunity for closure. Such an economy could never be expected to reach a state of equilibrium, although the tendency toward structural balance is one of the factors in its dynamics. Trade regulation may be embraced within this dynamic pattern as an attempt of certain groups to organize the market to their own advantage through political means. Entering into this political struggle to determine the structure of markets are some political leaders and some administrative officials who regard themselves as representing the consumer's interests. It seems reasonable to believe that the increasing sophistication and buying skill of consumers is one of the primary forces offsetting the tendency of the free market economy to turn into something else through the working out of its inherent dynamic forces. This was the destiny foreseen for the capitalistic system by Schumpeter, even though he was one of its staunchest advocates.

The household as an organized behavior system must be given special attention in creating an analytical framework for marketing. The household is an operating entity with an assortment of goods and assets and with economic functions to perform. Once a primary production unit, the household has lost a large part of these activities to manufacturing and service enterprises. Today its economic operations are chiefly expressed through earning and spending. In the typical household there is some specialization between the husband as primary earner and the wife as chief purchasing agent for the household. It may be assumed that she becomes increasingly competent in buying as she surrenders her production activities such as canning, baking and dressmaking, and devotes more of her time and attention to shopping. She is a rational problem solver as she samples what the market has to offer in her effort to maintain a balanced inventory or assortment of goods to meet expected occasions of use. This is not an attempt to substitute Economic Woman for the discredited fiction of Economic Man. It is only intended to assert that the decision structure of consumer buying is similar to that for industrial buying. Both business executive and housewife enter the market as rational problem solvers, even though there are other aspects of personality in either case.

An adequate perspective on the household for marketing purposes must recognize several facets of its activities. It is an organzied behavior system with its aspects of power, communication, and operating structure. It is the locus of forms of behavior other than instrumental or goal-seeking activities. A convenient three-way division, derived from the social sciences, recognizes instrumental, congenial, and symptomatic behavior. Congenial behavior is that kind of activity engaged in for its own sake and presumably yielding direct satisfactions. It is exemplified by the act of consumption as compared to all of the instrumental activities which prepare the way for consumption. Symptomatic behavior reflects maladjustment and is neither pleasure giving in itself nor an efficient pursuit of goals. Symptomatic behavior is functional only to the extent that it serves as a signal to others that the individual needs help.

Some studies of consumer motivation have given increasing attention to symptomatic behavior or to the projection of symptoms of personality adjustment which might affect consumer buying. The present view is that the effort to classify individuals by personality types is less urgent for marketing than the classification of families. Four family types with characteristically different buying behavior have been suggested growing out of the distinction between the instrumental and congenial aspects of normal behavior. Even individuals who are fairly well adjusted in themselves will form a less than perfect family if not fully adapted to each other.

On the instrumental side of household behavior it would seem to be desirable that the members be well coordinated as in any other operating system. If not, they will not deliver the maximum impact in pursuit of family goals. On the congenial side it would appear desirable for the members of a household to be compatible. That means enjoying the same things, cherishing the same goals, preferring joint activities to solitary pursuits or the company of others. These two distinctions yield an obvious four-way classification. The ideal is the family that is coordinated in its instrumental activities and compatible in its congenial activities. A rather joyless household which might nevertheless be well managed and prosperous in material terms is the coordinated but incompatible household. The compatible but uncoordinated family would tend to be happy-go-lucky and irresponsible with obvious consequences for buying behavior. The household which was both uncoordinated and incompatible would usually be tottering on the brink of dissolution. It might be held together formally by scruples against divorce, by concern for children, or by the dominant power of one member over the others. This symptomology of families does not exclude an interest in the readjustment of individuals exhibiting symptomatic behavior. Such remedial action lies in the sphere of the psychiatrist and the social worker, whereas the marketer is chiefly engaged in supplying goods to families which are still functioning as operating units.

All of the discussion of consumers so far limits itself to the activities of the household puchasing agent. Actually the term consumption as it appears in marketing and economic literature nearly always means consumer buying. Some day marketing may need to look beyond the act of purchasing to a study of consumption proper. The occasion for such studies will arise out of the problems of inducing consumers to accept innovations or the further proliferation of products to be included in the household assortment. Marketing studies at this depth will not only borrow from the social sciences but move into the realm of esthetic and ethical values. What is the use of a plethora of goods unless the buyer derives genuine satisfaction from them? What is the justification of surfeit if the acquisition of goods serves as a distraction from activities which are essential to the preservation of our culture and of the integrity of our personalities?

It has been suggested that a study of consumption might begin with the problem of choice in the presence of abundance. The scarce element then is the time or capacity for enjoyment. The bookworm confronted with the thousands of volumes available in a great library must choose in the face of this type of limitation.

The name hedonomics would appear to be appropriate for this field of study suggesting the management of the capacity to enjoy. Among the problems for hedonomics is the pleasure derived from the repetition of a familiar experience as compared with the enjoyment of a novel experience or an old experience with some novel element. Another is the problem of direct experience versus symbolic experience, with the advantages of intensity on the one hand and on other the possibility of embracing a greater range of possible ideas and sensations by relying on symbolic representations. Extensive basic research will probably be necessary before hedonomics can be put to work in marketing or for the enrichment of human life through other channels.

This paper barely suffices to sketch the analytical framework for marketing. It leaves out much of the area of executive decision-making in marketing on such matters as the weighing of uncertainties and the acceptance of risk in the commitment of resources. It leaves out market planning which is rapidly becoming a systematic discipline centering in the possibilities for economizing time and space as well as resources. It leaves out all but the most casual references to advertising and demand formation. Advertising is certainly one of the most difficult of marketing functions to embrace within a single analytical framework. It largely ignores the developing technology of physical distribution. Hopefully what it does accomplish is to show how the essentially economic problems of marketing may yield to a more comprehensive approach drawing on the basic social sciences for techniques and enriched perspective.

8

Marketing and Alderson's Functionalism *

Introduction

As the study of marketing has developed, scholars have increasingly felt the need to integrate the ever growing inventory of empirical data into some logical frame(s) of reference. Although this theoretical integration is a valuable goal, its attainment is, of course, most difficult.

In a half-century of taxonomic work (e.g., labeling commodities, agencies, functions, methods of operation) marketing scholars have used frames of reference which reflect their individual backgrounds and, frequently, the specific purpose of their inquiries. As the desire to conceptualize, observe, and measure has become stronger, these frames of reference have grown in number, type, and scope—to a point where one may justifiably question whether they can in fact be codified and eventually integrated into a "conceptual framework that will assist us in asking the right questions and in fitting facts into an orderly pattern with enlarged and significant meaning."[1]

A review of marketing studies repeatedly points to certain components or variables of marketing: for example, consumers, agencies, and their functions, products, and services; natural resources, governmental agencies, and society at large. Mere awareness of these variables, however,

Reprinted from the *Journal of Business,* Vol. 35 (October, 1962), pp. 403-413, by F. M. Nicosia by permission of The University of Chicago Press. Copyright 1962 by The University of Chicago.

* I am very grateful to Dean E. T. Grether for the many suggestions and constant encouragement generously given throughout the several drafts of this paper. Also I wish to thank Professors F. E. Balderston, C. W. Churchman, C. Y. Glock, and R. Olsen for their constructive criticism.

[1] E. T. Grether, "A Theoretical Approach to the Analysis of Marketing," in R. Cox and W. Alderson (eds.), *Theory in Marketing* (Chicago: Richard D. Irwin, Inc., 1950), p. 114.

cannot take us beyond a preliminary understanding. Interactions between mangement and technology, between management and consumer demand, and between socio-demographic factors and political settings—these and other relationships determine the nature and the dynamics of marketing. Thus, to understand marketing requires the study not only of its components but also of the sets and subsets of relationships among these components. In sum, it is valuable to conceive of marketing as a *system* of structural and dynamic *relationships*.

To conceive of a phenomenon as a system is a compelling need not peculiar to marketing. Biologists have devised concepts such as homeostasis and ecology; psychologists and sociologists speak of personality, Gestalt, the social psychological field, and culture. Even in the study of language, emphasis has shifted from grammar to communication (i.e., to the total design of a message). These are attempts to pinpoint not *properties of individual entities* but properties stemming from the modes by which entities mutually relate, that is, *properties of systems*. Considerable efforts have been devoted to studying the individual properties of marketing agencies (e.g., legal form, sales volume, number of employees, range of functions performed, location). The available techniques of aggregation, however, do not always allow us to depict many of the salient properties—systemic or global—inherent in a system of agencies.[2]

In the light of these observations, Alderson's functionalism[3] merits consideration as an approach or frame of reference which, while trying to get rid of what Drucker aptly calls the Cartesian vision of the world,[4] offers an all-encompassing integrating perspective of marketing entities *and* their interrelations—in short, of a marketing system. Alderson's func-

---

[2] For instance, the behavior of a marketing channel is affected by the individual characteristics of the participating agencies *and* by other systematic properties inherent to that channel. Thus, e.g., relationships of power and communication, which are critical in determining the channel's reactions to environmental changes, must also be considered.

[3] In this paper main attention is given to W. Alderson, *Marketing Behavior and Executive Action* (Homewood, Ill.: Richard D. Irwin, Inc., 1957). We shall also consider "The Analytical Framework for Marketing," in D. J. Duncan (ed.), *Conference of Marketing Teachers from Far Western States, Proceedings* (Berkeley: University of California Press, 1958); "Factors Governing the Development of Marketing Channels," in R. M. Clewett (ed.), *Marketing Channels* (Homewood, Ill.: Richard D. Irwin, Inc., 1945), chap. i; "Survival and Adjustment in Organized Behavior Systems," in Cox and Alderson (eds.), *op. cit.*, chap. iv; and "Scope and Place of Wholesaling in the United States," *Journal of Marketing*, XIV, No. 2 (September, 1949), 144-55. In the following pages, references to these five publications will be cited as follows: Alderson (1957) (or Alderson's book, or the author's book), Alderson (1958), Alderson (1954), Alderson (1950), and Alderson (1949), respectively.

[4] P. F. Drucker, "The New Philosophy Comes to Life," *Harper's*, July, 1957, pp. 38-39 (see also his "Nasce una Nuova Filosofia," *Tecnica e Organizzazione*, [September-October, 1958], p. 11).

tionalism underscores the importance of modifying our approach to the plethora of data now available. It indicates that we cannot further our understanding unless we think of marketing agencies *and* their relationships as components of a *system,* unless we conceptualize and observe them as such.

The purpose of this paper is to inquire into the nature of Alderson's functionalism. A brief sketch of the development of the functional*ist* approach and of its relations to earlier marketing approaches (the so-called functional, institutional, and commodity approaches) is presented in Section I. Then, in Section II, an attempt is made to isolate, summarize, and interpret the salient features of Alderson's formulation of functionalism. In this section, however, we shall refrain from investigating its "practical" implications for reasons clarified below.

I. Functionalism: An Approach to the Study of Marketing

This section will comment briefly on the relation of functionalism to earlier approaches to the study of marketing, so that we may reach a common understanding of the over-all nature and scope of functionalism. We may begin by considering the meaning of "marketing approach."

The meaning of this term may be clarified by observing a researcher who sets about the study of marketing.[5] After deciding what is to be considered "a marketing phenomenon," he starts by collecting as many observations as possible. If he were asked *what* has been observed, he would reply: "Commodities and services." If he were questioned as to *who* has been observed, his answer would be: "Agencies." One could also ask him *how* these agencies deal with commodities and services, and the researcher would say: "By performing functions." Over the years, scholars have attempted to study marketing with particular stress on the "what," or "who," or "how"—that is, on the so-called commodity, institutional,[6] and functional approaches, respectively.

---

[5] The meaning of "marketing approach" may also be understood by considering some developments in the economic studies of the properties of production and utility spaces or functions. Economists have learned that there are different ways to study these spaces: from the point of view of topology, different but not contradictory properties of a space can be established according to the *approach* used in cutting it. For instance, in the two-commodity case, if a utility space is cut horizontally, we obtain the so-called indifference curves; if it is cut vertically, we obtain the so-called processes of mathematical programming. Thus, in .general, the problem is to find the manner of cutting (i.e., an approach) which will yield either the most fundamental and comprehensive properties, or those properties most essential for the problem at hand.

[6] The term "institutional" is *not* used here in the sense of E. A. Duddy and D. A. Revzan, *Marketing: An Institutional Approach* (New York: McGraw-Hill Book Co., 1953).

Historically, basic agreement on the nature of, and the relations among, these approaches was a hard-won achievement. Consider, for instance, the "how" (functional) approach. Some European scholars in the early 1920's insisted that the "how" must be understood entirely on the basis of the legal and merchandising aspects of negotiation activities.[7] In the United States some scholars preferred to stress the study of the functions performed by the various agencies (e.g., transfer of title, physical supply, facilitating).[8] Others, rather than referring functions to agencies, took the whole marketing system as a unit of performance and thus attempted to conceptualize and study the "processes" (functions) inherent in such a system.[9]

In the course of time, however, the developments of the functional, institutional, and commodity approaches brought two main results. First, empirical studies based on these approaches produced a variety of data which enabled us to obtain a detailed morphological or anatomical description of the marketing system. Second, the reciprocal limitations of these studies led gradually to an awareness of the interdependence existing among various approaches to the study of marketing. Above all, as the understanding of the morphology (anatomy) of the marketing system became more adequate, the need for putting together the various pieces of the mosaic grew clearer and more urgent.

Thus, in the late 1940's, scholars trained their interest on the working (physiology) of the system. In 1947 Duddy and Revzan's institutional approach already conceived marketing as an "organic" whole. They emphasized that the "what," "who," and "how" are brought together by "biological" drives. In order to study marketing in its dynamic entirety, they devised new dimensions of analysis (structures and mechanisms of co-ordination and control).[10] Breyer, in turn, boldly attempted to study the workings of a particular component of the marketing system—the marketing channel.[11] Breyer's concepts of group, system, and network seem to share the perspective of the then newly born information theory, and these concepts immediately received sociological content in Alderson

---

[7] Particularly N. Garrone; for more details on the formation and development of the major European schools of thought on our subject see a brief but incisive article by C. Fabrizi, "L'Azienda e il Mercato," *Studi di Mercato* (Italian Association of Marketing Research), April, 1958, pp. 151 ff.

[8] Cf. P. T. Cherington, *The Elements of Marketing* (New York: Macmillan Co., 1920).

[9] Cf. F. E. Clark, *Principles of Marketing* (New York: Macmillan Co., 1922). On this topic see below, Sec. II, B.

[10] In this regard, the similarity of intent between the functionalist and Duddy and Revzan's institutionalist approaches is deep and substantial in spite of differences in forms and methods. This similarity of intent can be traced also in the recent work by D. A. Revzan, *Wholesaling in Marketing Organization* (New York: John Wiley & Sons, 1961).

[11] R. F. Breyer, *Quantitative Systemic Analysis and Control* (Philadelphia: College Press, 1949).

(1950), and broad politico-economic content in a study by Palamountain.[12] In conclusion, whether or not we agree fully with Alderson's formulation, marketing functionalism has already been with us for some time.

Functionalism represents a crucial evolution in our thinking because it goes beyond the collection and classification of marketing data and beyond the recognition that "the study of marketing centers around three basic factors: (1) commodities . . . ; (2) functions or services performed . . . ; and (3) institutions handling the various commodities and performing the functions."[13] Functionalism effectively merges and broadens the commodity, institutional, and functional approaches. It suggests a conception of marketing, and thus a methodology of research, which may be fruitful as a means of interpreting an advancing body of knowledge and, hopefully, as a means of building predictive and control devices.

In Alderson's formulation, functionalism "begins by identifying some systems of action, . . . stresses the whole system and undertakes to interpret the parts in terms of how they serve the system" [Alderson (1957), p. 16]. In a marketing system one must consider not only the nature and behavior of its units, but also the number, kind, and intensity of the networks of *functional relations* among them.[14] Furthermore, all marketing units have economic and sociopolitical ties with their environment. In general, multirelational webs connect them positionally (e.g., in a retail structure of a city) and functionally (e.g., in the task of delivering an appropriate assortment of goods). If marketing units are to be viable, then mutual adaptation and co-ordination become crucial. Conversely, each unit may also strive for viability by attempting to reach optimal degrees of relational autonomy—an objective pursued primarily through competition for differential advantages such as location, product differentiation, credit, etc. For instance, the units' attempt to control the formation and evolution of a marketing channel expresses their search for a balance between centripetal and centrifugal forces, that is, a balance between integration and autonomy.

---

[12] J. C. Palamountain, *The Politics of Distribution* (Cambridge, Mass.: Harvard University Press, 1955).

[13] C. F. Phillips and D. J. Duncan, *Marketing, Principles and Methods* (Homewood, Ill.: Richard D. Irwin, Inc., 1956), p. 6 (cf. also pp. 8-9 in 4th ed., 1960). See also P. D. Converse, H. W. Heugy, and R. W. Mitchell, *The Elements of Marketing* (New York: Prentice-Hall, Inc., 1952), pp. 15-16, and T. N. Beckman, H. H. Maynard, and W. R. Davidson, *Principles of Marketing* (New York: Ronald Press Co., 1957), pp. 18-19.

[14] With regard to units, Alderson thinks that the *elementary* units of marketing are households and business firms (1957, p. 15). That is, he seems to follow the dichotomy between production for consumption (households) and production for exchange (business firms) first suggested by Aristotle and constantly used since by economists of every school. Strict application of this dichotomy, however, may have several shortcomings; see, e.g., R. Cox, "Consumer Convenience and the Retail Structure of Cities," *Journal of Marketing*, XXIII, No. 4 (April, 1959), 356.

Relation networks and the capacity imputed to marketing units to initiate, alter, and terminate these relations become the conceptual tools used in studying the formation and existence of marketing subsystems, that is, higher-order units of marketing behavior such as the complex of wholesaling agencies. The units' membership in subsystems, as well as the subsystems' membership in the marketing system, is an index of functional relations among these units. Thus, in order to belong to a larger unit, each unit not only "must be effective in the subfunction it is expected to perform, but it must also be in balance with all of the other components" (1957, p. 28).

The following analogy may help to fix the differences between the marketing approaches discussed in this section. By using the institutional, functional, and commodity approaches to study the human body, a researcher will discover, for example, the presence of the pancreas and liver (the agencies) which produce (the function) certain enzymes (the commodities). The functionalist approach, however, leads the researcher to new questions concerning the dynamic properties of the phenomenon under investigation. For example, he may observe that both the liver and pancreas must work in harmony with respect to output productions and input consumptions (quantity, quality, timing, etc.); and he may then notice the importance of the relations between these two parts *and* their relations within the metabolic system, and so forth. In sum, investigation of these and other problems of dynamic equilibriums will lead to an operational definition of what can be called the system's "normal" behavior (i.e., its physiology). Only then may one proceed to identify the system's pathological manifestations, the probable determinants of such deviations and the necessary corrective actions. The implications of these remarks for private management and public policy are self-evident.

The present section has outlined how the study of marketing is undergoing an experience similar to those of other applied disciplines. Functionalism evolves from the early marketing approaches just as biochemistry and biophysics stem from chemistry and physics. Although the nature of functionalism cannot yet be spelled out in precise, axiomatic form, evidence leads us to hope that functionalism, in its marketing as well as in other contexts, will assume clearer formulations in the not too distant future.[15]

---

[15] Cf. e.g., R. K. Merton's attempt (*Social Theory and Social Structure* [Glencoe, Ill.: Free Press, 1957], pp. 50-84) to specify a paradigm for a functionalist analysis in sociology. See also the developments taking place in the General System Theory (from the early works by W. B. Cannon, *The Wisdom of the Body* [New York: W. W. Norton and Co., 1932], N. Wiener, *Cybernetics or Control and Communication in the Animal and Machine* [New York: John Wiley and Sons, 1948], R. W. Ashby, *Design for a Brain* [New York: John Wiley & Sons, 1952] and by members of the Society for General System Research).

II. Fundamentals of Alderson's Functionalism

The purpose of this section is to present and discuss some of the key features of Alderson's formulation of functionalism. Central to Alderson's functionalism are the all-pervasive concepts of the "organized behavior (i.e., ecological) system" and the "marketing process."[16] The definitions of these concepts are like the definitions of point, line, plane, and space set forth axiomatically in Euclidean geometry. Thus the author's concepts are not susceptible to operational evaluation, and therefore we shall refrain from it. The author's definitions of these two concepts, however, are rather fragmented and often blurred by distracting polemics.[17] We shall thus explore them by reconstructing and commenting upon their inner logic.

A. The Organized Behavior (Ecological) System

The concept of an ecological system rests on a sociological basis. Among the various analytical schemes of sociology, Alderson relies heavily on the so-called action frame of reference.[18] With the central notions of the action frame of reference (the act, the actor, the end, the situation, and the norm) he merges concepts originated by other behavioral sciences 'and then adjusts them to formulate propositions covering every aspect of marketing.

According to Alderson, an organized behavior system has the following salient features. The system's components are related by "their common or complementary participation in some operation" (1957, p. 26): for example, department stores in a city (common participation) and banks providing credit for consumer purchases in these stores (complementary participation). Performance of an operation requires co-ordination of each participant and, therefore, some structual organization among them. When the participants are neither associated in a random fashion

---

[16] The essential features of the former were first outlined in Alderson (1950); the latter, in Alderson (1949) and (1954).

[17] In some other cases, moreover, Alderson has not checked carefully the mutual consistency of some of his key statements. For instance, we are told that the ultimate goals of systems are survival and growth (1957, pp. 52-53). Then, we learn (pp. 55-60) that survival (a goal) can be obtained through status expectations, through competitive strategy and also through growth (p. 58). Growth, therefore, is presented both as an ultimate and an intermediate goal. Such a bivalent nature of growth cannot fully be justified by the known relativity involved in establishing a hierarchy of ends (on this relativity, cf., e.g., H. A. Simon, *Administrative Behavior* [2d ed., New York: Macmillan Co., 1957], pp. 62-66).

[18] See Talcott Parsons, *The Structure of Social Action* (2d ed., Glencoe, Ill.: Free Press, 1949), chap. ii.

nor rigidly connected, they constitute a system which may be called an organized behavior or ecological system.[19]

The two attributes "organized" and "behavior" deserve consideration. First, the system's components are "organized" both in a horizontal direction (cf. the economic concept of market structures and the similar concept of marketing level in marketing literature) and in a vertical direction (cf. the marketing concept of channel of distribution). The attribute "behavior," then, qualifies the dynamics of the bonds among the system's parts. These bonds allow a system to be open: that is, to *react to changes* in the environment. These reactions may involve replacing, adding, improving the system's parts, or changing inputs and outputs, or shifting the system's position (its "ecological niche") within the larger system to which it belongs, or, finally, acquiring new membership in some other system. Furthermore, the attribute "behavior" recognizes that a system can also *initiate change* by deliberate decisions.

How then do ecological systems come into being and persist? Alderson postulates that a system's behavior originates from purposeful action. Since a system presupposes a group of individuals, the rationale explaining the system's *formation and persistence* consists of the individuals' *common expectations* about the outcome of their association.[20] A business firm is an obvious example. Just as the association of some individuals gives rise to an ecological system, the merging of ecological systems creates still another ecological system. The formation of a voluntary chain among independent retailers shows that such systems also come together because of common expectations concerning the outcome of their union. Each member's position ("status") in a system determines his share of the association's outcome (e.g., the share of an employee in a firm's department, of a department in a firm, of a firm in a marketing channel). Members *co-operate* in order to increase the association's outcome, but they also *compete* to increase their share of the outcome (see, for effective examples, 1957, pp. 157 ff.).

All in all, an ecological system comes into being and perisists as

---

[19] Alderson states further that (*a*) if the relations among the system's parts are purely random, we have an atomistic system, and (*b*) if the parts' relations are established by a rigid blueprint—e.g., a car engine—we have a mechanical system. Note that the concepts of mechanical and ecological systems find their equivalent in the so-called rational and nature-system models developed by sociology. For a lucid treatment of problems and perspectives in this area see A. W. Gouldner, "Organizational Analysis," in R. K. Merton, L. Broom, and L. S. Cottrell, Jr. (eds.), *Sociology Today: Problems and Prospects* (New York: Basic Books, 1959), pp. 404-19.

[20] Although the stress on expectations introduces the important element of risk and uncertainty, Alderson's treatment of group formation is rather limited: cf., e.g., C. I. Barnard, *The Functions of the Executive* (Cambridge, Mass.: Harvard University Press, 1938), chaps. ii-v.

long as its members satisfy their individual goals. Thus, Alderson denies the existence of group or system goals apart from the goals of each member (1957, pp. 52-53). This point of view is striking not only in its unorthodoxy but also because it may conceal methodological issues crucial for the study of any system.[21]

In order to perform its operations, a system engaged in economic activities must arrange its parts in appropriate relational structures. Among the variety of structures possible in a marketing system, scholars are free to emphasize those which in their opinion appear most critical for the working of the whole.[22] For example. Duddy and Revzan postulate that the strategic sets of relations are agency structures (horizontal and vertical); area structures (i.e., relations among agencies according to the space dimension); price structures (i.e., relations in terms of systematic and non-systematic price formation); and control patterns (i.e., relational designs stemming from managerial devices aiming to control the firm's environment and governmental attempts to regulate management's decisions).

Alderson's functionalism recognizes four basic types of *structural relations:* power, communication, operations (input-output), and internal-external adjustments. The input-output relations are peculiar to systems engaged in economic activities. The performance of certain tasks calls for characteristic structures—that is, function determines structure. However, structures influence functions whenever structural possibilites are limited (1957, pp. 75 and 17).[23] Furthermore, we may add that changes in the centers where power, communication, and input-output processes take place modify structures and, ultimately, functions.

According to Alderson, *structuring* is any activity which establishes relational networks either within a system or between systems.[24] Structur-

---

[21] To the best of our knowledge, Alderson is the first marketing student who faces the issue and makes a clear-cut commitment. Reference to the possibility of groups without goals of their own can be found, e.g., in J. Marshak, "Towards an Economic Theory of Organization and Information," in R. M. Thrall, C. H. Coombs, and R. L. Davis (eds.), *Decision Processes* (New York: John Wiley & Sons, 1954), p. 188. See also D. Krech and R. S. Crutchfield, *Theory and Problems of Social Psychology* (New York: McGraw-Hill Book Co., 1948), p. 20; and Gouldner, *op. cit.,* p. 420. It is known, however, that distinguished scholars have spent much effort tracing the mechanism through which groups' goals are formulated: cf., e.g., K. J. Arrow, *Social Choice and Individual Values* (New York: John Wiley & Sons, 1951), and H. H. Goode, "The Greenhouse of Science for Management," *Management Science,* IV, No. 4 (July, 1958), 373-75.

[22] It is important to keep in mind that such systemic networks or structures should always be distinguished from the system's component units.

[23] For another effective discussion of structure versus function in marketing, see Duddy and Revzan, *op. cit.,* pp. 20-23.

[24] The features of structuring are seriality (and its special case of circularity) and concurrence, which includes parallelism and centrality (both divergent and convergent): cf. Alderson (1950, pp. 69 ff., and 1957, pp. 75 ff.) for examples.

ing can be realized in a variety of ways and, in this context, *efficiency* becomes relevant. Routinization, specialization, and versatility appear to be the most important areas in which marketing efficiency can manifest itself (1957, pp. 79-86). For instance, leasing, servicing, granting warranties, and prepacking are seen as forms of routinization of transactions guided by the efficiency criterion (pp. 302-4).

The study of the interactions among the power, communication, and input-output structures is basic to the understanding of the internal and external adjustments of a system. For example, the input-output operations call for *transactions* "between an organized behavior system and its environments" (1957, p. 66). More specifically, two systems relate to each other by means of *negotiations* (p. 130). In non-integrated systems, such as some froms of marketing channels, negotiations are the only means for co-ordination among the channel's units (p. 158). The power center of each system carries on this contacting and negotiating function. Thus, in a marketing system, contacts and negotiations not only involve issues of economic values but also imply efforts toward a balance of power both horizontally (e.g., among retailers, among wholesaling agencies) and vertically (between consumers, retailers, wholesaling agencies, manufacturers, service industries, extractive industries, and agriculture).

B. *The Marketing Process*

In Section I we have seen that functionalism is an approach to the study of marketing. In Section II, A, we have shown how functionalism conceives marketing as a complex ecological system, and we have identified the functionalist's major postulates with respect to (*a*) the formation and persistence of systems, and (*b*) the systems' major structures. Marketing is an ecological system engaged in economic operations. The purpose of this subsection is to investigate how Alderson studies such operations and assesses their nature and meaning.

Before beginning our inquiry, we should notice that there are *two basic ways* of studying a system's operation. On the one hand, a researcher relying on some sort of microanalysis may focus his attention on the operations (functions) performed by each agency in a system, and then he may in some way aggregate these operations into separate classes. Thus, thinking of the so-called marketing functions (buying, selling, transportation, etc.), we may define a marketing process as a "meaningful grouping" of some of these functions.[25] On the other hand, a researcher could begin by studying the total system and then attempt to identify some

---

[25] Cf. Revzan, *op. cit.*, pp. 6-7. Apropos of this definition, we entertain some doubts on (*a*) whether any "operational" grouping has ever been suggested, and (*b*) whether the so-called functions have helped beyond distinguishing and classifying marketing agencies by kind of operation.

basic types of operations (or processes) as they refer *directly* to such a system, rather than to the single agencies in the system. This latter approach could be named aggregate or *macroanalysis*. Alderson's processes, as well as those of Clark and Clark[26] and of Vaile, Grether, and Cox[27] are of this second type.

Let us see how Alderson arrives at the identification of his processes. By cutting across the marketing system, he singles out two major points: natural resources and final acquisition. Economic goods at the level of natural resources appear to the final buyer as *conglomerations,* having, by and large, no immediate economic usefulness for him. Conglomerations, therefore, can be defined as *meaningless assortments* (1957, p. 200). At the level of the final buyer, economic goods may be seen as a collection of goods "which either complement each other directly or in total possess some degree of potency for meeting future contingencies" 199). In other words, it is assumed that these goods were bought insofar as they were deemed capable of fulfilling the buyer's purposes; they are related by direct complementarity of use or by their capacity ("potency") to be used against estimated future patterns of consumption and contingencies. Such collections of goods can be called *assortments* and distinguished from conglomerations because of their immanent *economic meaning* to the user.

One is thus forced to reckon with the inherent *heterogeneity* of the original supplies and final demands. Goods acquire value only when in the basket of the ultimate user. In a primordial society goods reach the final buyer's assortment through a simple process of exchange (1957, pp. 292-95). As an economy evolves into industrialized forms, elements of ownership, time, space, and technology render the exchange process more complex. The gap between original supplies and final demands widens. Technology (and the increased variety of products derived from it) splits the flow of goods into several steps: goods must be associated in such ways as to satisfy the requirements of technological uses (technological assortments) before they can meet the patterns of final uses (ultimate buyers' assortments). Heterogeneity spreads throughout the exchange process, and the orginal *discrepancies* (pp. 215-17) between conglomerations and final assortments are accentuated. The flow of goods "may be described as a series of transformations from meaningless to meaningful heterogeneity" (Alderson, 1958, p. 16).

Marketing, because it creates meaningful assortments, is "the source of all ultimate value in use" (1957, p. 198). This implies, we may add,

---

[26] F. E. Clark and C. P. Clark, *Principles of Marketing* (New York: Macmillan Co., 1942).

[27] R. S. Vaile, E. T. Grether, and R. Cox, *Marketing in the American Economy* (New York: Ronald Press Co., 1952).

that the creation of ultimate value is the *raison d'être* of marketing in any kind of sociopolitical system—this provides its functional rapport with and within a society[28] From this perspective the author concludes that "manufacturing is a supplementary way of shaping goods to the needs of the consumer. It takes place within the structure of marketing operations rather than the reverse" (p. 198).[29] To summarize: all economic activities consist in *matching* the individual's needs with the right product, at the right place, time, price, and so on. The progressively larger distances between segments of supply and of demand, and the increasing number of producers, products, and final users, call for bringing together and aligning heterogeneous supplies and demands, qualitatively and quantitatively, over time and space.

It is interesting to note a subtle ambiguity and, perhaps, an overlapping of the two concepts of assortment creation and of matching heterogeneous supplies and demands: which one is the objective of the system's activities and which one is the process employed for attaining the objective? This issue is relevant if our search aims at concepts of marketing processes which can be operationally useful—for instance, measuring the cost and efficiency of a marketing system. Apparently, Alderson's commitment is that matching is carried out by the *sorting processes* (1957, pp. 202-11): sorting out, accumulation, allocation and assorting.[30] By sorting, marketing either *builds up* (by accumulation and assorting) or *breaks down* (by sorting and allocation) collections of goods. Alternatively, by sorting, marketing establishes either *qualitative relations* (sorting and assorting) or *quantitative relations* (accumulation and allocation) among goods. Under any circumstances, therefore, the end result of each sorting process is one or more assortments: "The building up of assort-

---

[28] In a sense, Alderson has limited his analysis to the marketing system without investigating its external relations. He never directly explores the place occupied by marketing in a society or its relations with the other society's systems. It is evident, furthermore, that Alderson thinks of marketing only as it exists in "associational" societies (*Gesellschaft* type) where inter- and intra-agency bonds are voluntary and typically based on contracts. Does he imply then that in a "communal" society (such as the U.S.S.R.) the activities involved in the flow of goods and services from production to consumption should not be thought of as making up a marketing system?

[29] Thus marketing may be thought of as the core of the total economic process: cf. G. M. Umemura, "The Classical School and a Theory of Marketing," in S. F. Otteson (ed.), *Marketing: Current Problems and Theories* (School of Business, Indiana University, Business Report No. 16 [Bloomington: Indiana University, 1952]), p. 27. In our opinion, it is more desirable to state that production is exchange internal to the firm, whereas marketing is external exchange with the firm's environment.

[30] More specifically, starting from the initial conglomeration of natural resources, the sequence of the basic marketing processes could be conceptualized as follows: *sorting out* from a heterogeneous supply to relatively homogeneous and separate stocks; *accumulation* of larger, relatively homogeneous stocks over time and/or space; *allocation*—breaking down of relatively homogeneous stocks into smaller ones through dispersion in terms of ownership, geographical location, etc.; *assorting*—bringing together different goods according to criteria of use association.

ments through the various stages of sorting is the essence of the economics of marketing" (p. 199).

It still remains to be seen how we can measure and evaluate such "economics" on the basis of the processes proposed by Alderson—and by other scholars. If marketing is the complex of all those activities involved in the flow of goods and services from production to consumption,[31] if its final objective is to satisfy human needs and to deliver a living standard,[32] then we may assert that the main task of marketing lies in (*a*) overcoming assortment discrepancies by a continuous process (sorting) of adaptation of assortments flow, and (*b*) by creating assortment discrepancies *ad hoc* (for efficiency in production, transportation, storage, etc.) in order to facilitate this adaptive process.

Assuming that Alderson's processes are the basic operations of the system, it should be possible to measure the system's effectiveness in terms of such operations. Alderson does not pursue this problem, but instead, for example, he states that intermediaries arise not because they can lead to a more economical performance of marketing processes, but because of considerations referring to contract, item flow, location pattern, storage capacity, goods and information handling, sorting balance and risk (1957, pp. 217-25). He has used the concept of marketing processes with reference to the operations of wholesaling (Alderson, 1949, pp. 150 ff.), marketing channels (Alderson, 1954, pp. 12-13), and the whole marketing system (Alderson, 1957, pp. 199-211), but only as expository devices rather than as clear-cut points of reference for observing marketing costs and their contributions to a society. And yet, in our opinion, the measurement of these costs and contributions is the implicit operational value of the concept of marketing processes.

Can we hope to reach a more penetrating explication of such a concept? The marketing processes (or tasks, functions) proposed by various scholars illustrate how far we have gone in this direction. Clark and Clark point at concentration, equalization and dispersion.[33] Breyer adds contact and negotiation.[34] Alderson prefers to emphasize searching, matching, and sorting.[35] McGarry suggests a six-fold classification (contacting, merchan-

---

[31] This is the standard definition of marketing accepted by the American Marketing Association; cf. Committee on Definitions, *Marketing Definitions* (Chicago: American Marketing Association, 1960), p. 15.

[32] A point of view accepted by most marketing scholars for more than two decades; cf. P. W. Stewart and J. F. Dewhurst, *Does Distribution Cost Too Much?* (New York: Twentieth Century Fund, 1939), p. 15.

[33] *Op. cit.*, pp. 4-7.

[34] R. F. Breyer, *The Marketing Institution* (New York: McGraw-Hill Book Co., 1934), pp. 5 ff.

[35] Alderson (1954), pp. 15-16. In his 1957 work the author left out the searching concept. We include it above because we do not think that searching is peculiar to marketing channels.

dising, pricing, propaganda, physical distribution, termination).[36] Vaile, Grether, and Cox underscore the processes of collecting, sorting, and dispersing.[37] By taking assortments as a unit of analysis, moreover, Alderson (1954 and 1957) implicitly offers another classification: the building up and breaking down of assortments. Similarities and overlapping among the above classifications seem quite substantial. Regardless of the reasons for which each scholar thinks of marketing processes as a useful concept, would it not be convenient to explore the extent to which such classifications can be reduced to a minimum common denominator? It could be done without resorting to too much Procrustean stretching. Perhaps the assortments-flows criterion may provide the answer.

Conclusion

Functionalism is an approach, an analytical framework, a frame of mind, which tries to cope with the same problems of substance and method encountered by other disciplines. Its main purpose is to go beyond the study of the *morphology* of a marketing system by conceptualizing the dynamic relations among the system's units—thus enabling us to study the *working* of the system itself.

The above sections have only explored the surface of fuctionalism in general and of Alderson's formulation in particular. However, it was still possible to identify the substance of the functionalist's message—a message which provides perspective and suggestions for model-building and empirical investigations.

But a great deal of introspection remains to be done. We must make explicit many of the tacit assumptions on which functionalism rests in order to discover gaps and contradictions, and we must state the functionalist's propositions in the form of testable hypotheses. In sum, the challenge facing the student of marketing is that of operationalizing the conceptual schemata suggested by functionalism—that is, of translating them into empirical research instruments.

---

[36] E. D. McGarry, "Some Functions of Marketing Reconsidered," in Cox and Alderson (eds.), *op. cit.*, pp. 269 ff.

[37] *Op. cit.*, chap. vi.

9

The Holistic-Institutional Approach
to Marketing

DAVID A. REVZAN

This lengthy essay is concerned mainly with a complete statement of the institutional approach, its component elements, and its implications. As such, it represents a refinement and expansion of the Duddy-Revzan original statements.

In addition to this expanded statement of the institutional approach, the essay will deal with a wide range of related topics: the background, definitions, evolution, and perspective of institutions and institutionalism; the environment of products and product assortments in the institutional approach; the components of agency, area, and price structures; the role of change versus stability; the role and types of coordination and control; and some evaluation with conclusions. By dealing in depth with many facets pertinent to the institutional approach, a special emphasis is placed on the term, "holistic," as it is included in the title. There is no inference in the use of this term, or the sequence of topics, of an encyclopedic treatment of all the materials. Especially in the discussion of institutionalism, the purpose is not to deal with the materials in any great depth. Rather, this dimension of the evolutionary perspective will be restricted to the more immediate backdrop and outreach of the twentieth century. The bibliography will include, however, a much broader range of material, sourcewise and timewise.

From David A. Revzan, *Perspectives for Research in Marketing: Seven Essays,* pp. 1-39; 152-155. Reprinted by permission of the author and the publisher, Institute of Business and Economic Research, University of California, Berkeley.

Institutions: Definitions, Origins, Types, and Evolutionary Aspects[1]

At the outset it is necessary to emphasize that the ideal and motivations in developing the institutional approach were neither to deny the existence and value of other valid approaches to the subject matter; to overthrow such existing economic theories as apply to marketing; nor to introduce yet another set of conceptual materials.

This holistic-institutional approach may best be presented as an intellectual perspective designed to offset, in part, the effects of the growing importance of splintered views and analyses presented in connection with increasing specialization. As such, it emphasizes the importance attaching to the generalist, overall, integrating views alongside those of the attempts of the various specialists.

It recognizes, accordingly, the need for maintaining the integrated and far-reaching treatment of the overall complexities where they exist, and the elimination wherever necessary of conceptual movements toward the orderly and normative which tend to destroy the overall perspective and the role of continuous change. Such an attempt is certainly not a move to intellectual simplicity as it searches for the central link between the categories of complexities.

From a different point of view, the institutional approach herein discussed is a lineal descendant of a long tradition manifest in many disciplines and writings. Suffice here to say that the emphasis of the approach is related to the emergence of the historical point of view, an increasing emphasis upon evolutionary patterns, and the corresponding deemphasis of the role and importance of the individual in society. Much of this shift in emphasis is traceable to the Marketing and Industrial Revolutions, the rise of urbanism, and the decline in importance of self-sustaining agrarian societies.

Basic definition of "institution." In defining the word, "institution," the importance of the historical reference point, and the contents of the particular subject matter or discipline, can neither be ignored nor underestimated. The range of types of institutions, in connection with definitions and classifications, is highly obvious, as is the feature of comparative complexity, and such aspects as cooperation in institutions versus competition. New analytical techniques and an expanding array of historical evidence help to contribute to these aspects. An analogy may be drawn here from the field of astronomy in terms of the structure of the Milky Way, based upon the use of optical versus radio telescopic observations.

---

[1] This section owes much of its content and organizational framework to Walton H. Hamilton [29, 84-89].

With the shift from the former to the latter, the number and complexity of its galaxies, among other things, were found to increase dramatically.

Hamilton [29, 84] defines an institution as: a symbol which describes a wide cluster of social usages; a connotation of a way of thought or action embedded in the habits and customs of a group or people; or, another word for a procedure, convention, arrangement, or particular mores or folkways. More specifically, he states: "Institutions fix the confines of and impose form upon the activities of human beings" [29, 84]. These various meanings, he adds, cover a range as wide as the interests of mankind.

Commons, the well-known figure in institutional economics, indicates the great uncertainty of the meaning of the word [20]. Among other meanings, it may be analogous to a framework of laws and regulations within which persons behave as inmates; or, it may signify the behavior of such persons. But whatever variations exist, he indicates this important universal principle; namely, *that an institution represents collective human action in control of individual action.* Institutions, so defined, range from unorganized forms such as custom, to such highly organized forms as the family, corporations, unions, the Federal Reserve System, and the state.[2] Later discussion will deal in more detail with the forms taken by and the purposes of these collective actions or institutions.

Park, one of the important figures in the field of sociology,[3] which subject matter field may, itself, be called a social science based almost completely on the study of institutions, develops a similar motif in the following statement:

> An institution embodies a social function. It is the form in which the individuals who constitute society seek to act collectively for the common, rather than the individual welfare. Neither plants nor animals have institutions, but plant communities have structure [44, 161-162].

In a later section he develops, also, a detailed relationship between institutions and collective behavior [44, 244-250].

Finally, in terms of basic definitions, that of John M. Clark, another important institutional economist, may be given:

> This [scientific] attitude regards institutions as means to ends, but not as sheer bits of social machinery to be tinkered with and altered wholly at the will of the tinkerer. They are themselves in a very real sense living things, evolving according to their own laws, and these laws the human understanding has not yet mastered. Yet their course is subject to some degree of direction, and man is continually calling on them to justify themselves by their results, and trying to improve them where they do not seem to meet this test [18, 5].

---

[2] Commons referred to these as organized "Going Concerns."

[3] This subject matter field may, itself, be called a social science based almost completely on the study of institutions.

Thus, based on the above, the emphasis on institutions and any systematic study of them, using them as the foundation and center of any approach, is the concern with individuals acting as members of groups in various forms of collective activity. The individual, in this framework, is no longer thought of as acting independently to arrive at decisions based on rational and subjective judgments and motivations. Instead, institutions arise as individuals, while still motivated by their respective self-interests, nevertheless tend to organize and cooperate consciously as groups, with dominant priority assigned to such group interest.

A group thus becomes opposed to other groups in a trial by strength, and accordingly there arises important competition between groups as well as between individuals. The individual acts, whether consciously or unconsciously, as a member of a group, *the institution;* and his decisions and functional activities become conditioned by the standards of the group or groups to which he belongs. Functional activity becomes primarily institutional rather than individual, and dominates all aspects of society— social, political, economic, and so forth.

This is not to say, however, that there is *not* any significant amount of activity which is individual in the sense that the individual involved has no formal affiliation with any institution. But, such individuals in these classes of activities are influenced, however, by the group or collective actions of others through their memberships in various types of institutions, as well as by other individuals. And, in the emphasis upon *collective action* as the root of the definition of institutions given above, the reader should not assign any given form of either political or economic organization.

The implications of these definitional characteristics for the institutional approach to marketing will be studied in later sections. Suffice to say here, that the members of any institution, if the institution is to survive and have any importance, must have an instinct for cooperation as the basic principle of internal organization. Each individual, in an environment of increasing risk, attempts to relate his self-interest to the benefits of collective security and authority to be found in an institution. Each may desire to compete, however, for a position of leadership in the institutional organization; and institutions may either cooperate with or compete against other institutions.

Types of institutions. Given the breadth of meaning inherent in the preceding definitions and discussions, it follows that institutions may be classified in several ways and upon diverse bases. Depending on their respective organizational structures, they may be classified as *formal, semiformal,* or *informal; diverse* or *narrow;* or *rigid* versus *flexible.* Similarly, they may be classified according to their main purpose, philosophy, and activity (such as religious, legal, political, marketing). They may be *complete* or *incomplete,* or *simple* versus *complex* in their structure and functioning.

Institutions, in their control over their constituent members, may be *exacting* or *lenient;* and *complete* or *incomplete.* In terms of such *size* criteria as number of members, or dollar volume, and so forth, they may range from very small to very large. And, related to size dimensions often is the factor of *geographical outreach:* from domestic to foreign; or within the domestic group, local, national, or regional; and, internationally, from two to several countries. Also, of importance within the size criterion, are the number of units in an institution from *single* to *multiple.* Further, institutions may be *limited function* or *full function* in relation to their other characteristics. They may be highly variable in their length of life, their breaks with the past, and in cycles of development.

Because of the way in which they originate, Sumner [57] has distinguished institutions according to whether they are enacted or crescive. *Enacted institutions* grow up and take form in some detectable historic process, and thus are a continuous link in such process. *Crescive institutions,* on the other hand, are the resultant of their members' reflective and rational purposes. As such, Sumner would label these more nearly artifact in nature than with the characteristics of organisms.

And, it follows from all that has been said, that institutions may be either *autocratic* or *democratic* both in philosophy and operation. Additionally, a given institution may be *dominant* or *subdominant* in some kind of hierarchical structure.[4] Finally, it may be said that many subject matter disciplines, in their formal intellectual structures, tend to assume many of the same attributes and forms of institutions.

The origin and growth of institutions [22] and [44]. With very few exceptions, the origins of institutions can rarely be isolated and discussed in any systematic fashion. They may arise as the results of accidental, arbitrary, or conscious action. But even when deliberately and consciously established, it may be stated that any institution's origin will be clouded usually in indefiniteness. The socio-political-economic culture surrounding the institution may supply ideas, formulas, sanctions, or patterns of habits. And, depending on the type of institution, there develop rituals, ceremonials, or cults; or, under more highly organized circumstances, there emerge "due process of law" or "sound" business policies and practices.

As an institution takes hold, it may shift so gradually from the usual or routine to the unusual or novel, that the pattern may not be readily visible or detectable, especially if the shift becomes copied by many other

---

[4] See the bibliography [44, Ch. 13], for some aspects of the sociological phenomenon of dominance in this connection.

competitive institutions. The existing institutional organization may serve as a ready cover for the beginning and development of new institutional arrangements. Very frequently, the new, the unique, the innovative, takes fast hold before the institutional changes, or the introduction of a new institution is detected and analyzed. As Hamilton has stated: "In institutional life, current realities are usually to be found behind ancient forms."

Thus, the development of institutions is associated very closely with the successive systems of ideas. As will be seen in later discussions of government regulation of the marketing system, changes in institutional arrangements involving such regulations follow closely upon changes in the philosophy of the relation of government to business, especially when the government itself becomes an active participant. It may be stated, accordingly, that the longer an institution survives, the more adaptable it has become to many systems of thought, social culture, and the like. And there arises an important institution of "common sense," and another of "public opinion," within which many other institutions must exist and conform.

In their evolutionary patterns, certain accepted institutions and their arrangements may lose their favorable position, while others not acceptable may suddenly, gain acceptance and respectability. Those that survive have responded through varying degrees and forms of adaptation to cultural changes in their environment. This degree of institutional accommodation is related to the nature of cultural changes; that is, whether gradual or abrupt, and peaceful, or with considerable friction. But as the changes take place the unfamiliar is treated as familiar, regardless of whether there is, in fact, complete understanding [29, 88].

At any given moment, then, in the survey of institutions, each important type as organic entities, are based upon notions, folkways, procedures, and so forth, deeply rooted in cultural patterns themselves of various origins and contents. Thus, as Hamilton states, each institution originates from elements, ideas, forms, and the like, originating in contemporary civilization, the eighteenth century, the medieval world, and the folkways from far-off, forgotten time periods [29, 88].

Park states it somewhat differently [44, 244-250]. Every institution may be described analytically as: (1) some type of movement that once was "active and eruptive," but which has, currently, achieved some level of routine and stability; (2) a form of collective action with more or less clearly defined aims; (3) reaching some level of importance and function, with formal or informal internal organization; and (4) providing itself with the necessary membership to execute its purposes, programs, policies, and so forth. An institution achieves that status when society knows what to expect of it; that is, tends to treat it as one of Commons' "Going Concerns."

As we have seen, this recognition is not even in time, place, or degree, but varies, in part and in composition, with the type and importance of the institution. Thus, there is implicit in every organization some concept and philosophy which may be stated in rational fashion; or which has evolved as a rationalization or justification for its existence.

We may close the discussion of this section with the following quotation:

Although there may be implicit in the practice of every institution an idea and a philosophy, it is only in a changing society where it becomes necessary to defend or redefine its functions that this philosophy is likely to achieve a formal and dogmatic statement; and even the body of sentiments and ideas which support these principles may remain, like an iceberg, more or less submerged in the 'collective unconscious,' whatever that is [44, 246].

Institutionalism

Institutionalism, in its broadest aspects in the present context, may be said to represent the systematic study of institutions, as defined above, in relation to a given discipline or subject matter. As such, it places emphasis, within the respective body of materials, on the structure and functioning of the various forms of collective action found in institutions, in lieu of an individualistic approach, or a nonpersonal, mechanistic emphasis. Every social science, or every behavioral science, is intimately involved in this search process as between the institutional or the noninstitutional emphasis, in its intellectual journey towards establishing and perfecting a body of theory.

The very nature of institutions raises in institutionalism several significant problems of priorities. How far can biological and organic analogies be useful? Can the matter of historical foundations and evolutionary patterns be discussed analytically and systematically? How quantitatively oriented can and should the institutional approach be made in any subject matter? Or is the approach fundamentally one of qualitative analytical description? Do the significant limitations of alternative approaches continue to exist, thus giving the institutional approach a significant advantage? Or does the institutional approach create even more serious limitations and handicaps? How can this approach in any subject matter be dovetailed with alternative aproaches, if at all? And, how can the treatment in one subject matter area of institutions be integrated with treatments in other subject matter areas? These are suggesive of some of the more significant problem and priority areas.

Institutionalism and the institutional approach have had long periods of development in the United States in terms of various social disciplines, as well as in other countries. As was indicated earlier, the whole subject matter of sociology may be called institutional, even though this may not always appear to be the case in practice. Whether emphasis is placed on human ecology, the study of human behavior in urban areas, on social classes, or on mass versus individual arrangements, the field has as its center core the study of institutions in a broad framework of society. In other words, the center of teaching and research is the human being in the environment of various formal and informal social institutions.

Other social sciences such as anthropology, law, history, and human psychology have the institutional orientation in varying degrees. Anthropology is almost as completely institutional in its composition is is sociology, albeit with much heavier emphasis on the comparative evolutionary aspects of institutions. Apart from such topics as practices and procedures, the field of law itself is almost a complete manifestation of the institutional arrangements involved in informal and formal bodies of law and their administration. Finally, history and human psychology deal with other aspects of institutions with varying depth, geographical, and chronological perspectives.

The development of institutionalism in the field of economics is almost completely an American phenomenon, and represents a "revolution" against the mechanistic and impersonal emphasis found in the assumptions of laissez-faire economics; in the theory of the classical and neoclassical economists; and in the theories of such writers as Chamberlin, Keynes, and others. It is not within the scope of this essay to investigate the many facets of institutional economics, but rather to recognize the lineal relationships of the institutional approach to marketing with these developments in economics as well as other social sciences.

From a historical viewpoint, institutional economics owes much, first of all, to the pioneer writings of John R. Commons, Wesley C. Mitchell, and Thorstein Veblen, but not excluding others as well.[5] This merely acknowledges the outstanding pioneers. But, just as was the case in the discussion of the origins of institutions, this mere listing ignores the continuum of ideas, theories, teachings, and so forth, which influenced each of these, as well as many others. More recently, the names of Clarence Ayres, John M. Clark, Morris Copeland, and Allen Gruchy are representative of the better-known institutional economists.[6]

The institutional approach to marketing, as it is developed in the remaining sections of this essay, owes much to these variegated sources while in the process of developing its own central identification so to speak. Much of the ascertainable debt has been and will continue to be identified

---

[5] Valuable materials on the contributions of these economists, plus pertinent bibliography, are given by Joseph Dorfman [23].

[6] See the bibliography for a representative sample of reference material.

wherever possible. But there is a residual part which cannot be identified with any certainty as to source, but which represents the whole stream of effects of individual and institutional education on those developing the approach.

The Holistic-Institutional Approach to Marketing

Basic definitions. The holistic-institutional approach, based upon and an extension of the writings of Edward A. Duddy and David A. Revzan, must be related to the framework presented in earlier sections of this essay. *The institutional approach to the study of marketing views the marketing system within the entire economic order as an organic whole functioning through a great variety of interrelated marketing structures to achieve the purposes attributed to marketing.* This emphasis on institutions and structures, and their functioning, is in sharp contrast to the mechanical concepts underlying many theoretical economists and others. The analogy in their analyses and theories is a balancing of the economic forces of supply and demand working through the mechanisms of the market to achieve either stable or unstable equilibrium [36, 179-201].

Given the previous background of the institution, it should not be surprising that the biological analogies inherent in the institutional approach are not perfect, although they have served and continue to serve as most useful descriptive-analytical devices.[7]

As a natural science economics is first of all a social science. It is not primarily concerned with individual behavior. . . . Secondly, economics is a biological science—it studies group [that is, institutional] relationships among living organisms of the genus *homo sapiens*. As such its generalizations must somehow make peace with the general theory of biological evolution. They can be true and relevant to some definitely specified period of social evolution [21, 67-79].

An important difference, however, between organisms in nature and institutions as part of social structures, is that natural organisms, being the product of their respective heredity and environment, have no individual power of initiating changes in their composition. Institutions comprising social structures, on the other hand, while also in large part inherited and subject to environmental influences, may be invented or modified at the will of those who constitute their membership (or, at least, the majority effective opinion).

Thus, human beings are of a different order of creation from animals and plants in this context; or, at least, we like to believe this is so. But, in

---

[7] Morris A. Copeland, as an important contemporary institutional economist, has long contended that economics *is a biological as well as a social science.*

harmony with the biological analogy, the institutional approach places primary emphasis upon a study of the structure and functioning—*the anatomy and physiology*— of the marketing system and its component parts, the institutional "organisms." Similarly, the institutional approach also calls attention to the growth and development of marketing structures, and thus the overall marketing system, through a process of evolutionary change.

When, in the opening statement, we speak of the economic order as functioning through a variety of structures in a process of marketing, there is implied in the term, "process," among other things, an important element of the intitutional approach which serves to relate the various kinds of functions and institutions each to the other in some kind of order, and thus gives overall organization to the market and marketing system. (A later definition of marketing organization will follow.) The institutionalist views the instrumentalities and institutions of coordination and control as including not only prices and profit margins, but managements using authoritarian and persuasive techniques, the regulatory forces of law and the government, and the important institutional elements of social conventions, customs, and folkways. The functioning of these institutions under their respective managements goes on within, and is a part of, the greater socio-economic environment of the groups whose interests are being served.

Thus, an institutional approach to marketing, in its holistic point of view, comprehends these elements:(1) *the functional activity of institutions;* (2) *structural organization of component institutions;* (3) *processes of structural change;* and (4) *coordination and control, including the economic and cultural environment.* Detailed definitional material pertinent to each element follows, with additional discussion of other aspects as well.

Definitions: functions. Based on the definition of marketing discussed earlier, marketing functions may be defined as homogeneous groups of activities, and their respective constituent elements, which are necessary to the performance of the marketing system. The analysis of functions not only calls attention to the basic nature of each group of activities and the component elements thereof, but to their interrelationship as well, and to the costs inherent in their performance. It is a basic assumption of such analysis in the present framework that forms of marketing organization and systems may change, and that the relative importance of the different sets of functions may be affected by changing conditions, but that the basic functions, as such, must be always present in any kind of marketing system.

Marketing functions operate through, and are executed by, various kinds of marketing agencies (institutions) or structures. Some of these are engaged exclusively in marketing; others, like banks and transportation companies, perform functions for a wide range of persons and institutions, in additions to those engaged only in marketing. The management of the marketing functions is through the control and direction of different types of structures in the marketing system. The operation of these organizations under their respective managements goes on within, and is part of the socio-economic environment of the group (or groups) whose interests are so served. And, it is through management, as well as other control institutions, that the coordination of the marketing system is achieved more or less efficiently and effectively.

Thus, functional activity is purposeful activity. Marketing institutions are functional in the sense that they give expression to the activities of groups of businessmen—activities which are necessary for the group's existence, or for its improvement, or for the achievement of its policies.

Definitions: marketing structures. *A marketing structure is the formal organization of the elements and activities of a marketing institution.* Thus, institutions become recognizable and differentiated only as they take different structural forms.[8] The *structural form* thus often comes to stand for the institution, as we may refer to the bank, the department store, or an insurance company as "institutions"; whereas the *actual institutions* for which these forms of business organization stand, are respectively, credit, retailing, and risk-bearing. Functional activity may be organized in many different ways with resulting variety in the structural forms. For example, the institution of retailing may find expression in many different types of retailing agencies. Other features of structures may be noted:

1. They are organic—thus subject to growth and change.
2. They have meaning only in relation to the functions they perform and the institutions of which they are a part.
3. Their activities are irrelated, and must be studied, accordingly, in relation to each other and to the total institutional situation.

The term "structure" in the context of the institutional approach, connotes something that has organization and dimension—shape, size, and complexity; a design that has evolved for the purpose of performing a function or a group of functions. The function, or functions, it performs helps, in turn, to influence its design. *Thus, function modifies structure.*

It is important to note in this definition that *the structure is the unit of management.* This remains true, whether the managing authority is the businessman, the consumer organization, government, or any other agency. The task of the management resolves itself into a series of problems, the solutions of which must be worked out to the extent that they are primarily or wholly marketing in nature, through the use of the structural organization of the market and the marketing system. *In this sense, then, marketing*

---

[8] The reader should relate this concept to the earlier discussion of institutions.

structures may be defined as tools of management used to accomplish their respective particular purposes.

Just as the functional activities of marketing are interrelated in a *process* of distribution of goods and services, so are the marketing structures coordinated into a *system* through which the process is carried on in a more-or-less orderly fashion under the control of management. "Management" as used in this context must be understood in its broadest significance, that is, as conditioned by the action of consumers, by government control, and the cultural environment.

Apart from what has been said above, a further discussion of the relationships of function to structure may be helpful at this point. Functions become institutionalized as they operate through the marketing system. *Between function and structure, action is reciprocal;* function modifies structure, and the nature of the existing marketing structure limits, in turn, the performance of marketing functions.

The analytical study of the structure of the marketing system deals with the institutional organization of the marketing process in terms of the respective functions performed and the agencies or marketing structures which have evolved for the performance of these functions. Many of the problem areas of the marketing system evolve out of the adjustment or maladjustment of these agencies to the functions they are expected to perform; and out of consideration of the usefulness or necessity of particular functions in given marketing situations. The managerial settings of those problems must be observed. But considerably more attention will be directed to the institutionalization of these functions within the wholesaling and retailing sectors, and in different commodity and geographical situations within and between sectors.

Definitions: structural change. In asserting the strategic role of structural change in the institutional approach, one is merely stating a truism, because of the fundamental nature of institutions as earlier defined. The viewpoint of this approach being organic, hence the structures, as defined above, are subject to laws of growth and change. They evolve as a result of economic and a wide range of other pressures under conditions not always ascertainable; they have growth periods of varying time lengths in which they flourish and expand; and they may then move into routinized levels at which they cease to be economically important, or they may disappear completely. *Structures, in their efforts to survive, are constantly being adapted to forces making for change, or trying to create and/or control them.*

The institutional approach is analogous to the biologist's approach to the study of living forms. In both cases there is interest in function and form; and these forms are organic, having life cycles with the characteristics previously noted. It is from this point of view that the institutional approach defines, classifies, and analyzes the phenomenon of change in and throughout the marketing system. Observations have demonstrated that processes of change may be analogous, indeed, to those in nature in varying degrees, depending upon the particular type. Through the impact of environmental forces on the individual structure (the organism), a variant of the original form may appear, but with new and different characteristics. These variants may be of lesser or greater significance to the entire marketing system. In a sense, these changes may be said to correspond to the process of mutation in natural forms. And, if the new form is better adapted to its socioeconomic environment, it survives and may generate additional variants; but, if it not, it is eliminated through a process of competition and selection. In addition, the scientific study of the marketing system may, itself, be said to be an institutional force making for change.

The process of structural change in the economic world may correspond, also, to these changes induced by the process of plant breeding. Thus, management may seek to hasten the process of adaption by developing new institutional forms building upon the characteristics of one or more existing forms. While the process of change often is marked, as in nature, by the evolution into more complex forms from the simple, the process, under management control, often works in the opposite direction of simplification of both function and structure.[9] *Change thus is universal in the marketing system as it is inevitably in nature, despite the attempts of some individual institutions to block change.* It penetrates into every part and functioning of the marketing system.[10]

Definitions: coordination and control. Just as the marketing functions interact in a process of distribution of goods and services, so the structures through which those functions get performed must work together to effect a marketing organization of these processes. The evidence of formal and systematic coordinated action is often difficult to discover when the individual marketing and facilitating agencies are left entirely free to determine their own policies. However, the pattern becomes quite distinct in those cases where the principle of institutional authority is invoked singly or collectively to compel cooperative action, or some type of conformity, or termination of certain activities.

Several institutional instrumentalities are at work to effect the coordination and control of the marketing system. The first of these is *price* and the *price structure,* behind which is the *free choice of consumers* at all levels of the marketing system functioning both as individuals and in

---

[9] Once again, the term "management" is used here in the broadest sense.

[10] Note the earlier definition of marketing which included emphasis on change.

institutional arrangements. In a *free* market, price is the impersonal factor that coordinates supply with demand through the rational behavior of consumers in that market. (The definition of markets will be given in a later section.) If we conceded, however, that the market is *not* free, and that consumers (individually and collectively) do not always act rationally and may be influenced in their choices by their emotional impulses and managements' persuasive techniques, then there may be good reason for considering other factors than price as means of coordination and control. But even in these cases consumers may be said to exert their influences on the marketing system through the mechanism of price and the price structure.

Another directing and coordinating force is the institution of *management* of the various marketing and facilitating agencies. Through management, the economic and noneconomic forces operating in the marketing system are interpreted and made effective in terms of definite organizational policies. These policies determine what marketing functions shall be performed, and those persons, within the organization, who shall be given authority for and held responsible in the execution of such policies. *Thus coordinated action and the exercise of control become the essence of managerial activities.* Management attempts to extend its control to every part of the marketing system, *including* price and the price structure. In turn, however, these attempts are limited by the other forces discussed in this section.

The entire range of *government control* is inherent in, and an integral part of, the institutional approach. Through legislation and judicial decisions, government sets limits to managerial action and freedom, and thus exercises a very potent and determining effect on the coordination of marketing institutions. Government may act positively to assist in the performance of marketing functions and in the creation and continuation of particular institutions; or may restrain and prohibit. Through its taxing powers, government may favor one type of marketing agency or a level of consumers, or particular products, while penalizing other categories. Much legislation and other governmental efforts may be directed towards preserving or restoring some philosophy of a "free" market and "workable" competition. On the other hand, government may act to stabilize other sets of prices, or permit deviations from competition by legalizing certain types of monopolies.

Finally, one must not overlook or underestimate the fact that much marketing behavior is based upon, and controlled by, social customs and habits. Management itself, continually controlled by these, is trying continually to break through this restraining environment so indigenous to all institutions. But to be successful in marketing, management must largely conform to customary modes of behavior on the part of consumers. In addition, customs and habits continue to govern the practices of business-men in their relations with each other. Indeed, every trade and industry may be said to be bound within its own framework of these. Therefore, custom and habit as important parts of the socioeconomic environment within which the institutions of the marketing system must work, become a determining factor in the coordination and control of the system and its structures.

Definitions: marketing organization. In the preceding discussion of the institutional approach, reference has been made from time to time to the concept of marketing organization. As used in the context of the institutional approach, the author's discussion is as follows (52, 17-18):

The concept as it is used in this introductory context is not concerned with the internal aspects of a particular firm. What is being emphasized here is the way in which many different kinds of individual firms and establish-ments array themselves in *formal, systematic* manner within various produc-ing, buying, selling, and facilitating agencies in making possible the systematic, continuous movement of goods and services from producing to using points, together with the necessary determination of prices and terms of sales for their exchange. Depending upon the ideology of the political environment, the maximization of alternatives for final users may or may not result, and the operation of the organization within some framework of "efficiency" may or may not take place.

The marketing organization is formal and systematic in the sense that there has evolved over a long period of time: (a) specialized production units both at the extractive and manufacturing levels which account for the highest percentage of all goods produced; (b) a series of specialized middlemen who, together with the integrated types, operate in various types of wholesale pri-mary and intermediate markets; (c) a series of specialized retail middlemen who, together with the integrated types, operate similarly in retail markets; and (d) many types of facilitating agencies (institutions) offering services to es-tablishments at all levels, and who act in a buying capacity as well, including professional transportation, storage, financial, communication, research, and related facilitating functions.

Thus, to summarize, the marketing organization is cross-sectional or dis-sectional study of the agencies and mechanisms of marketing as they array themselves in systematic fashion each to the other in moving goods and services from producing units.

Definitions: relation of channels to marketing organization. [11] To the above statement there must be added another discussing the relationship of channels of distribution to marketing organization [52, 18]: It may be

---

[11] The complete discussion of channels of distribution is given in a later section.

pointed out here that marketing organization is made effective through channels of distribution. Since the flow of goods and services through the marketing organization is not an automatic process, what must be recognized at the beginning is that marketing organization involves a complicated network of buying and selling agencies, of varying periods of negotiation, of physical handling agencies and intermediaries, and of facilitating business units of various sizes in various locations, grouped together in varying combinations to link particular producing units with particular using units. In addition, they combine in varying patterns of complexity to account for the over-all movement of particular commodity categories and groups of categories.

The channel thus becomes the linking vehicle by means of which marketing organization takes place and becomes effective. And as the marketing aspects of a nation grow in complexity parallel to the nation's total social and economic development, so do its channel aspects develop into more intricate patterns along functional, commodity, spatial, and control components.

The Institutional Approach and Homeostasis[12]

To the extent that the biological and organic attributes of the institutional approach have validity and applicability, so does the concept of *homeostasis* have equal validity and applicability. Just as the individual parts of the human body work together, in a state of dynamic equilibrium, to achieve an integrated whole when the body is healthy, or at least attempts to restore itself to such balance, so do the structural components of the marketing system attain, or strive to attain, this overall equilibrium and integration. In both cases, this takes place even while the component organisms have cycles of growth and possible subsequent stability or decline.

This concept of *homeostasis* in human biology thus has several aspects of the functioning and coordination of higher animal organisms which have some transferability to, and value for, the concept of the marketing system inherent in the institutional approach.[13] Some beginning aspects which indicate this relationship, and which appear to be of significance are:

1. The existence of a series of control mechanisms, thermostats if you will, which are interlocked internally and externally. These are referred to, also, as *homeostats*.

---

[12] For the definitive statement and discussion of homeostasis, see [15]. Also, of considerable value in developing the contents of this section is: [30, 300-309].

[13] The concept is having a widespread vogue currently in many social and behavioral sciences.

2. The existence of a *fluid matrix,* which is comparable in the marketing system to the roles of transportation, and money and credit agencies.

3. The existence of a *margin of safety;* that is, provision of "an allowance for contingencies."

4. The ability of the marketing system, as in the organism, to store surpluses created at any moment of time; and, when necessary, to eliminate such surpluses. Note, especially, the close relationship of this to the storage function and storage institutions.

5. The existence of a series of complementary interactions.

6. The existence in the marketing system, as in the individual organism, of defenses against unfavorable attacks.

7. Again, as in the human organisms, the continued consistency of certain characteristics of the marketing system, and the continuous attempts made to maintain these conditions.

8. The recognition of the conditions in (7) as basic to necessary elements of freedom and independence of individual institutions in the marketing system, as in the natural living organism.

9. The necessity for the individual institution, as well as the organism, to respond, internally, in positive or negative fashion to every external change.

10. The existence of sets of automatic sentinels or indicators related to, and in addition to the *homeostats* noted above.

11. The tendency for institutions, as well as organisms, to be resistant to certain types of change in the presence of constant change.

12. The tendency for certain effects to spiral.

13. The tendency of homeostasis to oppose or offset conditions of natural instability.

14. Finally, the tendency for the conditions of homeostasis to permit the organism to maintain itself at maximum efficiency, *under conditions which are naturally unstable.*

To the extent that this concept of homeostasis has validity, significance, and applicability for the present discussion, it can be said that, from within the marketing system and its component structures, come various signals of balance and imbalance often signaled through the price system by virtue of its role as the "brains and nervous structure" of the entire marketing system. As has been noted above, the managerial decisions of each institution working within the framework of this price structure become of key significance. But the materials in this essay will develop this relationship in more detail. In a sense, they represent one category of homeostats. These decisions, it should be noted, involve individual business units and group action in an environment both of competition and cooperation. Finally, the significance, once again of the coordinating and controlling aspects of the government, consumers, and custom and habit, should not be ignored in their homeostatic aspects.

The Environment of Product Assortments in the Institutional Approach[14]

Previous definitions of marketing and the marketing system invariably include a central position for goods and services as the *raison d'etre* for marketing and its functional and institutional components. The present discussion is restricted mainly to definitional and classification materials.

Basic definitions: products and product assortments. A product, for purpose of this definition, is the result of any specific extractive or manufacturing industry activity, which has a particular combination of specific physical and/or chemical characteristics designed to meet a specific need or an interrelated series of needs. Each product, in this concept, carries its own means of identification. Thus, if a given company packs and markets two separate brands of coffee (for instance, its own and a distributor's) each is considered a separate product for marketing purposes. The combination of all individual products satisfying a particular need (or customarily related needs) would constitute a product line for a given producer or middleman. An accumulation of several product lines having a common tie of homogeneity within a family of uses, establishes the basis for a family of products. Thus, one may speak of a *line* of canned peas, and a *family of lines* of canned vegetables.[15]

Product assortments can be approached from an internal managerial, and an external structural point of view, although these are not the only approaches. But for the institutional approach, this separation has great significance. Thus, product assortments can be viewed merely as a part of the discussion of product policies related to the manufacturing and marketing policies of a given producer. From an *internal management point of view,* a product assortment is:

1. The particular combination of individual products (as defined above), found as part of the production and/or marketing activities of a particular establishment at the extractive or manufacturing levels; or

2. The combination of individual products, item by item, and line by line, which are accumulated by given wholesale or retail middlemen

---

[14] The treatment in this section is based mainly on: [52, Chs. 7; 12, esp. 282-287; 13, esp. 303-305; and 14, esp. 336-337].

[15] In actual usage, however, the two terms may be used interchangeably and without distinction.

in order to execute as effectively as possible the marketing policies of their particular types of operation.

From the external point of view, product assortments represent the *sum total* of the internal assortments, as defined above, which are needed to meet the requirements of all middlemen and facilitating agencies involved in a given channel of distribution system of linkages for a stated kind of business.[16]

Variables in product assortments. Some indication of the more important variables in product assortments needs to be given here before discussing types of product assortments. One is the basic category of the product as indicated by some end-use designation; for example, stove, spoon, or motor. These end-use designations of products may be subclassified further according to whether the product has a single-use, few uses, or multiple and diverse uses. Next, are such important *physical characteristics* as model number, physical sizes, weight specifications, or color designations which lead, in turn, to product multiplication. Other variables include quality specifications, types of package, individual trade-mark or trade-name designations and identifications, or individual price-class-designations. More often than not, these variables affect product assortments by working in tandem, rather than being identified individually.[17]

Types of product assortments: internal management levels. The following outline indicates the principal types of product assortments at the extractive industry, manufacturing industry wholesale middlemen, and retail middlemen levels:

Type I—Extractive Industry Level
> IA—product assortments fixed by the nature of the available natural resources (for example: fish, coal, metal ores, diamonds)
> IB—product assortments in which some variety and quality range is introduced by: (a) producers' selections of breeds to be reared; or (b) botanical varieties of crops to be produced
> IC—product assortments based upon multi-product production situations (for example, mixed-crop and truck-crop farming)

Type II—Manufacturing Industry Levels (with either manufacturer's or distributor's brands, or none)
> IIA—short-line product assortments (for example, *only* canned peas, or fish, or corn)
> IIB—full-line or full-product family policies (for example, every conceivable type of canned vegetables)

---

[16] The meaning and types of channels of distribution will be discussed in a later section of this essay.

[17] Thus, a given brand name may designate a "fighting" price level to meet competition.

IIC—family of products with closely homogeneous production and/or end-use characteristics

IID—family of products with highly variable production and/or end-use characteristics

Types III, IV—Wholesale and Retail Middlemen's Levels (with manufacturers' and/or middlemen's brands, or none)

IIIA, IVA—by exclusive distributorship arrangements, product assortments limited to what the controlling manufacturer produces under Type II

IIIB, IVB—product assortments in depth achieved by carrying in inventory every output of a given homogeneous product-line or family of lines

IIIC, IVC—product assortments in breadth

IIID, IVD—combinations of product assortments in IIIB and IIIC, or IVB and IVC

Types of product assortments: channel perspective. The classification scheme presented below divides into two parts: the channel-level designation; and the type of product assortments for each level.

A. Channel-Level Designations (using the classifications of wholesale and retail middlemen, and of channels of distribution to be discussed in later sections)

I. *Extractive Industry—Edible Products Channel Levels*
   a. Producers' level—domestic and foreign
   b. Wholesale middlemen's level—stage #1
   c. Wholesale middlemen's level—stage #2
   d. Retail middlemen's level
   e. Consumer's level

II. *Industrial Goods Channel Levels*
   a. Producers' level—domestic and foreign
   b. Wholesale middlemen's level
   c. Manufacturers' level
   d. Wholesale middlemen's level—stage #1
   e. Wholesale middlemen's level—stage #2
   f. User's level—domestic and foreign

III. *Manufactured Consumers' Goods' Levels*
   a. Manufacturers' level—domestic and foreign
   b. Wholesale middlemen's level—stage #1
   c. Wholesale middlemen's level—stage #2
   d. Retail middlemen's level
   e. Consumer's level—domestic and foreign

B. *Changes Through the Channel* (12, 61)

Type I (band pattern: narrow, medium, or broad)—no change in product assortment as it moves through the channel.

Type II (diamond pattern)—narrow assortments at producers' level; wider assortments at wholesale middlemen's level; and narrow assortments again at retailers' level.

Type III (triangle pattern)—continuous *broadening* of product assortments at each channel level.

Type IV (*inverted* triangle pattern)—continuous *narrowing of* product assortments at each channel level.

Type V (picket pattern)—broadening of product assortments from the producers' level to the wholesale middlemen's level; and then a maintenance of such product assortment breadth through the remaining levels.

Type VI (*inverted* picket pattern)—a given breadth of product assortments at the beginning, with narrowing at the last channel level.

These classification patterns, and those that preceded, are of necessity generalizations, and make no allowance for the introduction of considerations of intanglible services. But even so-called intangible services frequently involve physical characteristics, or may be combined with tangible products. Generally, however, services as marketed frequently are limited in assortment possibilities because of the closeness of the service to the generating source. Thus, the services of a dentist are limited to his own professional abilities, except where an additional person may be used for a certain specialty.

The discussion of quality variables in relation to product assortments, and the measurement of product quality will be deferred until a later essay.

The Institutional (Agency) Structure: A System of Middlemen, Markets and Facilitating Agencies

Basic definitions. This category of structural components involves the various business units which perform, collectively, the entire range of maketing functions as defined earlier in connection with movements of and exchange of title to the product assortments noted above. Within the marketing system they are interrelated through the external aspects of marketing organization as links in channels of distribution. Thus, they are the institutional units performing functions as part of the physiological aspects of the marketing system. But, either individually, or in groups in channel patterns, they may be viewed anatomically as the working parts of the marketing "body." And, based on various criteria, these parts may be classified and assigned various orders of priority and importance.

The term "middleman" is very pertinent in marketing because it implies a group of business agencies that exist in the channel intermediate to the producing units at one end and the using ends at the other. The basic dictionary concept of the middleman as a go-between or intermediary is especially applicable. Although often viewed in historical perspective as parasites, middlemen are entirely differently evaluated in the modern marketing system. A result of a rapidly-evolving economic system in which producer and consumer are separated and unknown to each other in a personal sense, and in which an ever-widening assortment of goods must flow, the middleman is a constantly present example of growing specialization and complexity in trying to match what is being produced with what users need or can be convinced to buy.

In actuality, as shall be developed later in the discussion of channels, the middleman is not a single-level type of intermediary but represents several levels of intermediate relationships. These keep changing as business units which have not been intermediaries try to control or absorb such intermediaries, while the middlemen, in turn, frequently develop beyond their roles as intermediaries. Thus, as frequently happens when specialization continues to expand, increasing lines of friction develop between levels and categories of specialists; and these lead, in turn, to some overlappings and confusions. But despite these blurring developments, sight should not be lost of the fundamental meaning of middleman.

General aspects of classification. Apart from the tendencies noted in the preceding section, one may distinguish marketing agencies, first of all, as between those wholesale and retail middlemen who function at the heart of buying and selling functions, and those agencies which merely facilitate such functions. From an *organizational* point of view, a distinction may be made according to: (a) the type of legal form assumed; (b) the number of establishments units operated or controlled; and (c) the degree and types of integration effected.

On the basis of *risk elements,* middlemen agencies may be divided into those types which assume the full risks of ownership (so-called merchant middlemen), and those which function merely as agents without such risks. Given the analysis of the functional aspects of marketing, one may classify middlemen according to the degree of specialization. On the one hand there are those types which perform a full range of marketing functions (full-function types), and handle a general-line of product assortments; while, on the other hand, there are limited-function operations with specialty or limited-line product assortments.

Within each of the above classification bases, there are additional variations in the structural types occasioned by the following: (1) function in different commodity markets with different product assortments, thus determining various kinds of business; (2) operations at different levels of the marketing system—the wholesaling sector *versus* the retailing sector (to be discussed in the next section); (3) the different geographical outreaches—domestic *versus* foreign, and within the domestic, local, state, regional, or national; and (4) differences in the structure and degree of competition.

For most of the middleman agency structures, the characteristics that differentiate them are clearly identifiable. However, over the years hybrid types have emerged which have embraced more than one type of operation, and/or functioning in both the wholesaling and retailing sectors. Facilitating agencies may be related in valuable fashion to these classification bases; but, they also have close relationship to functional specialization (such as transportation, storage, financing, research, and communication).

The concept of wholesaling and retailing sectors. Given the framework of the marketing system as previously developed, there is considerable merit in dividing the system into sectors identified as wholesaling and retailing. Not only does such division emphasize differences in product assortments, but in types of middlemen, and types of facilitating agencies in terms of specialization and geographic characteristics. In addition, the division into two sectors introduces highly important variations in the motivations and shopping habits of buyers, as well as in the buying-selling sequences.

The *wholesaling sector* stresses, in an orthodox marketing sense, the nature and motivation of the buyer as the single most important criterion differentiating it from the retailing sector. Accordingly, based on this criterion, the wholesaling sector of the marketing system may be defined as that part in which goods and services move to various classes of buyers or their agents, who will: (1) engage in the sale and resale of such goods and services with profits in mind; (2) use the goods and services to facilitate the production of other goods and services, which then will be handled as in (1); (3) use the goods and services for various institutional purposes other than for profit-making (for example, charitable, educational, governmental).[18]

Two refinements need to be introduced in this beginning definition of the wholesaling sector. *First,* the prices charged for a given product sold at wholesale may or may *not* be lower than prices charged at retail;

---

[18] An important aspect to notice here is that transactions in wholesale markets frequently involve selling many types of goods more than one time.

although a lower price charged in the wholesaling sector *usually* is the prevailing situation. But, if, for example, a person operating an office or small business buys a single typewriter (a wholesale transaction), he may pay the identical price charged to a student buying the product for his own needs (a retail transaction). *Second,* the quantity purchased at wholesale *usually* is, but need not be, necessarily larger than the quantity purchased at a retail sales transaction. Many important variables affect this factor of the quantity purchased at each transaction by a given class of buyer.

From the preceding discussion, several criteria or characteristics emege, which *may be* useful in identifying and classifying transactions made in the wholesaling sector: (1) the motives and habits of the purchasers; (2) the quantity purchased at each transaction; (3) the wider varieties of goods offered for sale compared with retail sales; (4) the wider geographical bases for wholesale sales; (5) in most transactions, the lower prices per unit involved; and (6) the frequent occurrence of multiple buying-selling cycles for the same products.

On these bases, then the *retailing sector* involves all remaining sales and movements of goods and services to persons who will use these to satisfy their respective ultimate wants and desires. In the institutional tradition these persons can and do combine in any form of collective living-spending relationships, without affecting the essentially retail nature of the transaction. Thus, if the total quantitative measures of goods and services are determinable, and if data of the agency activities within each category are available, then the division in gross importance between the sectors can be approximated with reasonable accuracy.[19]

Given these two sectors, and their identifying criteria, it follows that the movements of goods and services do not all involve regular progressions from producers→to wholesale middlemen→to retail middlemen →to ultimate consumers. The larger proportion of goods and services, as will be discussed later, move in various channel patterns. The following are, of course, merely suggestive of categories of transactions generalized from numerous actual patterns:

1. From extractive industry producers (raw materials)→to processing manufacturers;

2. From extractive industry producers→to wholesale middlemen in one or more channel combinations→to nonmanufacturer categories of users, *excluding* ultimate consumers;

3. From manufacturers→to wholesale middlemen in one or more channel combinations→to extractive industry producers and/or other producers; and

---

[19] One gross measure is to relate the gross volume of wholesale sales, based on available Census data, to the gross volume of retail sales.

4. From one establishment to another in the same levels as (3), based upon highly integrated and interlocking ownership and control patterns.

Definitions: markets. Marketing, as an applied subject matter field, must consider the definition of "market" in both its theoretical and applied aspects. Accordingly, this section will present both points of view, together with a discussion of types and some evolutionary aspects. In all of this discussion, the relationship of markets to both agency structures should not be forgotten [25, 4-5, 8-11].

"Market" is a term rich in theoretical and practical connotations, and susceptible of many different uses and interpretations. Under the assumptions of perfect competition, a market is a place or region where informed buyers and sellers meet for the purpose of buying and selling goods; and where a single price tends to prevail at a given time for the same grade of product. It is assumed, further, that *all* units of a good of the same grade *are alike;* that buyers and sellers are *equally* well informed about offerings of products and available current price data; and, that they are *equal* in bargaining power, the famous assumption of atomistic competition. It is obvious that, under such ideal conditions, a *single* price will prevail at any given point in the market area. Where price differences do exist, they tend to conform to differences in transportation and handling costs.

Fetter states:

Free access, common knowledge, two-sidedness of competition, capacity (*i.e.,* capacity of the economic system to perform the services or to produce the goods)—these are the essential conditions of a true market in which there can be *effective* competition. When all these conditions are present the law of supply and demand fully operates and uniform market prices result [26, 263].

He makes a distinction, accordingly, between the market place and "the regions from which goods are bought for sale, and to which they will be shipped after sale" [25, 279].[20]

Inherent in the economists' concept of a perfectly competitive market is the concept of the market as *a mechanism,* the chief purpose of which is the determination of the exchange values of goods and services in prices. It is a mechanism that registers the value estimates of buyers and sellers for a given commodity in terms of money prices, the result of the bargaining process being *market price*—a measure of the exchange value of that product. All considerations of place, or time, or commodity, are subordinate to this essential process of price determination. For the economist, also,

---

[20] These regions will be discussed in a later section as market-tributary areas, or simply as market areas.

it is through the market mechanism that the work of specialists in production is coordinated through their response to prices and profits.[21]

If uniformity of price for the same grade of product be accepted as the criterion of the existence of a market, then there are as many different markets in the marketing system as there are different prices. Different prices to different classes of buyers may be justified on the basis of differences in costs of selling to them; or because of the different marketing functions they perform; or such differences in prices as may arise purely from the sellers' discriminatory policies. In any case, each class of buyer constitutes, in effect, a separate market for the seller. From the standpoint of the businessman, there is for any one commodity a single market with price differentials for different grades and for different buyers, through a system of discounts or allowances.

The idea of *place* as applied to the term "market," has acquired a wide range of meaning and applications. It may be a neighborhood retail store; the shopping center of a city, a region, or a country; or, as in the case of such staples as wheat and cotton, the whole civilized world. The extent of the market for a given product is dependent upon differential costs and prices at a market center with respect to other market centers, upon the degree of organization of communication service, and upon a number of psychological and managerial considerations.

From what has been said up to this point, it is clear that, to have a market, the goods bought and sold need *not* be physically present, nor do the buyers and sellers have to be in actual *physical* contact. Merchandise may be sold by description or by sample, as well as by inspection; *provided,* that there exists an effective medium of designation and grade specification, and an equally effective system of communication of other information. *In the last analysis, it is the concept of the market as a zone of influence— the meeting of buyers' and sellers' minds—that is important for the marketing system.*

Types of markets. The preceding definitions of market have indicated, already, some idea of the range of type of markets. At the outset, we may add differentiation between the wholesaling and retailing sectors, and between types of products traded at each level within these sectors. But within each of these categories, there are many additional gradations and differentiations.

The marketing executive may begin with the concept that "markets are people with money to spend—and the desire to spend it." In this popular concept of a market, he is able, with the use of many research methods and techniques, to detect psychological differences among various

---

[21] In this connection, reference should be made to the later section on price structures.

buying groups in their purchasing power (both "gross" and "effective"), their motivations, and in their willingness to buy both categories of products and individual brand within the categories. This approach emphasizes, among other things, the market to the marketing executive, both in terms of size at the present time, and future potentialities and expectancies. His attitude towards these present and expected markets may emphasize, accordingly, aggressive exploitation, persuasion, and development, rather than *passive* acceptance.

In the roundabout system of manufacture that is so dominant today, most goods, of necessity, are produced for a *future* market. This is peculiarly and particularly true of goods produced to satisfy a seasonal demand. Agricultural products, seasonally produced, must be carried through the period of consumption which may be of several years in duration. Thus, this *time notion* of the market enters into the practical thinking of all businessmen in their buying and selling operations. Kinds of goods, quantities to be produced, and prices are largely determined in the present; delivery and payment are largely in the future.

In the case of certain agricultural and industrial commodities for which trading in *future contracts* is practiced, the distinction in time has become the basis of a separate institutional organization of *cash and futures* commodity markets. Transactions in which immediate delivery of the commodity to the buyer is contemplated, are said to be in the *cash market*. Where contracts are entered into in the present, with delivery and payment in the future, and where the transactions are governed by the rules of a trading exchange (one type of organized commodity market), the market is referred to as a *futures trading,* or merely *futures, market*.

Finally, for purposes of this section, we may refer to *buying markets* and *selling markets*. There are two essential senses or meanings in which these subdivisions are used: the *first* refers to a condition of the market at a particular time; and the *second* characterizes the market with respect to the direction of movement of goods, either *to* or *from* the market in a tributary area.

In the first of these senses, a *buyers' market* is one in which supply is so large in relation to the effective demand, that buyers are able to exercise a dominant influence in the determination of market price. Conversely, a *sellers' market* is one in which the supply of goods is in such short supply relative to demand that sellers are able to demand and receive price premiums. Under competition, the assumptions underlying these types of markets are that the demand for the product is generally inelastic, and that both buyers and sellers have knowledge of these supply gluts or shortages when they occur, and are willing to take any advantage they can. In the case of particular products, the condition tends to be, generally, of short duration, and, usually, is self-corrective. When monopoly is present, or the conditions of a great war, sellers' markets tend to prevail for considerable periods of time. In fact, in time of war, this condition may so extend to wide classes of goods that rationing and price controls are invoked. During periods of an extended business depression, widespread buyers' markets may continue for long time periods.

Turning to the second sense in which these terms are used, the best examples of *buying markets* are the central markets for agricultural products to which products are shipped from scattered small producers. The movement of goods is *centripetal,* and these wholesale markets sometimes are referred to by the same term. Conversely, where scattered buyers buy from a centrally-located market, or from a fixed point of production or supply, the market is looked upon primarily as a *selling market;* and, the movement of goods away from the market as a center justifies designation of these movements and markets as *centrifugal.*[22] Examples are manufacturing or large merchandise centers; and the reshipping or distribution area aspects of agricultural goods wholesale markets.[23]

The "mucilage" of the agency structure: channels of distribution [52, Chs. 1, esp. 16-22; 5-6; and 24]. The concept of channels of distribution or marketing channels, has been mentioned briefly in the preceding discussion of marketing organization. This section explores, in more depth, the meaning, types, and selected implications.

"Channel" connotes, in its marketing meaning and application, a pathway taken by goods and services as they flow from point of production to points of intermediate and final use. But, in these flows, there is a further connotation of a sequence of marketing agencies; namely the wholesale and retail middlemen who perform, type by type, various combinations of marketing functions at various points in the channel in order to facilitate such flows. In addition, there is a connotation of a sequence of facilitating agencies which perform auxiliary functions at one or more points within the channel.[24]

The channel is, therefore, the vehicle, conceptually speaking, for viewing marketing organization in its external aspects, and for bridging the physical and nonphysical gaps which exist in moving goods from producers to consumers through the exchange process, including the determination of prices.

---

[22] Centripetal and centrifugal movements may characterize two different time aspects of the same wholesale market.

[23] Space does not permit adequate discussion here of the evolution of the market within the marketing system. Interested readers will find the following references most useful: [48, esp. 68-69, 115; 49, Chs. 5, 14-16]. Attention is directed, also, to the relationship of this material and the later discussion of prices and price structures.

[24] Some writers view each functional or sub-functional grouping as giving rise to flows.

Geographically speaking, the channel thus bridges the gap between producers and users. In this sense, distance is involved not only in the usual units and terminology of measurement, but also in terms of the time involved in transit, and the costs of both transportation and communication. In addition to time in relation to distance, the channel has a function to perform in bridging time gaps in the pure storage sense. Thus, within the channel, certain types of middlemen and certain special institutions arise both to carry physical inventories, and to change their physical characteristics over periods of time.

In addition, channels are useful in bridging gaps in product assortment patterns (as disclosed earlier in this essay), by matching sellers' inventories, in both physical and qualitative aspects, with buyers' inventory intentions. Channels, also, are means of bridging gaps in knowledge, and the communication of such knowledge as is available. *They become, accordingly, a structural arrangement whereby sellers, or their middlemen representatives, search for customer prospects with whom to communicate and to whom sales ultimately can be made; and whereby buyers, in turn, search for sellers carrying the assortments desired, and from whom purchases ultimately can be made.*

The concept of the channel of distribution involves, in addition to these characteristics, sets of vertical and horizontal relationships between various types of wholesale and retail middlemen, in various kinds of business and types of markets. As such, it can be used as the keystone for the analyses of various "circuit" and "flow" arrangements centering around these managerial aspects. Based upon all of these considerations, there can evolve systematic analyses of various managerial policies and problems.

Finally, we may summarize the types of channels of distribution. Classification according to the *number of links* in the channel—the intervening marketing and facilitating agencies—is the oldest and most orthodox basis, and yields, accordingly, *direct, semi-direct,* and *indirect channels.* Where a set of channels exists which makes use of more than combination of agencies, a differentiation may be made between that part which is a *primary level of importance,* and that part which is of *secondary,* or *auxiliary* importance. Channels, *by type of managerial control,* introduce elements of *integrated versus nonintegrated*; and, further, subdivides channels into producer-controlled, wholesale-middlemen-controlled, and retail-middlemen-controlled. Significant subclassifications emerge, within these catagories, by type of operation, and horizontal and vertical integration [52, 117-119; 31, 159-165]. Finally, channels may be classified, also, by *breadth of business penetration,* and by each kind of *physcial* and *nonphysical* flows.[25]

---

[25] For illustrations of channels by the nature of the commodity and commodity flows see: [52, 121-140], and the references given.

The Area Structure of the Marketing System

Comprehensive definition. In viewing the marketing system in its geographical aspects, it may be pointed out that exchange of goods, geographically, will depend on two sets of considerations, fundamentally. *First,* an area (such as city, region, or some other unit of space) which has no *nearby supply,* or at least an *insufficient* supply, of goods for the needs of its population, must offer a money price, or its equivalent in goods and services, sufficient to generate movements of needed goods from the area, or areas, which have surpluses. This geographical exchange must consider, of course, all transportation or transfer costs, together with differences in each area's demand based upon its want patterns, its income size and distribution per capita, the social characteristics of its population, other sources of demands, and any conscious social controls exerted over its demands.

In addition, this exchange must consider differences in costs of production between areas based on differences in resources, differences in the scale and technology of production, and related factors. Included in this, as a significant analytical detail, are the theory and economics of plant location. The burden placed upon the marketing agencies will vary with the distance of the plant from the center of gravity—the consuming area (or areas). The marketing processes involved in moving raw materials and supplies are essentially much simpler than those required for finished goods. Finally, there must be, in this set of considerations, some kind of economic mutuality of wants between the areas, so that each may have the monetary means for paying for what it wants in terms of what it can sell.

The second set of considerations reflects, in addition to the prime factors just mentioned, trade between areas based upon the managerial policies of businessmen as they pertain to type of operation, location of establishments, and price and nonprice policies. This trade reflects, also, the role of the various governmental levels and agencies as evidenced in promotional, regulatory, and impeding types of legislation and other activities as they relate to the marketing of goods interregionally and intraregionally, as well as in international patterns.

Area structure, in this context, calls attention, first of all, to the basic geographical specialization of location of extractive industry resources, and to the expected marketing returns based on them—the basic conditions of this locational inequality. Building upon this inequality, it emphasizes next that, for each agency in the overall agency discussed above, there is the necessity of selecting a particular location. These locational alternatives have exclusive trading areas, respectively, in which each is dominant in terms of buying and/or selling importance—*the primary trading area.*

The same concept may be used for clusters of agencies in a given geographical context.

A zone surrounding the primary trading area offers less-than-proportionate returns than the primary zone, and is designated as the *secondary trading area.* A final zone may exist in certain area structures in which the particular trading centers and their constituent agencies have no distinct and outstanding advantages over competing centers and their component agencies—*the zone of trading indifference.* As the geographical unit becomes more complex, and as the marketing system expands, a hierarchy of super trading areas may encompass several subordinate trading areas in a metropolitan area context.[26] These trading areas, and their boundaries, are, in the organic tradition of the institutional approach, dynamic and not static.

Types of area structures. Based on the above, the area structure of the marketing system involves many component types. One may, first of all, detect and analyze geographical patterns in the location of extractive industry resources. Secondly, manufacturing establishments may become resource-oriented; market-oriented; intermediately located between resources and markets; or "footloose." Third, wholesale middlemen and facilitating agencies may follow substantially the same patterns as for manufacturing establishments. Retail middlemen may follow patterns of centralization in downtown shopping areas; varying degrees of decentralization in the remaining areas of the city (neighborhood shopping areas and centers, string street locations, and isolated neighborhoods); and an extension of these into the suburbs of the metropolitan areas.

A second type of area structure emphasizes the patterns of geographical flows of goods and services. These may show total physical and value flows of commodities by type of transportation agencies; or they may show aggregates of flows for several commodities. In such flow analyses, variable geographical units may be used (for example, local, regional, national, or international). Refinements may be introduced into these flow analyses, once again, by relating commodity flows to the various channels of distribution utilized, in terms of the spatial configurations.

When the trading area becomes the center and basis of analysis, a number of classifications may be used. The most common is the distinction between *buying and selling areas.* (These coincide with the preceding treatment of markets.) *Buying,* or *supply areas,* are those from which supplies are drawn to a given market, centripetally, in more important quantities than any other competing buying markets. Conversely, selling markets reverse this process to establish *distribution areas.*

---

[26] Note the New York and Chicago metropolitan areas.

Trading areas may be differentiated, also, as *wholesale versus retail.* With the conspicuous exception of the areas serviced by large mail-order warehouses, *wholesale trade areas* for a given commodity or class of commodities are uniformly more extensive, geographically, than for retail trade areas. *Retail trade* areas, with the important exception noted above, tend to be confined to a more narrow range mainly within metropolitan areas, within a section of the city, or within some other restricted range.

Where speed is an important consideration, the boundaries of supply and distribution trading areas may divide on a time-zone pattern. And, in certain situations in which distribution of goods is governed by trade associations, or controlled price systems, the marketing areas resulting may be for specified points of supply. In such cases, area structures become inseparable from price structures as discussed in the section which follows. And a distinction may be made in trading area analyses between *actual* and *potential* boundary situations.

Prices and Price Structures

Definitions and related materials. This structural element, within the institutional approach, deals with the "brain and nervous system" of the overall marketing system and its component institutions, as has been noted. Thus, the price structure is the integrating force through which the exchange of goods and services takes place within a mass marketing system. Thousands upon thousands of individual prices are interrelated to form threads of prices; and these, in turn, are woven together into an intricate fabric of price structures in the wholesaling and retailing sectors, respectively. The importance of each price varies within each strand of thread; and the strands of thread vary, in turn, in thickness within the price fabric. And, while the overall price structure tends to be dynamic, individual prices may show wide variations in their respective responsiveness to change over time. Their determination takes place in the types of wholesale and retail markets discussed earlier under conditions ranging from some form of "workable" competition to those of absolute monopoly, with many intermediate gradations.

Studies of prices and price structures may fall into one of three possible categories: (1) those which consider individual prices and their determination as primarily important, and which either neglect or subordinate the study of any interrelationships with other prices; (2) those which consider individual prices only as a segment of an interrelated structure of prices; and (3) those which deal with the relationships of levels of prices to monetary factors [14, 3-16].

Proponents of the individual price approach, if they arrive at any conclusions at all concerning the existence of a system of prices, do so on the basis of those price patterns which evolve from the uncontrollable actions of prices in a freely competitive market.[27] In the phrase of equilibrium economics, price is thought of as a quantity of money which equilibrates supply with demand rather than as a structure. The institutional approach, however, takes the view that a general price structure does exist, and that the individual prices, rather than determining such a structure, tend to be determined by forces operating within and as part of this overall structural environment.

A general price structure represents the unification of the prices of individual goods and services into an overall price series reflecting interrelationships of demand (analyzed as competing, completing, or complementary over time, among other types of analyses, according to degree); interrelationships of time factors; institutional factors in terms of types and level of operation; spatial relationships within the framework of area structure as discussed earlier; varying degrees of control by management and government; and, finally, the presence of erratic forces. Thus, the concept of a price structure has additional utility in showing the effects of various variables on price as it works to effect the coordination and control of buyers and sellers in the marketing system.

The concept of price structure has in back of it the important assumption of a series of individual price threads from which an entire price fabric is knit, as has been noticed. Accordingly, individual prices, viewed in the perspective of the marketing system, tends to have real meaning only in relation to the overall price structure. Stated another way, if the present economic order in the United States is primarily, but not completely, one of individual exchange cooperation working through a system of markets and prices, then the price structure is a useful concept in explaining the degree to which there are systematic relationships present which are sufficient enough to constitute the overall pattern of prices and price movements herein designated as a structure.

The conflict in thinking between classical and institutional economics in present analyses of price structures justifies further treatment here of the place occupied by institutions in relation to price-making.[28] From an economic viewpoint, institutions reflect steps taken by individuals to organize and operate collective activities, in order better to accomplish the end of want satisfaction and maximization. From both the supply and demand sides, individuals as producers, middlemen, facilitating or other

---

[27] "In any ideal competitive market there tends to be a definite pattern of prices *over time* just as there is over space. But the difficulties of predicting the future make this pattern a less perfect one, so that we have an equilibrium that is constantly being disturbed but is always in the process of reforming itself—not unlike the surface of the ocean" [53, 570].

[28] The contents of the early discussion dealing with institutions should be reviewed at this point, together with the sources cited.

agencies, or as consumers, express their price decisions in an environment of usages, traditions, and formal and informal controls, which are at the heart of institutional organization.

Because of this, the institutions themselves create a peculiar set of structural elements within the confines of the general price level—the overall price structure. Some institutions reinforce and expand the competitive elements in the price structure and the marketing system; other institutions, emphasizing such things as services and brand preferences, prefer to steer away from price competition toward product differentiation and administered prices—so-called nonprice competition. As the variety of institutions expands, in order to adapt to the exercise of freedom of choice by individuals, the complexities of the existing price structures for the products being marketed likewise become more involved. Developments in transportation and communication cause such complexities to expand spatially.[29]

The component elements of price structure. Space limitations will permit only a summary listing here of the principal component elements of price structures.[30] These elements may be classified as follows: (1) competitive factors; (2) management and other administrative controls which lead to various price policies; (3) product and product assortment factors, including the contents of the earlier discussion; (4) inter-product relationships; (5) time factors; and (6) spatial factors.

Types of price structures. One possible classification scheme under this heading would include the following:

1. *Price structures measuring time variability:* daily, weekly, seasonal, cyclical, secular, and erratic movements

2. *Price structures measuring price flexibility:* flexible, semiflexible; and inflexible

3. *Price structures that measure spreads or margins, which reflect differences in costs or value:*
    a. *horizontal price structures*—regional, locational
    b. *vertical price structures*
        (1) spreads between prices of raw materials, semi-processed goods, and related finished goods
        (2) comparisons of wholesale and retail price levels—composite and related categories

---

[29] For a pertinent summary of the relationship between institutions and price structure, and a critical view of the role of institutions, see [35, 137-139].

[30] For a more complete discussion, see (25, 446-457), and the references cited therein.

(3) quality or grade differentials for homogeneous categories

(4) cash *versus* futures prices

4. *Price structures resulting from the use of price as an instrument of managerial control*

    a. individual businesses, by channel level

    b. groups of business, by channel level

5. Combinations of (1), (2), (3), and (4)

A somewhat different classification scheme is based on a series of interrelationships which involve Mitchell's concept of "a system of prices" [42, 108-116]. He has recognized the following sets:

1. Between the prices of consumers' goods in the hands of retailers, wholesalers, and manufacturers (what might be referred to in a marketing context as the "channel view").

2. Between the prices of consumers' goods in (1) and the prices of producers' goods (a) used directly in making consumers' goods, and (b) used indirectly in manufacturing consumers' goods.

3. Between the buying and selling prices in any branch of trade and the prices of the firm's securities engaged in it.

4. Between the prices of services to persons and the larger field of business dealings.

Finally, it may be valuable to note here how he ties together any given price change and its subsequent chain of effects.

1. That changes in the price of one product are passed on in turn to the prices of its substitutes (if any), and then on to the prices of the substitutes of the substitutes, and so forth.

2. That changes in the price of any one of the universally important types of producers' goods in any important use will cause price changes in a wide variety of other uses, and in the prices of goods utilizing these producers' goods.

3. That, ultimately, all prices in a business economy are continually influencing one another.[31]

Conclusions: Some Theoretical Aspects of the Institutional Approach

There is no question but that the institutional approach introduces elements into the study of marketing which makes the realization of a body of theory much more difficult than in the "pure" economic approach. But, in such aspects as area structure, agency structure, and price structure, the institutional approach can and has introduced many aspects of

---

[31] For a historic study analyzing some of these price structure attributes see: [41].

quantitative analyses which represent considerably more than elementary description; and a much more analytical framework than is found in alternative approaches. The wealth of Census data, together with a new perspective of the channel, have done much to strengthen the analyses relating to both agency and area structures. Similarly, various marketing research techniques and studies are constantly enlarging the quantitative attributes of the marketing system.

The following propositions may represent a satisfactory conclusion to the view of the institutional approach presented in this essay.

Proposition # 1. The marketing organization is thought of as the functioning of a system of interrelated structures or organisms; and, its functioning is conditioned by the cultural and political patterns of the geographic unit in which it operates at any given period of time.

Proposition # 2. The marketing system, in the above context, cannot be segmented and considered effectively apart from its relationships to the whole economy. At the same time, it must be viewed as an entity for study representing one aspect of economic specialization.

Proposition # 3. Each institution operating in the overall marketing system must be analyzed in terms of an evolutionary pattern—a life cycle so to speak—which has pertinency only with reference to a particular socio-economic-cultural environment.

Proposition # 4. The indivdual, instead of considered as acting independently in making judgments, is considered instead to be operating as a member of one or more institutions; and, that his actions and decisions are both conditioned and determined within the collective action of the institution.

Proposition # 5. Individuals, as members of these institutions, sacrifice some of their respective areas of freedom of choice, even while continuing to maintain and to exercise a large degree of self-interest, in a search for cooperation and security stemming from collective group action.

Proposition # 6. The tendency towards group action leads to an effort at conscious control by institutions: (a) imposition of group authority on the individual's freedom of action; (b) exercise of control by government agencies at various levels of administration and authority; (c) the controlling forces of tradition and customs operating for various institutions within the pressure of mass markets; (d) ever-growing and widening evidence of monopoly power, and other deviations from competition; and (e) attempts at control at all channel levels.

Proposition # 7. The substitution of institutional collective action for much of individual action leads, inevitably, to conflicts between various institutions acting in various capacities. These conflicts may intensify the need and demand for increased government control; and they create, in turn, rivalry among the economic groups seeking, within their respective institutions, to exercise such authority and control.

Proposition # 8. Finally, if institutions exercise various forms of coercion and control in their collective actions, then ethical problems of responsibility for such actions arise, and need to be evaluated.

REFERENCES

1. Alderson, Wroe, *Marketing Behavior and Executive Action: A Functionalist Approach to Marketing Theory.* Homewood, Ill.: Richard D. Irwin, Inc., 1957.
2. Alexander, Ralph S., "Key Marketing Words—What they Mean," C. J. Dirksen, A. Kroeger, and L. C. Lockley (eds.), *Readings in Marketing.* Homewood, Ill.: Richard D. Irwin, Inc., 1963, pp. 64-65.
3. ————, "Report of the (A.M.A.) Definitions Committee," *The Journal of Marketing.* XIII, October 1948, p. 214.
4. Bain, Joe S., *Barriers to New Competition: Their Character and Consequences in Manufacturing Industries.* Cambridge, Mass.: Harvard University Press, 1956.
5. Barger, Harold, *Distribution's Place in the American Economy Since 1869.* Princeton, N.J.: Princeton University Press, 1955.
6. Barnes, Harry Elmer, *A History of Historical Writing,* 2d rev. ed. Dover paper No. T-104. New York: Dover Publications, Inc., 1963.
7. Beckman, Theodore N., "The Value Added Concept as applied to Marketing and Its Implications." in Seelye (ed.), *Marketing in Transition.* New York: Harper and Bros., 1958, pp. 236-249.
8. Beckman, Theodore N., Engle, Nathanael H., and Buzzell, Robert D., *Wholesaling: Principles and Practice,* 3d ed. New York: The Ronald Press Co., 1959.
9. Blankenship, A. B., "Needed: A Broader Concept of Marketing Research," *The Journal of Marketing.* XIII, January 1949, pp. 305-310.
10. Borden, Neil H., "Notes on Concept of the Marketing Mix," in E. J. Kelley and W. Lazer (eds.), *Managerial Marketing: Perspectives and Viewpoints.* Homewood, Ill.: Richard D. Irwin, Inc., 1958, pp. 272-275.
11. Bowden, Witt, Karpovich, Michael, and Usher, Abbot P., *An Economic History of Europe Since 1750.* New York: American Book Co., 1937.
12. Breyer, Ralph F., *Quantitative Systemic Analysis and Control: Study No. 1—Channel and Channel Group Costing.* Philadelphia: The Author, 1949.

13. Bursk, Edward C., *Text and Cases in Marketing: A Scientific Approach.* Englewood Cliffs, N.J.: Prentice-Hall, Inc., 1962.

14. Bye, Raymond T., *Critiques of Research in the Social Sciences: II—An Appraisal of Frederick C. Mills' "The Behavior of Prices."* Social Science Research Council Bulletin No. 45. New York: The Council, 1940, pp. 3-16.

15. Cannon, Walter B., *The Widsom of the Body,* rev. and enlarged ed. New York: W. W. Norton and Co., 1939. (Reprinted as paperback N-205, 1963.)

16. Cassady, Ralph Jr., and Jones, Wylie L., *The Changing Competitive Structure in the Wholesale Grocery Trade: A Case Study of the Los Angeles Market, 1920-1946.* Berkeley and Los Angeles: *University of California Press,* 1949.

17. ———, *The Journal of Marketing.* XIV, September 1949, pp. 176-177.

18. Clark, John M., *Social Control of Business,* 1st ed. Chicago: The University of Chicago Press, 1926.

19. Clewett, Richard M. (ed.), *Marketing Channels for Manufactured Products.* Homewood, Ill.: Richard D. Irwin, Inc., 1954.

20. Commons, John R., *Institutional Economics: Its Place in Political Economics.* paperback reissue, two vols. Madison, Wis.: The University of Wisconsin Press, 1959, 1961. (First published in 1934 in New York: The Macmillan Co.)

21. Copeland, Morris A., "Economic Theory and the Natural Science Point of View," *The American Economic Review.* XXI, March 1931, pp. 67-79.

22. Cox, Reavis, "The Meaning and Measurement of Productivity in Distribution," *The Journal of Marketing.* XII, April 1948, pp. 433-441.

23. Dorfman, Joseph; *et al., Institutional Economics: Veblen, Commons and Mitchell Reconsidered.* Berkeley and Los Angeles: University of California Press, 1963.

24. Duddy, Edward A,. "The Place of Terminal Markets," in *Marketing: The Yearbook of Agriculture—1954.* Washington, D.C., U.S. Government Printing Office, 1955.

25. Duddy, Edward A., and Revzan, David A., *Marketing: An Institutional Approach,* 2d ed. New York: McGraw Hill Book Co., Inc., 1953.

26. Fetter, Frank A., *The Masquerade of Monopoly.* New York: Harcourt, Brace and Co., Inc., 1931.

27. Giffin, R. R., "Changing Output per Person Employed in Trade, 1900 to 1940, *The Journal of Marketing.* XII, October 1947, pp. 242-245.

28. Gilmore, Harlan W., *Transportation and the Growth of Cities.* Glencoe, Ill.: The Free Press, 1953.

29. Hamilton, Walton H., "Institution," *Encyclopedia of the Social Sciences.* VIII, pp. 84-89.

30. Henry, Jules, "Homeostasis, Society, and Evolution: A Critique," *The Scientific Monthly.* 81, December 1955, pp. 300-309.

31. Hirsch, Werner Z., "Toward a Definition of Integration," *The Southern Economic Journal.* XXV, October 1950, pp. 159-165.

32. Howard, John A., *Marketing Management: Analysis and Decision*. Homewood, Ill.: Richard D. Irwin, Inc., 1957.

33. *The Journal of Marketing*. XIV, September 1949, pp. 145-155,169-177.

34. Kelley, Eugene J., and Lazer, William (eds.), *Managerial Marketing: Perspectives and Viewpoints—A Source Book*. Homewood, Ill.: Richard D. Irwin, Inc., 1958.

35. Knight, Frank H., "The Limitations of Scientific Method in Economics," in *The Ethics of Competition*. New York: Harper & Bros., 1935, pp. 137-139.

36. ———, "Statics and Dynamics: Some Queries Regarding the Mechanical Analogy in Economics," reprinted in *On the History and Method of Economics: Selected Essays*. Chicago: The University of Chicago Press, 1956, pp. 179-201.

37. Lane, Frederic C., and Riemersma, Jelle C. (eds.), *Enterprise and Secular Change: Readings in Economic History*. Homewood, Ill.: Richard D. Irwin, Inc., 1953, Section I, pp. 3-195.

38. Lyon, Leverett S., *Salesmen in Marketing Strategy*. New York: The Macmillan Co., 1926.

39. McCarthy, Jerome, *Basic Marketing: A Managerial Approach*. Homewood, Ill.: Richard D. Irwin, Inc., 1960.

40. McNeill, William H., *The Rise of the West: A History of the Human Community*. Chicago and London: The University of Chicago Press, 1963.

41. Mills, Frederick C., *The Behavior of Prices*. New York: National Bureau of Economic Research, Inc., 1927.

42. Mitchell, Wesley C., *Business Cycles: The Problem and Its Setting*. New York: National Bureau of Economic Research, Inc., 1927.

43. Mund, Vernon A., *Open Markets: An Essential of Free Enterprise*. New York: Harper and Bros., 1948.

44. Park, Robert E., *Human Communities: The City and Human Ecology*. Glencoe, Ill.: The Free Press, 1952.

45. Phelps, D., M., *Sales Management: Policies and Procedures*. Homewood, Ill.: Richard D. Irwin, Inc., 1951.

46. Phelps, D. Maynard, and Westing, J. Howard, *Marketing Management*. Homewood, Ill.: Richard D. Irwin, Inc., 1960.

47. Phillips, Charles F., and Duncan, Delbert J., *Marketing: Principles and Methods*, 4th ed. Homewood, Ill.: Richard D. Irwin, Inc., 1960.

48. Pirenne, Henri, *Medieval Cities*. Princeton, N.J.: Princeton University Press, 1945. (Also reprinted as paperback edition, New York: Doubleday and Co., Inc., 1956.)

49. Polanyi, Karl, *The Great Transformation: The Political and Economic Origins of Our Times*, paper Beacon BP No. 45. Boston: Beacon Press, 1957.

50. Revzan, David A., *A Comprehensive Classified Marketing Bibliography*, Part I, Berkeley: University of California Press, 1951; Part II, *ibid.;* and Supplements No. 1 to these. Berkeley: Institute of Business and Economic Research, 1963.

51. ———, "An Integrated Approach to Marketing Management: Some Introductory Thoughts," delivered to the Research Workshop in Marketing, 1963.

52. ———, *Wholesaling in Marketing Organization.* New York: John Wiley and Sons, Inc., 1961.

53. Samuelson, Paul A., *Economics: An Introductory Analysis,* 1st ed. New York: McGraw-Hill Book Co., Inc., 1948.

54. Social Science Research Council, Advisory Committee on Economic and Social Research in Agriculture, *Research Methods and Procedure in Agricultural Economics,* 2 vols. mimeographed. New York: The Council, August 1928, 1, pp. 3-5.

55. Sombart, Werner, *The Quintessence of Capitalism.* New York: E. P. Dutton, 1915.

56. Stewart, Paul W., and Dewhurst, J. Frederic, *Does Distribution Cost Too Much?* New York: The Twentieth Century Fund, Inc., 1939.

57. Sumner, William G., *Folkways.* New York: Ginn and Co., 1906.

58. Tosdal, Harry R., *Introduction to Sales Management,* 4th ed. New York: McGraw-Hill Book Co., Inc., 1957.

59. ———, *Problems in Sales Management,* 4th ed. New York: McGraw-Hill Book Co., Inc., 1939.

60. Williamson, Harold F. (ed.), *The Growth of the American Economy,* 2d ed. New York: Prentice-Hall, Inc., 1951.

III

CONSUMER THEORY

10

Toward a Model of Consumer
Decision Making

FRANCESCO M. NICOSIA

*A thorough review of the theories and empirical findings on consumer be-
havior in the fields of marketing, economics, and the behavioral sciences leads
the author to conclude that each field contributes its part to our understanding
and, when taken together, these parts seem to emerge into a conceptualization
of consumer behavior as a decision process. A major aim of this study is the
explicit construction of an integrated and comprehensive decision process of
consumer behavior. The decision process is described over a behavior space
defined by five variables and by four functional relations among these variables. The variables are: the act of buying; the consumer's motivation and
attitude; the advertisement; and time.*

In the course of my marketing practice, I frequently investigated empirical questions about several aspects of consumer behavior. The answers
were often useful—at least in furthering my professional career. But the
more aspects I studied, the more I became aware of the limitations of my
answers and of my understanding of consumer behavior in its complex
entirety.

Therefore, for my dissertation, I chose to consider a question of a
different nature—one which is perhaps ultimately at the basis of all research on consumer behavior. In a few words, I asked myself: why do
consumers behave the way they do?

This question, of course, has been studied for several decades from
the points of view of different disciplines, for different purposes, and with
the help of different research methods. I believe we are all aware, however,

Reprinted with permission from *Emerging Concepts in Marketing,* William S.
Decker, ed. (Chicago: American Marketing Association, 1963), pp. 422-437.

that the conclusions obtained so far are unrelated and throw light on only fragmentary aspects of consumer behavior. Further, the problem itself seems to become more blurred as the amount of published and unpublished data increases. The current proliferation of work—highly detailed, circumscribed in conception and often atheoretical—may soon cause us to lose sight of our main concern. If future research is to be charted intelligently and economically, we must begin to assess our present knowledge.

The first objective of my dissertation, therefore, was to take stock of our understanding of consumer behavior. Toward this end I reviewed some extant theories and empirical findings on consumer behavior in the fields of marketing, economics and the behavioral sciences.[1]

This review led to several conclusions. One of them was that each field contributes its part to our understanding and, when taken together, these parts seem to emerge into a conceptualization of consumer behavior as a decision process. The explicit construction of an integrated and comprehensive decision process thus became the second aim of my dissertation.

I propose to make these two objectives—a review of the literature, and the construction and analysis of an overall model of consumer decision making—the grounds for the organization of my presentation. For clarity of exposition, however, let me make a few prefatory remarks on the notion of decision process.

On the Meaning of "Decision Process"

As is known, social phenomena can be studied from two points of view according to a prevalent distinction in the social sciences: aggregate or macro-analysis, or individual or micro-analysis. I have used the second approach: my study is an attempt to conceptualize the decision process of an *individual* consumer. This does not imply, however, that the influences of social processes are overlooked.

Several notions of the term "decision process' prevail in the social sciences, ranging from formally precise definitions to those which construe the term as a primitive one. To give the term an approximate location, I may anticipate two major findings of my review. First, much of the literature conceptualizes the consumer's act of choice as the result of a decision. Then, the decision in itself is seen either as a simple association between a stimulus and a response, or at the other extreme, as a very complex process of interaction among many behavior determinants.

---

[1] The empirical findings I reviewed were made available to me by the library of the Consumer Behavior Program, sponsored jointly by the School of Business Administration and the Survey Research Center of the University of California at Berkeley.

To be comprehensive, let us agree that by decision process we mean a description of the phenomenon of consumer behavior in terms of the following:

a. A list of the variables (e.g., physiological, psychological and social) which make up the content or morphology of the phenomenon; and

b. A *mechanism* (or flow chart, or network of interactions) through which the variables listed in (a) come in contact with and affect each other over a period of time.

It should be clear that I visualize a decision process as a structure, for instance, a system of equations. Later we shall see some of the consequences that derive from this view which may be of relevance to marketers. By way of analogy one may say that the "list of variables" and the "mechanism of their interaction" represent respectively the anatomy and the physiology of the decision making process underlying the phenomenon of consumer behavior.

A Review of the Literature on Consumer Decision Making

It is obviously impossible to present today a fair summary of my assessment of our present knowledge of consumer behavior in the fields of marketing, economics and the behavioral sciences.[2] Here I shall only touch upon some points. In each field we shall investigate (a) what variables or classes of variables have been suggested as morphological components of consumer decision processes; and (b) what fuctional relations, if any, have been visualized as the working mechanism(s) of such processes.

Marketing Literature

Marketing encompasses many fields of specialization. In these fields there are often views of consumer decision making which are decisively based on notions of an economic or behavioral nature. We shall consider them later in the two subsections on economics and the behavioral sciences. For the moment we shall restrict ourselves to marketing treatises.

Marketing interest in consumer behavior has been keen since the early works by Shaw, Cherington, Clark, Copeland and, of course, Starch and Nystrom. Yet the notion of consumer decision making entertained by marketing scholars is elusive. By and large, a decision seems to be conceived as a set of a great many ill-defined activities—both mental and

---

[2] This assessment will be presented in my forthcoming manuscript to be published by Prentice-Hall (H. Simon series). [EDITORS' NOTE: The book referred to is Francesco M. Nicosia, *Consumer Decision Processes,* 1966.]

physical—which in some way interact and lead to the act of buying a certain product and brand.

The treatment of the subject differs a great deal from author to author. There are, however, a few common points underlying marketing thinking which suggest a wide acceptance of the following classes of variables as components of consumer decision processes.

1. Variables external to the consumer. These include social, economic, geographic and like variables. The emphasis placed on the importance of each of these variables changes according to each author. In the main, the basis for the assignment of the importance is not clear; it also is not clear whether and how this assignment varies according to types of consumers and classes of products and brands. Probably, this lack of clarity derives from the fact that the mechanism(s) through which environmental variables come to impinge upon a consumer decision are not considered explicitly.

2. Variables internal to the consumer. These include variables of the so-called physical and psychological nature. The list of these variables is practically endless. There seems to be agreement only on grouping the psychological variables into two classes:

2.1. *Rational orientations.* The consumer is always thought of as rational—either very, somewhat, or little. But the literature never goes on to say which specific variables are elements of this class. At best, one may conclude that the class includes only one variable: rationality; at worst, this class is empty because, as long as we do not know the dimensions of rationality, one may say that whatever the consumer does, he does it rationally.

2.2. *Orientations other than rational.* Contrary to the case of rational orientations, this class is crowded: impulses, drives, motives, habits and so on almost *ad infinitum,* all are elements of this class. Meaning and use of these terms also vary a great deal from author to author. The only generalization we can make is that many authors experience a diffuse aura of irrationality in these terms.

With respect to the functional relations among the variables just listed, it is safe to state that they are never objects of consideration—explicitly or implicitly. In fact, we should expect this; if the components of a decision process are not spelled out precisely, one cannot design the mechanism (or flow chart) which describes the network of interaction among these components.[3]

---

[3] I shall not report on a few speculative flow charts of consumer decision processes I obtained by analyzing some of the attributes most frequently used in the literature to describe consumer behavior, and by identifying the dimensions underlying these attributes.

The elusiveness of the marketing notions of consumer decision making probably originates from the recognition that the phenomenon consists of a large number of physical and mental activities interacting among themselves and with environmental stimuli over time. But an integrated description of the phenomenon cannot be formulated as long as the study of these activities is fragmented and the investigation of their mechanism(s) of interaction is not undertaken.

This elusiveness can be also attributed to the fact that these notions seem to emerge from a compromise between the differing points of view offered by economics and the behavioral sciences. Thus, the consumer is seen to be rational, and he decides by skillfully applying the techniques of marginal analysis.[4] Then, the consumer is *also* said to be irrational, behaving according to a colorful list of motives such as romantic needs, aesthetic needs, *et alia.*[5]

Finally, this elusiveness may also derive from marketing attempts to be "scientific." Here the theory of consumer decision making consists of any set of correlations which happen to pass a test of statistical significance and a conglomeration of *ad hoc* hypotheses formulated for the purpose of explaining such correlations.[6]

To sum up, marketing is confronted with a wide heterogeneity of consumer acts of choice and factors which seemingly affect them. In its quest for explanation, marketing relies upon notions borrowed from economics and the behavioral sciences in different degrees. It is clear, however, that to grasp the complexities of consumer decision and processes and to construct useful models of them, marketing must carefully assess the nature and limitations of these notions. With this aim in mind, I turned my work toward an analysis of economics and the behavioral sciences.

Economic Literature

Economists have collected and interpreted an impressive amount of data on consumers. Also, many suggestions for policy have been offered, and many decisions have been made by public and private institutions on the basis of these economic studies. Let us here focus on only one field of economics—demand or choice theory. Since different versions of

---

[4] In this respect, for example, the borrowing from economics is inappropriate because the normative nature of the economic image of man is usually not distinguished from the computational meaning of marginal analysis.

[5] The borrowing from the behavioral sciences is frequently unsystematic. And it becomes superficial, if not erroneous, when we see that, explicitly or implicitly, psychological variables are ultimately equated with the class of "irrational" variables mentioned above.

[6] Incidentally, we may note that as long as the consumer is visualized as behaving according to significant statistical associations, *de facto* the "king" is not the consumer but a "level of significance" somehow chosen by the researcher.

demand theory exist, I shall restrict my remarks to what may be called the neo-classical version of demand theory under conditions of certainty.[7]

Economic theory of demand suggests that one possible way of describing a decision process is to postulate the following major morphological components.

1. Variables concerning the consumer. These include his preferences, his endowment or purchasing power, and his desire to maximize (or satisfy) his preferences.

2. Variables concerning the environment. They include goods and services in scarce quantities, and their transformation rates (i.e., prices).

As to the mechanism of the decision process, its components seem to interact in the following general way. *Given* a certain number of goods available at certain *given* prices, and *given* the consumer's preferences and his endowment, his desire (also given) to satisfy his preferences will (must) lead him to buy certain combinations and amounts of the available goods.

The clarity with which this economic model is postulated should help the researcher who wants to adopt it as a basis for his investigation. He is made aware of the model's possibilities and thus may decide when to use it; he will be able to interpret empirical data gathered on the basis of the theory expressed by the model and on the qualifications that stem from it.

This economic conception does not particularly help us to understand the content and the dynamics of consumer decision processes.[8] Consider, for example, the fact that the goods and services from which he chooses are given. This means that the model does not describe how a consumer determines what goods are available. His decision is a choice among givens, and searching is thus eliminated.

As for consumer preferences, an analysis of the postulates concerning them shows that, as a group, these postulates lead to an elegant bypassing of all the problems connected with the consumer's social psychological field. In a word, the model considers neither the content nor the dynamics of the preference field; they are simply assumed away. It is

---

[7] During the last twenty years the notions of man, behavior and decision process portrayed in neo-classical theory have been revised in many ways. With reference to our concern, the comments made in the text also apply to the types of economic man generated by these revisions.

[8] The point of whether economics does offer a theory of choice has been argued for some time. Recently, it has been suggested that economics as well as game theory, statistical decision theory and the like do not offer theories of choice but rather techniques which show the chooser, before he chooses, some consequences of the facts and premises from which he starts. See C. K. Ramond, "Theories of Choice in Business," paper presented to a meeting of the American Psychological Association, September 5, 1962, St. Louis, Missouri.

thus clear that, for instance, the model cannot describe how the act of consumption is translated into satisfaction, that is, how preferences change (learning) as the result of experiences with products and brands. Further, by assuming away the nature of preferences and the paths of their evolution, the model does not suggest descriptions of, for example, how a stimulus (prices, advertisements, etc.) is internalized and operated upon by the preference field.

From an empirical point of view, therefore, the model leads the researcher to gather data concerning only environmental variables and to overlook the psychological make-up of the consumer. This closely resembles the so-called behavioristic (Stimulus-Response) view of man. Indeed, most economic research on the consumer is in practice a study of the empirical associations between variables external to the consumer (e.g., prices, incomes, saving, assets, inventories, advertising expenditures) and the consumer's final overt behavior, that is, his act of buying or not buying.

At this point of my work, it became clear that my original question "why do consumers behave the way they do?" could be qualified in the following manner. Would our understanding of consumer decision making be improved if we were more explicit about the properties of the consumer and his environment, and about the types of interactions among these properties over time? I therefore turned my attention to the behavioral sciences with this question in mind.

Literature in the Behavioral Sciences

Given the purpose of formulating comprehensive models of consumer decision making, the major and most pervasive difficulty I encountered in my review was the lack of an integrated view of human behavior despite the vast amount of literature (*vis à vis* the relative scarcity of literature on consumer behavior, particularly of published results). The large number of classifications and sub-classifications of the behavioral sciences results in fragmentation of research and a high degree of institutionalization of such fragmentation.

However, some views of human behavior—most of them to be found under the name of theory of action—offer valuable suggestions.[9] Although they differ with respect to their emphasis on the morphology or on the mechanisms of behavior, these views and the empirical work informed by them do attempt to portray the *entirety* of the process underlying an act of overt behavior.

Let me summarize what I learned in my review. Without exception the components of consumer decision processes are divided into two

---

[9] These views emerge from the various writings by Lazarsfeld, Katona, Parsons, Simon and the psychologists of the so-called Wurzburg School.

major groups: the variables referring to and thus describing the actor, and those referring to and thus describing the actor's environment. The main classes of actor-variables that emerge from theoretical and empirical work are as follows.

A.1. Physiological variables. Their role in a decision process is largely two-fold: (a) they may be seen as broad and generalized motivational forces (e.g., thirst); and (b) they may also participate as constraints (e.g., motor abilities). As you know, these variables received a great deal of attention in the early studies of consumer behavior. However, a large number of studies suggests that they could be useful in a model of consumer decision making only if and when they appear decisively to determine the actor's physical perception of environmental stimuli and to affect the final overt choice of means that will satisfy his need.

A.2. Disposition, attitude and motive variables. Their presence in consumer decision processes has been identified empirically in the following phases: (a) determination of the perception of object-stimuli (e.g., product attributes); (b) determination of the perception of other environmental stimuli (e.g., advertisements); (c) participation in the formation of generalized needs; and (d) participation in the transformation of generalized needs into specific object-needs.

A.3. Cognitive variables. These variables describe the organization of the actor's social psychological field. That is, they establish the functional relations among the field's component variables, where such relations provide the ultimate means for the actor to adapt his psychological reality to his environmental reality.

As for the environmental variables, the following groups emerge as the most salient components of consumer decision processes.

B.1. Interpersonal relations. The role of these variables in small group research has been ascertained for a large number of human decisions. Unfortunately, they have received little attention in consumer research, despite their proven promise of aiding our understanding of consumer decisions in some classical studies by Lewin, Katona and Mueller, Katz and Lazarsfeld, and Menzel, Coleman and Katz.

B.2. Channels of information and influence. Much data on mass media channels are published regularly (e.g., circulation, readership, recall). These data, however, offer very few suggestions, if any, for our purposes of conceptualizing the morphology and the dynamics of consumer decision processes. The studies on the two- or multi-step flow of information and influence are probably the only ones which have thrown some new light on the technical and social processes through which a marketer may reach his audience.

B.3. Product attributes. The nature and role of these variables have been conceptualized in different ways. For instance, one reads of "objective" and "subjectively perceived" product attributes, and of "socially" and "personally" perceived attributes. From our point of view, it should be clear that, ultimately, what counts is the presence or absence of these perceptions (variables) in the decision process. In other words, what describes the actor's cathectic-cognitive orientations toward the world and thus toward a particular product and brand is only the presence or absence of certain variables in his decision process.

To conclude this review of the process' morphological components, we may note that almost all the studies I have examined consider the act of buying as the *final act,* that is, as the dependent variable. It is clear, however, that consumer behavior does not stop here; it is followed by a series of activities which may lead to the act of consumption. With the noticeable exceptions of the theoretical notions of Lewin's "gate keeper" and of Alderson's "purchasing agent," this transition from buying to consumption has received very little attention. The act of consumption then is followed by some reactions which may or may not change (learning) the orientation of the subject toward a particular product and brand. Here, too, I have found neither theoretical nor empirical research of relevance.

These considerations on the "final" act lead us to a group of remarks concerning the dynamic aspect of consumer decision making. Like marketers and economists, although to a lesser extent, behavioral scientists have generally overlooked the study of the functional relations among the components of the decision processes. At best, their interactions are visualized as a sequence of relations through time, but they are not stated precisely enough to be included directly in any model without reservations. All the mechanisms of consumer decision making I have built so far essentially rely on my own interpretations of the literature reviewed. I should mention that in building models, these interpretations must be specified operationally and thus they become hypotheses waiting for empirical test.

A Model of Consumer Decision Making

My review of the literature led to the following conclusions: (a) the views of consumer decision processes in marketing, economics and the behavioral sciences usually explain only parts of the phenomenon; (b) research informed by these views has yielded a wealth of findings about the many components of these processes; (c) but this wealth, in turn, has created the need, still unfulfilled, for describing the dynamic relations among the processes' components—that is, ultimately, a need for reconstructing a total picture of our phenomenon.[10]

A reconstruction of the whole decision process thus became the second phase of my dissertation. By using the theoretical and empirical evidence available to me, I developed a very articulated flow chart describing the morphology and the dynamic mechanism of a consumer decision process.

The general logic of the flow chart can perhaps be best summarized by the following figure. As can be seen, consumer behavior is described by two major circular flows: a "loop" from the firm to the consumer and back to the firm; and a "loop" from the consumer's social psychological field before the firm's message, to his reactions, and back to his social psychological field.

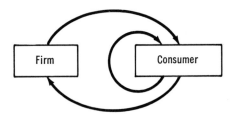

In its final version, the flow chart is a large set of variables interacting in many *circular system-like flows*. Obviously, this flow chart is not a capstone; rather it is a step which attempts to distill the many bits of evidence, to bring into a systematic picture, and to indicate fruitful paths of research in order to gain a fuller understanding of the morphology and dynamics of consumer behavior.

The comprehensiveness of the flow chart is such that it can be used as a basic frame of reference for the study of particular as well as overall properties of consumer decision making. That is, one may behave "experimentally" with it. Today, I propose to study "experimentally" some of the overall properties of consumer decision processes and a few of their implications for research designs and marketing decisions.

If we divide the entire flow chart into four major fields, and summarize the various mechanisms in each field, the overall decision process can be described in the following manner.

---

[10] There are, of course, other gaps in the research concerned with identifying and assessing the components of these processes. For example, what are the differences, if any, between variables such as the "opinion leaders" (Lazarsfeld) and the "taste maker" (Opinion Research Corporation)? Or, what variables are present in the decision by what types of consumers for what types of products and brands?

1. The field concerned with the consumer's act of buying. Specifically, let us summarize this field by postulating that the time rate of change of the buying B of a certain brand at time t is some function b of the consumer's motivation M toward that brand and the level B of buying it at time t.

2. The field concerned with the formation of the consumer's motivation to buy a certain brand. As a summary of this field, let us state that his motivation M toward a certain brand at time t is some function m of his attitude A toward that brand at time t.

3. The field concerned with the formation of the consumer's attitude. Let us assume that the time rate of change of his attitude A toward a certain brand at time t is some function a of his buying B of that brand, of his attitude A toward that brand, and of the advertisement C of that brand, all at time t.

4. The field concerned with the advertising policy of a business firm. Given our experimental purpose, let us assume that the nature of the advertisement C at time t is not determined by any of the above variables, but rather is exogenously chosen by the firm.

You will notice that the above decision process is described over a behavior space defined by five coordinates or variables and by four functional relations among those variables. The variables are: the act of buying B; the consumer's motivation M and attitude A; the advertisement C; and time t. The functional relations are those expressed in the four points above.[11] We can thus describe the decision process in the (B, M, A, C)-space at time t with the following four equations:

$$1. \quad \frac{dB(t)}{dt} = b[M(t), B(t)]$$

$$2. \quad M(t) = m[A(t)]$$

$$3. \quad \frac{dA(t)}{dt} = a[B(t), A(t); C(t)]$$

$$4. \quad C(t) = \overline{C}$$

Observe that the model formalizes the usual sequence: from an independent variable (C), through intervening variables (M, A), to the dependent variable (B). In other words, it expresses our "experimental" interest in understanding the impact of an advertisement on buying be-

---

[11] The five variables, in other words, are the morphological components, and the four functional relations the dynamic mechanism of the process. The variables B and C could be measured in dollars; and M and A could be measured, for example, on the basis of the dimensions (a) scope, general or specific, (b) time perspective, present or future referents, and (c) dynamics, passive or driving. Several problems connected with measurement criteria are discussed in my forthcoming publication by Prentice-Hall, mentioned earlier.

havior. Of course, we may easily rewrite the model for the purpose of studying, for instance, the impact of buying behavior on the advertising policy of a firm.

Once the forms of the functions (b, m, a) are empirically determined, we could ask several questions. For example, the value of B (total sales volume) for a given value of C (advertising expenditures) is obtained by solving the above system of equations for B as a function of C. The value of B is given by the integral equation

$$B = J(t, k_1, k_2)$$

where the constants of integration depend on the respective intervals of integration, and the function J depends on the original functions (b, m, a).

With respect to research designs aiming at the collection of empirical observations, note that both the values of B and A depend on the respective intervals of integration; that is, the size(s) of the time intervals at which the observations are taken. It follows that we must have repeated observations of the variables' values at time intervals whose size varies a great deal—this is particularly important if the phenomenon exhibits oscillatory properties even in the case of uniform applications of the stimulus C over time. In the research reports of the longitudinal type (panel) I have examined, the researcher has overlooked the fact that the observed values of B and A do depend on his own choice of the size of the time interval. This is an area where experimental and empirical research is needed very badly.

Now, suppose that the decision process has the property of oscillating over time (and I suspect that this is a most frequent case for a large part of consumer goods and services). It follows that the firm's decisions concerned with the applications of the stimulus (e.g., intensity and timing of its advertising) should be planned accordingly. In my opinion, a great deal of research and marketing decisions do not even raise this question.

To illustrate another implication of the model for marketing and advertising decisions, let us investigate the conditions under which the consumer will continue to buy a certain value B when a certain amount of advertising C is applied uniformly through time. If we look at the above system of equations and state the conditions of stability which must be satisfied, we find that it must be:

$$1.1. \ b \ (A, B) = 0$$
$$3.1. \ a \ (B, A; \overline{C}) = 0$$

The behavioral meaning of these stability conditions is that, for a given amount of advertising expenditures $\overline{C}$, a consumer will not change his buying behavior over time if there exist at least a pair of values $A = \overline{A}$ and $B = \overline{B}$ satisfying such conditions. That is, the underlying attitude toward a brand and the amount bought must be mutually consistent. Here we may say, for instance, that if some automakers had systematic observations of the values of A, they might have been able to predict earlier the sudden decrease of the demand for medium price cars in the second half of the fifties.

The above stability conditions can answer other problems as well. For example, given the values of B and C at a certain time, one may determine the value C′ necessary to increase sales to a level B′ > B.

The analysis of the above system of non-linear equations could be profitably continued. If we assume that the functions (b, m, a) are linear in their respective variables, we restrict the model's range of generality, but may undertake some analyses of greater depths.

Among the findings of these analyses, I shall mention a few of those which can be presented without having to consider too many technical prerequisites. Let us write the following *simplified* and *linear* version of the above system of equations:

$$\text{I.} \quad \frac{dB(t)}{dt} = b \cdot [A(t) - \beta \cdot B(t)]$$

$$\text{II.} \quad \frac{dA(t)}{dt} = g \cdot [B(t) - \gamma \cdot A(t)] + cC_o$$

The decision process is now described by three variables (B, A, $C \geqslant 0$) and by the "personality" coefficients (b, β, g, γ, c) characteristic of our consumer (or type of consumer).

The meaning of the personality coefficient is the following. The coefficients b and g determine how rapidly the consumer will resolve the differences (or if you wish, conflicts) in equations (I.) and (II.). The coefficient $1/\beta$ may be called the "attitude" coefficient in that it measures the impact of an attitude toward a brand on the amount bought. The coefficient $1/\gamma$ may be called the "behavioral" coefficient in that it measures the impact of the amount bought of a brand on the attitude toward it. Finally, the coefficient c determines the impact of the advertisement C on the attitude A. The values and signs of these coefficients have different behavioral implications, and they are too numerous to be considered here. Let us assume that

$$C \gtrless 0; \text{ and b, g, } \beta, \gamma > 0$$

Once we have determined the amount B_o bought of the advertised brand when the level of advertising expenditures is C_o, we may ask under what conditions the decision process will repeat itself and lead our consumer to buy the same amount B_0. By examining the stability conditions on our solution B_0, we find that

$$\text{I.1. } b\beta + g\gamma > 0 \text{ and}$$
$$\text{II.1. } gb(\beta\gamma - 1) > 0$$

Remembering our stipulations on the signs of the personality coefficients, condition (II.1.) can be written as

$$\text{II.2. } \beta\gamma > 1$$

The importance of these relations consists above all in the fact that they state properties of consumer decision processes not previously evident in the literature. They are new hypotheses and could be contradicted by empirical observations. Further, they also indicate some of the directions that research must take to improve our understanding of consumer behavior. For instance, one could determine for what kind of consumers and for what kind of products and brands these relations are or are not satisfied.

We could now discuss whether and how the decision process reaches the equilibrium point B_0 (i.e., the consumer will continue to buy that amount) by analyzing the characteristics of the system's path, for example, oscillatory, underdamped, critically damped, and overdamped cases. The analysis leads to new hypotheses and, again, points out crucial considerations for the improvement of research designs. Since the performance of this analysis involves rather routine operations, I shall conclude with another example which illustrates the "experimental" flexibility of precise models of consumer decision making.

Consider the personality coefficient c. This coefficient could be written as the difference between the impacts of two advertisements, that is, $c = c_x - c_y$, where c_x indicates the impact of the advertisement C_x for brand X and c_y indicates the impact of the advertisement C_y for brand Y which competes with brand X.[12] Now, it is reasonable to assume that in this case at least one of the other personality coefficients is different for the two brands. Assume that the "behavioral" coefficient γ is different. By reanalyzing the relation determining the value of B_0, we find that it must be

$$\frac{c_x}{c_y} = \frac{\gamma_x}{\gamma_y}$$

---

[12] Note that instead of competing brands we could consider two or more different media, e.g., two mass media, or a mass medium and personal selling, etc.

This implies that the equilibrium buying of brand X may depend: (i) on the mechanisms (summarized in this model by c_x and c_y) operating upon and internalizing the stimuli C_x and C_y; and (ii) on the other personal attributes of the consumer—in our example, the "behavioral" coefficient.

Conclusions

Let me try to conclude. The plethora of empirical data on consumer behavior continues to increase. However, as has been also observed in another recent review, there has been a hiatus in consumer research for some time.[13]

Taking stock, introspection and conceptualization are certainly prerequisites for charting more useful empirical work and, in this respect, the building of formal models is highly relevant.

These models are the core of precise theories about the morphology and the dynamics of consumer behavior and can thus direct research toward meaningful observations and analyses and, eventually, greatly enrich our understanding of the problems encountered by public and private institutions in the field of marketing.

---

[13] L. Guest, "Consumer Analysis," *Annual Review of Psychology,* Vol. 13, (1962).

11

Summary of the Theory
of Buyer Behavior

JOHN A. HOWARD
JAGDISH N. SHETH

1. Introduction

1.1 Need for Theory

Marketing management can be viewed as the art of converting truth about human behavior—qua buying—into a profitable marketing policy. This view puts the significance of buyer behavior into useful perspective, and in line with this perspective a brief summary of the theory of buying behavior is presented here.[1] The model is complex in the sense that it incorporates both consumer and industrial buying and such diverse marketing influences as product innovation, merchandising, advertising and sales effects, price of the brand, and availability of the brand.

The particular aspect of buying behavior to which the model addresses itself is brand or supplier choice. The central mechanisms contained here, however, apply just as well to the choice among generic products, but some of the details might be less appropriate. In product choice, perceptual complications might, for example, make less of a difference than with brand choice.

The executive's need for theory in buyer behavior has become increasingly crucial in recent years as (1) technological change has speeded up product change which raises far greater marketing uncertainties than

---

Not previously published; prepared especially for this volume by Professors Howard and Sheth.

[1] The complete statement of the theory appears in John A. Howard and Jagdish N. Sheth, *The Theory of Buyer Behavior,* which is just now being readied for publication.

do established products, (2) the increasing development and widened use of market research techniques have increased the flow of market facts, (3) the computer has increased a thousand-fold the power to store, retrieve, and analyze market facts providing someone has the requisite theory to guide the formulation of the required computer programs, and (4) the company organizational structure has grown in complexity so that the various information collectors and decision makers in a company must have a common way of looking at marketing problems if the company is to behave in a coordinated, goal-directed manner. A model is necessary to provide the simplification that an executive must have to grasp the *essential* elements of his many-sided problems in a *hurry* and to *communicate* his ideas to subordinates, peers, and superiors.

The need for theory to guide basic research is obvious. The model as set forth here, for example, is providing the intellectual foundations for a large, three-year program of research in buyer behavior at Columbia University as a joint project between the Bureau of Applied Social Research and the Graduate School of Business. It is also guiding other research.

1.2 Summary of Content

Here we set forth a systematic set of ideas—a theory of buying behavior which applies to most people buying most products.

First, it explains the process by which a buyer may develop habitual preferences for brands. In other words, how does a buyer achieve a brand preference equilibrium? Relative to the economic theory of choice, the equilibrium analysis provides an explanation for attaining equilibrium or stable preference. This is generally not explained in economic analysis and is part of the *ceteris paribus* assumption. The process of achieving equilibrium in brand preference is considered a learning phenomenon over time. Because of the time element, it is a dynamic process. We will call it "purchase preference dynamism."

Second, it explains the process by which the buyer, in effect, changes his environment by considering brands which, though they were actually available before, he did not consider as possible alternatives. This, too, is a second dynamic element in the sense that by bringing a new brand into his purview he may destroy the equilibrium—his asymptotic position on the learning curve—and must now learn a new equilibrium position. In a sense this results in changing the buyer's subjective environment; hence, we will call it "environmental dynamism."

Two general topics will be discussed: the elements that constitute a buyer's given psychological state, and the processes which can change that psychological state and thereby lead to change in his purchasing behavior.

2. Central Elements of Buyer's Psychological State

Let us begin by describing the buyer's psychological state as a first step toward comprehending the total number of elements making up this complex model.

There are five central elements or variables that constitute the buyer's psychological state. These are shown in Figure 1. The only directly observable variable is the act of purchase.

Figure 1. Feedback From Brand Usage

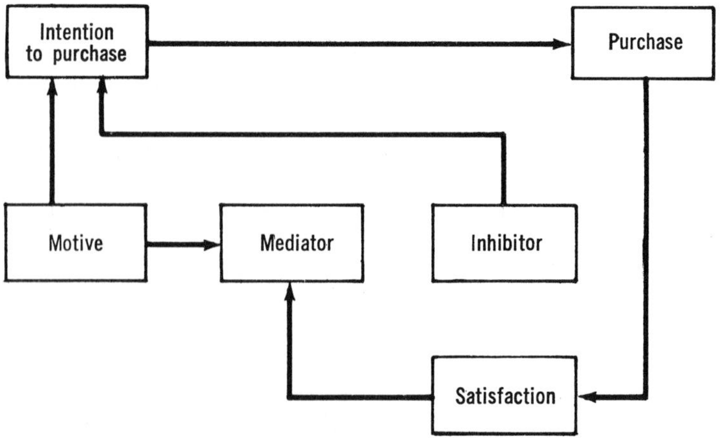

There are three causal variables: Motive, Attitude, and Inhibitor.[2] Finally, there is Intention to Purchase which is the link between the causal variables and Purchase. Empirically there is often a delay in purchasing so that Intention measured at one point in time is a poor predictor of Purchase because the overt behavior may occur later and in the meantime events in the buyer's environment change the values of the causal variables. Hence, some variable which summarizes all of the psychological effects and yet is short of actual purchase is very useful in identifying the influence of marketing variables.

---

[2] To simplify this general exposition we use "Attitude" in lieu of the more fundamental variable "Mediator" of which attitude is only a surrogate variable. In terms of analysis the use of "attitude" constitutes a serious oversimplification; for example, in many buying situations the analyst focuses on a long sequence of behavior, or the housewife talks to a friend today, sees an ad next week, and only needs a unit of the product two weeks hence. The concept of attitude does not lend itself to the examination of this sequence. It does greatly facilitate exposition, however, because "attitude" has far greater popular currency than "mediator."

Motive(s) summarizes the needs of the buyer that can be served by the purchase of a brand from this product class. First, motivation is the energizing element in behavior (it has no directional effect) which when described in simplest terms means that motivation does not influence which brand will be chosen. Instead, it merely causes some brand of the product class to be bought. We assume here that the buyer has a set of needs—which are uniquely satisfied by a given product class and that brands of this product class serve no other needs. This assumption is necessary to avoid the confusion that appears in consumer panel data where it is found that different brands of the same product class are bought to serve different needs. These data have often been mistakenly interpreted as indicating an absence of brand loyalty. Second, multiple goals complicate motivation analysis further because one goal may conflict with another. Third, when all the complexities of motivation are incorporated, however, we find that it can exert a directional as well as an energizing effect. Fourth, purchase-influencing motives seem to be learned instead of innate, and knowledge of the learned motives is not nearly as well developed. Finally, to be operational we must think of a structure of motivation where an *end*—a goal—becomes a *means* to a higher level goal in the motivation structure. Most market research attempts to measure motives are aimed at the lower, more specific and concrete level of this structure.

Attitude represents the buyer's evaluation of the attributes of the brand in satisfying his needs. There is a separate attitude for each brand; and as implied by "attribute*s*," attitude is multidimensional. It can be visualized as a point in n-dimensional market space in which the attributes of the brand constitute the dimensions. Other things being equal, the distances between these points in space represent degrees of substitution that the buyer will make among the brands. To speak of brands as having positions in n-dimensional space is, of course, merely another way of describing more precisely the concept of product differentiation introduced into economic theory in the 1930's by Chamberlin and Robinson; and it is also an essential element of the concept of market structure that has served so usefully in the study of industrial organization pioneered by Edward S. Mason.

Carlson and Rosenberg have shown that an attitude includes both a motivational as well as a directional element, and for this reason there is an arrow in Figure 1 connecting Motives and Attitude, indicating that motivational effects can be indirect through Attitude as well as direct to Intention. It may seem a little strange to some readers that the concept of attitude should be set in this behavioristic framework.[3] There is evidence

---

[3] The implicit assumption is that attitude is a partial cause of behavior. Although widely accepted for a long time, this relation is not obviously true. A number of years ago, the lack of evidence was pointed out in Howard, *Marketing:*

from the laboratory, however, that attitudes can be modified by the conditioning techniques that learning theorists have used for years to change behavior. Hence, we are justified in treating the concept of attitude in these behavioristic terms.[4]

3. Changing Psychological State

3.1 Introduction

The buyer in making his brand choice is often confronted with elements in the situation which inhibit the choice of some brands or suppliers more than others. The two most common and conspicous practical examples of Inhibitor (I) are brand price and brand availability. These, however, are merely special cases of two of the three very general psychological influences. The first is *discrimination*. To the extent the housewife is able to discriminate among the brands, such as when large price differences exist among them, Inhibition is low and her attitude will be a good predictor of her behavior. This is a stimulus-oriented influence which can be contrasted with the response-oriented nature of the other two influences: *energy expenditure* and *interference*. To the extent that the purchase of a brand requires energy expenditure, such as in shopping for it, attitude will be a poor predictor of behavior. To the extent that the purchase of a brand interferes with her ongoing shopping behavior, for example, inhibition will be high, which is to say that there will be a greater discrepancy between the attitude toward that brand and the purchase of that brand.

Finally, we believe there are temporary nonrandom shifts in Intention when Attitude and Inhibitor are constant. These shifts are due to changes in motives, and hence, there is an arrow directly from Motive(s) to Intention.

3.2 Feedback from Brand Usage

Satisfaction from experience with the brand is probably by all odds the most important single determinant of the buyer brand preference (Atti-

---

Executive and Buyer Behavior (New York, Columbia University Press, 1963), pp. 139-147. The development of dissonance theory has provided evidence that changes in behavior can cause a change in attitude. This more complex two-way relationship does complicate matters. However, the work in dissonance theory has dealt with relatively unimportant issues, and hence the conclusions may or may not hold in marketing. Even if they do, the concept of attitude still can be highly useful to marketing practice as long as attitude can be used as an indicator of behavior.

[4] In fact, the same phenomenon that partial reinforcement is more effective than continuous reinforcement has been found to operate with attitudes as it does with behavior.

tude). The amount of this satisfaction is captured in Satisfaction as shown in Figure 1. Satisfaction is another application of the widely held principle of reward or reinforcement: a buyer follows a given course of action because it is most rewarding to him. The evidence that reinforcement affects Attitude was cited above.

The effects of reinforcement are sometimes limited, however, because the buyer must make many choices in situations where he has little or no direct experience with the particular brand being chosen. On the other hand, an experienced, sophisticated adult has had an enormous amount of experience in a given culture which he brings to bear in evaluating an unfamiliar brand. Hence, few new brands are entirely new to the buyer, and new product classes are fewer still.

This past experience is transferred to the new purchasing situation—either the stimulus or response or both are new—by means of the mechanism of generalization. First, we must distinguish between stimulus generalization—a given response to a particular stimulus is transferred to a similar stimulus—and response generalization in which a given stimulus which has been associated with a particular response becomes associated with a similar response. Stimulus generalization is of two kinds —physical and semantic. If the buyer sees a new brand which is physically similar to the brand he has been buying, the sight of the new brand is more likely to cause him to buy the new brand than if the new brand is different.

Even more important, however, is semantic or mediated generalization in which the buyer is more likely to transfer his old purchasing response to a new ad if the ad has a *meaning* that is similar to the old ad. With semantic or mediated generalization the "meaning" of the stimulus (as measured by Attitude) instead of physical similarity mediates between the stimulus and the response. An example of semantic generalization is seen when a company's "company image" influences the sales of its brands by means of a common brand name across all products, but the extent to which company image is actually effective in changing Attitude is not known. Most executives believe that company image makes a difference in sales.[5]

Response generalization, too, can be distinguished according to whether it is physical or semantic (mediated). Let us deal with semantic generalization alone since physical generalization is merely a simpler version of it. Assume that a given ad having a certain meaning stimulates the buyer to purchase Brand A, but that when he sees the ad, A is not available. Consequently, under the principle of semantic generalization he will transfer his purchasing response to Brand B, toward which as a result of other

---

[5] William A. Mindak, "Fitting the Semantic Differential to the Marketing Problem," *Journal of Marketing* (April, 1961), pp. 28-33.

ads and conversations with friends he has come to have an attitude similar (to attach a similar meaning) to that he has toward A.

An extension of mediated response generalization is that if the buyer encounters a new product which has come to have a "better meaning than his regular brand (his attitude indicates it has better attributes), he is more likely to buy the new brand the more it is similar to his regular brand.

These various generalization mechanisms provide immense flexibility and continuity in buying behavior.

3.3 Product Cues

Two kinds of nonfeedback effects are distinguished: (1) Cues emanate from the physical brand itself, and they are effective because they call up memories of the satisfaction to be derived from the brand. (2) Other cues consist of symbols that *stand for the brand* such as advertising and discussions with friends, salesmen, etc. They are labeled "information," and are usually quite ambiguous. Effects in the form of cues emanating directly from the brand (product cues) are typically much less ambiguous and more effective in stimulating behavior.

The physical brand can serve as a set of product cues, however, only if the buyer is sufficiently familiar with it. In the case of a radically new brand in the market, the physical brand itself provides very few meaningful cues; and hence, it can serve only to a limited extent as product cues. As the buyer becomes more and more familiar with the brand, its potential as the source of product cues is enhanced. In the case where a person is thoroughly familiar with a brand, the mere color of the package may be sufficient to conjure up in the buyer's mind all of the brand's want-satisfying capacities.

Some essential concepts will aid the discussion. State of the Alternatives is the variable which specifies the brands physically in objective terms by whatever dimensions are appropriate to the specific buyer. Attitude and Inhibitor together constitute the subjective counterparts of this objective variable. It is shown in Figure 2. The variable also incorporates other elements of the market structure such as price and availability. Quality can also be included, but objective measures of it are less easy to come by.

A central concept having to do with State of Alternatives is "evoked set." It is defined as those brands which, out of all of the brands objectively available in the market, the buyer calls to mind when he is motivated to think of buying the product. Unless a buyer's evoked set is known, it is difficult to understand his behavior.

This idea of evoked set—what it is that buyers really choose from in the market such as in the supermarket where there is a great number of

brands actually available—has not been well studied in either buying behavior or other kinds of behavior. In industrial buying the "list" (list of
acceptable suppliers) that the industrial buyer maintains in his memory
or in a written record is a very obvious element in determining who he
will buy from. It can be observed in consumer purchase panel data where few
consumers are found to buy more than two or three brands in any given
product class of a frequently purchased item. Some general psychological
studies bear upon the concept, e.g., those having to do with categorization.

The concept of evoked set plays an essential role in the theory because brand choice within a given evoked set is assumed to be a significantly different process from that of choosing a brand to add to the
evoked set. The equilibrium analysis (preference dynamism) up to and
including Sec. 3.4.3.2. assumes a given set, whereas the changing equilibrium analysis of Sec. 3.4.3.3 (environmental dynamism) assumes that
the content of the set changes and that this change can at least be affected
by, perhaps even be brought about by, the buyer himself.

An arrow in Figure 2 indicates that the State of the Alternatives
influences Attitude and Inhibitor. In this way the objective facts of the

Figure 2. Product Cues

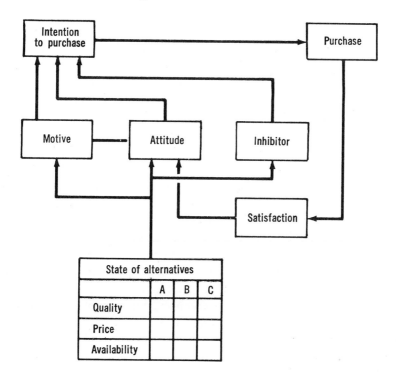

marketplace are converted into the buyer's subjective facts, that is, into his decision premises. Finally, the brand also stimulates Motive. Anyone who has smelled cooking food can attest to the fact that contact with the product can stimulate an appetite (a need, a motive) which before the event was nonexistent.

While on the topic of essential concepts of the theory, let us make some distinctions commonly made in model building. First, among all of the forces that empirically play upon the buyer we must distinguish between those we will incorporate and those we will ignore and hence implicitly treat as random. The variables in the model represent the former class of forces.

Second among those forces that we do incorporate, we must distinguish between those variables the changes in which we will attempt to explain and those the changes in which we take as given, that is, do not attempt to explain. The variables incorporating the former are called "endogenous variables"; the latter, "exogenous variables." One of the key functions of an exogenous variable is to explain differences among individual buyers in the nature of their buying responses. State of the Alternatives which we have just discussed is an example of an exogenous variable.

3.4 Information Cues

3.4.1 Introduction. The third avenue of influence upon the buyer's behavior—information cues—is to many the glamour part of marketing: television, radio, newspapers, salesmen, interaction with friends, etc. Most of the stimuli here are words, and human language is a phenomenon which psychologists have only recently begun to study systematically, drawing upon the discipline of linguistics. Further, growing evidence suggests that the buyer often deliberately subjects himself to new stimuli—he seeks information—in order to find the necessary information upon which to make his brand choice. The latter process seems to operate in almost all marketing situations, but it becomes especially significant in the marketing of new products.

Also, when language and other symbols are introduced, it becomes imperative that human perceptual limitations be recognized. In passing it should be noted that many of the perceptual complications presented here may also apply to product cues and to feedback from experience. Because feedback and product cues, however, are typically far less ambiguous than information cues, we expect these complications to apply much less; and hence we ignore perception involving these two effects. If the reader encounters a situation where he believes perceptual limitations exist in either or both the feedback and product cue effects, he can apply the analysis merely by extending the arrows from Satisfaction and State of Alternatives, respectively, through the information cue channel of Figure 3.

Let us examine the passive buyer first.

Figure 3. Passive Buyer: Perfect Information

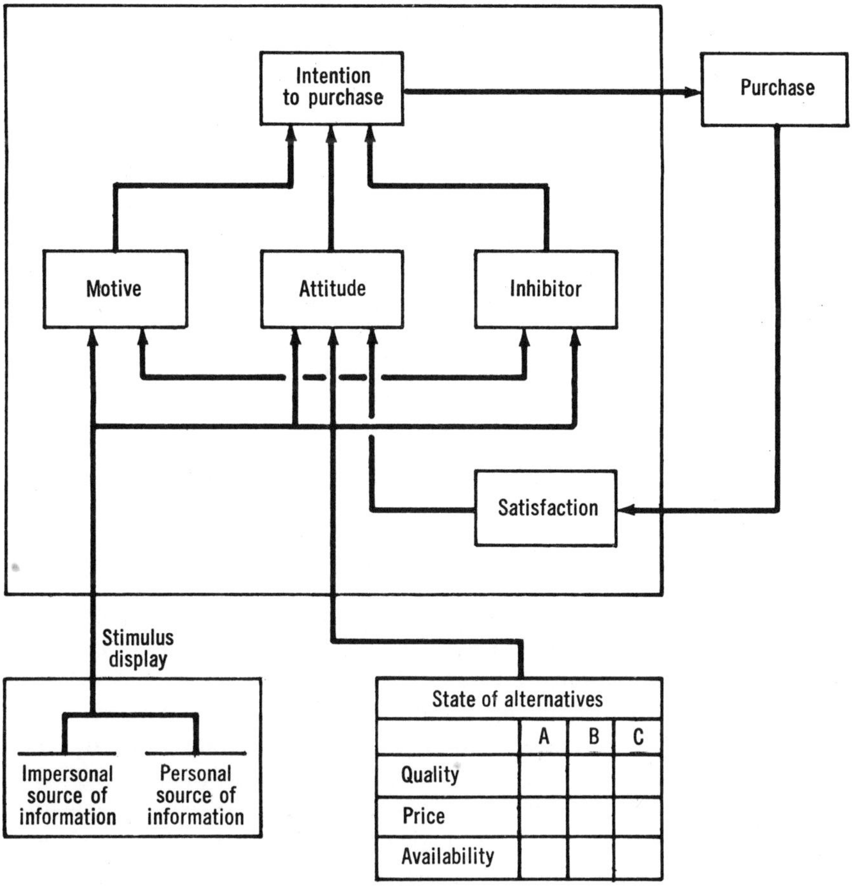

3.4.2 Passive buyer. *3.4.2.1 Introduction.* Clearly much brand choice instead of occurring from a deliberate act on the buyer's part does seem to result from the chance exposure of the buyer to information; for example, a friend merely by chance happens to mention that he has purchased a particular brand. In these instances we think of the buyer as passively responding to his environment.

Before proceeding with the discussion, it will be helpful to distinguish between two kinds of situations which the passive buyer encounters: perfect information and imperfect information. One of the main distinctions between product cues and information cues is that information cues are more ambiguous. Even within information cues, however, there is a great variation in degrees of ambiguity, or in "uncertainty," as the economist would call it. Hence, by distinguishing between those cases where the buyer perceives the passively received information with objective accuracy and those in which he markedly misperceives it, the effects of information can be presented in a more orderly way. Let us first discuss the case of high objective accuracy, which by economists is labeled "perfect information."[6]

3.4.2.2 Perfect information. As shown in Figure 3 information is received from the Stimulus Display, which is an objective description of the stimuli: of "what is really out there." For marketing purposes one of the most difficult problems is to specify the content of the stimulus display, and our inability to do this greatly hinders progress toward the understanding of buyer behavior. Try to describe a television ad in objective terms, for example.

Stimulus Display at the left side of Figure 3 contains two parts, Impersonal Sources of Information and Personal Sources of Information because there is some evidence that information from other people (Personal Sources of Information) is more influential than information from advertising (Impersonal Sources of Information), for example.

Information from Stimulus Display as shown in Figure 3 influences all three of the causal central variables: Motive, Attitude, and Inhibitor.

3.4.2.3 Imperfect information. Information cues typically constitute exceedingly complex stimuli. This complexity and the resulting ambiguity make it possible for a great variety of perceptual phenomena to obscure the effects of these stimuli upon behavior and to complicate the simple picture portrayed in Perfect Information. To illustrate the exquisitely selective capacity of the housewife, it has been reported that as high as 30 percent of the women do not "see" an ad on a Sunday evening television spectacular even though they are known to be in the room and can recall the parts of the show surrounding the ad. These perceptual complications occur because ambiguity increases the potential for misperception; and equally important, ambiguity leads to discrimination conflict and to goal conflict, both of which affect motivational intensity which further influences perception.[7]

---

[6] However, the economist in his use of "perfect information" incorporates the additional condition that the information itself is objectively accurate in fact.

[7] All of the analysis about conflict set forth here applies to before-the-decision situations. After-the-decision conflict is covered by dissonance theory, which to simplify the exposition will be dealt with later.

It is important to recognize that ambiguity of information is highly subjective. Its complexity makes a difference; but even with some objectively given level of complexity, we find great differences among buyers as to how ambiguous the stimulus is thought to be.

One of the consequences of complex stimuli for perception is merely to change the amount of effects the physical stimuli—the *quantity* of the information—which the buyer admits into his body: the extent to which he opens and closes his receptors. This is contained in Sensitivity to Information now shown in Figure 4. One determinant of the level of Sensitivity to Information is the degree of ambiguity of the stimulus, be it an ad (signs that stand for the product) or the brand (the significate) itself. The ambiguity exerts an influence upon the extent to which the

Figure 4. Passive Buyer: Imperfect Information

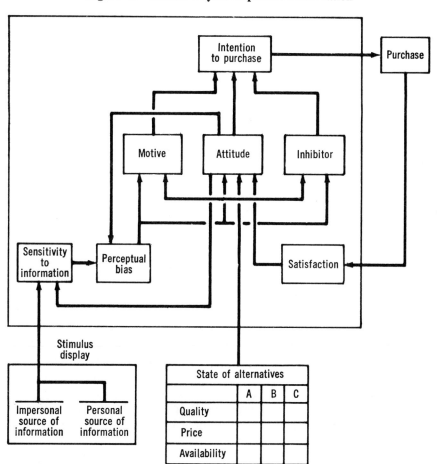

buyer "pays attention" to the stimulus. "Attention getting" is one of the most talked about problems in advertising, and yet the advertising literature quickly reveals that little is known about it. It is central to all marketing. The specific relation between ambiguity and attention is very complex, as we will see in Figure 6 below. Communication researchers have shown some of the significance of attention in the proposition that a communication which presents the motivation first and then the "reason why" (cognitive element) will more likely influence the person than when the order is reversed.[8] The implication is that the motivation increases the receiver's attention so that he is more likely to comprehend the "reason why" of the communication.

Another determinant of Sensitivity to Information is how interesting the stimulus is to the buyer as shown by the arrow from Attitude. Hess has well documented the effect of this upon a person's visual intake. He has found that a human expands his eye pupils when he sees a stimulus that is interesting. Presumably it applies to the other senses of taste, smell, touch, and hearing, as well as to the visual sense. This principle is now being used by the Interpublic advertising agency to test the effectiveness of various advertisements. It also suggests that the often-questioned but time-honored criterion of whether a person likes an ad may have some validity as a measure of the ad's ability to influence purchasing behavior.

The second effect of complex stimuli is not only to modify the amount of information that is received but also to modify the nature of its content—the *quality* of the information—and even to distort it seriously. This effect is caught in Perceptual Bias, which is a further complicating factor. There seem to be at least four mechanisms operating here to bring about this distorting effect. One of these—stimulus integration—will be described by way of illustration. The other mechanisms are discussed in the complete statement of the theory. There is evidence that when a person repeatedly sees a complex stimulus, he tends to come to associate (to integrate) the elements together. If later he is exposed to these familiar elements in a background containing less familiar elements, he will perceive the familiar ones much more easily than he will the unfamiliar elements: he filters out the unfamiliar. Further, he may "see" the familiar even when it is not "out" there. For example, if he is only *partially* exposed to a very familiar ad such as might occur when he is rapidly thumbing through a magazine, he will in fact perceive the entire ad and it will have the same effect on his behavior as though he had been exposed to the entire ad. The principle of stimulus integration has implications for the arrangement of products in a supermarket. The housewife is so familiar with the shelf location of a brand based on frequency of

---

[8] Arthur R. Cohen, *Attitude Change and Social Influence* (New York, Basic Books, 1964), p. 11.

having seen it that she is confused if the item is moved only a few feet away.

Another practical implication of the principle of stimulus integration is in the process of identifying attitude scales necessary to deriving n-dimensional market space. For example, in using word-association measures, the integration principle is being invoked.

Response integration is an important analogue to the stimulus integration phenomenon.[9]

3.4.3 Active buyer. *3.4.3.1 Introduction.* A buyer who deliberately seeks information is labeled an "active buyer." This active buyer, however, can seek infomation about either of two different phenomena. First, he can seek information about the brands in his evoked set. Second, he can seek information about a brand not now in his evoked set, which, in effect, means to explore the possibility of putting a new brand into his evoked set. Let us discuss the first case.

3.4.3.2 Constant evoked set. Let us assume that our buyer has a given evoked set, say X, of brands. We know that at least for some products a buyer overtly and actively seeks information from a variety of sources. The specific mechanism that describes this process is shown in Figure 5 by an arrow to Ambiguity which is merely a measure of the degree of ambiguity (uncertainty) of the information being received. The reader will recall that to simplify we show here only those effects that occur in the form of information cues, but the analysis applies just as well to product cues. To illustrate the Ambiguity variable, a new brand can be viewed as having decreasing ambiguity as the buyer learns more and more about it.

This ambiguity leads to conflict which creates tension (Arousal), an effect related to motivation. The increase in Arousal, for example, causes the person to seek new information (to exhibit exploratory behavior). Among adults exploratory behavior with respect to product cues seems to appear in the following cases: (1) In underdeveloped countries, where there is no labeling or branded goods, exploratory behavior with respect to the product is visible; (2) For many unbranded fruits and vegetables it exists among American housewives: twisting, polishing, smelling, rubbing,

---

[9] Through her shopping experience a housewife comes to develop a pattern of overt behavior such as going to Store A and another for going to Store B. Each of these patterns represents a separate sequence of integrated acts which are developed by the contiguity principle of learning—things are learned merely because they occur together irrespective of reinforcement—just as is true of the stimulus aspect of behavior. This is the integration of elements over time, however, instead of the integration as of a point in time implied in the earlier discussion of stimulus integration.

Figure 5. Active Buyer

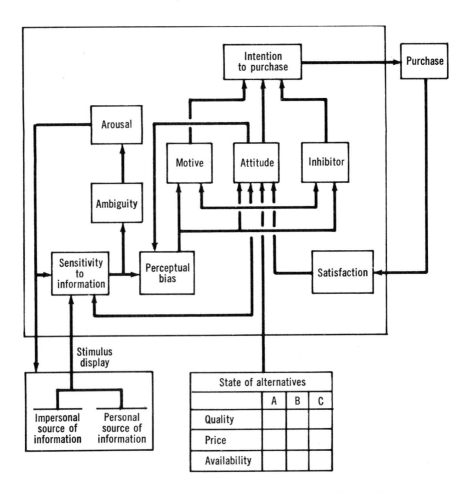

pinching, etc.; (3) For *novelty* items, most of us exhibit exploratory behavior.

Exploratory behavior manifests itself in two ways. First, it will increase the buyer's sensitivity to existing stimuli; he will open his receptors as represented by Sensitivity to Information.

Second, assuming that increasing Sensitivity to Information does not suffice to reduce the ambiguity of the information to a satisfactory level, the buyer will change Stimulus Display by seeking out friends to discuss the purchase with, looking for advertising that he would not otherwise expose himself to, etc. Increases in Sensitivity to Information will occur first because the change in it requires less energy expenditure than does a change in Stimulus Display.

The relation between Ambiguity and Arousal, however, is nonmonotonic, as shown in Figure 6. First, there is a certain mid-level of ambiguity of information which is the least arousing and which is represented by X_1. Second, we expect most situations to be in the range of X_2 and as the buyer receives information about a brand in his evoked set, he moves away from X_2 toward X_1.

Figure 6. Ambiguity-Arousal Relation

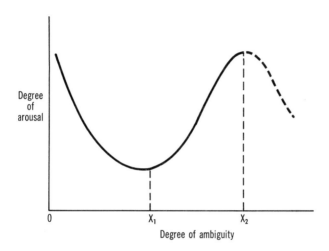

More complex stimuli represented by the range beyond X_2 tend to be too complex to be perceived; and he will avoid them, which is an example of ego defense.

Finally, there are differences among people with respect to the Ambiguity-Arousal relation. An example of individual differences that is relevant here is represented in the work of Donald Cox, who found a nonmonotonic relation between women's self-confidence and their susceptibility to persuasion in a purchasing context. According to the theory here, the women of high confidence view the product as being located in the area of X_1 to X_2, and those of low confidence in the range beyond X_2. These differences have usually been thought of as due to differences in individual personality; and no doubt, to an extent this is true. In addition to this personality difference, however, it has been found that people who are more highly integrated into their social structure are more likely to adopt brands first. Going beyond this essentially sociological difference and based upon other evidence, we postulate that a buyer has degrees of self-confidence with respect to each of three levels: the general or personality level, the product class level, and the individual brand level. Each is relevant to buying behavior.

In summary, with a given evoked set of brands, the buyer has two interrelated types of mechanisms which cause him to "zero in on a brand" and to achieve a state of equilibrium in which he continues to purchase the brand unless there is some change in his environment or in the content or intensity of his need. Reinforcement effects from using the brand constitutes the first of these. The second is made up of a number of perceptual mechanisms which cause the buyer to "close off" information with respect to competitive brands as he finds a brand that meets his need. This "closing off" occurs as his preferred brand moves from X_2 toward X_1. These two varieties of mechanisms are interrelated in that reinforcement gives rise to more intense attitudes which in turn cause the person to perceive (to be sensitive to) favorable but not unfavorable bits of information about his preferred brand.

A company policy implication of these two mechanisms is that if a company makes its information available when the buyer is receptive to information—he is between X_1 and X_2 of Figure 6—the company's information is more likely to be perceived. It is important to remember that both his motivation and his cognition can be influenced. If the buyer is not in a receptive state, some major jolt of information will be required to have an effect.

3.4.3.3 Changing evoked set. Analysis that assumes a given evoked set as does Sec. 3.4.3.2 will not carry us far in a world so fraught with change in the available alternatives, change which somehow must be incorporated directly and systematically. The appropriate analysis is already implied in Figure 6 showing the nonmonotonic relation between Ambiguity and Arousal. The 0 to X_1 range of the figure to some extent holds the key to the fascinating practical problem of how buyers come to accept new products, how the buyer breaks out of his state of equilibrium, out of the confines of his current evoked set, and adds a new brand to that set.

The empirical basis for this assertion is the large number of studies which have shown that people do not like a completely known environment. They appear to prefer a certain minimum of ambiguity. As a buyer continues to use a brand he becomes more and more familiar with it—it becomes less and less ambiguous—and at some point the ambiguity decreases to a level below the minimum level of Arousal, X_1. As Ambiguity declines further, Arousal begins to increase; and he exhibits exploratory behavior by searching for something new, something novel, in this product class. Finding the new brand will provide the desired ambiguity and thus place him in a new situation in which he will be in the X_1 to X_2 range of a new Figure 6 in which the new brand is an element in this evoked set.

The process of changing his evoked set can be seen when it is compared with the learning process as depicted by the traditional learning curve which relates the number of purchases of a given brand that a buyer has made to the probability of his purchasing that brand the next time. This relation which has received so much attention in conventional psychology is shown in Figure 7. By means of the learning curve we can express our ideas with greater precision. First, the asymptote may occur at any level of probability. The only necessary condition is that it be greater than chance where chance is defined in terms of the number of brands in the buyer's evoked set. Second, the asymptote is normally attained by degrees as illustrated in Figure 7, but there is the phenomenon

Figure 7.   Learning Curve for Brand A

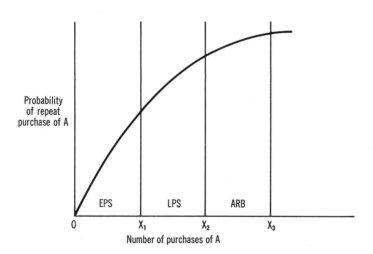

of "all-or-none" learning where the buyer goes immediately to the asymptote. Third, the learning curve can be defined as consisting of three stages: Extensive Problem Solving, Limited Problem Solving, and Automative Response Behavior. In the first stage the buyer has no evoked set, the probability of his repeat purchase is low, his buying activity requires some thinking, and much time is consumed in his choice process. In the second stage the buyer has an evoked set but its elements change, the probability of his repeat purchase is at a medium level, limited thinking is involved, and not much time is involved in the choice. In the third stage, the buyer has a constant evoked set, a high probability of repeat purchase, no thinking, and no time required for the decision. Hence, we would expect the foreigner, a newlywed housewife, etc. to be in Extensive Problem Solving. Most of American supermarket buying would occur in the latter two stages.

Having related the perceptual processes to the conventional learning view of behavior, let us proceed. The buyer acquires information as a part of the learning process in progressing toward the asymptotic position. Simultaneously he is reducing the ambiguity that the brand holds for him, and so in Figure 6, in terms of the Ambiguity-Arousal relation, his is progressing in the *opposite* direction to that in Figure 7. His confidence in judging the brand is increasing; but, and this is very important, after a time at the asymptote of the learning curve, and as his knowledge and confidence increase still further, he becomes bored and begins to look around for a new brand.

It is interesting to note that we see contrasted here the psychology of simplification and the psychology of complication. In the learning process he tends to simplify his world particularly by means of reaction to dissonance; for example, perhaps he "sees" evidence to support his past purchase. On the other hand, he also likes, up to a point, to complicate his world by looking for new alternatives.

One possibility, however, is that he will never drop below the X_1 position because sufficient information is difficult to come by. Instead he will reduce his level of aspiration and be satisfied with his current brand (remain brand loyal), but he will do this only after he has tried unsuccessfully to obtain information.

In summary, there are two kinds of forces operating on the buyer's decision process but at different times. One encourages him to seek new brands—to change his evoked set—whenever he becomes too familiar with existing brands. The other—arising from feedback and perceptual effects—encourages him to continue selecting the brand that he regularly tends to choose from his given evoked set. Which of these forces are dominant in governing his behavior depends among other things upon the degree of ambiguity of the brand and its associated stimuli, namely, feedback, product cues, and information cues. The "other things" are the importance of the product in its use to the buyer either in a functional or social sense, how easy it is to evaluate the product, and the personality of the buyer which has already been referred to. Empirical evidence suggests that in some situations the buyer reaches a state of equilibrium and stays there: he is brand loyal. In other situations, the state of equilibrium is short-lived.

A company policy implication of these two kinds of opposing forces is that with new products repeatedly appearing in an industry, the market as a whole goes through cycles of decreasing ambiguity, acceptance of a new brand, etc. Fashion products represent an example of a short cycle.

If a company will identify these cycles and introduce its new product at a period of high receptivity, e.g., when a majority of the buyers are in the X_1 range of Figure 6, the company will be more successful.

4. Exogenous Variables

The idea of exogenous variables as those influences on buying behavior, the change in which we do not wish to explain, was mentioned when State of Alternatives was introduced. By using the concept of exogenous variables we are able to carry the analysis further; for example, additional exogenous variables were just referred to: Importance of Purchase and Ease of Evaluation of Product. These were used to explain at what level we might expect the asymptote to occur. Others can be included to further refine the analysis. All of them taken together constitute the buyer's frame of reference which charactrizes him as the unique individual that he is. The practical significance of this is that if in studying buyers we do not control for these influences, the error effects will be so great that we can have little hope of understanding the buyer's behavior. They explain differences in buying behavior among products, among buyers, and over time for a given buyer.

5. Summary

In the foregoing pages a theory of buyer behavior has been set out in summary form. Also, according to the current evidence, it conforms to the facts of how buyers make their decisions. In addition, it deals with many of the problems that the practicing company executives and public policy makers encounter. It raises a host of questions for fundamental research to answer. Finally, it suggests that the two dominant areas of marketing activity are communication and innovation.

12

Behavioral Models for Analyzing Buyers

PHILIP KOTLER

In times past, management could arrive at a fair understanding of its buyers through the daily experience of selling to them. But the growth in the size of firms and markets has removed many decision-makers from direct contact with buyers. Increasingly, decision-makers have had to turn to summary statistics and to behavioral theory, and are spending more money today than ever before to try to understand their buyers.

Who buys? How do they buy? And why? The first two questions relate to relatively overt aspects of buyer behavior, and can be learned about through direct observation and interviewing.

But uncovering *why* people buy is an extremely difficult task. The answer will tend to vary with the investigator's behavioral frame of reference.

The buyer is subject to many influences which trace a complex course through his psyche and lead eventually to overt purchasing responses. This conception of the buying process is illustrated in Figure 1. Various influences and their modes of transmission are shown at the left. At the right are the buyer's responses in choice of product, brand, dealer, quantities, and frequency. In the center stands the buyer and his mysterious psychological processes. The buyer's psyche is a "black box" whose workings can be only partially deduced. The marketing strategist's challenge to the behavioral scientist is to construct a more specific model of the mechanism in the black box.

Unfortunately no generally accepted model of the mechanism exists. The human mind, the only entity in nature with deep powers of understanding, still remains the least understood. Scientists can explain plane-

Reprinted with permission from the *Journal of Marketing*, national quarterly publication of the American Marketing Association, Vol. 29 (October, 1965), pp. 37-45.

Figure 1. The Buying Process Conceived as a System of Inputs and Outputs

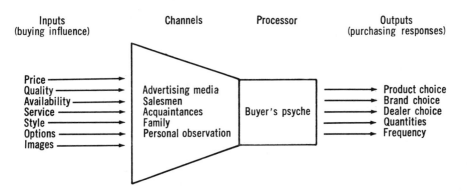

tary motion, genetic determination, and molecular behavior. Yet they have only partial, and often partisan, models of *human* behavior.

Nevertheless, the marketing strategist should recognize the potential interpretative contributions of different partial models for explaining buyer behavior. Depending upon the product, different variables and behavioral mechanisms may assume particular importance. A psychoanalytic behavioral model might throw much light on the factors operating in cigarette demand, while an economic behavioral model might be useful in explaining machine-tool purchasing. Sometimes alternative models may shed light on different demand aspects of the same product.

What are the most useful behavioral models for interpreting the transformation of buying influences into purchasing responses? Five different models of the buyer's "black box" are presented in the present article, along with their respective marketing applications: (1) the Marshallian model, stressing economic motivations; (2) the Pavlovian model, learning; (3) the Freudian model, psychoanalytic motivations; (4) the Veblenian model, social-psychological factors; and (5) the Hobbesian model, organizational factors. These models represent radically different conceptions of the mainsprings of human behavior.

The Marshallian Economic Model

Economists were the first professional group to construct a specific theory of buyer behavior. The theory holds that purchasing decisions are the result of largely "rational" and conscious economic calculations. The individual buyer seeks to spend his income on those goods that will deliver the most utility (satisfaction) according to his tastes and relative prices.

The antecedents for this view trace back to the writings of Adam Smith and Jeremy Bentham. Smith set the tone by developing a doctrine of economic growth based on the principle that man is motivated by self-interest in all his actions.[1] Bentham refined this view and saw man as finely calculating and weighing the expected pleasures and pains of every contemplated action.[2]

Bentham's "felicific calculus" was not applied to consumer behavior (as opposed to entrepreneurial behavior) until the late 19th century. Then, the "marginal-utility" theory of value was formulated independently and almost simultaneously by Jevons[3] and Marshall[4] in England, Menger[5] in Austria, and Walras[6] in Switzerland.

Alfred Marshall was the great consolidator of the classical and neo-classical tradition in economics; and his synthesis in the form of demand-supply analysis constitutes the main source of modern micro-economic thought in the English-speaking world. His theoretical work aimed at realism, but his method was to start with simplifying assumptions and to examine the effect of a change in a single variable (say, price) when all other variables were held constant.

He would "reason out" the consequences of the provisional assumptions and in subsequent steps modify his assumptions in the direction of more realism. He employed the "measuring rod of money" as an indicator of the intensity of human psychological desires. Over the years his methods and assumptions have been refined into what is now known as *modern utility theory*: economic man is bent on maximizing his utility, and does this by carefully calculating the "felicific" consequences of any purchase.

As an example, suppose on a particular evening that John is considering whether to prepare his own dinner or dine out. He estimates that a restaurant meal would cost $2.00 and a home-cooked meal 50 cents. According to the Marshallian model, if John expects less than four times as much satisfaction from the restaurant meal as the home-cooked meal, he will eat at home. The economist typically is not concerned with how these relative preferences are formed by John, or how they may be psychologically modified by new stimuli.

---

[1] Adam Smith, *An Inquiry into the Nature and Causes of the Wealth of Nations,* 1776 (New York: The Modern Library, 1937).

[2] Jeremy Bentham, *An Introduction to the Principles of Morals and Legislation,* 1780 (Oxford, England: Clarendon Press, 1907).

[3] William S. Jevons, *The Theory of Political Economy* (New York: The Macmillan Company, 1871).

[4] Alfred Marshall, *Principles of Economics,* 1890 (London: The Macmillan Company, 1927).

[5] Karl Menger, *Principles of Economics,* 1871 (Glencoe, Illinois: Free Press, 1950).

[6] Leon Walras, *Elements of Pure Economics,* 1874 (Homewood, Illinois: Richard D. Irwin, Inc., 1954).

Yet John will not always cook at home. The principle of diminishing marginal utility operates. Within a given time interval—say, a week—the utility of each additional home-cooked meal diminishes. John gets tired of home meals and other products become relatively more attractive.

John's *efficiency* in maximizing his utility depends on the adequacy of his freedom of choice. If he is not perfectly aware of costs, if he misestimates the relative delectability of the two meals, or if he is barred from entering the restaurant, he will not maximize his potential utility. His choice processes are rational, but the results are inefficient.

Marketing Applications of Marshallian Model

Marketers usually have dismissed the Marshallian model as an absurd figment of ivory-tower imagination. Certainly the behavioral essence of the situation is omitted, in viewing man as calculating the marginal utility of a restaurant meal over a home-cooked meal.

Eva Mueller has reported a study where only one-fourth of the consumers in her sample bought with any substantial degree of deliberation.[7] Yet there are a number of ways to view the model.

From one point of view the Marshallian model is tautological and therefore neither true nor false. The model holds that the buyer acts in the light of his best "interest." But this is not very informative.

A second view is that this is a *normative* rather than a *descriptive* model of behavior. The model provides logical norms for buyers who want to be "rational." Although the consumer is not likely to employ economic analysis to decide between a box of Kleenex and Scotties, he may apply economic analysis in deciding whether to buy a new car. Industrial buyers even more clearly would want an economic calculus for making good decisions.

A third view is that economic factors operate to a greater or lesser extent in all markets, and, therefore, must be included in any comprehensive description of buyer behavior.

Furthermore, the model suggests useful behavioral hypotheses such as: (a) The lower the price of the product, the higher the sales. (b) The lower the price of substitute products, the lower the sales of this product; and the lower the price of complementary products, the higher the sales of this product. (c) The higher the real income, the higher the sales of this product, provided that it is not an "inferior" good. (d) The higher the promotional expenditures, the higher the sales.

The validity of these hypotheses does not rest on whether *all* individuals act as economic calculating machines in making their purchasing

---

[7] Eva Mueller, "A Study of Purchase Decisions," Part 2, *Consumer Behavior, The Dynamics of Consumer Reaction,* edited by Lincoln H. Clark (New York: New York University Press, 1954), pp. 36-87.

decisions. For example, some individuals may buy *less* of a product when its price is reduced. They may think that the quality has gone down, or that ownership has less status value. If a majority of buyers view price reductions negatively, then sales may fall, contrary to the first hypothesis.

But for most goods a price reduction increases the relative value of the goods in many buyers' minds and leads to increased sales. This and the other hypotheses are intended to describe average effects.

The impact of economic factors in actual buying situations is studied through experimental design or statistical analyses of past data. Demand equations have been fitted to a wide variety of products—including beer, refrigerators, and chemical fertilizers.[8] More recently, the impact of economic variables on the fortunes of different brands has been pursued with significant results, particularly in the case of coffee, frozen orange juice, and margarine.[9]

But economic factors alone cannot explain all the variations in sales. The Marshallian model ignores the fundamental question of how product and brand preferences are formed. It represents a useful frame of reference for analyzing only one small corner of the "black box."

The Pavlovian Learning Model

The designation of a Pavlovian learning model has its origin in the experiments of the Russian psychologist Pavlov, who rang a bell each time before feeding a dog. Soon he was able to induce the dog to salivate by ringing the bell whether or not food was supplied. Pavlov concluded that learning was largely an associative process and that a large component of behavior was conditioned in this way.

Experimental psychologists have continued this mode of research with rats and other animals, including people. Laboratory experiments have been designed to explore such phenomena as learning, forgetting, and the ability to discriminate. The results have been integrated into a stimulus-response model of human behavior, or as someone has "wisecracked," the substitution of a rat psychology for a rational psychology.

The model has been refined over the years, and today is based on four central concepts—those of *drive, cue, response,* and *reinforcement*.[10]

---

[8] See Erwin E. Nemmers, *Managerial Economics* (New York: John Wiley & Sons, Inc., 1962), Part II.

[9] See Lester G. Telser, "The Demand for Branded Goods as Estimated from Consumer Panel Data," *Review of Economics and Statistics,* Vol. 44 (August, 1962), pp. 300-324; and William F. Massy and Ronald E. Frank, "Short Term Price and Dealing Effects in Selected Market Segments," *Journal of Marketing Research,* Vol. 2 (May, 1965), pp. 171-185.

[10] See John Dollard and Neal E. Miller, *Personality and Psychotherapy* (New York: McGraw-Hill Book Company, Inc., 1950), Chapter III.

Drive. Also called needs or motives, drive refers to strong stimuli internal to the individual which impels action. Psychologists draw a distinction between primary physiological drives—such as hunger, thirst, cold, pain, and sex—and learned drives which are derived socially—such as cooperation, fear, and acquisitiveness.

Cue. A drive is very general and impels a particular response only in relation to a particular configuration of cues. Cues are weaker stimuli in the environment and/or in the individual which determine when, where, and how the subject responds. Thus, a coffee advertisement can serve as a cue which stimulates the thirst drive in a housewife. Her response will depend upon this cue and other cues, such as the time of day, the availability of other thirst-quenchers, and the cue's intensity. Often a relative change in a cue's intensity can be more impelling than its absolute level. The housewife may be more motivated by a 2-cents-off sale on a brand of coffee than the fact that this brand's price was low in the first place.

Response. The response is the organism's reaction to the configuration of cues. Yet the same configuration of cues will not necessarily produce the same response in the individual. This depends on the degree to which the experience was rewarding, that is, drive-reducing.

Reinforcement. If the experience is rewarding, a particular response is reinforced; that is, it is strengthened and there is a tendency for it to be repeated when the same configuration of cues appears again. The housewife, for example, will tend to purchase the same brand of coffee each time she goes to her supermarket so long as it is rewarding and the cue configuration does not change. But if a learned response or habit is not reinforced, the strength of the habit diminishes and may be extinguished eventually. Thus, a housewife's preference for a certain coffee may become extinct if she finds the brand out of stock for a number of weeks.

Forgetting, in contrast to extinction, is the tendency for learned associations to weaken, not because of the lack of reinforcement but because of nonuse.

Cue configurations are constantly changing. The housewife sees a new brand of coffee next to her habitual brand, or notes a special price deal on a rival brand. Experimental psychologists have found that the same learned response will be elicited by similar patterns of cues; that is, learned responses are *generalized*. The housewife shifts to a similar brand when her favorite brand is out of stock. This tendency toward generalization over less similar cue configurations is increased in proportion to the strength of the drive. A housewife may buy an inferior coffee if it is the only brand left and if her drive is sufficiently strong.

A counter-tendency to generalization is *discrimination*. When a housewife tries two similar brands and finds one more rewarding, her ability to discriminate between similar cue configurations improves. Discrimination increases the specificity of the cue-response connection, while generalization decreases the specificity.

Marketing Applications of Pavlovian Model

The modern version of the Pavlovian model makes no claim to provide a complete theory of behavior—indeed, such important phenomena as perception, the subconscious, and interpersonal influence are inadequately treated. Yet the model does offer a substantial number of insights about some aspects of behavior of considerable interest to marketers.[11]

An example would be in the problem of introducing a new brand into a highly competitive market. The company's goal is to extinguish existing brand habits and form new habits among consumers for its brand. But the company must first get customers to try its brand; and it has to decide between using weak and strong cues.

Light introductory advertising is a weak cue compared with distributing free samples. Strong cues, although costing more, may be necessary in markets characterized by strong brand loyalties. For example, Folger went into the coffee market by distributing over a million pounds of free coffee.

To build a brand habit, it helps to provide for an extended period of introductory dealing. Furthermore, sufficient quality must be built into the brand so that the experience is reinforcing. Since buyers are more likely to transfer allegiance to similar brands than dissimilar brands (generalization), the company should also investigate what cues in the leading brands have been most effective. Although outright imitation would not necessarily effect the most transference, the question of providing enough similarity should be considered.

The Pavlovian model also provides guide lines in the area of advertising strategy. The American behaviorist, John B. Watson, was a great exponent of repetitive stimuli; in his writings man is viewed as a creature who can be conditioned through repetition and reinforcement to respond in particular ways.[12] The Pavlovian model emphasizes the desirability of repetition in advertising. A single exposure is likely to be a very weak cue,

---

[11] The most consistent application of learning-theory concepts to marketing situations is found in John A. Howard, *Marketing Management: Analysis and Planning* (Homewood, Illinois: Richard D. Irwin, Inc., revised edition, 1963).

[12] John B. Watson, *Behaviorism* (New York: The People's Institute Publishing Company, 1925).

hardly able to penetrate the individual's consciousness sufficiently to excite his drives above the threshold level.

Repetition in advertising has two desirable effects. It "fights" forgetting, the tendency for learned responses to weaken in the absence of practice. It provides reinforcement, because after the purchase the consumer becomes selectively exposed to advertisements of the product.

The model also provides guide lines for copy strategy. To be effective as a cue, an advertisement must arouse strong drives in the person. The strongest product-related drives must be identified. For candy bars, it may be hunger; for safety belts, fear; for hair tonics, sex; for automobiles, status. The advertising practitioner must dip into his cue box—words, colors, pictures—and select that configuration of cues that provides the strongest stimulus to these drives.

The Freudian Psychoanalytic Model

The Freudian model of man is well known, so profound has been its impact on 20th century thought. It is the latest of a series of philosophical "blows" to which man has been exposed in the last 500 years. Copernicus destroyed the idea that man stood at the center of the universe; Darwin tried to refute the idea that man was a special creation; and Freud attacked the idea that man even reigned over his own psyche.

According to Freud, the child enters the world driven by instinctual needs which he cannot gratify by himself. Very quickly and painfully he realizes his separateness from the rest of the world and yet his dependence on it.

He tries to get others to gratify his needs through a variety of blatant means, including intimidation and supplication. Continual frustration leads him to perfect more subtle mechanisms for gratifying his instincts.

As he grows, his psyche becomes increasingly complex. A part of his psyche—the id—remains the reservoir of his strong drives and urges. Another part—the ego—becomes his conscious planning center for finding outlets for his drives. And a third part—his super-ego—channels his instinctive drives into socially approved outlets to avoid the pain of guilt or shame.

The guilt or shame which man feels toward some of his urges—especially his sexual urges—causes him to repress them from his consciousness. Through such defense mechanisms as rationalization and sublimation, these urges are denied or become transmuted into socially approved expressions. Yet these urges are never eliminated or under perfect control; and they emerge, sometimes with a vengeance, in dreams, in slips-of-the-tongue, in neurotic and obsessional behavior, or ultimately in mental breakdown where the ego can no longer maintain the delicate balance between the impulsive power of the id and the oppressive power of the super-ego.

The individual's behavior, therefore, is never simple. His motivational wellsprings are not obvious to a casual observer nor deeply understood by the individual himself. If he is asked why he purchased an expensive foreign sports-car, he may reply that he likes its maneuverability and its looks. At a deeper level he may have purchased the car to impress others, or to feel young again. At a still deeper level, he may be purchasing the sports-car to achieve substitute gratification for unsatisfied sexual strivings.

Many refinements and changes in emphasis have occurred in this model since the time of Freud. The instinct concept has been replaced by a more careful delineation of basic drives; the three parts of the psyche are regarded now as theoretical concepts rather than actual entities; and the behavioral perspective has been extended to include cultural as well as biological mechanisms.

Instead of the role of the sexual urge in psychic development— Freud's discussion of oral, anal, and genital stages and possible fixations and traumas—Adler[13] emphasized the urge for power and how its thwarting manifests itself in superiority and inferiority complexes; Horney[14] emphasized cultural mechanisms; and Fromm[15] and Erickson[16] emphasized the role of existential crises in personality development. These philosophical divergencies, rather than debilitating the model, have enriched and extended its interpretative value to a wider range of behavioral phenomena.

Marketing Applications of Freudian Model

Perhaps the most important marketing implication of this model is that buyers are motivated by *symbolic* as well as *economic-functional* product concerns. The change of a bar of soap from a square to a round shape may be more important in its sexual than its functional connotations. A cake mix that is advertised as involving practically no labor may alienate housewives because the easy life may evoke a sense of guilt.

Motivational research has produced some interesting and occasionally some bizarre hypotheses about what may be in the buyer's mind regard-

[13] Alfred Adler, *The Science of Living* (New York: Greenberg, 1929).

[14] Karen Horney, *The Neurotic Personality of Our Time* (New York: W. W. Norton & Co., 1937).

[15] Erich Fromm, *Man For Himself* (New York: Holt, Rinehart & Winston, Inc., 1947).

[16] Erik Erikson, *Childhood and Society* (New York: W. W. Norton & Co., 1949).

ing certain purchases. Thus, it has been suggested at one time or another that

Many a businessman doesn't fly because of a fear of posthumous guilt—if he crashed, his wife would think of him as stupid for not taking a train.

Men want their cigars to be odoriferous, in order to prove that they (the men) are masculine.

A woman is very serious when she bakes a cake because unconsciously she is going through the symbolic act of giving birth.

A man buys a convertible as a substitute "mistress."

Consumers prefer vegetable shortening because animal fats stimulate a sense of sin.

Men who wear suspenders are reacting to an unresolved castration complex.

There are admitted difficulties in proving these assertions. Two prominent motivational researchers, Ernest Dichter and James Vicary, were employed independently by two separate groups in the prune industry to determine why so many people dislike prunes. Dichter found, among other things, that the prune aroused feelings of old age and insecurity in people, whereas Vicary's main finding was that Americans had an emotional block about prunes' laxative qualities.[17] Which is the more valid interpretation? Or if they are both operative, which motive is found with greater statistical frequency in the population?

Unfortunately the usual survey techniques—direct observation and interviewing—can be used to establish the representativeness of more superficial characteristics—age and family size, for example—but are not feasible for establishing the frequency of mental states which are presumed to be deeply "buried" within each individual.

Motivational researchers have to employ time-consuming projective techniques in the hope of throwing individual "egos" off guard. When carefully administered and interpreted, techniques such as word association, sentence completion, picture interpretation, and role-playing can provide some insights into the minds of the small group of examined individuals; but a "leap of faith" is sometimes necessary to generalize these findings to the population.

Nevertheless, motivation research can lead to useful insights and provide inspiration to creative men in the advertising and packaging world.

---

[17] L. Edward Scriven, "Rationality and Irrationality in Motivation Research," in Robert Ferber and Hugh G. Wales, editors, *Motivation and Marketing Behavior* (Homewood, Illinois: Richard D. Irwin, Inc., 1958), pp. 69-70.

Appeals aimed at the buyer's private world of hopes, dreams, and fears can often be as effective in stimulating purchase as more rationally-directed appeals.

The Veblenian Social-Psychological Model

While most economists have been content to interpret buyer behavior in Marshallian terms, Thorstein Veblen struck out in different directions.

Veblen was trained as an orthodox economist, but evolved into a social thinker greatly influenced by the new science of social anthropology. He saw man as primarily a *social animal*—conforming to the general forms and norms of his larger culture and to the more specific standards of the subcultures and face-to-face groupings to which his life is bound. His wants and behavior are largely molded by his present group-memberships and his aspired group-memberships.

Veblen's best-known example of this is in his description of the leisure class.[18] His hypothesis is that much of economic consumption is motivated not by intrinsic needs or satisfaction so much as by prestige-seeking. He emphasized the strong emulative factors operating in the choice of conspicuous goods like clothes, cars, and houses.

Some of his points, however, seem overstated by today's perspective. The leisure class does not serve as everyone's reference group; many persons aspire to the social patterns of the class immediately above it. And important segments of the affluent class practice conspicuous underconsumption rather than overconsumption. There are many people in all classes who are more anxious to "fit in" than to "stand out." As an example, William H. Whyte found that many families avoided buying air conditioners and other appliances before their neighbors did.[19]

Veblen was not the first nor the only investigator to comment on social influences in behavior; but the incisive quality of his observations did much to stimulate further investigations. Another stimulus came from Karl Marx, who held that each man's world-view was determined largely by his relationship to the "means of production."[20] The early field-work in primitive societies by social anthropologists like Boas[21] and Malinow-

---

[18] Thorstein Veblen, *The Theory of the Leisure Class* (New York: The Macmillan Company, 1899).

[19] William H. Whyte, Jr., "The Web of Word of Mouth," *Fortune,* Vol. 50 (November, 1954), pp. 140 ff.

[20] Karl Marx, *The Communist Manifesto,* 1848 (London: Martin Lawrence, Ltd., 1934).

[21] Franz Boas, *The Mind of Primitive Man* (New York: The Macmillan Company, 1922).

ski[22] and the later field-work in urban societies by men like Park[23] and Thomas[24] contributed much to understanding the influence of society and culture. The research of early Gestalt psychologists—men like Wertheimer,[25] Köhler,[26] and Koffka[27]—into the mechanisms of perception led eventually to investigations of small-group influence on perception.

Marketing Applications of Veblenian Model

The various streams of thought crystallized into the modern social sciences of sociology, cultural anthropology, and social psychology. Basic to them is the view that man's attitudes and behavior are influenced by several levels of society—culture, subcultures, social classes, reference groups, and face-to-face groups. The challenge to the marketer is to determine which of these social levels are the most important in influencing the demand for his product.

Culture

The most enduring influences are from culture. Man tends to assimilate his culture's mores and folkways, and to believe in their absolute rightness until deviants appear within his culture or until he confronts members of another culture.

Subcultures

A culture tends to lose its homogeneity as its population increases. When people no longer are able to maintain face-to-face relationships with more than a small proportion of other members of a culture, smaller units or subcultures develop, which help to satisfy the individual's needs for more specific identity.

The subcultures are often regional entities, because the people of a region, as a result of more frequent interactions, tend to think and act alike. But subcultures also take the form of religions, nationalities, fraternal orders, and other institutional complexes which provide a broad identification for people who may otherwise be strangers. The subcultures

---

[22] Bronislaw Malinowski, *Sex and Repression in Savage Society* (New York: Meridian Books, 1955).

[23] Robert E. Park, *Human Communities* (Glencoe, Illinois: Free Press, 1952).

[24] William I. Thomas, *The Unadjusted Girl* (Boston: Little, Brown and Company, 1928).

[25] Max Wertheimer, *Productive Thinking* (New York; Harper & Brothers, 1945).

[26] Wolfgang Köhler, *Gestalt Psychology* (New York: Liveright Publishing Co., 1947).

[27] Kurt Koffka, *Principles of Gestalt Psychology* (New York: Harcourt, Brace and Co., 1935).

of a person play a large role in his attitude formation and become another important predictor of certain values he is likely to hold.

Social Class

People become differentiated not only horizontally but also vertically through a division of labor. The society becomes stratified socially on the basis of wealth, skill, and power. Sometimes castes develop in which the members are reared for certain roles, or social classes develop in which the members feel empathy with others sharing similar values and economic circumstances.

Because social class involves different attitudinal configurations, it becomes a useful independent variable for segmenting markets and predicting reactions. Significant differences have been found among different social classes with respect to magazine readership, leisure activities, food imagery, fashion interests, and acceptance of innovations. A sampling of attitudinal differences in class is the following:

Members of the *upper-middle* class place an emphasis on professional competence; indulge in expensive status symbols; and more often than not show a taste, real or otherwise, for theater and the arts. They want their children to show high achievement and precocity and develop into physicists, vice-presidents, and judges. This class likes to deal in ideas and symbols.

Members of the *lower-middle* class cherish respectability, savings, a college education, and good housekeeping. They want their children to show self-control and prepare for careers as accountants, lawyers, and engineers.

Members of the *upper-lower* class try to keep up with the times, if not with the Joneses. They stay in older neighborhoods but buy new kitchen appliances. They spend proportionately less than the middle class on major clothing articles, buying a new suit mainly for an important ceremonial occasion. They also spend proportionately less on services, preferring to do their own plumbing and other work around the house. They tend to raise large families and their children generally enter manual occupations. This class also supplies many local businessmen, politicians, sports stars, and labor-union leaders.

Reference Groups

There are groups in which the individual has no membership but with which he identifies and may aspire to—reference groups. Many young boys identify with big-league baseball players or astronauts, and many young girls identify with Hollywood stars. The activities of these popular heroes are carefully watched and frequently imitated. These reference figures become important transmitters of influence, although more along lines of taste and hobby than basic attitudes.

Face-to-Face Groups

Groups that have the most immediate influence on a person's tastes and opinions are face-to-face groups. This includes all the small "societies" with which he comes into frequent contact: his family, close friends, neighbors, fellow workers, fraternal associates, and so forth. His informal group memberships are influenced largely by his occupation, residence, and stage in the life cycle.

The powerful influence of small groups on individual attitudes has been demonstrated in a number of social psychological experiments.[28] There is also evidence that this influence may be growing. David Riesman and his coauthors have pointed to signs which indicate a growing amount of *other-direction,* that is, a tendency for individuals to be increasingly influenced by their peers in the definition of their values rather than by their parents and elders.[29]

For the marketer, this means that brand choice may increasingly be influenced by one's peers. For such products as cigarettes and automobiles, the influence of peers is unmistakable.

The role of face-to-face groups has been recognized in recent industry campaigns attempting to change basic product attitudes. For years the milk industry has been trying to overcome the image of milk as a "sissified" drink by portraying its use in social and active situations. The men's-wear industry is trying to increase male interest in clothes by advertisements indicating that business associates judge a man by how well he dresses.

Of all face-to-face groups, the person's family undoubtedly plays the largest and most enduring role in basic attitude formation. From them he acquires a mental set not only toward religion and politics, but also toward thrift, chastity, food, human relations, and so forth. Although he often rebels against parental values in his teens, he often accepts these values eventually. Their formative influence on his eventual attitudes is undeniably great.

Family members differ in the types of product messages they carry to other family members. Most of what parents know about cereals, candy, and toys comes from their children. The wife stimulates family consideration of household appliances, furniture, and vacations. The husband tends

---

[28] See, for example, Solomon E. Asch, "Effects of Group Pressure Upon the Modification & Distortion of Judgments," in Dorwin Cartwright and Alvin Zander, *Group Dynamics* (Evanston, Illinois: Row, Peterson & Co., 1953), pp. 151-162; and Kurt Lewin, "Group Decision and Social Change," in Theodore M. Newcomb and Eugene L. Hartley, editors, *Readings in Social Psychology* (New York: Henry Holt Co., 1952).

[29] David Riesman, Reuel Denney, and Nathan Glazer, *The Lonely Crowd* (New Haven, Connecticut: Yale University Press, 1950).

to stimulate the fewest purchase ideas, with the exception of the automobile and perhaps the home.

The marketer must be alert to what attitudinal configurations dominate in different types of families, and also to how these change over time. For example, the parent's conception of the child's rights and privileges has undergone a radical shift in the last 30 years. The child has become the center of attention and orientation in a great number of households, leading some writers to label the modern family a "filiarchy." This has important implications not only for how to market to today's family, but also on how to market to tomorrow's family when the indulged child of today becomes the parent.

The Person

Social influences determine much but not all of the behavioral variations in people. Two individuals subject to the same influences are not likely to have identical attitudes, although these attitudes will probably converge at more points than those of two strangers selected at random. Attitudes are really the product of social forces interacting with the individual's unique temperament and abilities.

Furthermore, attitudes do not automatically guarantee certain types of behavior. Attitudes are predispositions felt by buyers before they enter the buying process. The buying process itself is a learning experience and can lead to a change in attitudes.

Alfred Politz noted at one time that women stated a clear preference for G.E. refrigerators over Frigidaire, but that Frigidaire continued to outsell G.E.[30] The answer to this paradox was that preference was only one factor entering into behavior. When the consumer preferring G.E. actually undertook to purchase a new refrigerator, her curiosity led her to examine the other brands. Her perception was sensitized to refrigerator advertisements, sales arguments, and different product features. This led to learning and a change in attitudes.

The Hobbesian Organizational-Factors Model

The foregoing models throw light mainly on the behavior of family buyers.

But what of the large number of people who are organizational buyers? They are engaged in the purchase of goods not for the sake of consumption, but for further production or distribution. Their common

---

[30] Alfred Politz, "Motivation Research—Opportunity or Dilemma?", in Ferber and Wales, same reference as footnote 17, at pp. 57-58.

denominator is the fact that they (1) are paid to make purchases for others and (2) operate within an organizational environment.

How do organizational buyers make their decisions? There seem to be two competing views. Many marketing writers have emphasized the predominance of rational motives in organizational buying.[31] Organizational buyers are represented as being most impressed by cost, quality, dependability, and service factors. They are portrayed as dedicated servants of the organization, seeking to secure the best terms. This view has led to an emphasis on performance and use characteristics in much industrial advertising.

Other writers have emphasized personal motives in organizational buyer behavior. The purchasing agent's interest to do the best for his company is tempered by his interest to do the best for himself. He may be tempted to choose among salesmen according to the extent they entertain or offer gifts. He may choose a particular vendor because this will ingratiate him with certain company officers. He may shortcut his study of alternative suppliers to make his work day easier.

In truth, the buyer is guided by both personal and group goals; and this is the essential point. The political model of Thomas Hobbes comes closest of any model to suggesting the relationship between the two goals.[32] Hobbes held that man is "instinctively" oriented toward preserving and enhancing his own well-being. But this would produce a "war of every man against every man." This fear leads men to unite with others in a corporate body. The corporate man tries to steer a careful course between satisfying his own needs and those of the organization.

Marketing Applications of Hobbesian Model

The import of the Hobbesian model is that organizational buyers can be appealed to on both personal and organizational grounds. The buyer has his private aims, and yet he tries to do a satisfactory job for his corporation. He will respond to persuasive salesmen and he will respond to rational product arguments. However, the best "mix" of the two is not a fixed quantity; it varies with the nature of the product, the type of organization, and the relative strength of the two drives in the particular buyer.

Where there is substantial similarity in what suppliers offer in the way of products, price, and service, the purchasing agent has less basis for rational choice. Since he can satisfy his organizational obligations with any one of a number of suppliers, he can be swayed by personal motives.

---

[31] See Melvin T. Copeland, *Principles of Merchandising* (New York: McGraw-Hill Book Co., Inc., 1924).

[32] Thomas Hobbes, *Leviathan,* 1651 (London: G. Routledge and Sons, 1887).

On the other hand, where there are pronounced differences among the competing vendors' products, the purchasing agent is held more account-able for his choice and probably pays more attention to rational factors. Short-run personal gain becomes less motivating than the long-run gain which comes from serving the organization with distinction.

The marketing strategist must appreciate these goal conflicts of the organizational buyer. Behind all the ferment of purchasing agents to develop standards and employ value analysis lies their desire to avoid being thought of as order-clerks, and to develop better skills in reconcil-ing personal and organizational objectives.[33]

Summary

Think back over the five different behavioral models of how the buyer translates buying influences into purchasing responses.

Marshallian man is concerned chiefly with economic cues—prices and income—and makes a fresh utility calculation before each purchase.

Pavlovian man behaves in a largely habitual rather than thoughtful way; certain configurations of cues will set off the same behavior because of rewarded learning in the past.

Freudian man's choices are influenced strongly by motives and fan-tasies which take place deep within his private world.

Veblenian man acts in a way which is shaped largely by past and present social groups.

And finally, Hobbesian man seeks to reconcile individual gain with organizational gain.

Thus, it turns out that the "black box" of the buyer is not so black after all. Light is thrown in various corners by these models. Yet no one has succeeded in putting all these pieces of truth together into one coher-ent instrument for behavioral analysis. This, of course, is the goal of behavioral science.

---

[33] For an insightful account, see George Strauss, "Tactics of Lateral Relation-ship: The Purchasing Agent," *Administrative Science Quarterly,* Vol. 7 (September, 1962), pp. 161-186.

13

A Time for Propositions

W. T. TUCKER

As one considers Juan's shirt, Peter Rigby's furniture, the peach-faced parrot, or Barbara's new dress, there is an enormous temptation to describe consumer behavior in terms of a decision model suggested by economic theory, decision theory, and some portions of psychological theory. This might be stated as:

$$D_a \equiv \frac{AR_a}{AE_a} \geqslant \frac{AR_x}{AE_x}$$

This reads simply decision A will be made, if, and only if, the anticipated reward for the decision divided by the anticipated effort required by the action is at least as great as the anticipated reward of any other decision, divided by the anticipated effort required by that action.[1]

There are a number of problems involved in starting a theory at such a point. First, it suggests that the subject under consideration relates to purchases that are made and need consider little or nothing subsequent to that event. Second, it seems to be an assumption itself and to rest on certain other assumptions that are highly questionable, such as the ability of the human mind to carry out rather difficult mathematical procedures such as the ascription of some sort of reward units to varying situations and effort units to different forms of effort, to say nothing of carrying out a

From FOUNDATIONS FOR A THEORY OF CONSUMER BEHAVIOR by W. T. Tucker, pp. 133-144. Copyright © 1967 by Holt, Rinehart and Winston, Inc. Reprinted by permission of Holt, Rinehart and Winston, Inc.

[1] There are, of course, alternative formulations. The most obvious using the same notations is: $D_a \equiv AR_a - AE_a > AR_x - AE_x$, but minor changes could incorporate the notion of variable reward outcomes, each associated with some predicted probability or other such relative subtleties.

fairly large number of long division problems subconsciously.[2] Further it suggests that what we should be engaged in is a study of human anticipations and evaluation, neither of which is readily accessible to study.

In all probability the implicit assumption that such a model should be the basis for a study of consumer behavior has had more than a little to do with current distortions common to discussions of human behavior. Any beginning effort, should, it would seem, start with a simple listing of the factors, or elements or processes that seem relevant, taking considerable care not to imply relationships for which there is little supporting evidence. I would like to assert two propositions.

> Proposition 1. *Someone goes through some process and acquires something with some effect.*
> Proposition 2. *Someone uses something in some way with some effect.*

I believe that the important character of these propositions lies in what is *not* said, as much as in what is said. The elements of the first proposition are the individual, the product or service acquired, the process that includes acquisition, and the effect. Notice that the proposition does not suggest that the process is directed toward acquisition, but merely includes it. Nor is there any suggestion of what causes the effect or what is effected. Proposition 2 is similarly stripped of many possible implications. The term "uses" is meant in a reasonably broad sense.

Let it be clear that both propositions are required to cover any instance of consumer behavior and that both the *someone* and the *something* remain constant for an individual instance of consumer behavior. An example may help. Imagine a woman purchasing a box of corn flakes that she herself does not eat. We should consider first the "someone." The woman must be characterized by some definitional system unless one wishes to characterize her simply in terms of her behavior in the consumer situation. It would not be irrelevant to describe her in terms of her age, her anxieties or her social class if one were concerned with the possible relationship between these and any other element contained in the propositions. The process that includes purchase could well include putting on a coat, getting out car keys and all the other activities included in going to the store, selecting the product, paying for it, and returning home. The "something" must also be defined in relevant terms. For instance, one might include the grocery bag and savings stamps in the "something" which would then mean that throwing the bag away or folding it up and putting it in a drawer and that licking the stamps, and so forth, would have to be included in the use. The effect could include effects on the

---

[2] "In part this may be attributed to the realization that game theory is inadequate as a descriptive theory; human beings simply do not have the perception, the memory, or the logical facility assumed by any of the theories," R. Duncan Luce and Howard Raiffa, *Games and Decisions*. New York: Wiley, 1957, p. 259.

someone, the something, the process, or any other element of the situation. In fact, the assumption could well be made that there are effects on all elements included in the proposition and quite probably on other elements of the total situation such as the store or the automobile tires or the cashier.

The conclusion is that if any three elements of Proposition 1 are defined, the fourth is also defined. And the adequacy of the definition of the fourth element is a function of the adequacy of the independent definitions of the other three elements. A box of corn flakes is completely defined by the individual who purchases it, the processes involved in the purchase, and the various effects consequent in this behavioral package. For instance, on a fairly trivial level, the box of corn flakes is partially defined by the change in inventory of the store.

The portion of the behavior included in Proposition 2 for the same case includes both the woman and the corn flakes. Her use of the product may consist largely of placing it on a shelf and at some later time throwing the empty box away. (This suggests that the husband or children acquire the corn flakes from the shelf and use them in some way.) Again, a definition of the effects involved in this portion of consumer behavior, combined with definitions of the "someone" and the "something," defines the use. And any one element of the second proposition can be defined in terms of the other three.

The two propositions are, of course, simultaneous propositions. This means that an adequate definition of the someone and the something must satisfy both propositions. There is nothing at all novel in the notion. Its primary value lies in suggesting the range and direction of research required for the development of a theory of consumer behavior.

It should be obvious to any student of the subject that some elements of the propositions have been studied with considerable ingenuity and care by marketing specialists while others have received little attention. Further, some disciplines have tended to develop relatively powerful methodologies that apply to one or two elements or to interrelation between specific elements that are commonly known or utilized by students of consumer behavior. Lastly, it is obvious that very few attempts have been made to tie all of the elements together into any systematic construct.

In my opinion there is not enough reliable information available for the construction of an operational theory. While models that have aesthetic or intellectual appeal are among the delights of a computer-mathematics age, they can, when misunderstood, delay progress toward viable theory through their almost sirenlike attraction.

The closest thing to a theory of consumer behavior that exists currently is probably some decision model somewhat like that stated at the beginning of this chapter. The elements normally included in one way or another are the cost or effort involved in various actions, the relative rewards anticipated, and the perceived probability that such rewards will in fact follow. Without going into the mathematics of decision making, I would like to suggest why decision theory should be regarded as wrong-headed for the prediction of individual decisions. (I believe that it is, at its present stage of development, also inadequate as a standard for the evaluation of institutional decisions, but the basis for that belief requires a rather involved explanation that is not appropriate here.)

It is common knowledge that human-choice experiments show that people in general do not maximize their chances for reward in any usual sense, but this is often overlooked since it is intuitively obvious that they should.[3] Two of my own recent experiments seem relevant.

In the first, women were offered their choice of any one of four loaves of bread, each marked with a different symbol.[4] Twice-a-week deliveries were made to each woman's door and each made at least twelve repeated selections. In spite of the fact that all loaves of bread were as close to identical as modern, quality-control methods could assure, half of the women developed a marked brand loyalty to one of the symbols. And this brand loyalty was not easily upset by premiums (in the form of coins) placed on other brands. Further, most women tried all or several of the brands prior to demonstrating brand loyalty. There are, of course, numerous explanations for such behavior. Most of them deal with the difference between anticipated reward and objectively measured reward in one way or another. The individual cases of two of the subjects suggest some of the difficulties involved. Subject 1 chose brand P on the first trial and every subsequent trial despite premiums ranging from one to seven cents placed on another loaf. Subject 2 chose brand M on her first trial and alternated her choice each time so that no one of the four brands was ever selected on either of the two trials following its last selection. The first subject's actions can be explained in terms of habit strength, which may be conceived as increased reward anticipation or decreased effort. The second subject's behavior seems to deny either of these explanations. First, the willingness to select any loaf seems to suggest that the anticipated reward for any loaf was identical. If this were true, why should she go to the trouble of remembering which loaf she chose last time in order to avoid it on the next trial? Does one have to refer to the anticipated rewards of novelty where novelty is in fact minimized? Or should one suggest that the subject is continually exploring to determine what the char-

---

[3] R. R. Bush and F. Mosteller, *Stochastic Models for Learning.* New York: Wiley, 1955, pp. 294-300.

[4] W. T. Tucker, "The Development of Brand Loyalty," *Journal of Marketing Research,* 1, August 1964, pp. 32-35.

acteristics of the different brands are? Whatever one suggests, decision theory in the process seems to lose applicability to consumer behavior.

The second experiment attempts to test the relationship of reward, the probability of reward and effort in the most direct fashion.[5] The apparatus used is a rather large box with three lifting handles. The subject is given essentially the following instructions: Your task during the next hour is to produce 120 buzzes using this apparatus. Select any of the handles you wish and raise it; if it is the correct handle, a buzzer will sound. If the buzzer sounds, stop until the machine is reset for you to make another buzz. If the buzzer does not sound, select either of the two remaining handles. If it causes the buzzer to sound, wait for the apparatus to be reset. If it does not cause the buzzer to sound, raise the third handle, which will cause the buzzer to sound, and wait for the instructions to begin to produce the next buzz.

Since each of the handles is equally likely to be "correct" on any trial, and since the handles weigh 10, 20, and 30 pounds respectively, it would seem sensible to lift the lightest handle first, the next lightest second and the heaviest last on all trials. Subjects (college males) have shown no inclination to use that solution even when they grow tired and ask to rest. On the average, subjects have made no apparent attempt to minimize the total work required, even when given as many as 240 trials at a single session. We have a saying in our culture, "work is its own reward." There are other possible explanations involving the gambler's fallacy, the nature of the social situation, or the desire to show off one's muscularity. But, if such things influence a situation as simple as the production of buzzes on an apparatus of this sort, one might conclude that something is always operating in complex consumer behavior to confound decision-theory analysis.

It is exactly in order to prevent unwarranted reliance on algebraic models as essentially accurate explanations for behavior without empirical evidence that the two propositions suggested here are kept almost unbearably general. They do imply an element of certainty that many would not posit in relationship to any human behavior. The statement that any element in either proposition is fully defined by the other three elements is quite possibly untenable. Certainly a number of theorists would prefer to say that any element in either proposition is *probabilistically* defined by the other three elements. The restriction is surely legitimate, given the concepts and measuring instruments with which we have to deal.

---

[5] W. T. Tucker, "Human Choice Behavior: The Relationship Between Effort and Probability of Reward," *Marketing and Economic Development:* Proceedings of the American Marketing Association 1965 Fall Conference; Chicago, American Marketing Association, 1965, pp. 411-418 reports a subsequent experiment that supports the same conclusions.

One other seeming rigidity of the paradigm is its insistence that the someone and something of both propositions are identical. If there are effects included in the matter covered by Proposition 1, is it not likely that either the someone or the something may be effected and therefore become different from the someone or the something that operates in Proposition 1 before the subsequent time period covered by Proposition 2? Much as I dislike admitting this difficulty, there seems no way around it. Some change, even critical change, could occur between the purchase act and the use act. It would be hard to claim that the man who buys an engagement ring is identical with the one who breaks the engagement and returns it. The analogy with simultaneous equations is overstated, but I do not believe that it is a useless analogy.

The propositions are simply organizing and suggestive schemes or perhaps formats. It might be of interest to examine their elements and possible relations in terms of present knowledge and methodology.

Someone

The "someone" element, like the others, craves definition. The number of possible concepts and measuring instruments that can be applied to the task of definition is unbelievably large. With increasing evidence that such things as memory and intelligence have a biochemical base, a whole new range of potential measurement seems to lie just over the horizon. At present most of the paraphernalia of sociology and psychology apply, and the problem is to determine their relevance. Marketing has done most with socioeconomic variables, including geographic location, setting up descriptions or definitions that relate people to product acquisition or use in terms of markets. The enormous amount or work of this sort that has been carried out is of theoretical as well as practical value in that it has developed a reasonably broad perspective of the definitional systems applicable to the someone. Age, sex, life-cycle stage, subculture, and socioeconomic variables are clearly relevant. Work on the relevance of psychological variables has been less persuasive with studies by Westfall, Evans, and myself suggesting that we have been trying to examine appropriate variables without adequate measuring instruments or conceptual frames.[6] The oft-mentioned study by Mason Haire of instant coffee nonusers

---

[6] F. B. Evans, "Psychological and Objective Factors in The Prediction of Brand Choice: Ford Versus Chevrolet," *The Journal of Business,* 32, October, 1959, pp. 340-369.

Ralph Westfall, "Psychological Factors in Predicting Product Choice," *Journal of Marketing,* 26, April 1962, pp. 34-41.

W. T. Tucker and J. J. Painter, "Personality and Product Use," *Journal of Applied Psychology,* 45, 1961, pp. 325-329.

clearly implies that cognitions, attitudes, beliefs, and opinions form a range of constructs with which students of the subject should attempt to deal meaningfully.[7] No study has so clearly verified this as Al E. Birdwell's examination of the relationship between self-image and product image.[8]

There has long been an implicit concept that consumers can be defined in terms of either the products they acquire or use or in terms of the meanings products have for them or their attitudes toward products. Montrose S. Sommers' study is, perhaps, as explicit on this as any recent work.[9] Both he and Bob S. Hodges are currently engaged in research that should suggest how valid and useful definitional systems of this sort may be.

The Process That Includes Acquisition

The cases included in this book are highly persuasive that the process of acquisition is a much more extensive and richer process than we usually think. Juan's shirt, Paul's peach-faced parrot, or Mrs. Superscript's secondhand Cadillac seem deeply imbedded in some total-life process. To speak of the process as though it included only those actions directed toward acquisition is to misunderstand the character of consumer behavior. And to speak of the process only in terms of intentions of instrumental actions may be one of the more ridiculous conclusions of a *post hoc* sort. Attending to a Ford commercial is almost surely a significant portion of the process that includes, or passes through, the acquisition and use of a Chevrolet. It might as easily be a portion of the process that includes the purchase of a camera or the eating of an avocado. The conceptual dangers seem to be of two sorts. First there is the danger of reducing all present behavior to a function of some common past event such as toilet training. The second is the danger of excluding from the study of present behavior those portions of the process that do not seem to be instrumentally or causally linked to it, but which are nonetheless critical to an understanding of the process.

There is no intention here to deny the existence of cause-effect relationships in consumer behavior. The suggestion is simply that other sorts

---

[7] Maison Haire, "Projective Techniques in Marketing Research," *Journal of Marketing,* 14, April 1950, p. 649.

[8] Al E. Birdwell, Jr., *A Study of the Influence of Image Congruence on Consumer Choice,* Unpublished Doctoral Dissertation, University of Texas. (A summary is to appear in Proceedings American Marketing Association Conference Dec. 1964.)

[9] Montrose S. Sommers, "The Use of Product Symbolism to Differentiate Social Strata," *University of Houston Business Review,* 11, Fall 1964, pp. 1-102.

of relationships may be more common, more available to research or more critical to an understanding of the process.

Whatever the process is, it should not be considered simply a set of physical actions, although this subset may be one that can be approached most readily. Cognitive processes and interactions are surely as relevant to the process as cognitions are to the definition of consumers. It seems almost redundant to mention that social dynamics may describe portions of the process with greater accuracy than any other conceptual frames. Communications theory and all of the work on audience measurement generally impinge upon the process.

It is necessary to admit the artificiality of a distinction between the individual and what he does. Analysis always seems to sever the most important connective tissue. The legitimizing assumption about the relationship of the elements of both propositions is that any one is defined by an adequate definition of the other three. In effect, this demands the kinds of definitions that will bind the wounds of analysis. In effect, the process must be defined in terms of the someone if it is to satisfy the demands of the propositional form. Of course, it is further assumed that none of the elements can be defined out of situational context.

Reference to Margaret Mead's recent work in Indonesia may suggest the conceptual requirements without implying that hers is the only adequate methodology or even the preferred one. Not only does her work describing the activities of the people being studied include full accounts of behavioral sequences, the individuals involved, and the circumstances under which they occurred; her research team took thousands of feet of film to preserve the connectedness that even the most thorough verbal description loses.[10]

Something

The thing acquired has been variously categorized according to its class, brand, the nature of the one who acquired it, or the presumed character of the acquisition process, narrowly defined. Classification systems that divide goods into large subgroups such as durables and nondurables have uses and should not be derided for their simplicity. Nor should the customary categories such as furniture, hardware, foods, or clothing be disregarded for their obviousness. While neither system satisfies the conditions of clarity and completeness required of a nominal scale, either is so much more precise than the more pretentious nonsense of the marketing text that its directness is refreshing.

---

[10] Margaret Mead, "Retrospects and Prospects," *Anthropology and Human Behavior*. Washington, D.C.; The Anthropological Association of Washington, 1963.

More complex systems such as the categories described in terms of presumed acquisition behavior (convenience, shopping, specialty and impulse) or the new continua (red-yellow) essay considerably more than they can handle. And such casually used adjectives as "fashion" or "unwanted" should hardly be tolerated by students of the subject. There may even be doubt that marketing practitioners find them of real use except for the convenience of disregarding the fashion or unwanted aspects of certain products.

A study by Keith Cox showing the different effect on sales of different display widths for different products suggests that some existing product definitional systems may be largely unoperational.[11]

Of course, there has been almost no help from the behavioral sciences in the definition of contemporary artifacts. The result is that rather than having product definitional systems that can be utilized in the process of understanding the other elements mentioned in the propositions, it seems necessary to use the definitional systems that deal with individuals or processes in the examination of products. Since the definitional systems for individuals is probably the most extensive and possibly valid, it seems probable that our best methods for product description lie in the nature of purchasers and users and in terms of the meanings various sorts of people associate with products. For instance, we might take social class as a variable and discuss the question of whether a specific product is purchased more frequently by one class than another, used more frequently by one class than another, or takes different forms in one class than another.

The statement that 98 percent of the homes in the United States have television sets suggests that one is considering an essenially classless product. And we may assume that the sets are somehow the same since we refer to them all in the same way. But they may be quite different in nature (age, size, original cost, and such other obvious characteristics), in use, or in the meaning assigned them by their owners or users. All of this merely indicates that we are too sophisticated to classify goods in the simplest physical terms such as size or compositions and have no other useful labels or relevant continua for more appropriate definition.

The availability of the computer and the range of techniques suggested by multivariate analysis makes it clear that we can at least proceed to define products in terms of their similarity to other products in a fairly systematic manner. While some current work germaine to the problem is underway, I know of no efforts being made to tackle the question of product similarity directly.

---

[11] Keith Cox, "The Responsiveness of Food Sales to Shelf Space Changes in Supermarkets," *Journal of Marketing Research,* May 1964, pp. 63-67.

While no mention has been made of services, it should be clear that these are acquired also. In fact, what is most often acquired is some combination or package of services and products more difficult to describe than either alone. Nor is anyone sure where products leave off and services begin. It is not difficult to foresee enormous problems arising out of inadequate attempts to separate products and services or failures to take the service aura of particular products into account. At the simplest level, the presence of a guarantee may differentiate otherwise similar products.

The additional consideration of service is conceptually negligible in the total scheme of consumer behavior. It does, however, pose research considerations of no mean measure. There are no ready simplifications; only the *caveat*.

Effects

Effects *within* the system are at once the most difficult and the simplest to discuss. What can be affected? Only those things discussed as other elements. How can they be affected? Only in the terms in which they are defined.

These statements are not as trivial as they may at first appear. The cases in this volume are rather fully described, but in few of them is there more than slight opportunity to understand effects within the system. For instance, the processes involved in the Rigbys' purchase of furniture for their sons almost certainly were accompanied by cognitive changes about furniture, furniture retailers, the merchants of their own town, and a host of other things. It is not difficult to imagine what some of these were since the article itself is suggestive of their nature. But such suggestions are a far cry from measurement and satisfactory quantification of effect.

The case discussed by Pullins ends with a statement, *"At this time,* the values that Bob has placed on Budweiser and Michelob coincide with his conception of his social position." But any changes that may occur through future behavior can be located only if one measures the values with an instrument sensitive enough to examine changes, only if one has a clear definition of "coincidence," only if one can define social position with accuracy and measure Bob's conception of it.

The presence of the effect element in the propositions places major demands on the definitional system for each of the other elements, demands that might otherwise be unnoticed.

Few attempts have been made to study effects of purchase or use. The most dramatic studies relate to the purchase and use of TV sets and describe behavioral changes in relatively gross ways. Others have studied such limited relationships as that of automobile ownership and academic performance in high-school students. And there have been incidental findings such as the fact that a recent purchaser of a product is one of the most attentive persons to advertisements of the product he has purchased, suggesting that the mere act of purchase may involve particular anxieties, ambivalences, cognitive dissonance or the like. The findings could as easily suggest the individual was merely restimulating certain pleasurable processes or fantasies usually associated with the prepurchase period.

Of course, there are effects that relate to other individuals who may appear in the contextual situations of purchase or use or to other aspects of the physical situation. For instance, if the woman who purchased the corn flakes mentioned earlier purchased the last box on the supermarket shelf, her purchase could influence the behavior of a number of subsequent customers.

There seems to be little reason for going into further examples of the many sorts of effects possible.

All of the elements of Proposition 2 are like the elements in the first proposition. The consumer and the individual are identical (within the suggested limits), use is viewed as imbedded in processes just as acquisition was, and effects of the same kinds are possible; but, while it may be possible to assume identity of the individual and the product from purchase to use in many or most cases, there is the strong presumption that a subsequent instance of purchase may find many of the elements changed by the effects of the previous purchase or use or both. The propositions merely form a system for the segmentation of what is an ongoing process. The product purchased may play an important role in the process of purchasing a subsequent product as the use of an automobile implicates the purchase of gasoline and facilitates the visit to a shopping center. Processes that include the purchase of one item may include the purchase of several. Or the processes involved in the purchase of some item such as a house may span the processes involved in the purchase of a large number of others. And so the segmentation is to some extent arbitrary.

The nature of the suggested elements may tend to minimize the importance of special subportions of the purchase or use activities. A summary of the cases included in this volume would have to emphasize the lack of adequate information apparently available to the purchaser, since most of the examples stress the way in which the consumer searches for relevant knowledge, yet remains incompletely informed at the time of purchase.

An apparent shortcoming of the propositional forms used is that they insist upon both acquisition and use. The case of ToNiri's attempt to buy a house, which seems to be a coherent and complete case of consumer behavior, lacks both, if one considers the time period through the failure of his bid. Great as the temptation may be to include nonacquiring behavior sequences as consumer behavior, even relatively cursory analysis demonstrates the madness involved in attempting to discuss products not purchased. A house was not the only thing ToNiri failed to acquire. The sequence of events reported so ably by Salisbury, insofar as they are a part of some consumer behavior, refer to the purchases of lumber, nails, and other materials with which ToNiri has begun to build.

None of these shortcomings seem vital to the purposes for which the propositions are designed. Their intention is to delimit the subject of consumer behavior clearly, to state where the relevant parameters lie in relation to one another, to suggest the research that could provide satisfactory raw material for a theory, and to provide a set of standards against which any posited theory can be evaluated.

IV

MARKETING THEORY AND MARKETING MANAGEMENT

14

Marketing Theory as Marketing Management

C. WEST CHURCHMAN

Of all the ideas that man's genius has created, perhaps none have been so frustratingly elusive as "theory" and "fact." The frustration comes about because we seem so sure at times what these ideas must mean, only to have them shattered by the next breakthrough in man's history.

As Professor Martin's essay assumes, there is a perfectly reasonable sense, historically justifiable, in which "theoretical" is a property of the language man uses to describe and predict the world about him. But there is also a reasonable sense, also historically justifiable, in which "theoretical" is a property of the way in which man makes decisions in his world. It is this second sense that will concern us here. We wish to explore the concept of theoretical behavior.

The historical justification of the concept of theoretical behavior goes back many centuries, to the early Greeks. In more modern times, it arises in the fascinating notion that knowledge is a way of doing, or, as we shall prefer to say it, a certain kind of management of affairs. The underlying philosophy is pragmatism, itself an elusive but highly profitable idea occurring in man's intellectual development.

To say that knowledge is a type of management is to imply that the validity of our ideas can only be tested in the context of decision making. If the decision making is uniformly good, then the principles that led to the decisions are valid, i.e., known.

Now "theory" and "fact" are aspects of knowledge; they represent some of the things that are known well or badly. If we regard knowing to be a type of management, then we will feel impelled to regard "theory" itself as a certain kind of management activity.

In other words, to discuss a "theory of marketing" is to discuss a mode of managing marketing functions. Thus, our aim is to distinguish between "theoretical" and "nontheoretical" marketing management, and to judge to what extent the distinction makes a difference in the practical management of marketing in firms.

In order to find some guidelines, we should traverse briefly the old pathways of man's pursuit of the elusive concept of theory. Perhaps the best beginning is Democritus of the fifth century B.C. Here was an attempt to describe the behavior of all Nature in terms of a very few properties; the size, shape, and velocity of particles. Few would deny that Democritus sought a "theory" of Nature. What makes his work seem theoretical is (1) the parsimony of properties (Nature is "basically" made up of very few properties) and (2) the utter rationality of the laws (events must happen in one way only).

Both points are important in the subsequent history of ideas. When Plato describes the universe in his *Timaeus* and Euclid writes his *Elements,* both writers try to reconstruct the whole or a part of Nature by means of the fewest basic properties, and both writers assume that Nature is inherently rational in its structure.

If we were to characterize Euclid as a manager, we would say that he operated his enterprise with a strong policy theme based on an assumption that the underlying structure of the world could be recognized, and, once recognized, that his policy would operate successfully thereafter.

This conviction that Nature is inherently rational characterized the early theorists of the Greek period. The irrational for them is inherent in men and their attitudes towards Nature; the goodness of man consists in man's learning the true rationality of his environment and adapting the right attitude towards it.

The same spirit pervades in the renaissance of science and philosophy in the seventeenth century. Leibniz tells us that there are various ways in which decision makers manage their affairs, but the most perfect manager is God. God requires no information from outside and perceives all things analytically, i.e., deduces all events precisely and perfectly. He is an ideal, self-contained inquiring system; for example, the time required to compute any finding, no matter how complicated, is exactly zero. The less ideal minds of Leibniz' world perceive less clearly, compute more slowly, make more errors, and have to use information as a crutch to compensate for their inadequacies. Reality is supremely rational: minds of finite intelligence introduce noise, uncertainty, obscurity, irrationality.

It was the empiricists of the seventeenth and eighteenth centuries who argued so strongly against this type of theoretical manager. For John

Locke, the mind starts with very little, and only after a long struggle does it come to learn about the rationality of the world. It starts by being meagerly theoretical. Nevertheless, Locke did maintain the other facet of Platonic theory: there are only a few basic qualities with which the mind begins. Everything is constructed from these few types of inputs for the system.

The most significant thing that Locke did was to place the rationality of the world in the inquirer himself. Or, rather, to be historically accurate, it was Hume and especially Kant who showed that a mind that learns only from raw inputs must construct its own connections between these inputs. In Kant's philosophy, the inputs are so raw that the inquiring system cannot tell them apart unless it imposes a rationality upon them. "Telling apart" requires a concept of space and time, and the laws of space and time are the contribution of the inquirer.

In management terms, Kant's thesis is that information is as much a matter of managing as are the other practical decisions the manager makes. The most important managerial decision to be made about information is interpretation. The interpretation of information is a matter of inferring what the information means. If the manager is willing to assume a great deal about reality, he will interpret information in very rich terms, whereas if he is skeptical about how reality is going to behave, he will interpret information in very sparse terms. For example, a sales manager may assume that his markets are all stable; he interprets last year's data to imply an accurate picture of this year's demand. Another manager may not want to assume anything at all about the stability of demand; he interprets last year's sales to be last year's sales and nothing else. It is to be emphasized that these two managers could not resolve their conflict by hiring an expert statistician according to today's concept of statistics. The statistician himself adopts either strong assumptions about reality or very weak assumptions; what makes him an expert is not contained in his willingness to assume or not to assume.

Now, both these managers understand their problem to be one of using information that is in some sense "given." The question is: "given" by what? By a rational outside world? If all we have is what is given, then this "outside" world is unknown, unconscious, unreflective, and (as Berkeley put it) unnecessary.

David Hume tried to show that the so-called regularity of these inputs and the conviction that they will reoccur in the same patterns as they had in the past is a matter of habit for the mind. The manager simply becomes used to regularity.

The tactical problem of these managers is, therefore, one of deciding how much order to impose on what is given. Immanuel Kant tried to provide one guide for the manager in this connection. His thesis is that the manager must impose a minimal rationality, because otherwise he won't be able to recognize any information at all. Specifically, he must assume that he can divide the world into the past and the future and that objects can be structured in space. In order to do this, the information system requires a clock and geometrical measuring rods. The clocks and the rods presuppose a modicum of logic, arithmetic, geometry, kinematics, and mechanics. In other words, numbers, points, lines, planes, spaces, times, and masses exist because the information system operates that way, and we know of no other way for it to operate.

Although Kant showed to his own satisfaction that there must be a future if there is a past, he provided no help in showing what this future must be. It must be a future with a clock, a ruler, and a compass. But this is small consolation to a skittish manager who believes that Nature—including his competitors—may trick him, unless one could show (which Kant could not) that a world with a clock must be highly predictable.

Thus, there are two types of information managers: the bold and the cautious. Since neither manager is "theoretical," in the sense of Democritus, Plato, and Leibniz, let us call the bold one the generalizer, and the cautious one the particularizer.

The particularizer says that one cannot forecast. He likes to show how past attempts to forecast prices have been no better than random predictions, and then—very inconsistently to be sure—he asserts that therefore no one can forecast: *he* forecasts an infinity of failures to beat chance. The generalizer believes that the task is to interpret the data, and that interpretation includes the art of making a priori assumptions. So he tries—over and over—to predict what will happen, and he acts on his assumptions. Both particularizer and generalizer are fundamentally skeptical about the basic rationality of Nature: the flow of inputs may be—or may not be—a pattern. The flow itself is essentially nonrational, that is, does not originate from known rational causes.

Thus, the bit of the history of thought we have just reviewed reveals three types of management:

1. Theorizer—A management based on the assumption that reality is rational (predictable), and hence the task of the manager is to remove the randomness and obscurity of his own thinking in order to become as much like reality as possible.

2. Generalizer—A management based on the assumption that reality is nonrational, but that the task of the manager is to construct a strong structure within which the raw inputs from reality may be given the fullest possible weight.

3. Particularizer—A management based on the assumption that reality is irrelevant, and that the task of the manager is to permit maximum flexibility of decision making so as to meet the requirements imposed by the data.

In language more familiar to the student of management, the particularizer is an opportunist; the generalizer, a planner; the theoretician, an idealist.

As is true of all lessons learned from history, it is necessary to go beyond what our forebearers said and try to capture their intent in our own language. The three descriptions given above are vague and somewhat useless, until we couch them in a language more familiar to current analysis.

The life of any decision maker may be considered as a string of decisions made at specific points of time. At these points of time, the decision maker has choices. Therefore, throughout his history he is creating his life by choosing one decision rather than another. At the beginning, he confronts a fantastic array of alternatives lives; as he near the end, he finally decides just one life, which is his biography.

Attached to any life-in-prospect for the decision maker is a value or perhaps a set of values, depending upon the viewpoint of the observer. For purposes of discussion, assume that this value, or these values, can be fully described by a number on a scale, or a vector of numbers. Thus, each life L_1, L_2, L_3, etc., is a member of a set L. Associated with each L_i is a value V_i. Each L_i is a string of decisions D_{jk}. The subscript j refers to the point in time, the subscript k to the particular, physical decision that might occur at such a point. Thus j ranges over the decision-making episodes of the life, while k ranges over the alternative decisions that can be made at any episode. The total set of D_{jk} is designated by D.

We shall want to assume some things about decision-making lives. Indeed, we have already assumed that their values can be represented along appropriate scales. Furthermore, we shall want to say that an act is a decision only if its adoption changes the value of the life to which it belongs. Suppose L_i is a life with a string of decisions D_{jk}. The notation "$L_i - D_{jk}$" designates a class of lives in which, at time t_j, the decision D_{jk} does not occur, though every other decision in L_i remains. In other words, at time t_j, $L_i - D_{jk}$ contains a decision other than D_{jk}. We note that the operator "$-$" is intended to be closed with respect to L; that is, given any L_i with D_{jk} at time t_k, there exists at least one L_m belonging to L which is like L_i in all respects except that it contains no D_{jk} at t_k. The assumption we have made about decisions is that the value of L_i differs from the value of any member of $L_i - D_{jk}$. In effect, this assumption simply groups together into one decision all physically distinct acts that have the same effect on the value of a life. We assume that the points of time are so chosen that every life contains a decision at every point of time.

Next, we introduce the concept of a policy. A policy is a life with an underlying theme. That is, an observer of the life can depict the pattern of the life by some rule. He sees, for example, that the life was trying to accomplish a goal or avoid a certain kind of act. Apparently, we are struggling to define something here that is quite obscure. To avoid the obscurity, without really solving the problem, we introduce a set of rules R. A rule is a device that, at any time t_k, selects a proper nonempty subset of the alternative decisions. If it selects one and only one decision at each t, it is a rigid rule; if it selects more than one (but not all), it is a constraining rule. Thus, each rule selects a proper subclass of L. We say that a life is governed by a policy if it belongs to the subclass selected by some member of R.

This way of defining policies does not really solve the basic problem, because one can always define a rigid rule for any given life by simply having the rule select the decisions that actually were made. The intent, of course, is that R contains only rules that the decision maker himself generated at the outset of a series of decisions.

In order to make this stipulation more precise, we introduce the concept of a "preparatory" decision. One decision prepares the way for another decision if it makes the latter possible. This notion is not too difficult to capture within the symbolism already adopted. Imagine a life with decision D_{11} at time t_1 and D_{22} at time t_2. Suppose D_{11} is removed; i.e., we consider the class of all lives $L - D_{11}$. If none of these contain D_{22}, we say that D_{11} prepared for D_{22}. A more general and more useful way to define preparation is to say that D_{11} prepares for D_{22}, if all lives containing both have higher value than the corresponding lives containing D_{22} but not D_{11}.

I have chosen this fairly elaborate way to define preparatory decisions in order to be able to describe any kind of decision maker and his life, whether living or machine, individual or social. In lives with a heavy emphasis on preparatory decisions, the decision maker is a planner. He devotes a greater deal of his potential resources to setting up for later decisions. Indeed, if we think of preparatory decisions in the same way in which we think of setup procedures in production, then we can say that the setup cost is a decision itself, and that the planner tends to decide to make this cost high. Continuing the analogy with production, this means that he tends to make strong commitments, just as a high setup in inventory theory implies large inventories.

In order to make the concept of a commitment clearer, we can return to the formalism introduced above. The lives of decision makers are pathways of decisions. Sometimes the pathways break into many choices at each episode, while at other times, there are very few choices. In some cases, the decision maker will start to follow one path, i.e., to adopt one theme, but may find that this theme is unsatisfactory. If he has left himself flexible, he can change his theme without drastically changing the overall value of his life; if he has committed himself, he cannot feasibly reverse his theme. Thus, a life is reversible if, once a decision has been made, it is possible later on to adopt other decisions that nullify the cost of the first decision.

To make this concept of reversibility clearer, suppose a decision maker has adopted decision D_{11} at time t_1. He now pursues his life until time t_j, when he comes to regret his earlier choice. At this point, there may be a decision D_{jk} available to him that nullifies the effect of D_{11}. In other words, at t_j he can choose a life containing D_{jk} with a value equal to a life not containing D_{11}. He can pursue his life "as though" D_{11} had never occurred. Thus, a decision D_{11} is reversible at time t_j if there exists in L two lives with the following properties: (a) one contains D_{11} and the other does not; (b) both contain the same decisions between t_1 and t_j; (c) the one containing D_{11} does not contain D_{jk} at time t_j, while the other does; (d) the lives are the same after t_j; and (e) the value of the two lives is the same.

A decision is irreversible if no decision can reverse it at a later period of time during the life of the decision maker. Evidently, reversibility could become a matter of degree, depending on how much a later decision can erase the value introduced by an earlier one. I assume that the more a life tends towards preparatory decisions, the greater the irreversibility of its decisions. In other words, one who plans thoroughly commits himself to the decisions his plan dictates.

The planner, then, is one who adopts policies (lives with a theme) with preparatory and consequently irreversible decisions. The opportunist prepares minimally and commits himself least; the theme of his life is much more difficult to discern, except in vague terms like happiness or profit maximization. The opportunist, therefore, lets the day-to-day data tell him how to respond. He is the operationally oriented manager in the sense that he tries to overcome the difficulties as they occur. One could find a theme for his life only if one could forecast the difficulties; but forecasting is a preparatory decision he tends to shun.

Nothing in the above discussion indicates which manager is "best," and man has always recognized the problem of prejudging by posing contradictory maxims: "Rome (O Great Irreversible Decision!) was not built in a day," and "He who hesitates (plans?) is lost."

The planning manager leads a life very much like the cognitive life of a so-called theoretical scientist. The opportunistic scientist plans minimally for the next experiment and lets the results of the experiment tell him what to do next. Nowadays, he finds contentment in the application of experimental designs and the analysis of variance and covariance. He thinks of himself as exploring a vast area and being able to travel from one site to another with no loss of energy. Since he has no real a priori conviction about the outcome of an experiment, he is rarely disappointed intellectually. The generalizer, on the other hand, works for months building up an elaborate conceptual structure; only then does he permit himself to test his concepts. He can be terribly disappointed or marvelously overjoyed. But in either event, the next choice becomes an outcome of his preparatory structure building. Like it or not, his intellectual decisions tend to become less and less reversible the older he gets. A single datum, on the other hand, tends to become more and more important.

As for the generalizing manager, he believes in long-range planning, operations research, systems design, and all the other tools of management that emphasize the larger point of view. The opportunist believes in cases, daily or weekly accounts, and other factual reports. He believes in seeing his subordinates on the scene. He believes that on-the-spot tactics are more important than vague and general strategies.

If one were to try to characterize the shift in management that has occurred in the last two decades in America, it would be safe to say that it has become less opportunist and more planning. In recent years, the shift has become most apparent in marketing management.

What of marketing theory, then? At the beginning of the essay, it was argued that there is a distinction between the true theorizer and the generalizer. In ordinary academic discussions, the distinction is rarely made. This is because the American scientific community has practically forgotten the rationalist philosophy that initiated its modern history. The theorizer believes that reality is rational, and that irrationality, randomness, and the like are the making of the inquiring mind. The generalizer, on the other hand, believes in order, too, but he believes that order is what he imposes on chaos.

To the mind of Leibniz's God, there is no "given." "Data," for Leibniz, are the devices that poorer minds use to cope with reality; data are contingent, uncertain, obscure. Yet, a modern scientist would argue that objectivity, the cornerstone of science, is to be found in data—what is given. The planning manager tries his best to prepare for what will come, but he ultimately believes that what will come will be given to him, as an "input." "Information" is the input he cannot plan. Or can he?

Suppose he asks himself this question: after all, since my plans do change the world and hence also the information I eventually receive, what is it that my plans cannot change? What is really, fundamentally, irretrievably given? If he does ask himself this question, he is on the way to becoming a theorizer as well as a generalizer.

One response he may make is this: the past is irretrievably given. It is *given* that last year we sold 1,000 items of so-and-so. But is it? In the life of the manager, it is not what was sold that matters but why it was sold. Can he create an answer to the "why"?

Suppose we are observing a man looking at a white swan. One question the man could pose to himself is: *given* this white swan, are all swans white? Another and more interesting question is this: to what degree is this a white swan? A manager may ask: *given* these sales last year, what will the sales be next year? Another and far more interesting question is: to what degree is this a sale? As soon as we begin to regard nature in depth rather than extension, we ask why rather than what. To learn that a swan has degrees of whiteness is to learn why the swan appears white to our eyes. To learn that a customer is sold in degrees of conviction is to learn why he appears to be someone we sold to last year. In both cases, the "given" becomes the start of a problem, not the answer. To ask why a swan appears white is the start of an inquiry in which the so-called induction to "all swans are white" is irrelevant. It is to understand that recording a swan as white is a delicate decision. To ask why a customer appears to be sold is also the start of an inquiry in which forecasts of next year's sales based on this year's sales are irrelevant. It is to understand that recording a sale is a delicate decision. To record some transaction as a sale when the customer is truly dissatisfied, or truly erratic, or truly dead, is to make a foolish decision.

The theorizer is therefore the supreme questioner. He questions in depth as well as extension. One of the greatest insights of modern philosophy is E. A. Singer's dictum that to ask a question is to assume an answer. The question-asker assumes that answers "exist." He also assumes that any reply he may give to a question is no more than one response among many. *The* answer is an ideal, and yet, it must exist. Reality is the ideal end of all question asking.

When a decision maker lives his life, he asks a question. The empiricist believes that when the life is over, then finally the answer to the question will be given. At this point, at life's end, the question asker is, for the planner and opportunist, completely passive. To the theorizer, a life is also a question, but at its end, there is only a response, one part of the whole that makes up the final answer. He believes that all these responses, in some rational but obscure way, go to make up the meaning of a life. The way is obscure, because we cannot accept the simple rationality of our philosophical predecessors, who defined the rational in terms of the logically consistent. Whatever modern rationality is, it must be far richer in meaning than the logically consistent: it must include contradiction, opposition, conflict, evil, as well as consistency, sameness, cooperation, and good.

Marketing theory is at least a proposal for a generalizing rather than a particularizing marketing management—for planning rather than for opportunity. It may sometime become a proposal for a theorizing marketing management as well—for a management that knows how to ask questions.

15

Development of a Framework for a Theory of Marketing Planning

PRESTON P. LE BRETON

At all levels of business and government we are witnessing a renewed interest in the important activity of planning. This current interest highlights again the need for a theoretical framework which would be useful as a guide for all planners regardless of their institutional affiliation (wholesale, retail, manufacturing, banking), functional assignment (advertising, selling, marketing research, buying), or level within an organization (president, vice-president of marketing, sales manager, advertising manager). One conceptual scheme found useful to the author is developed in this paper. It has as its components three parts: the planning process, the dimensions or characteristics of a plan, and the influence a given set of dimensions have on the planning process.

In developing a framework for a Theory of Marketing Planning we are faced with two major questions: (1) What is meant by a Theory of Marketing Planning? (2) How might the usefulness of a particular Theory of Marketing Planning be judged? To understand the meaning of a Theory of Marketing Planning it is helpful first to examine the definitions of "theory," "marketing," and "planning."

The definition of a theory as presented in Webster's New Collegiate Dictionary would appear to be quite satisfactory. A theory is defined there as "A more or less plausible or scientifically acceptable principle offered to explain phenomena." A plan can be thought of as a predetermined course of action. Planning is the process fol-

Reprinted with permission from *Emerging Concepts in Marketing*, William S. Decker, ed. (Chicago: American Marketing Association, 1963), pp. 265-278. Professor Le Breton wishes to note that much of the material used in this paper came from his book *Planning Theory*, Prentice-Hall, Inc., 1961.

lowed in preparing a course of action. In the 1957 issue of the *Journal of Marketing,*[1] a useful definition of marketing is given: "Marketing implies integration of all functions in moving any type of goods or services from production to the final user."

A Theory of Marketing Planning can thus be defined as an attempt at an explanation of how a course of action is or may be determined for the various functions of marketing.

How To Judge The Usefulness of A Theory

In answering the second question as to how to best judge the usefulness of a particular theory of marketing planning, reference can be made to the views of Professor H. Koontz, who was speaking with reference to the same problem in the field of management. His observations are equally applicable to the field of marketing. They appeared in a recent issue of the *Harvard Business Review* [2] in an article entitled, "Making Sense of Management Theory." His comments were as follows:

If we are to clarify management theory, as I hope we eventually will (with the help of experienced managers), we will need special criteria to make our studies more understandable and useful to the business man. Here are the yardsticks by which such a theory might be judged:

1. A theory should deal with an area of knowledge and inquiry that is "manageable"; no great advances in scientific knowledge were made as long as man contemplated the whole universe.

2. A theory should be useful in improving management practice, and the tasks and needs of the executive himself must be the central focus.

3. No theory should be hampered by semantic obstacles; useless jargon not understandable to the practicing manager should be eliminated.

4. An effective theory should give direction and efficiency to management research and teaching.

5. Finally, a worthwhile theory must recognize that it is but a part of a large universe of knowledge and theory and need not actually encompass that universe.

Although Professor Koontz is talking about management theory, his position is transferable to a discussion of marketing planning theory.

---

[1] H. Bund and J. W. Carroll, "The Changing Role of the Marketing Function," *Journal of Marketing,* (1957), Vol. 21, p. 271.

[2] Harold Koontz, "Making Sense of Management Theory," *Harvard Business Review,* (1962), Vol. 40, p. 46.

Where Does the Planning Concept Fit?

The basic model to be used is made up of two parts—planning and implementation. Most scholars will recognize this model as a variation of the process model which usually includes planning, organizing, controlling, staffing, directing and perhaps coordinating. This model can be called a modified process model.

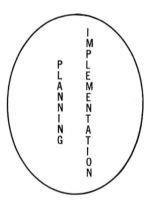

In the context of the discussion at hand, the model can be viewed under two broad conditions: (1) within an institution which is primarily a marketing institution, such as wholesale or retail establishments, or (2) within another economic institution where marketing is simply one of many functions performed, such as manufacturing or finance institutions.

This modified-process model will assist anyone interested in obtaining a better understanding of a marketing institution, a marketing division or department or a sub-unit of a marketing division or department. The discussion up to this point has dealt with the overall modified process model which consists of both planning and implementation. The remainder of the paper will be concerned solely with the planning phase of the model, specifically as it applied to marketing planning.

The Planning Model—Basic Framework[3]

The planning model is made up of two significant components: the Planning Procedure and Dimensions or characteristics of a Plan. The key to the development of a theory of planning is found in the relationship of

---

[3] Preston P. LeBreton and Dale A. Henning, *Planning Theory,* (New Jersey: Prentice-Hall, Inc., 1961).

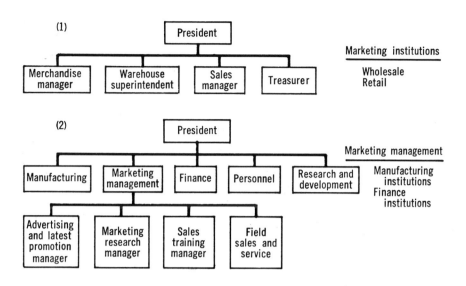

(1) President — Merchandise manager, Warehouse superintendent, Sales manager, Treasurer

Marketing institutions
Wholesale
Retail

(2) President — Manufacturing, Marketing management, Finance, Personnel, Research and development

Marketing management
Manufacturing institutions
Finance institutions

Marketing management — Advertising and latest promotion manager, Marketing research manager, Sales training manager, Field sales and service

The modified process model is universal in application in that it applies at all levels:

☐ President
☐ Division head
☐ Department head
☐ Section head

across all functions:

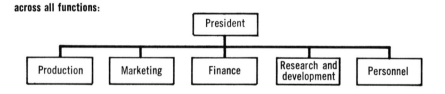

President — Production, Marketing, Finance, Research and development, Personnel

to all organizations:

both economic

Bank   Retail hardware   Wholesale drug

and non-economic

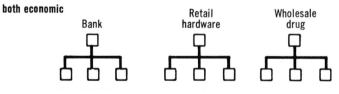

Medical   Educational   Political

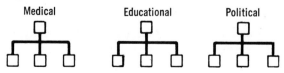

the dimensions of a plan to the planning procedure. As stated previously, the basic responsibility of a marketing executive consists of the preparation and implementation of a wide variety of plans. Some plans are fairly simple, of little significance to the operation and occur infrequently. Other plans are highly complex, of great importance and occur fairly frequently. The intensity with which each dimension or characteristic occurs in a given plan has an important influence on the way in which the marketing executive is likely to carry out his planning activity.

Dimensions of a Plan

The number of dimensions of a plan is determined by how restrictive or elaborate a definition one wishes to give the basic descriptive characteristics of any plan. Sixteen dimensions have been found to be useful for purposes of analysis. All plans have the following dimensions:

1.	Complexity	9.	Flexibility
2.	Significance	10.	Frequency
3.	Comprehensiveness	11.	Confidential nature
4.	Time	12.	Formality
5.	Duration	13.	Authorization
6.	Uniqueness	14.	Ease of gaining approval
7.	Specificity	15.	Ease of implementation
8.	Completeness	16.	Ease of control

A useful way of defining each dimension is to view the various factors which influence the degree of intensity with which each dimension occurs.

The *complexity* or simplicity of a plan is a function of the number of major components within a plan, the number of alternatives useful in evaluating each component, the established objectives, policies and procedures of the company, the technical nature of the subject matter, and the divisibility of the plan and its components.

The *significance* or lack of importance of a plan is a function of the cost of preparing and/or implementing a plan, the anticipated increase in efficiency and quality of service or increase in savings or revenue.

The *comprehensiveness* or narrowness of organizational impact of the plan is a function of the number of organization units likely to be significantly effected by the plan and the number of organization units from which data will be furnished or acquired.

The *time* available for preparing a given plan relative to the normal time requirement is a function of the rapidity of unexpected change occurring within the environment, the nature of the plan and the effectiveness of the internal and external control system.

The *duration* or life expectancy of a plan is a function of the nature of the plan, the dynamics of the environment, the leadership role and philosophy of the organization and the accuracy of the existing plan.

The *uniqueness* or similarity of a plan is a function of the lack of similarity of the present plan to previous plans in one or more significant phases of the planning procedure.

The *specificity* or generalness of a plan is a function of the nature of the assignment, the nature and availability of the data to be used, the nature of useful alternatives, and the existing company policies and procedures.

The *completeness* or incompleteness of a plan is a function of the nature of the assignment, the nature and availability of data to be used and the existing company policies and procedures.

The *flexibility* or restrictiveness of a plan is a function of the nature of the assignment, the nature of data to be used, the nature of useful alternatives and the existing company policies and procedures.

The *frequency* or infrequency of a plan is a function of the degree of permanence associated with the elements of a plan, the dynamics of the economy and/or environment, the institution's policy regarding innovation, the leadership role in areas of competition and the total capacity of the firm, human and material.

The *confidential* nature or non-confidential nature of a plan is a function of the competitive advantage that lies in secrecy, the extent of ill-will that would be created among all persons connected with the organization if the plans were known in advance and the personal nature of the information contained in the plan.

The *formality* or informality of a plan is a function of the level of authorization for preparation of the plan, the level of contacts required within or outside the organization, the level at which plan will be approved, the company policies and procedures, the data requirements for the plan and the decision requirements and their influence on planning tools and techniques.

The *authorization* or non-authorization of a plan is a function of the explicit authority of the planner, the company policies and procedures, and the general philosophy of management relative to decentralization of authority.

The ease or difficulty of *gaining approval* of a plan is a function of the complexity of subject matter covered, the emotional response likely to be engendered in those responsible for its approval, the internal logic of the plan, the way in which the planning process is performed, the degree of change to be brought about as a result of the new plan, and the magnitude of gain or loss relative to the degree of likelihood of success or failure.

The ease or difficulty of *implementation* of a plan is a function of the complexity of subject matter covered, the emotional response likely to be engendered in those responsible for its implementation, the internal logic of the plan, the way in which the planning process is performed and the degree of change to be brought about as a result of the new plan.

The ease or difficulty of *control* of a plan is a function of the preciseness and accuracy with which premises can be established, the accuracy of the plan, the preciseness and accuracy with which standards of performance can be established, the effectiveness of measuring tools available and the feed-back mechanism provided in the plan.

The range of intensity with which a dimension might occur across many plans is illustrated below.

COMPLEXITY

Simple	Fairly Complex	Complex	Highly Complex	Extremely Complex

SIGNIFICANCE

Insignificant	Fairly Significant	Significant	Highly Significant	Extremely Significant

COMPREHENSIVENESS

Restricted (One organization level)	Fairly	Comprehensive	Highly	Extremely Comprehensive (Entire organization)

DURATION OF THE PLAN

Short Range	Fairly Long Range	Long Range	Very Long Range	Extremely Long Range

Planning Procedure

For purposes of analysis, the planning procedure can be divided into the following fourteen steps:

1. Becoming aware of a possible need for formulating a plan.
2. Formulating a precise statement of the objective of the plan to be prepared.
3. Preparing a broad outline of the proposal.
4. Obtaining approval of the proposal.
5. Organizing planning staff and assigning responsibility.
6. Determining the specific outline of the plan.
7. Establishing contact with all cooperating units.
8. Obtaining necessary data.
9. Evaluating data.

10. Formulating tentative conclusions and preparing tentative plans.

11. Testing components of tentative plans and making adjustments where appropriate.

12. Preparing the final plan.

13. Testing the plan and making adjustments where necessary.

14. Obtaining approval of the plan.

Most of the steps in the planning procedure are easily understood. A few steps deserve additional explanation. Steps 3 and 4 are appropriate only when the initiative is taken by the planner or it is deemed important by him to get prior approval before embarking on the remaining steps of the planning procedure. With some plans, it may be very difficult to prepare a specific outline for all components of the plan. Step 6 is still valuable and practicable if the interpretation is "determining as far as possible" the specific outline of the plan. At times steps 8 and 9 can be treated almost simultaneously because some information may be discussed and evaluated at the time it is gathered. Components of tentative plans are tested for "acceptance level" as well as accuracy of data and intellectual soundness of a decision.

The testing of a final plan may be of little practical importance when the various components are not intimately related and when the components have been properly tested before the final plan is prepared.

A step by step progression within the planning procedure worked out extremely well when tested against actual practice.[4] However, the accomplishment of one step may be satisfactory at a given stage in the planning procedure but may require revision in the light of activities performed at a more advanced stage of the planning procedure. For example, as a result of testing components of a tentative plan, Step 11, it may be necessary to repeat Steps 8, 9, and 10.

Influence of Dimensions Upon the Planning Process

Central to the thesis of this paper is the proposition that as the dimensions of a plan vary significantly in intensity, their influence on one or more steps of the planning process will also vary. For ease of analysis the recommended fourteen steps in the planning procedure have been reduced to eight parts as follows:

A. Establish means for the early determination of need for formulating a new plan or revising an existing plan.

B. Take special care to prepare the proposal in terms easily understood by the approving agent. This may include the use of non-technical terms and examples to clarify the proposal.

---

[4] Refinement of the original planning theory resulted from a research project undertaken in 1961. "Dimensions of a Plan and Their Influence on the Planning Process," *Western Management Science Institute,* (1961).

C. Include on the planning staff representatives or consultants who possess the necessary technical knowledge and experience not possessed by the planner.

D. Include on the planning staff representatives from major organization units which will be affected by the plan.

E. Make formal contact with cooperating units to insure understanding of the nature of the project and the role to be played by the cooperating units.

F. Use sophisticated tools for data collection and processing as well as for decision-making.

G. Subject significant components of the plan to careful tests to determine the soundness of the plan and to discover possible difficulties in attempting to gain approval of the plan.

H. Prepare the final plan in such a way that it is not only technically accurate but also persuasive in nature and easy to understand by approving and implementing units.

To avoid excessive repetition of each part of the planning procedure, as it occurs, only the letters A, B, C, D, E, F, G, or H are used to designate the areas of influence. Research suggests the following hypotheses stand up satisfactorily under empirical testing:

As a plan becomes highly *complex* there is a greater likelihood that the planner will find it advantageous to take special care to prepare the proposal in terms easily understood by the approving agent, (this may include the use of non-technical terms and examples to clarify the proposal), to include on the planning staff representatives or consultants who possess the necessary technical knowledge and experience not possessed by the planner, to make formal contact with cooperating units to insure understanding of the nature of the project and the role to be played by the cooperating units, to use sophisticated tools for data collection and processing as well as for decision-making, to subject significant components of the plan to careful tests to determine the soundness of the plan and to discover possible difficulties in attempting to gain approval of the plan, and to prepare the final plan in such a way that it is not only technically accurate but also persuasive in nature and easy to understand by approving and implementing units.

As a plan becomes highly *significant* there is a greater likelihood that the planner could gain considerable benefit from Items A, B, C, D, E, G, H.

As the effect of a plan *extends* across several organizational lines there is a greater likelihood that the planner could gain considerable benefit from Item D.

As the available planning *time* relative to normal planning time is significantly reduced there is a greater likelihood that the planner could gain considerable benefit from Item C.

As the *duration* of the plan extends over a considerable period of time there is a greater likelihood that the planner could gain considerable benefit from Items A, B, C, D, E, F, G, and H.

When a plan is *unique* there is a greater likelihood that the planner could gain considerable benefit from Items A, B, C, D, E, F, G, and H.

When a plan is highly *general* there is a greater likelihood that the planner could gain considerable benefit from Items C, D, G, and H.

When a plan is highly *incomplete* there is a greater likelihood that the planner could gain considerable benefit from Items C, D, G, and H.

When a plan is highly *flexible* there is a greater likelihood that the planner could gain considerable benefit from Items B and H.

When a plan is prepared very *frequently* there is a greater likelihood that the planner could gain considerable benefit from Item A.

When a plan becomes highly *confidential* there is a greater likelihood that the planner could gain considerable benefit from Items E and G.

As a plan becomes highly *formal* there is a greater likelihood that the planner could gain considerable benefit from Item E.

When the preparation of a plan is *approved* from high authority there is a greater likelihood that the planner could gain considerable benefit from Items A, C, E, G, and H.

As a planner anticipates considerable difficulty in *gaining approval* of a plan there is a greater likelihood that the planner could gain considerable benefit from Items A, B, C, D, E, F, G, and H.

As a planner anticipates considerable difficulty of *implementation* there is a greater likelihood that the planner could gain considerable benefit from Items A, C, D, F, G, and H.

As a planner anticipates considerable difficulty of *control* there is a greater likelihood that the planner could gain considerable benefit from Items A, C, D, E, F, G, and H.

It should be noted that it is extremely difficult, if not impossible, to measure the impact of a slight degree of change in intensity of dimensions upon steps within the planning procedure.

Subtheories of Planning

Once the planner has determined the intensity of each dimension and its likely impact on the planning procedure, he is in a position to begin the planning process. At this point the planner has only a general guide to direct him. He knows, for example, that for a highly comprehensive plan he should consider the reasonableness of seeking the assistance of representatives of several sub-units within the organization. If the plan under consideration should also be highly complex and significant, he might wish to consider bringing in consultants or, at least, adding internal specialists to the planning group.

For the planner to be in a position to maximize his contribution to the planning process, he should know something more in addition to the above. For example, he should know how to organize and motivate specialists, how to gather and interpret information needed for a plan, and how to select a desirable course of action from many alternatives.

The knowledge needed by the planner to carry out his total responsibility can be obtained in large part from several sub-theories which relate directly to planning. Over-all planning theory can be divided into the following sub-theories:

> Theory of need determination
> Theory of choice
> Theory of data collection and processing
> Theory of testing
> Theory of organizing for planning
> The role of communication theory in planning
> The role of persuasion theory in planning

The relationship of the sub-theories of planning to the planning procedure can be illustrated as shown on the following page.

Dimensions of a Plan—Relationship to Sub-Theories

Once the planner has a complete grasp of the above theories, he is in a position to relate more specifically the dimensions of a plan to each step in the planning procedure. Three examples will serve to illustrate this point:

The greater the significance of a plan, the greater the likelihood that the planner will find it advantageous to

> —use formal controls and audits to gauge the progress of an existing plan

Need —use perpetual study, management observation and contemplation, and management suggestions to seek out ideas for new plans or to make present plans obsolete

> —spend considerable time, effort and money to develop a rapid, accurate feedback on results of current plans and to develop all useful sources of new ideas
> —include a greater variety of alternatives

Choice   —use sophisticated techniques to project the value and degree of certainty of future inputs and outputs

—use sophisticated techniques of decision-making

—add to the planning staff members specifically qualified to perform the testing function

—use sophisticated tools and techniques for testing

Testing   —spend considerable time, effort and money in testing

—supply elaborate test results with the basic plan when it is submitted for approval.

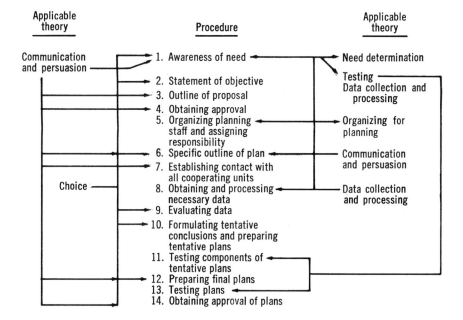

Principle of Interrelation of Dimensions

The principle can be stated as follows: All dimensions of a plan are inter-related and thus exert a combined influence on the planning process.

The greater the ease of implementation, ease of control, specificity, frequency, authority, completeness, the easier the obtaining of coopera-tion at all stages, the shorter the full period between authorization of a major project and its completion.

The greater the comprehensiveness, complexity, and significance, the higher the level in the organization for approving a plan, the greater the need for exercising tight control and coordination, the greater the likeli-hood that the planner will use group or committee action rather than single action in carrying out the planning process.

Principle of Primacy of Dimensions

The principle can be stated as follows: When two or more dimensions occur with one or more relatively high and one or more relatively low on the intensity scale (complexity high-significance low, for example) one or more dimensions will take priority over other dimensions and thus exert a primary influence over the planning process. Primacy of a dimension is a function of the nature of the plan, the dimension itself, the intensity of the dimension, and the direction and intensity of other dimensions.

Summary and Conclusion

The basic planning framework which was examined in this paper consisted of three parts: the planning procedure, the dimensions of a plan, and the relationship of dimensions of a plan to the planning procedure. The planning framework was viewed as part of a larger management model which also included implementation.

The assumption was made that the planning-implementation model is a useful model for viewing the basic responsibilities of all executives within all organizations. The marketing executive faced with the task of preparing a multiplicity of plans might benefit from following the recommended steps. One of his first acts would be to separate his total task into major components such as market research, advertising, and selling. For each of these major components he may wish to determine the intensity with which each dimension occurs and the likely impact of each dimension upon the planning procedure he has chosen. With the above determination as a guide, he is then able to maximize the likelihood that a good plan will be prepared.

The development of a theory of planning allows the planner to gain a better understanding of why things happen as they do. At best, a good theory will allow the planner to predict the likely results of a given course of action.

16

Uncertainty, Information, and Marketing Decisions

PAUL E. GREEN

Marketing's potential as a scientific discipline is the subject of much current debate. Probably less moot, however, is the assertion that the continued development of marketing theory will depend in large part on the adaptation of concepts and techniques drawn from other fields.

The present state of marketing theory already reflects the impact of other disciplines. Portions of microeconomic theory play a large part in contemporary normative marketing. The value of a behavioralistic approach to marketing has been ably demonstrated by Alderson.[1] The efforts of Kuehn and other mathematically oriented researchers have resulted in the use of Markov processes as models for the prediction of brand-share levels over time.[2] The area of physical distribution appears particularly amenable to the construction and testing of mathematical models.

Still another pair of disciplines, decision theory and information theory, show promise for contributing to the growth of marketing theory. The nature of these new developments and their potential applicability to managerial decision making in marketing are discussed in this essay. Considerable emphasis will be placed on the applicability of these techniques to the theory and design of marketing research activity. At times describ-

Reprinted from *Theory in Marketing: Second Series,* Reavis Cox, Wroe Alderson, and Stanley J. Shapiro, eds. (Homewood, Illinois: Richard D. Irwin, Inc., 1964), pp. 333-354, by permission of the American Marketing Association. Copyright © 1964 by American Marketing Association.

[1] Wroe Alderson, *Marketing Behavior and Executive Action* (Homewood, Ill.: Richard D. Irwin, Inc., 1957).

[2] R. E. Frank, A. A. Kuehn, and W. F. Massy, *Quantitative Techniques in Marketing Analysis* (Homewood, Ill.: Richard D. Irwin, Inc., 1962).

ing, at other times exhorting, the author attempts to show how applied decision theory and information theory can provide a useful prescriptive framework within which the data gathering and cost incurring activity of marketing research can be fruitfully analyzed. The *informational value* of marketing research rather than the mechanics of carrying out such research—given that its anticipated value is worth the cost—is emphasized in this essay.

Although these techniques are of rather recent development, the literature on both decision theory and information theory is already extensive. No attempt is made herein to cover even a modest portion of this literature.[3] Rather, emphasis is placed on Bayesian decision theory, a specific segment of the literature in which concepts of both decision and information theory have been combined in an effective and elegant form. The contributions made by Schlaifer and Raiffa to developing the relevance of Bayesian theory to both information theory and decision making under uncertainty are so exhaustive that any one writing on this subject is obliged to consider his own efforts as largely expository or slightly extensive to their more basic work.[4]

A brief overview of information theory as propounded by Shannon, Weiner, Nyquist, and other noted contributors is provided at the beginning of this essay. Initial efforts focused on the development of concepts to measure the amount of information. Shannon concentrated on those aspects of information dealing with the design of *physical systems* and the relationship of information to the technical problems of encoding, transmitting, and receiving the symbols of communication. In the discussion of Shannon's contributions, some rudimentary concepts of information theory, such as the logarithmic measure of information, the amount of average information, and noisy and lossy information channels, are described in a marketing context. Both in its own right and as an analogue to some of the information concepts of Bayesian decision theory, this earlier work constituted a significant breakthrough.

Attention then shifts to a discussion of the *value* of information in decision making under uncertainty. Concepts of information theory become imbedded in the broader framework of decision theory. Once marketing research is recognized as an important area for the application of these techniques, both decision theory and the modified concepts of

---

[3] In particular, an apology is offered for our failure (due to space constraints) to include a description of the behavioralistic theory of communication as developed by Ackoff. Readers interested in this specific extension of information theory should see R. L. Ackoff, "Toward a Behavioral Theory of Communication," *Management Science*, Vol. 4, No. 3 (April, 1958).

[4] R. Schlaifer, *Probability and Statistics for Business Decisions* (New York: McGraw-Hill Book Co., Inc., 1959); and H. Raiffa and R. Schlaifer, *Applied Statistical Decision Theory* (Cambridge, Mass.: Harvard Business School Press, 1961).

information theory can be used in the evaluation of the three main information-gathering functions of marketing research:

1. Information gathered to support the existence of a business problem.
2. Information gathered in the developmental process of structuring a problem, i.e., the activity incurred in searching for alternative courses of action, identification of objectives to be achieved, etc.
3. Information gathered (or capable of being gathered) in the evaluative process of choosing among alternative courses of action.[5]

Such decision theory concepts as the expected value of perfect information, the expected value of sample information, the cost of obtaining information, and the employment of preposterior analyses in determining how much (if any) marketing research should be undertaken are illustrated by simple numerical examples.

In the final section, the author comments in a more philosophical and speculative manner on the potential contribution of decision and information theory to the advancement of both descriptive and normative marketing theory.

Information Theory From the Systems' Viewpoint

Probably most of us have some intuitive idea as to what is meant by possessing "a lot" versus "a little" information. We might expect that a primary objective of information is *to reduce our uncertainty* as to the occurrence of several possible events. For example, if we were driving along some relatively unknown route and came to a fork in the road, the statement of a seemingly reliable gasoline station attendant as to which road we should take in order to proceed to our destination would be informative. If the attendant not only assisted us in making this choice but, in the spirit of true service, proceeded to tell us the name of the best restaurant in the town which was our destination, we would consider this combined message as constituting even greater information (assuming our notions about the best eating place in town were also subject to uncertainty).

This illustration suggests that the *amount* of information is relative to our degree of uncertainty. That is, the greater our uncertainty as to which possible event will occur, the greater is the amount of information conveyed by the occurrence of the event. Being told the correct route out of five equally likely routes should be more "informative" than being told the correct route out of two equally likely possibilities. And, if we

---

[5] In effect, all three categories involve choice. Our reason for separately identifying these activities is that the *character* of choice is quite different among classifications. These distinctions will be brought out in a later section of the chapter.

already know which fork to take in order to reach our destination, being told that this route is "correct" provides *no* information.

In the special case where all contingencies are considered equally likely, it would seem reasonable to assume that the amount of information contained in a particular message could be measured as some function of the *number* of possibilities which we envision *before* that particular message is conveyed. However, we might also desire that our measure of the amount of information be additive. That is, whether the message conveyed to us consisted of two simple parts, route number and best restaurant in town or the compound expression of these two events, we should like to end up with the same total amount of information. Fortunately, the logarithmic function provides this desirable property of additivity when we deal with the joint occurrence of independent events.

Information theory, as developed by Shannon, is concerned with the *amount* of information measured by the extent of the change in event probability produced by the message, whether or not the message is perfect.[6] In words, the measure for this general case is

$$I(X) = \log_2\left[\frac{\text{Probability of event after message is received}}{\text{Probability of event before message is received}}\right]$$

In the *special* case of a perfect message (or the actual occurrence of the event), the above expression reduces to

$$I(X) = \log_2 1 - \log_2 p(X) = 0 - \log_2 p(X) = -\log_2 p(X)$$

where $I(X)$ equals the informational content of the event X, and $p(X)$ equals the probability assigned to its occurrence prior to the receipt of the perfect message.

As a marketing setting for our discussion, consider the case of a marketing manager concerned with forecasting unit sales volume for the coming month. Suppose that the manager is certain that forcasted sales will be within ± 10,000 units of actual sales, but as he considers more narrow ranges of error, his forecasting ability diminishes, as shown in the first portion of Table 1. Columns (1), (2), and (3) refer to the forecasting accuracy of our hypothetical marketing manager. In past endeavors, he has always managed to be within ± 10,000 units of actual sales, i.e., $p(X_1)$ equals unity. The probability of his forecast being within ± 5,000 units drops to .75, however, while the probability that his forecast is within ± 500 units of actual sales is only .05.

---

[6] C. E. Shannon and W. Weaver, *The Mathematical Theory of Communication* (Urbana, Ill.: University of Illinois Press, 1949). Also, see S. Goldman, *Information Theory* (New York: Prentice-Hall, Inc., 1953).

Table 1. Calculation of Information Content—Sales Forecasting Illustration

(1) Event X_i	(2) Description of Event	(3) Probabilities $p(X_i)$	(4) Units of Information $I(X_i)$
X_1	± 10,000 units	1.00	.00
X_2	± 5,000 units	.75	.42
X_3	± 2,000 units	.50	1.00
X_4	± 1,000 units	.25	2.00
X_5	± 500 units	.05	4.32

Suppose the manager were to receive a "message" that his forecast will really be within ±500 units of actual sales. Intuitively, we would suspect that more information is contained in this message than in a message indicating that his forecast is within ± 10,000 units. As noted earlier, information theory, as developed by Shannon, formalizes this notion of the amount of information contained in a "perfect" message and expresses it as a number defined as:

$$I(X) = -\log_2 p(X)$$

To illustrate, the informational content of $-\log_2 1$ is zero, while $-\log_2 .05$ is 4.32 units or, more typically, 4.32 bits (an abbreviation for binits, since logarithms to the base 2 are used). If the message is perfect, the number representing $I(X)$ specifies the informational content of this special case or, equivalently, the information after the event X has occurred. As intuition would suggest, if one were certain that an event was going to occur, being told that the event has occurred provides no information. It does not alter the probability attached to the occurrence of the event before the message was received. On the other hand, if the chances attached to the occurrence of an event were very low, a communication that the event has occurred (or is certain to occur) carries a large amount of information.

The Shannon measure can be easily extended to deal with both (1) imperfect messages, and (2) the receipt of more than one message. To illustrate the first case, suppose that before final sales results are tallied, a preliminary report is received by the marketing manager which indicates that his forecast will be within ± 1,000 units. Based upon the past experience with preliminary figures, the probability that sales will really be within ± 1,000 units, given the results of the preliminary report, is .75. The informational content of this message can be defined as either the difference between the perfect information potential before the message and after the message or the logarithm of the ratio of the after-message probability to the before-message probability. That is, if $p_1(X)$ equals the prior probability (.25 from Table 1) that the manager's forecast will be within $\pm$ 1,000 units of actual sales, and if $p_2(X)$ equals the probability, after the message, that the manager's forecast will be within $\pm$ 1,000 units of actual, then

$$I(M) = \{-\log_2 p_1(X)\} - \{-\log_2 p_2(X)\}$$

$$= \log_2 \frac{p_2(X)}{p_1(X)} = \log_2 \frac{.75}{.25} = \log_2 3$$

$$= 1.58 \text{ bits.}$$

Had the message been perfect, its informational content would have amounted, of course, to 2 bits $(-\log_2 .25 = 2)$.

The Calculation of Average Information

To extend the Shannon measure to deal with the possible occurrence of several events, a few new concepts are needed. To illustrate this extension, suppose our marketing manager assumes that the sales potential of a given marketing area will fall within one of the intervals noted in Table 2.

Table 2. Calculation of Average Information (Annual Sales Potential)

(1) Event X_i	(2) Description of Event (000's of Units)	(3) Probabilities $p(X_i)$	(4) Information $I(X_i)$	(5) Weighted Information $p(X_i) \cdot I(X_i)$
X_1	$100 < X \leqslant 120$	.10	3.322	.3322
X_2	$120 < X \leqslant 140$	.40	1.322	.5288
X_3	$140 < X \leqslant 160$	.25	2.000	.5000
X_4	$160 < X \leqslant 180$	.20	2.322	.4644
X_5	$180 < X \leqslant 200$	.05	4.322	.2161
			$H(X) =$	2.0415 bits

As noted in Table 2, the marketing manager assumes that the events of column (2) are mutually exclusive and collectively exhaustive, i.e., they form a partition over the set of all possible events. Column (3) represents the probabilities assigned to the occurrence of each event, while column (4) represents the informational content of a perfect message regarding the occurrence of each possible event, respectively.

Although the manager can receive messages regarding the occurrence of *any* of the events, he might well be more interested in the amount of information received *on the average*. For example, a message could be received indicating the occurrence of X_5 (resulting in a large amount of information). Before the fact, however, it is more likely that a message indicating, say, X_2 (resulting in a smaller amount of information) would be received. The *average* information, called $H(X)$, is defined in the general case as

$$H(X) = -\sum_{i=1}^{n} p(X_i) \log_2 p(X_i)$$

or, since $I(X) = -\log_2 p(X)$, the average information is, equivalently,

$$H(X) = \sum_{i=1}^{n} p(X_i) \cdot I(X_i)$$

The average information for the hypothetical data of Table 2 is obtained as the sum of column (5), a figure which was derived by multiplying each perfect message entry of column (4) by its respective probability of occurring.

Lossy and Noisy Channels

Information theory can also be easily extended to deal with the situations of channel loss and/or channel noise. These concepts can be explained in terms of the following illustration. Assume that customer attitudes toward a specific firm can be expressed as either "good" or "poor." Assume further that the firm's salesmen purportedly convey these attitudes (e.g., by means of call reports) to the marketing manager. In terms of this simple illustration, the information "transmitted" in the channel can be viewed as the attiture toward the firm which the consumer really expresses to the salesman. The call report which the marketing manager gets from the salesman can be considered as the information "received" in the channel. From the marketing manager's point of view, the interesting feature is the extent to which the salesman serves as a lossy and/or noisy channel in communicating—via the call report—the attitude actually expressed by the customer.

To be more specific, let us first assume that the probability that a customer's attitude toward the firm falls in the "good" state is .50 and, similarly, the probability that his attitude toward the firm is "poor" is .50.

We shall also suppose that the salesman serves as a perfect channel, i.e., a channel which contains neither loss of information nor noise. These assumptions are noted in Table 3.

The entries of Table 3 are joint probabilities, i.e., $p(X_i$ and $Y_j)$. In the loss-free and noise-free case, the salesman is assumed to convey the "true" attitude of the customer without error. In terms of conditional probabilities, $p(Y_1|X_1) = p(Y_2|X_2) = 1.0$; and $p(Y_1|X_2) = p(Y_2|X_1) = 0$. Hence, the joint probability of, say, Y_1 *and* X_1 occurring is $p(Y_1|X_1)$. $p(X_1)$, or $1.0 \times .50 = .50$, as noted in the first cell of Table 3.

We can next examine the question regarding how much information is generated, on the average, by X_i and/or Y_j. To do this, we shall have to introduce four new measures: $H(X,Y)$, $T(X,Y)$, $H(X|Y)$, and $H(Y|X)$. The first measure, $H(X,Y)$, is the information contained in the *joint* occurrence of the stimulus (attitude actually expressed by a customer) and the response (customer's attitude as reported by the salesman). The measure $T(X,Y)$ stands for the amount of information *shared* by X and Y. The measure $H(X|Y)$ is that portion of the stimulus which is lost in the salesman's report, the average uncertainty still attached to the stimulus when the response is known, and is typically called the *equivocation* of the channel or channel loss.[7] Finally, $H(Y|X)$ measures the average uncertainty of the response, given the stimulus. This measure is usually referred to as ambiguity or channel *noise*.

The calculation of these measures first proceeds by specific application of the more general formula for determining the amount of average information:

$$H(X) = - \sum_i p(X_i) \log_2 p(X_i)$$

$$H(Y) = - \sum_j p(Y_j) \log_2 p(Y_j)$$

$$H(X,Y) = - \sum_{i,j} p(X_i \text{ and } Y_j) \log_2 p(X_i \text{ and } Y_j)$$

When the appropriate entries of Table 3 are substituted in the three preceding formulas, we arrive at $H(X) = 1$ bit; $H(Y) = 1$ bit; and $H(X,Y) = 1$ bit.

---

[7] Expressed somewhat more technically, $H(X|Y)$ is the *prior* expectation of the information potential in the posterior distribution of X; more will be said on this point in the second section of this essay.

Table 3. Loss-Free and Noise-Free Channel—Joint Probabilities

Customer Attitude–X_i	Salesman's Report–Y_j		Marginal Probabilities
	Good	*Poor*	
Good	.50	0	.50
Poor	0	.50	.50
Marginal Probabilities	.50	.50	1.00

The measures $T(X,Y)$, $H(X|Y)$, and $H(Y|X)$ are derived from the proceding measures as follows:

$$T(X,Y) = H(X) + H(Y) - H(X,Y) = 1 + 1 - 1 = 1$$
$$H(X|Y) = H(X,Y) - H(Y) = H(X) - T(X,Y) = 1 - 1 = 0$$
$$H(Y|X) = H(X,Y) - H(X) = H(Y) - T(X,Y) = 1 - 1 = 0$$

The data in Table 3 illustrate the case of perfect transmission and, hence, a loss-free and noise-free channel. In this case, $H(X) = H(Y) = H(X,Y) = T(X,Y) = 1$, while both $H(X|Y)$ and $H(Y|X)$ are zero. This should agree with what we would intuitively expect. If the sales manager knows *either* the stimulus or the response, he, in effect, knows both inasmuch as the call report perfectly "calls" the customer's attitude. (Incidentally, if the salesman consistently transposed results by calling *all* "good" attitudes, "poor," and vice versa, no change in the measures would result. This reflects the fact that the manager has merely to reverse the labels in order to have a perfect predictor of stimulus, given response.)

In the case of this specific loss-free and noise-free channel, both $H(X)$ and $H(Y)$ contribute 1 bit each. However, their *joint* information, $H(X,Y)$, is less than the sum of $H(X)$ and $H(Y)$ indicating that X_i and Y_j share information; that is, $T(X,Y)$ is greater than zero. In fact, in this case, $T(X,Y) = 1$. We can now consider the other three logical possibilities which remain: lossy and noisy; lossy and noise-free; and loss-free and noisy. The appropriate joint probabilities for these variations are shown in Table 4.

Calculation of appropriate measures for the other three cases proceeds analogously. In the lossy and noisy case, the salesman's response is independent of the attitude expressed by the customer. Hence, $H(X,Y) = H(X) + H(Y) = 2$ bits and *no* information is shared; $T(X,Y) = 0$. Moreover, $H(X|Y)$ and $H(Y|X)$ produce 1 bit each. In this case, knowledge of some response, Y_j, provides no predictive help about stimulus, and vice versa.

Table 4. Tables of Joint and Marginal Probabilities

Customer Attitude–X_i	Good	Poor	Marginal Probabilities	Type
		Salesman's Report–Y_j		
Good	.25	.25	.50	Lossy and Noisy
Poor	.25	.25	.50	
Marginal Probabilities	.50	.50	1.00	
Good	.50	0	.50	Lossy and Noise-Free
Poor	.50	0	.50	
Marginal Probabilities	1.00	0	1.00	
Good	.50	.50	1.00	Loss-Free and Noisy
Poor	0	0	0	
Marginal Probabilities	.50	.50	1.00	

In the lossy but noise-free case, the salesman provided just one response, "good," whether the attitude expressed by the customer was good or bad. Although there exists no ambiguity about the response, i.e., $H(Y|X) = 0$, neither is any information provided by the response; $H(Y)$ also equals zero. The stimulus and response share no information and, hence, $T(X,Y) = 0$. The other measures, $H(X)$, $H(X,Y)$, and $H(X|Y)$, equal 1 bit each. The sole source of uncertainty is then provided by the stimulus X_i.

In the loss-free but noisy case, the opposite conditions prevail. In this instance, we assume that the stimulus is always X_1 (the customer's attitude is "good") and, hence, knowledge that X_i equals X_1 provides no information. However, the salesman is assumed to have a .50 probability of responding with "good" and a .50 probability of responding with "poor." The measure $H(Y)$ thus provides 1 bit of information and $H(Y|X)$ and $H(X,Y)$ equal 1 bit each. Analogous to the preceding case, the other measures, $H(X)$, $T(X,Y)$, and $H(X|Y)$, equal zero.

Information measures of the type illustrated in the simple cases above can be extended to deal with more than two variables at some increase in computational labor. Measures analogous to partial correlation coefficients can be calculated without the need to satisfy the latter's assumption of interval scales.[8] This suggests that some of the measurement techniques of information theory may be useful in statistical analysis, independent of

---

[8] A discussion of the similarities between information measures and the analysis of variance may be found in W. J. McGill's paper, "Isomorphism in Statistical Analysis," in H. Quastler's *Information Theory and Psychology* (Glencoe, Ill.: The Free Press, 1955), pp. 56-62.

their potential for dealing with some of the theoretical aspects of information in marketing.

Limitations of Information Theory in Decision Making

Information theory as developed by Shannon goes well beyond the simple, introductory treatment found in the preceding paragraphs. For present purposes, it is sufficient to note that Shannon is primarily concerned with the informational aspects of physical systems—channel capacity, message encoding and decoding, channel noise, channel loss, and the like. Emphasis is placed on the *amount* of information rather than on whatever *value* it may have to the receiver.

To illustrate the difference between these two points of view, suppose that our marketing manager of Table 2 is now concerned with only two possible levels of annual sales potential, viz., $100 < X \leqslant 140$ and $140 < X \leqslant 200$ (in thousands of units). If the former event occurs, the sales manager would not wish to market some new product in the territory; if the latter event were to occur, he would. Suppose further that if the former event (which we shall call X_a) occurs and the producer *does* market the product, he would lose $10,000, while if the latter event (X_b) occurs and the manager markets the product, he can gain only $2,000. These highly simplified ground rules are noted in Table 5.

Table 5. Payoff Table—Sales Potential Illustration (Payoffs Refer to the Act—"Market the Product")

(1) Event: X in 000's of Units	(2) $p(X)$	(3) $V(X)$	(4) $I(X)$
X_a: $100 < X \leqslant 140$	.50	$-10,000$	1.0
X_b: $140 < X \leqslant 200$	.50	2,000	1.0

If we were concerned with only the amount of information generated by a perfect message, Table 5 indicates that such a message indicating event X_a would be equivalent in *amount* of information with a perfect message indicating event X_b. From the standpoint of value, however, the manager who received—before he marketed the product—a perfect message (e.g., the result of a "perfectly reliable" market survey) indicating X_a might well consider this a much more valuable message than one indicating X_b. In the former case, he could avoid a loss of $10,000; in the latter case he could gain only $2,000. This distinction between the amount of information and the value of information becomes quite important as we now turn to the use of Bayesian theory and the information concepts which are associated with this normative approach to decision making under uncertainty.

Bayesian Decision Theory and the Value of Information

Bayesian decision theory represents one prescriptive procedure for making decisions under uncertainty. Like other theories of rational decision making, certain assumptions underlie application of the theory. Specifically, a decision problem under uncertainty is made up of the following components (1) a decision maker; (2) a set ($n \geqslant 2$) of alternative courses of action; (3) a set ($n \geqslant 2$) of mutually exclusive and collectively exhaustive events which can occur; (4) a payoff function which assigns a value to the occurrence of each event; and (5) an element of doubt regarding which one of the possible events will occur.[9]

Bayesian decision theory assumes that the decision maker can assign numerical weights (which obey the postulates of probability theory) to each of the possible events. These probabilities may be based on either long-run experience with the event in question, or, in the case of unique events, they may reflect the more subjective judgments of the decision maker, or a combination of the two.[10] In either instance, the theory assumes that the decision maker chooses that act which maximizes expected value (or, more generally, expected utility), where expected value is a weighted average over all possible payoffs for a given act. Hence, maximization of expected value is the rationality criterion of Bayesian theory.

A key feature of this theory is the notion that the decision maker may elect to secure more information regarding the probabilities attached to each possible event by conducting "experiments." In the context of marketing, these experiments may consist of market surveys, pretests of new products, trial pricing studies, and so on. Typically, these experiments will cost something to conduct and seldom will they yield perfect information concerning the probabilities attached to alternative events. Bayesian decision theory provides a prescription for determining the size and type of experiment to conduct (if any should be conducted at all) and a means of using the sample findings of the experiment to modify prior probabilities attached to the alternative events.

---

[9] In the general case, payoffs are expressed in von Neumann-Morgenstern utilities, a function which measures the decision maker's attitudes toward risky outcomes. In practice, monetary measures (e.g., net profits, discounted cash flow) are usually employed. An introductory discussion of utility theory may be found in Schlaifer, *op. cit.*, pp. 24-49.

[10] A discussion of the "subjective" school of probability may be found in L. J. Savage, *The Foundations of Statistics* (New York: John Wiley & Sons, Inc., 1954).

The application of Bayesian procedures to marketing decisions offers provocative possibilities. Marketing problems are noted for high uncertainty attached to the occurrence of alternative events, paucity of relevant information, and lack of control over the outcomes of decisions. Consequently, the marketing manager must frequently resort to hunch and intuition in choosing among courses of action. The primary function of marketing research is to reduce this uncertainty by providing information relevant to decisions. Bayesian decision theory provides a systematic framework which considers both aspects, viz., the role of judgment *and* "objective" information (actual or potential) in choosing among alternative courses of action.

But marketing research is a more continuous activity than the preceding paragraph would suggest. Marketing research activity may be undertaken for purposes of (1) providing feedback information on currently pursued courses of action; (2) developing new courses of action (and the possible consequences related thereto) when a need to change present policies may exist; and (3) providing information on the likelihood of possible events, given the choice of each alternative course of action. It is also apparent, however, that each of these activities involves decisions and, consequently, the possibility of erroneous choice.

To illustrate, suppose the sales volume of a supermarket is declining relative to some goal level. A marketing research report which ascribed the decline in sales to failure of the store's merchandising policy could be in error. Sales could be declining as a consequence of a falloff in total sales for all supermarkets in the trading area. This particular supermarket may even be increasing its share of total sales. Another case in point is the nylon leotard craze in 1960. Producers of textile nylon suddenly faced a marked downward shift in demand from knitting mills, a development which producers initially took to indicate that the fad had run its course. Actually, consumer demand was still holding up well. Inventory imbalances in the long channel from fiber producer to consumer had created the sharp fall in the derived demand for the fiber used in the leotards. Demand at the fiber producer level later increased and then gradually leveled off.

The task of marketing research in correctly interpreting feedback is not easy. Marketing research can be compared to a noisy and lossy channel that produces two types of errors: (1) failure to signal a problem when one really exists; and (2) false signaling of a problem when none really exists.

The marketing research manager is also faced with choices in the search for alternative courses of action when there is a possible need for changing the currently pursued course. Search activity delays decisions and incurs cost.[11] In addition, all problems are subject to incomplete optimization. The marketing researcher must somehow try to chart a middle course, which balances the cost of too extensive a search with the lost opportunity costs attached to terminating his search too quickly. A pricing problem encountered by a firm introducing a new man-made fiber illustrates this difficulty. In the haste of introducing the new fiber, a price was chosen which turned out to be too low relative to customer demand and the firm's ability to supply. A (purportedly superior) alternative course of action which involved coupling a somewhat higher price with a prestige labeling policy was uncovered *after* the original pricing decision had been implemented.

After courses of action are formulated, marketing research can play an important role in the evaluative process—the estimation of probabilities attached to the consequences of taking alternative courses of action. Most pretests are designed to facilitate this aspect of the problem solving process.[12] Again, the decision maker must weigh the cost of securing additional information against the cost of taking action in the light of his current uncertainties. As an illustration of the Bayesian approach, the remainder of this section is devoted to a discussion of this third or evaluative stage in the problem-solving process. By means of a simple and hypothetical example, we introduce such concepts as: (1) the cost of uncertainty; (2) the expected value of perfect information; (3) the expected value of sample information; (4) sequential decision making; and (5) the use of preposterior analysis in evaluating the effectiveness of alternative strategies.

A Numerical Illustration

Consider the following oversimplified problem. The marketing manager for the Beedle Brothers Brewery is concerned with the sales appeal of the firm's present label for its quart-size bottled beer. Marketing research studies indicate that supermarket consumers find little "eye-appeal" in the drab, somewhat cluttered appearance of the label. The firm has hired a

---

[11] The reader interested in the relationship of both information theory and search theory to decision theory should see D. F. Mela, "Information Theory and Search Theory as Special Cases of Decision Theory," *Operations Research,* Vol. 9, No. 6 (1961), pp. 907-9. In addition, a path-breaking paper concerned with the value of information is J. Marshak's "Towards an Economic Theory of Organization and Information" in R. M. Thrall, C. H. Coombs, and R. L. Davis (eds.), *Decision Processes* (New York: John Wiley & Sons, Inc., 1954).

[12] What is described above as an orderly, sequential process of problem recognition, structuring and evaluation is obviously a gross simplification of the real world. In reality, a problem may undergo almost continuous reformulation. Identification of just when a decision was made is frequently a difficult task, as well.

design artist who has produced some prototype labels, all of which have been evaluated by the firm's executives. One label design has consistently won out in all preference tests which have been conducted among Beedle executives. But the marketing manager is still in doubt as to whether the new label would increase sales appreciably. He considers the costs associated with converting his firm's machinery, inventory, point-of-purchase displays, etc., to the new label and notes that an out-of-pocket cost of $500,000 would be involved.

If the new label were really "superior" to the old, Beedle's marketing manager estimates that the present value of all *net* cash flows related to increased sales generated over the next three years by the more attractive label would exceed by $800,000 the cash flows anticipated under the old label.[13] Based on his prior experience with merchandising changes of this type, he is only willing to assign a 50-50 chance to the event "new label is superior to old." Table 6 summarizes these data.

As noted in Table 6, calculation of expected monetary value for this simple two-act, two-state case merely involves calculation of a weighted

Table 6. Beer Label Problem—Calculation of Expected Monetary Value (Payoff Entries in $000's)

Acts	$p(S_1)$	S_1–New Label Is "Superior"	$p(S_2)$	S_2–New Label Is Not "Superior"	Expected Monetary Value
A_1–adopt new	.5	800	.5	−500	150
A_2–keep old	.5	0	.5	0	0

average payoff for each act, i.e., E.M.V. $= \sum_{j} p_{ij} O(A_i, S_j)$ for the A_ith

act, where $O(A_i, S_j)$ represents the payoff associated with the conjunction of the ith act and jth state of nature. In the absence of any further information, the marketing manager who wished to maximize expected monetary value would choose act A_1; he would adopt the new label.

More realistically, the decision maker may elect to delay his terminal decision in order to gather more information regarding the probabilities

---

[13] In practice, of course, incremental cash flow would be a function of how "superior" the new label turned out to be. (Moreover, selection of the appropriate planning horizon over which to discount future revenues would require study.) In the interest of keeping this illustration reasonably tractable, we shall heroically assume a two-event structure and a three-year planning horizon.

attached to alternative consequences of each course of action. For purposes of exposition, suppose that the decision maker possessed four data-gathering alternatives prior to making a terminal choice.

1. Experiment e_0—do not experiment; make terminal choice now.
2. Experiment e_1—purchase a "perfect" survey service; cost of this service equals $300,000.
3. Experiment e_2—purchase a survey which is 80% reliable; cost equals $100,000.
4. Experiment e_3—purchase a survey which is only 70% reliable in the first stage, but if a second stage is required, the reliability increases to 80%; cost of first stage equals $50,000 while cost of second stage, if needed, equals $80,000. (Since some setup costs need not be duplicated, the second stage, 80% reliability survey can be done cheaper if preceded by a first-stage survey than if conducted alone.)

Under these simplified ground rules, we can now proceed to a discussion of some of the measures of information underlying Bayesian decision theory.

Figures 1 and 2 represent tree diagrams which summarize the pertinent payoffs and probabilities associated with each experiment. By following the path, e_0 (the dummy experiment) of Figure 1, we note the same data which were shown in Table 6. It is clear that in the absence of experimentation, the decision maker would select A_1 leading to an expected monetary payoff of $150,000; hence, the path labeled A_2 is blocked off by the double slash.

The path labeled e_1 traces out the strategy associated with the opportunity to conduct a perfectly reliable survey at a cost of $300,000. By "perfect" survey is meant one which would disclose without error which event, S_1 or S_2 is the correct state of nature. If $Z_1(e_1)$ and $Z_2(e_1)$ are the outcomes which indicate S_1 and S_2, respectively, in a perfectly reliable survey, the conditional probabilities $p\ [Z_1(e_1)\ |\ S_1]$ and $p\ [Z_2(e_1)\ |\ S_2]$ equal unity; $p\ [Z_1(e_1)\ |\ S_2]$ and $p\ [Z_2(e_1)\ |\ S_1]$ equal zero. Analogous to the channel loss and channel noise concepts of information theory, a perfectly reliable survey would be both loss-free and noise-free. Given each survey response, the decision maker would take the best act for that response—A_1, if the survey results indicate $Z_1(e_1)$, and A_2, should the survey results indicate $Z_2(e_1)$.

Before the fact, however, the decision maker must still apply the prior probabilities attached to S_1 and S_2, since the survey result can report results related to either state. (The calculation of these marginal probabilities is shown in the first part of Table 7). When the prior probabilities

Figure 1. Tree Diagrams—Brewery Problem Payoffs in $ 000's

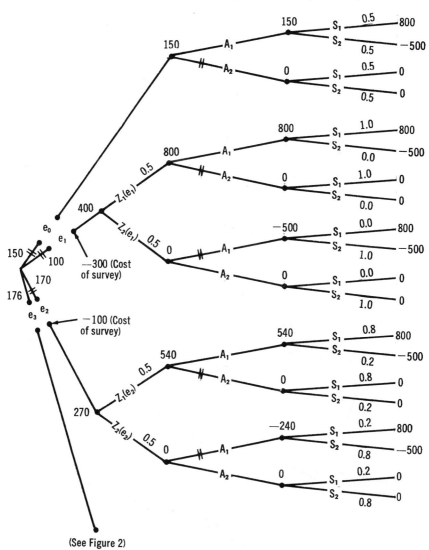

(See Figure 2)

are applied, the gross expected monetary value of the e_1 strategy is $400,000. But without conducting the perfect survey, the decision maker's expected value associated with taking A_1 is $150,000. The difference of $250,000 represents the *cost of uncertainty* associated with taking A_1 and also the *expected value of perfect information*—the upper limit which a decision maker could afford to spend for a perfectly reliable survey. Inasmuch as the perfect survey costs $300,000, the strategy e_1 is definitely inferior to e_0. The perfect information costs more than it is worth.

Figure 2.   Tree Diagrams—Brewery Problem Payoffs in $ 000's

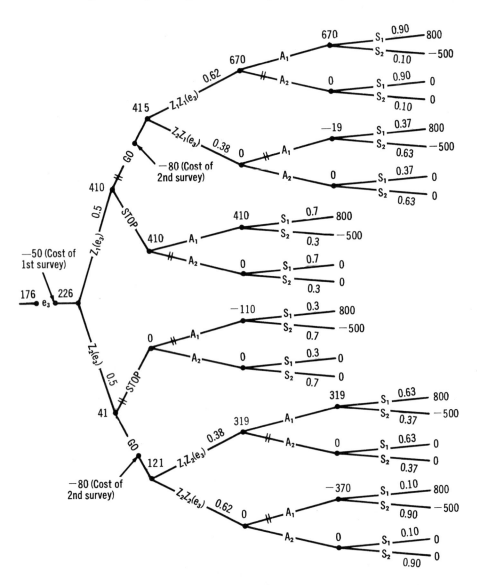

The branch labeled e_2 traces the path of the next strategy under consideration. This survey, which, more realistically, carries only an 80% reliability, is assumed to cost $100,000 rather than the $300,000 associated with the attempt to gather "perfect" information. Conditional probabilities, $p\ [Z_1(e_2)\ |\ S_1]$ and $p\ [Z_2(e_2)\ |\ S_2]$ equal .8 and $p\ [Z_1(e_2)\ |\ S_2]$ and $p\ [Z_2(e_2)\ |\ S_1]$ equal .2. In terms of information theory, we are dealing with both a noisy and lossy channel since the stimuli, S_1 and S_2, can imply either "response," Z_1 or Z_2, and conversely.

The probabilities attached to the branches emanating from experiment e_2 are derived from Table 7. The entries labeled joint probabilities

Table 7. Calculation of Relevant Probabilities Associated With Experiments e_1, e_2, e_3

		Joint Probabilities		Marginal	Posterior Probabilities	
		S_1	S_2	Probabilities	$P(S_1|Z_i)$	$P(S_2|Z_i)$
e_1	Z_1	.5	0	.5	1.0	0
	Z_2	0	.5	.5	0	1.0
		.5	.5	1.0		
	Z_1					
e_2	Z_1	.4	.1	.5	.8	.2
	Z_2	.1	.4	.5	.2	.8
		.5	.5	1.0		
e_3 (first stage)	Z_1	.35	.15	.5	.7	.3
	Z_2	.15	.35	.5	.3	.7
		.50	.50	1.0		
		$S_1|Z_1(e_3)$	$S_2|Z_1(e_3)$		$P(S_1|Z_i,Z_j)$	$P(S_2|Z_iZ_j)$
	Z_1Z_1	.56	.06	.62	.90	.10
e_3 (second stage)	Z_2Z_1	.14	.24	.38	.37	.63
		.70	.30	1.00		
		$S_1|Z_2(e_3)$	$S_2|Z_2(e_3)$			
	Z_1Z_2	.24	.14	.38	.63	.37
	Z_2Z_2	.06	.56	.62	.10	.90
		.30	.70	1.00		

(e.g., .4, .1, etc.) represent the probability attached to the combination of each survey result, Z_1 or Z_2, with each state of nature, S_1 and S_2. For example, the joint probability, $p[Z_1(e_2)$ and $S_1] = p[Z_1(e_2) \mid S_1] \cdot p(S_1) = .8 \times .5 = .4$. Marginal probabilities are also calculated in a manner analogous to the examples covered under the section on information theory. The posterior probabilities, however, are found through application of

Bayes' theorem.[14] To illustrate, suppose $Z_1(e_2)$ *is* observed. This survey result suggests (with less than perfect reliability) that S_1 is the underlying state of nature. Intuitively, we should wish to revise our prior probabilities, .5 and .5 associated with S_1 and S_2, respectively, in the light of this survey result. This can be done by merely dividing the joint probabilities making up the $Z_1(e_2)$ row by the marginal probability, i.e., $p\ [S_1 \mid Z_1(e_2)]$ $= p\ [Z_1(e_2)$ and $S_1]\ /\ p\ [Z_1(e_2)] = .4/.5 = .8$ and $p\ [S_2 \mid Z_1(e_2)] =$ $p\ [Z_1(e_2)$ and $S_2]\ /\ p\ [Z_1(e_2)] = .1/.5 = .2$. If $Z_1(e_2)$ is observed, then act A_1 would be selected leading to an expected payoff of \$540,000, and if $Z_2(e_2)$ is observed, then act A_2 would be selected leading to a zero payoff. Since before the survey is undertaken each sample result could be observed, the marginal probabilities, $p\ [Z_i(e_2)]$ are next applied leading to the expected payoff of \$270,000. The \$100,000 cost of the survey is deducted from this payoff with the result being a net expected monetary payoff of \$170,000.

Strategy, e_3, is traced out in Figure 2; associated probability calculations are shown in Table 7. No new principles are involved in this sequential strategy. Notice, however, that the decision maker *again* revises his posterior probability after the first-stage survey *if* he decides to undertake the second stage. If $Z_1(e_3)$ is observed (a survey result favorable to S_1), the decision maker would not undertake a second survey but would proceed with act A_1 and change over to the new design. If $Z_2(e_3)$ is observed (a survey result favorable to S_2), the decision maker should undertake the second survey. When, if another Z_2 is observed, i.e., $Z_2, Z_2(e_3)$, the decision maker should select A_2; while, if $Z_1, Z_2(e_3)$ is observed, he should select act A_1. By starting from the right and working backwards, and always choosing the highest payoff path, the expected value of this whole strategy turns out to be \$176,000; hence, all other main paths are blocked off. (In practice, of course, it is not mandatory that the decision maker stop at a two-stage experiment. An evaluation of additional stages would involve calculating the expected payoff of proceeding, i.e., the expected value of additional sample information versus the cost incurred to obtain the additional information.)

In following through the preceding illustration, the reader has probably observed that both probabilities *and* conditional payoffs affect the

---

[14] What is shown above descriptively may be computed by application of Bayes' formula:

$$p(S_i|E) = \frac{p(E|S_i) \cdot p(S_i)}{\sum_{j=1}^{n} p(E|S_j) \cdot p(S_j)}$$

where the S_j form a partition over some set of "states of nature" and E stands for some event where an S_j is a necessary condition for its occurrence.

value of information as formulated under Bayesian theory. Furthermore, this value is an expectation rather than a sum certain.[15] Roughly speaking, the expected value of new information represents the difference between the expected payoff associated with taking the *best* act in the absence of the new information and the expected value of the strategy involving both information collection and best terminal action. The *net gain* from information collection is the expected value of the information less the cost of obtaining it. If the net gain is positive, the decision maker—according to Bayesian theory—should "purchase" the additional information.

Many additional complications could have been included in the illustration. The costs associated with information collection could have been treated as a random variable. Sensitivity analyses could have been run in which probabilities and/or payoffs were changed in order to ascertain the sensitivity of the payoff associated with the best strategy to these changes in assumptions. Hopefully, however, enough has been covered to give the reader at least a basic grasp of the concepts underlying Bayesian theory and the mechanics of applying it.

The Amount Versus Value of Information

As has been described, information theory as developed by Shannon is concerned with the *amount* of information. The information measures of Bayesian decision theory are concerned with the *value* of information. Although application of both schemata involves revision of probabilities, Bayesian theory considers payoffs as well as probabilities. In this latter theory, information measures are imbedded in a much broader framework.

Many similarities, however, exist between the two theories. For example, the concepts of a channel loss and channel noise are common to both schemata. Bayes' theorem enters into the calculation of the measure of equivocation, as discussed in the section devoted to Shannon's information theory. Equivocation, $H(X|Y)$, can be defined as the prior expectation of the information potential in the posterior distribution of the stimulus X given Y, the response. On the other hand, the concepts of channel loss and noise can be useful in the interpretation of Bayesian theory. The conditional probabilities associated with the results of a "perfectly reliable" survey are analogous to those related to a channel which is both loss-free and noise-free. In more realistic cases, however, the "channels" in Bayesian decision problems will be both lossy (given a particular survey result, uncertainty may still exist regarding the underlying state of nature) and noisy (given a particular state of nature, uncertainty may still exist regarding the sample outcome).

---

[15] This distinction is important if the individual's utility were not linear with money.

The purposes for which these two theories have been designed are quite different. Information theory was developed by Shannon to cope with design problems involved in the construction of physical systems and to provide predictive criteria useful in channel transmission and receiving and in message encoding and decoding. Schlaifer used information measures to provide criteria of a prescriptive nature which would enable the decision maker to approach the problem of buying information as part of the overall framework of making rational decisions in the face of uncertainty. Although neither theory has been applied extensively as yet to actual marketing problems, the potential of both appears promising.[16]

Potential Usefulness of Information Measures in Marketing

Information theory has already been employed as a descriptive measure by several experimental psychologists.[17] From the psychologist's viewpoint, information theory has provided measures useful in experimental studies of learning, perception, and stimulus discrimination. As far as marketing is concerned, information theory might be useful in measuring the informational content of advertising messages and in determining the effect of various levels of redundancy on reader interest and recall. For example, how is consumer recall of various advertisements related to their informational content? How is a consumer's loyalty to a given brand related to the level of his information about this brand versus other brands? Do advertising messages containing relatively high information content attract and hold the reader's initial attention and favorably affect his attitudes? Is the informational content of advertising related to the price of an item and/or its length of time on the market?

The use of information theory in the study of marketing organizations and industrial systems would also seem to offer potential as a descriptive measure. For example, the design of such routinized documents as salesmen's call reports, sales forecasts, reports on competitive activity, and various sales statistics might be aided by a conceptual understanding of information theory. It would also appear that some concepts, e.g., the principle of "management by exception" and budget variances (in the accountant's sense of the word), might be studied within the framework of information theory. These areas, of course, are only illustrative of the potential contribution of information theory as an analytical technique in the study of business communication. Suffice it to say that an operational

---

[16] For some early applications of Bayesian decision theory to actual marketing problems, the following articles by the author might be of interest: (1) "Bayesian Decision Theory in Pricing Strategy," *Journal of Marketing,* January, 1963; and (2) "Decision Making in Chemical Marketing," *Industrial and Engineering Chemistry,* September, 1962.

[17] See Quastler, *op. cit.*

definition of information is now available for coping at least partially with the complexities of these problems.

Bayesian theory and its related information concepts might hold even greater potential as a device for dealing with decisions under uncertainty and as an analytical framework in which the data gathering services of marketing research can be evaluated from an economic standpoint.

Although the applicability of traditional statistical techniques is well known to many marketing researchers, it is interesting to note that Bayesian decision theory provides a useful bridge between conventional statistical reasoning and economic reasoning. By explicitly introducing the economic costs of wrong decisions and the decision maker's prior judgments, Bayesian theory offers a direct rationale for choosing among alternative sampling plans and provides insight into the determination of economical sample sizes. In classical statistics, with its emphasis on hypothesis testing and type I and type II errors, losses due to wrong decisions enter the model only externally and incompletely through selection of appropriate alpha and beta risks. (Some levels of significance like .05 and .01 have achieved almost sacred status.) In contrast, Bayesian decision theory enables the researcher to view the costs of wrong decisions that are associated with values of the parameter(s) of interest and, by assigning prior probabilities over the values of these parameters, to choose that act leading to the lowest opportunity loss. Bayesian statistics also provides a natural procedure for statistical estimation which is not restricted to the usual assumption of a quadratic loss function.

Of especial interest to the market researcher, however, is the potential value of preposterior analysis in determining whether any survey is worth the cost and, if so, the type and size of survey in order. Bayesian procedures can be extended in a natural fashion to deal with the important case of making sequential decisions where various information states exist between decision steps.

Although the outlook may appear sanguine for the future application of Bayesian decision theory to real marketing problems, this is not to say that these procedures will be—or should be—speedily adopted without reservation. Bayesian computations are frequently complex and time consuming. In the author's experience, most problems of any size required computer simulation in order to determine the relevant conditional payoff functions. In addition, Bayesian procedures do not yet exist for all traditional statistical procedures with which the analyst works. Nor in many cases can the relevant prior distributions be developed easily. In practice, the analyst will frequently resort to sensitivity analyses of prior distributions and payoff entries in order to show the decision maker how the "best" choice is affected by changes in the variables of interest.

In summary, Bayesian decision theory is entirely consonant with the incorporation of new data provided by activities like marketing research. Marketing research is thus viewed as a potentially valuable—but cost incurring—source for reducing the costs of uncertainty associated with decisions made in the absence of the research findings. Research can then be channeled into those areas where the potential informational gain is worth the cost of obtaining it. Somewhat ironically, considering the current trend toward greater use of the behavioral sciences in marketing, the venerable marginal analysis of microeconomic theory may find regained stature in the modified garb of statistical decision theory.

17

A Comparison of Management Theory Y With the Marketing Concept

JOHN DOUGLAS

One of the most important problems faced by men in all professions is that of "keeping up." For the executive, this means reading in a multitude of areas. Wendell Willkie's One World concept has descended upon business. As interrelationships and interdependencies appear, the scope of the businessman's "specialty" broadens. To keep up in his reading, the executive must not only read but also develop the criteria for sifting through the volume of materials.

The acquisition of an up-to-date posture is difficult at best. So time-consuming can this be that the most important questions rarely are formed. How does this report relate to the one read last week? What implications do the new empirical research findings pose for the future? How valid are the assumptions underlying the newer theories?

This article represents an attempt to gain this broader vision. In an effort to approach current business topics in such a manner, this writer focuses upon two recent major developments in business—the newer management and marketing theories. The following paragraphs contain a discussion of these theories organized around four basic questions. What are the management and marketing theories that are receiving attention in current literature? What are the similarities of these theories that suggest a more basic trend or characteristic? How is this basic trend identified? What are the implications of this trend for marketing and management operations and therefore for society? Starting with the first question, then, the following discussion will attempt to relate these theories and to present possible implications.

Reprinted with permission from the *Quarterly Review of Economics and Business,* Vol. 4 (Autumn, 1964), pp. 21-32.

The Contemporary Theories

The New Management Theory

In 1960, Douglas McGregor of the Massachusetts Institute of Technology presented in book form some ideas that represented the more advanced management thought of the time.[1] In particular, Professor McGregor emphasized the management thought that related to the managing of the human resources of the firm—a topic appearing in more and more academic and professional journals[2] and one which gains international attention daily. In McGregor's words,

This volume is an attempt to substantiate the thesis that the human side of enterprise is "all of a piece"—that the theoretical assumptions management holds about controlling its human resources determine the whole character of the enterprise. They determine also the quality of its successive generations of management.[3]

In his book McGregor stated that every managerial act rests on theory and that theory and practice are inseparable; thus, he suggested that the assumptions about human nature and human behavior (and so also the statements underlying managerial decisions and thus theory) should be clearly delineated and expressed. In short, McGregor contended that the traditional management practice (Theory X) should give way to a more contemporary Theory Y.[4] He built his case by analyzing the basic assumptions of both the traditional and the "called for." A brief summary of the major points will provide a common reference point.

Theory X Assumptions

The assumptions about human behavior are

1. The average human being has an inherent dislike of work and will avoid it if he can.

2. Because of this human characteristic of dislike of work, most people must be coerced, controlled, directed, threatened with punishment to

---

[1] Douglas McGregor, *The Human Side of Enterprise* (New York: McGraw-Hill, 1960).

[2] See, for example, David W. Belcher, "Toward a Behavioral Science Theory of Wages," *Journal of the Academy of Management,* Vol. 5, No. 5 (August, 1962), pp. 102-17; Perry Bliss, *Marketing and the Behavioral Sciences* (Boston: Allyn, 1963); Rensis Likert, *New Patterns of Management* (New York: McGraw-Hill, 1961).

[3] McGregor, *op. cit.,* pp. vi-vii.

[4] When McGregor uses the term "theory" he means certain managerial assumptions about the behavior of subordinates.

get them to put forth adequate effort toward the achievement of organizational objectives.

3. The average human being prefers to be directed, wishes to avoid responsibility, has relatively little ambition, wants security above all.[5]

With these assumptions as a base, McGregor held that traditional methods actually stress direction and control of subordinates since the direction and control of operations includes people as well as things. Although this pattern seems to have expressed the management practice of past years, McGregor contended that these practices should change because the basic assumptions of Theory X are in error and also are lacking in validity.

This is a brief summary of some of the characteristics of the traditional theory of management; a review of what McGregor hoped would replace it will follow.

Theory Y Assumptions and Practice

The more appropriate assumptions about man should be

1. The expenditure of physical and mental effort in work is as natural as play or rest.

2. External control and the threat of punishment are not the only means for bringing about effort toward organizational objectives. Man will exercise self-direction and self-control in the service of objectives to which he is committed.

3. Commitment to objectives is a function of the rewards associated with their achievement.

4. The average human being learns, under proper conditions, not only to accept but to seek responsibility

5. The capacity to exercise a relatively high degree of imagination, ingenuity, and creativity in the solution of organizational problems is widely, not narrowly, distributed in the population.

6. Under the conditions of modern industrial life, the intellectual potentialities of the average human being are only partially utilized.[6] The central principle which derives from these assumptions is that conditions should be created to encourage subordinates to achieve their own goals best by working for the success of the enterprise.

In summary, McGregor believed that the traditional management practice is based upon assumptions about human nature which are the *consequences* of a management practice using organizational concepts derived from early military and church organizations—authority through

---

[5] McGregor, *op. cit.,* pp. 33-34
[6] *Ibid.,* pp. 47-48.

direction and control. If management were to change its practices, the proponents of Theory Y say, the truer nature of man would be revealed. This position, of course, gains support from psychology and sociology research. The manager under Theory Y would create positive conditions or a climate wherein the subordinate would see that fulfilling the needs of the organization would in turn enable him to fulfill his own personal needs. The subordinate, therefore, would become much more involved in the matters that affect his work behavior. He would plan, organize, direct, and maintain self-control over work that was his responsibility.

This review presents only the highlights of the newer management theory presented by Douglas McGregor—a theory finding widespread acclaim, acceptance, and expression in other articles, in executive development courses, and in graduate and undergraduate curricula.

Now, let us turn to the development of another new theory—one representing changing thought in the marketing field. At the moment, there should be no attempt by the reader to compare the new marketing concept with Theory Y; this discussion will occur later in the article.

The New Marketing Concept

This new theory sounds almost naive in its simplicity; that is, all marketing activity should start with the consumer. While the consumer has always been important, he has not always been the key figure in the design and manufacture of the product. In past years, the problems of reducing cost and increasing efficiency have required the major efforts of the corporation; however, a new focal point is being discussed. No longer can the engineer demand the most attention. The important man on the emerging scene is now the consumer.

In some instances, men have expressed the newer concept as part of an evolutionary process.[7]

The function of marketing is still growing within the corporate organization, and it will continue to grow for some time to come. Business has come a long way since the day when most corporations were production-oriented manufacturing companies. The swing to the customer-minded philosophy has brought the marketing-oriented manufacturing company into full bloom today.[8]

But not all the experts hold the newer marketing theory to be a natural evolutionary outgrowth. Much more urgency and change is expressed by such persons as Robert J. Keith. In his article, "The Marketing

---

[7] The evolutionary character of the concept found expression in a recent article "AMA Beats the Drum for Innovation," *Business Week,* No. 1764 (June 22, 1963), pp. 88-91. The retiring president of the American Marketing Association, Donald R. Longman, said, "It's not a revolution, but a rapid evolution."

[8] "Transition To A Marketing Company," *Sales Management,* Vol. 87, No. 2 (July 21, 1961), pp. 36-38 and 102.

Revolution,"[9] Mr. Keith likens the relationship between the new marketing concept and the traditional one to the revolution in science created by Nicolaus Copernicus. "The market is the center of the economic universe as the sun is the center of our universe." A similar picture is expressed by Fred J. Borch, new president of the General Electric Company. "Under marketing, the customer becomes the fulcrum, the pivot point about which the business moves in operating for the balanced best interests of all concerned."[10]

The operating idea in the last statement quoted is supported by those persons who look at the marketing concept in terms of the decision process of the corporation. Peter Drucker, long associated with dealing with the managerial problems of firms, suggests that even (perhaps he meant to say especially) the corporate officers should view marketing as the starting place for policy, for criteria in decision-making, and for the testing of corporate effectiveness.[11] Professors Lazo and Corbin go so far as to say that the new marketing concept means that all business decisions (whether made by marketing personnel, engineers, research and development workers, or financiers) should be made with the market in mind; the decision should be viewed in terms of the impact upon the market.[12] And finally, A. P. Felton has stated that the marketing concept is

A corporate state of mind that insists on the integration and coordination of all the marketing functions which, in turn, are melded with all other corporate functions, for the basic objectives of producing maximum long-range corporate profits.[13]

Thus, the marketing concept has been viewed from a number of different bases: an evolutionary concept, a revolutionary concept, an integrating concept, and others. Common to all views is this important thought: while the movement toward the new theory or concept will be a function

---

[9] Robert J. Keith, "The Marketing Revolution," reprinted from the *Journal of Marketing,* Vol. 24, No. 3 (January, 1960), pp. 35-38, in Parker M. Holmes, Ralph E. Brownlee, and Robert Bartels (eds.), *Readings in Marketing* (Columbus: Merrill, 1963), pp. 65-70.

[10] Fred J. Borch, "The Marketing Philosophy as a Way of Business Life," in *The Marketing Concept: Its Meaning to Management,* Marketing Series, No. 99 (New York: American Management Association, 1957), p. 4.

[11] Peter Drucker, *The Practice of Management* (New York: Harper, 1954), pp. 37-41.

[12] Hector Lazo and Arnold Corbin, *Management in Marketing* (New York: McGraw-Hill, 1961). These authors also mention that some persons believed it was not the early efforts of educators like Paul Converse, J. F. Pyle, and R. S. Vaile nor the efforts by Ralph Cordiner at General Electric to act on marketing matters that ushered in the marketing concept. Rather, it may have been "the graduated taxes, high wages, and inflation which followed in the wake of World War II which finally made management focus its attention on the importance of marketing" (p. 9).

[13] Arthur P. Felton, "Making the Marketing Concept Work," *Harvard Business Review,* Vol. 37, No. 4 (July-August, 1959), p.55.

of the type of industry, the character and vision of top management, the nature of the product, and other factors, the movement is inevitable. Marketing in its many ramifications must start with the customer.

The preceding paragraphs have served the purpose of answering the first question: What are the contemporary management and marketing theories that represent newer trends of thought? With this material as a framework, we are now ready to ask, What are the similarities of these theories that suggest a more basic trend or movement?

Similarities of the New Theories

Timing

Perhaps it was not unusual that the new management theory and the new marketing concept came on the scene about the same time. The fields of management and marketing almost by definition tend to overlap each other in both day-to-day operations and longer-range policy matters. Because the marketing activity of a firm must be managed, the management concepts relate to all processes of marketing. Similarly, the higher levels of management (divisional level and up) must be concerned with marketing matters—products, prices, markets, competition, and so on. This relationship probably explains the emergence of the two new ideas at approximately the same time—the early fifties.

Heralds of New Truth

Both theories have received so much attention and acclaim that the outsider might feel that major breakthroughs had been accomplished and that the search for truth had ended. Theory X represented the traditional management thought and although no analogy has been made to the coin, there is the feeling that the other side of Theory X is Theory Y. Theory Y is presented as *the* theory for the management of human resources.

Often the new marketing concept, too, is presented as an absolute or ultimate law: " . . . once the importance of marketing has been accepted *as a matter of survival,* the company creed itself will undergo vital changes . . ."[14] A business executive of General Electric has said that the reason many older business firms had been successful was that "their businesses were customer-oriented because they knew that this was the only way to run a business!"[15] As a final example of the critical nature of the concept, J. W. Keener believes that "the marketing-oriented organizations will be

---

[14] Lazo and Corbin, *op. cit.,* p. 30.
[15] Borch, *loc. cit.*

the winners in the exciting, risk-filled, and opportunity-filled decade ahead."[16]

Both these concepts, therefore, represent advanced stages in the respective fields. Both also are described as major changes in emphasis and direction incorporating the latest information from the allied fields of economics, psychology, and sociology.

Shift in Emphasis

Figure 1 shows the pre-concept relationship of both the marketing area in its relationship to the market and the management area in its relationship through supervision.

Figure 1. Relationships Under Theory X and Production Orientation

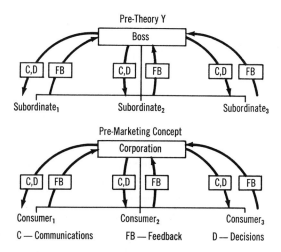

From Figure 1, we see that communications and decisions have flowed downward through the organization, the subordinate and the consumer responding with feedback. In management circles, the subordinate feedback has been in the form of productivity; in the marketing context, the consumer has responded with his feedback in terms of the purchasing dollar.

Theory Y and the new marketing concept seem to suggest that the orientation needs revision; the new emphasis should be on customer or market orientation. In management, the new emphasis should be on employee orientation to the management process. In both these concepts

---

[16] J. W. Keener, "Marketing's Job for the 1960s," reprinted from the *Journal of Marketing,* Vol. 24, No. 3 (January, 1960), pp. 1-6, in Holmes *et al., op. cit.,* p. 174.

the call is for greater involvement by the lower-level units (i.e., the subordinate or the consumer).

If the new relationships were to be diagrammed, they would appear as in Figure 2.

Figure 2. Relationships Under Theory Y and Consumer Orientation

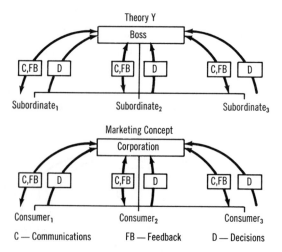

Communications are now (or would be) originating in two areas: the boss and the corporation; the subordinate and the market or consumer. Each is to be a more equal partner in the relationship. Feedback also stems from both as information concerning needs and wants as well as reactions to decisions are continually transmitted to both parties. Decisions emanate from the bottom and flow upward with the subordinate and the consumer having a more direct influence in the decision process. These figures should illustrate the influence of the newer concepts upon communication and decision patterns. No longer would the main stream of ideas and communication be downward. Under the new plans, the pattern would be modified in favor of a bottom-to-top direction.

The preceding paragraphs have served to suggest that many similarities exist between the new marketing and management theories. These newer theories began to be discussed about the same time. The supporters of both the management and the marketing theories claim the presence of new or ultimate truth in these ideas. And both theories represent a shift of emphasis in decision and communication patterns.

The presence of many common elements, then, points to the possibility of a more basic relationship or factor common to both movements.

Thus far, such a relationship has merely been suggested but the following section will directly support a case for the common element. This time the question is, How is this basic characteristic identified?

The Common Characteristic

To me the underlying theme permeating both the marketing concept and the management concept is the dependence upon participation. The new concepts call for the subordinate and the consumer to participate in activities once reserved for those persons in higher management levels and positions.

Participation in Management

The rationale in management thought follows logically in this way. Who should perform the management process? Who should do the planning, organizing, directing, and controlling of activities? In earlier days the answer might have been a resounding "the boss," but today many would say "the subordinate." Many consultants know that solutions to company problems exist within the ranks of the company personnel and that the consultant's job is to clarify the problem, locate the persons with the solutions to these problems, and then convince top management of the value of the solutions. This very characteristic is basic to the participation concept. Theoretically, the subordinate manager, who has to work on the project, is best able to plan the project and set the objectives he believes are attainable. If the subordinate manager is best able to plan the operation that he will perform, it follows that he will be the one who can best organize and direct it. In the process of performing these management functions, the subordinate applies control, which has become self-control. Under this kind of system of subordinate participation in the management process, the primary role of the executive manager or boss is in the *coaching* of the subordinates as they participate and in the *coordination* of the activities of the subordinates.

Participation in Marketing

The American economic system has always had an element of consumer participation in it. As put forth in the basic economic texts or even in the contemporary language of Robert Heilbroner's *The Making of Economic Society*,[17] America chose the market system (as opposed to tradition and command) for finding an economic answer to such questions as what is to

---

[17] Robert Heilbroner, *The Making of Economic Society* (Englewood Cliffs: Prentice-Hall, 1962).

be produced, how it is to be produced, and to whom it should be distributed. In the market system, the consumer is supposed to have the greatest voice by actually deciding whether to purchase or not. The dollar is the consumer vote. This point is relevant to the marketing concept.

The role of the consumer is theoretically elevated through the implementation of the new marketing concept. This is not a drastic step, as the consumer role is already on a high plane. In 1944, Ludwig von Mises wrote:

> Within the market society the working of the price mechanism makes the consumers supreme. They determine through the prices they pay and through the amount of their purchases both the quantity and quality of production. They determine directly the prices of consumers' goods, and thereby indirectly the prices of all material factors of production and the wages of all hands employed.
>
> . . . in that endless rotating mechanism the entrepreneurs and capitalists are the servants of the consumers. The consumers are the masters, to whose whims the entrepreneurs and capitalists must adjust their investments and methods of production.[18]

If the American economic system has already given the consumer such an elevated role, how does the newer theory stress greater participation by the consumer?

It appears that the major difference between the consumer roles under the traditional market system and under the new marketing concept is that the consumer in the past has participated in response to corporate activity (through buying or not buying the products) whereas the new marketing concept describes consumer participation in the *planning phases* of production as well as in the setting of the criteria for decision-making throughout the total enterprise.

This participation in the new marketing concept is manifested in two ways.[19] The consumer now assumes a much greater role and voice in the decision-making processes of the firm *and* those persons involved with the marketing activity assume a much more important place among the executive elite. Most writers, when describing the implementation of the marketing concept in the firm, speak in terms of the change that must take place within the organization. The "proper state of mind" or the "changed attitude" refers to that of the corporate officials, who must be willing to see the significance of operating *from* the market rather than *to* the market. Thus this type of participation (the other was consumer par-

---

[18] Ludwig von Mises, *Omnipotent Government* (New Haven: Yale University Press, 1944), pp. 49-50.

[19] In the Foreword to Lazo and Corbin, *op. cit.*, p. v, Peter Drucker uses the terms "marketing view" and the "management of marketing" to convey a similar idea.

ticipation) is an internal type where the person in charge of marketing activities becomes more involved.

Considerable effort has been devoted to illustrating where this new, greater stress upon participation occurs in the new marketing and management theories. This is not to say that these newer theories contain no other factors or ideas in common; however, basic to them both and crucial to their implementation is consumer or subordinate participation. It is this dominant characteristic which permeates both trends.

The identification of this common denominator is important for two reasons. First, it enables us to see more easily the relationship of these newer theories to others outside the business area. Certainly, participation or ego involvement is an important term in many fields. The newer art expression rests upon it; education and training insist upon it; and psychology thrives upon it. To this extent, then, Theory Y and the new marketing concept are part of a broader social trend. This insight helps us to understand better the "why" of the newer theories.

The second reason for identifying the common characteristic is more directly relevant to the final topic of the implications of the newer theories. If the theories are perceived as being related to other movements also stressing participation, a possible danger presents itself. Because of the inertia created by similar movements, the newer theories may be acclaimed and accepted before their merits have been investigated extensively. Participation is neither good nor bad. It must be weighed with a specific set of conditions in mind. There are many questions of limitations and extent. Therefore, the next question is, What are the implications of this increased participation for marketing and management and indirectly for the whole of society?

The following discussion is intended to locate probable problems if the greater-participation trend is supported. This is not to say that the raising of questions necessarily denies the point. In other words, the succeeding paragraphs are not included to condemn participation but to provide an awareness of the more far-reaching consequences of participation by greater numbers of people in decisive areas of management and marketing. It is hoped that such an examination of problem areas may aid the reader in evaluating the newer theories from a broader and wiser base.

Implications of Participation

Benefits

Many claims have been made by the proponents of the participation movement as to its advantages. These proponents, coming primarily from the university ranks as social scientists, believe participation provides significant benefits for both the individual participating and the corporation. Included in these advantages are such items as productivity increases, improvements in morale and motivation, a greater sense of well-being for the participating subordinate, and enhancement of the individual's identification with the corporation goals.[20] The picture that emerges is of an individual growing and developing through participation in the decision process of the enterprise. This individual is a cooperative person and is thus able to find much more meaning in his work and the work of others around him.

These benefits to the individual are not at the expense of the corporation, however, since it too benefits from this participation. The productivity increases of the individual will also improve the cost picture of the corporation; efficiencies from the cooperation of the subordinates should be more attainable; the corporate image becomes more easily accepted by all parties, who, because of their participation, become salesmen for the enterprise.

Problems and Criticisms

Not everyone agrees that the benefits just described are the natural extension of participation. The first charge thrown at the participation proponents is that of manipulation.[21] The social scientists, particularly the newer group of behavioral scientists who have worked in industry, have been labeled by Lorin Baritz as the "servants of power."[22] The behavioral servants respond to the wishes of their masters, the corporation executives, who have hired them at salaries far above their meager university earnings to conduct "research studies" that will "uncover the truth." Baritz maintains that most of these "findings" are really *post facto* findings: a company needs data to support some point and data are found. The Harwood studies, for example, which are purported to exemplify the benefits to be derived from participation, are seen by Baritz as ingenious methods for having the employees "participate" in a management-planned situation so that the goals of the corporation would be better achieved.[23]

---

[20] See, for example, Victor H. Vroom, *Some Personality Determinants of the Effects of Participation* (Englewood Cliffs: Prentice-Hall, 1960).

[21] Douglas McGregor was well aware of the criticisms of participation. In his Chapter 9, "Participation in Perspective," he criticizes those proponents of participation who believe that the magic formula has been found for the elimination of conflict and disagreement; he also attacks the critics who believe participation is merely manipulation. In his words, ". . . participation is not a panacea, a manipulative device, a gimmick, or a threat. Used wisely, and with understanding, it is a natural concomitant of management by integration and self-control." See McGregor, *op. cit.,* p. 131.

[22] Loren Baritz, *The Servants of Power* (Middletown, Conn.: Wesleyan University Press, 1960).

[23] Others have raised their voices in protest. See the writings of Arthur Kornhauser, C. Wright Mills, and Wilbert E. Moore.

Baritz' criticism has been used here to exemplify some thinking and uneasiness about the use of social findings. Actually, one of two possible assumptions must be made before carrying the discussion further. One assumes that subordinate units can help set objectives in the best interests of the firm or one assumes that they cannot. If the latter position is held, then efforts to guide behavior in the direction of predetermined patterns must be vulnerable to the charge of manipulation. The control of individual behavior is beset with many problems of ethics. The reader can surely extend his thinking along these lines to see how involved this charge of manipulation can become.

But the other assumption may also hold. Perhaps the majority of the proponents of the newer management and marketing theories sincerely believe that goals and methods advocated by subordinate units will in fact work for the greatest good of the organization. What then?

If subordinate units in fact were encouraged to make corporate plans and decisions, the mind would immediately turn to difficulties emerging in many directions. How could responsible leadership be encouraged?[24] How could such units handle complex commodities such as defense mechanisms or drugs? Does the consumer know what he wants?[25] These are only some of the pertinent questions. Even though such reflections conjure up a multitude of problems, the discussion here will center about a broader area. Perhaps the most serious and far-reaching implication of the participation movement is the subtle impact it would have upon the standards of society.

The Social System

It has been suggested that the pursuit and questioning of implications is important because so many forces in society (management and marketing, in this case) are striving toward the goal of participation. True, not all factions of the business society may completely achieve this end but because of the striving, the question of direction is critical.

If a corporation actually becomes consumer oriented, it takes on the values of the consumers. This transformation does not come overnight but in the day-to-day attempts to have "the customer's wants become the very criteria for corporate decision-making." What will happen to society when participation encourages the acceptance of mass values? Can society's goals be achieved when mass values may delay the process of innovation and individual creativity? And as Irving Kristol suggests,[26] if segments of

---

[24] John Douglas, "Our Lopsided Concept of Accomplishment," *Business Quarterly,* Vol. 28, No. 1 (Spring, 1963), pp. 10-18 and 77.

[25] "Tiffany's Off On a Spree," *Business Week,* No. 1727 (October 6, 1962), p. 56.

[26] Irving Kristol, "Is the Welfare State Obsolete?" *Harper's Magazine,* Vol. 226, No. 1357 (June, 1963), pp. 39-43.

our nation resist taking on the values of the masses, the government may become the protector or guardian of these segments—resulting in increased bureaucratic organization.

The point is that the very process of placing participation as *the* goal may erode the forces within this nation that have been balanced basically by our Constitution (the doctrine of checks and balances). The individual's values can be lost to those of the mass. Can minority or individual rights continue to be respected with this greater emphasis upon mass values?

In the same way that followership should be viewed as the countervailing[27] force to leadership, participation should be viewed as the countervailing force to autocratic decision-making, and cooperation the countervailing force to conflict. In more specific terms, the two new theories being discussed contain an emphasis upon participation by subordinate units. In effect, this movement would invest new power in these groups. If the pendulum swings radically to one side, then it would be possible for the new power groups to overbalance the power of the executive organization. To provide an effective and constructive change, then, the new theories must include more specific corollaries relating to limitations, extent, and scope.

Summary

Two concepts, one in marketing and one in management, were reviewed with special attention given to the relationship of each to a more fundamental movement of the times. Stress upon participation by subordinate units in management and marketing and the resulting aim of cooperation among the forces appeared as primary goals. The implications of such goals suggested that the newer theories in marketing and management— indeed, in all areas—need to be extended to their broader ramifications before widespread endorsement occurs.

---

[27] See John Kenneth Galbraith, *American Capitalism* (Cambridge, Mass.: Riverside Press, 1962) for the development of the countervailing power concept.

18

The Analysis of Market Efficiency

LEE E. PRESTON
NORMAN R. COLLINS

Marketing efficiency has been appraised primarily in terms of the relationship between trading costs and volume, although this simplification has been criticized for neglecting qualitative factors. Four more specific indicators of market efficiency are identified: (1) viability-stability, (2) ratio of units traded to marketing effort, (3) revenues of market participants and (4) realization of potential transactions. Results of simulation analysis show that these indicators are, at least in principle, measurable, and that they are not closely correlated with each other.

The principal criterion for appraising the efficiency of marketing activities appears to be the minimizing of measured costs per unit of marketing work over calendar time periods. The cost standard, usually stated in terms of labor time, has been the primary focus of the major empirical studies of marketing activitiy on an economy-wide basis;[1] and, so far as one can discover, costs are a principal element in designing and appraising marketing organization alternatives within the firm. Even Alderson, who was a principal critic of the cost approach to marketing analysis [2, Chs. 3 and 11], tied his last conceptual innovation to the cost standard. He and Miles Martin defined the "transvection" as "the unit of action for the system by which a single end product . . . is placed in the hands of the consumer after moving through all the intermediate sorts and transformations from the original raw materials [3, p. 118]." Although remarking that a "distribution network quickly becomes too complicated for complete evalua-

Reprinted from Lee E. Preston and Norman R. Collins, "The Analysis of Market Efficiency," the *Journal of Marketing Research,* a publication of the American Marketing Association, Vol. III (May, 1966), pp. 154-162.

[1] Principal references are [8, 10, 12, 13, 16, 20, and 21].

tion of marketing effectiveness," they further stated that a "transvection has the optimal number of steps if costs cannot be decreased, either by increasing or decreasing the number of steps [3, p. 124]." The principal analysts of marketing efficiency, particularly Barger, Cox and Sevin, tried to emphasize the variability of the quality-service features that may be offered in the market under different cost conditions. In spite of these qualifications, critics of the cost standard have stressed the overwhelming importance of the qualitative dimension, the scope for variety and adaptation in the system, and the standard of living delivered, as ultimate appraisal criteria.[2]

This article suggests extending the criteria for analyzing market efficiency beyond the cost standard, as currently understood, but stopping well short of the qualitative appraisal of the product-promotion-service results in final markets. The article does not argue that these ultimate results are not overwhelmingly important. Rather, it argues that these results grow out of the entire socioeconomic system in which they are observed, and thus cannot reasonably be appraised in terms of market or economic activity alone. Nor does the article argue that *cost,* in the broadest sense, is not the appropriate basis for efficiency analysis. However, the many cost dimensions —incurred *vs.* opportunity costs, the timing and incidence of expenditures, and the special costs of market activity associated with communication and risk reduction—render any attempt to arrive at a single composite cost figure subject to overwhelming conceptual, as well as statistical, limitations.

This article therefore, proposes some specific criteria that might be adopted for appraising the efficiency of market activities, and it uses data drawn from simulation experiments to examine some indicators of market performance with respect to these criteria. It is concluded from this analysis that extending criteria for appraising market efficiency, both within the firm and in a larger systemic context, beyond the cost standard is both feasible and necessary, and that specifying and measuring a range of appropriate efficiency criteria is a major task of marketing research.

Criteria of Market Efficiency

For purposes of this analysis, a market is defined as a potential exchange relationship among buyers and sellers, and market efficiency as the facility and effectiveness with which the potential exchanges are accomplished.

---

[2] An excellent short review of the issues is presented in [14], and a more extensive consideration in [10, Chapters 10-14]. An attempt at analytical integration of all elements of marketing effectiveness into a cost framework at the level of the firm was made by Verdoorn [27] and extended by Allison [4] and Howard [15, Chapter 7]. These latter presentations are so general as to represent formalizations of judgmental analysis rather than guides to substantive research.

This concept of market efficiency is thus divorced from the specific character or quality of goods or services subject to exchange, the volume of goods or services either supplied or demanded, and the exchange ratio (*i.e.,* the trading price).

Market efficiency in economic literature has been equated with market outcomes generated by perfect competition.[3] Under perfectly competitive conditions, the interplay of sellers and buyers leads to the establishment of a unique market price in which the marginal cost of supply is equal to the marginal satisfaction obtained by buyers; supply costs are everywhere minimized, and no market participant can gain without loss to another. This pareto-optimal outcome has come to be regarded as *the* efficient one from the resource allocation viewpoint, and the failure of actual markets to meet the requirements of perfect competition has been said to bring about inefficiency. The significance of this result has been variously assessed, and the relative magnitude of the resulting welfare losses has been estimated as rather small in some studies. Further, it has been frequently argued that these short-run allocative inefficiencies are more than offset by the innovative activity, and increased qualitative variety and range of product choice associated with market imperfections.

In any event, neither the theoretical standard of perfect competition nor the principal qualifications surrounding its use as a norm for appraising actual market performance include specific consideration of the efficiency of market activity itself. Phillips has said:

Economic theory largely neglects organizational aspects of markets, emphasizing instead structural characteristics. Competitive markets in particular are defined in theory in terms of their structure, not their organization, by reference to the number of firms, the homogeneity of the product, freedom of entry, *etc.* This is curious since the markets of the real world which are used as illustrations of competitive price setting are not unorganized, unregulated meetings of buyers and sellers. They are organized in rather extreme detail [18, p. 175].

Not only is a market an organizational structure, it is also, as Adelman [1] has emphasized, "a system of information on cost and demand." It has been frequently noted that this information system is not costless and that information, communication, and transaction costs conditions may vary considerably under different institutional arrangements, with important effects on both marketing structure and performance [6, 25].

These issues were drawn together by Sosnick in the concept of "exchange efficiency." He noted that:

The level of output is not the only issue raised by asking about the impact of a market on the allocation of resources among users. Also important is how

---

[3] A rigorous presentation of this analysis, highly suggestive in terms of the argument in this paper, is [17], especially Chapter 3.

well the quantity available . . . leaves the hands of persons who value the commodity least and ends up in the hands of persons who value it most.

. . . the exchange function of markets seems to have been forgotten. The explanation may lie in the fact that the exchange process is quasi-automatic in certain administered-price markets, so that all interesting attributes of the outcome can be summarized merely by the level of output, price, or profit. In general, however, to omit the subject of exchange efficiency will neglect something that is in all markets relevant and in some markets critical [24, p. 88-9].

Sosnick has suggested some tests of exchange efficiency with primary reference to agricultural markets and without attempting direct empirical application [24, p. 112-16]. Two important recent contributions have combined organization and information considerations in developing market efficiency tests for specific empirical research purposes. Balderston and Hoggatt [7] give a series of specific efficiency tests for analyzing their market simulation model, and Stigler [26] uses three principal criteria in his recent appraisal of public regulation in the securities markets. It is significant that both these instances in which attention was focused on the efficiency of *market* operations, as different from cost reduction or "low" prices, were characterized by the absence of tangible production costs and consumable products. In the Balderston-Hoggatt simulation model, production costs are parameters of the system, and the product is not specified in detail. In the securities market neither the production cost of shares nor of the physical assets they represent is the primary determinant of stock market values, and the shares themselves are used for trading purposes only. Thus, in these contexts the problem of market efficiency was placed in clear relief.

Independent analysis and a search of the literature leads to a proposal of the following characteristics as potential criteria for appraising efficiency of marketing networks or transactions-transvections systems, considering both buying and selling sides, multiple-level marketing organizations and interaction patterns.

Viability—Stability

Viability is the first market characteristic examined by Balderston and Hoggatt in their analysis of the simulation model, and is the first consideration cited by Stigler—"The basic function a market serves is to bring buyers and sellers together [26, p. 126]." A market that functions only spasmodically, or exhibits such unstable behavior patterns as to be constantly on the verge of explosion or discontinuance, or operates in a manner that excludes large numbers of potential participants from the exchange environment, is clearly not performing this primary task. However, the *existence* of a market is a logical requisite to analyzing its efficiency, and the *continuity* of market activity is more readily analyzed in terms of *stability*. Thus, the viability of market activity over time appears to be a necessary, but not sufficient, condition for market efficiency.

The aspect of market performance most frequently cited in the general literature as related to market efficiency, in the sense discussed here, is the stability of prices and trading quantities. The importance of stability follows directly from the association between instability and risk, and between risk and cost. It is not simple, however, to specify in a particular market context the degree of stability that is, in fact, associated with risk reduction for all parties in the market, or to separate risk reduction benefiting all from rigidities benefiting only particular market participants. The contrast between these two possibilities accounts for the development of two quite different views in the literature. From one perspective, relative stability in market activity and price levels is desirable and, indeed, a requirement for continuous market operation and attaining maximum benefit from using a *market* rather than some other (governmental or intra-firm) mechanism for resource allocation. Futures markets and other forms of risk-reduction and risk-shifting through forward trading have been thought desirable because of their stabilizing influence on market results. On the other hand, flexibility, particularly of prices, in response to changes in cost and demand is frequently cited as a requirement for effectively competitive market activity, and argument from this principle has led to a conclusion that stability (usually termed "rigidity" in this context) is associated with inefficiency. These two different ideas may be formally joined in a statement such as the following: A market is efficient when cost changes are readily reflected in price changes, demand changes reflected in volume changes, and random instability not associated with fundamental readjustments is at a minimum.

Stigler has emphasized the importance of the volume response to demand changes, which he terms *resilience,* "an unfamiliar word for a property whose absence is called 'thinness' [26, p. 127]." Many other writers have repeatedly stressed the efficiency aspects of price and volume stability in general, as opposed to erratic and partially random patterns of fluctuation. For example, Phillips comments:

Equilibrium among interdependent firms . . . requires an organization of sufficient formality to prevent independent behavior from destablizing the market. That is, markets with large numbers of equipowerful firms and very informal organizations tend to have excessive rivalry and poor performance [18, p. 37].

Carrying out a stability test cast in these terms requires, of course, an ability to measure demand and cost changes apart from the market response to them, and thus to separate functional adjustments from residual instability. A simulation model readily permits this type of measurement; in actual markets it is considerably more difficult.

These comments on market stability have been fairly unspecific for the particular magnitudes to be stabilized. The literature tends to emphasize stabilization of price levels, and this criterion may be extended to cover price-cost relationships, and thus take account of the difference between market responses to changes in cost and demand. The existence of decentralized markets, interrelated markets and multi-product markets introduces the further complication of price *dispersion*—that is, the distribution of prices among transactions, over space, or among products related by cost or demand. The stability criterion may be broadened to include these price structure relationships as well. Of course, as additional relationships are introduced, the specification of stability conditions and the identification of functional and random fluctuations become increasingly difficult. In addition to prices, one might also examine the stability of numbers of market participants, trading volume, profits, *etc.,* with the relevant activity variables measured on both an aggregate and per-firm basis.

Number of Units Traded and Amount of Market Effort

The engineering definition of efficiency in terms of physical output per unit of input has been widely adopted in economic analysis, and the appropriateness of this criterion for analysis of distributive activity on an economy-wide basis has been argued by Barger [8], Cox [10], and others. Some variant of this approach is generally applied in the analysis of marketing costs at the firm level. The problems involved in using this criterion—principally with the definition of the quality of input effort and the associated changes in product quality—are well known. However, insofar as units of market effort, such as amount of communication activity, number of transactions, *etc.,* may be measured and unambiguously interpreted, direct output/input efficiency measures may be obtained.

Revenues of Market Participants

It has been suggested by Balderston [5] that one criterion of the efficiency of marketing organization may be the maximization of total net revenues of all market participants other than final buyers. This is an appropriate criterion for managerial appraisal, although it specifically neglects the welfare of consumer participants (unless their revenues can be explicitly estimated in terms of "reservation prices" and "consumers' surplus"). It may be useful, however, to consider the revenue criterion against gross measures of trading volume and price levels to determine the net trade-offs involved in the choice of market organizational patterns. Of course, the distribution of revenue gains both among market levels and among individual enterprise units is a matter of considerable concern to the market participants themselves, and changes in the relative as well as the absolute amounts of revenues and profits may be significant. In particular, if the number and size of firms is subject to variation, the direct measurement of revenue or profit per firm may be a misleading indicator of the effectiveness of the total marketing system.

Realization of Potential Transactions

A centralized market assures the realization of all potential transactions between buyers who are willing to pay at least as much as the market price and sellers willing to sell for no more than the market price, unless there are artificial barriers to entry. In a decentralized market, transactions may take place at any viable combination of bid and offer prices. As a result, there is no "market price," but only some central tendency or average of actual prices. Further, there may be mutually compatible bid and offer combinations that fail to result in transactions because of the absence of full communication and information. It is, therefore, relevant to examine such markets to determine the extent to which they result in the consummation of all potential transactions indicated by bid and offer conditions on both sides, and the conditions under which such transactions are consummated. In addition, one might consider *which* potential transactions were left unconsummated, and why.[4]

The conceptual problem involved here is not as obvious as it seems. If we consider the intersection of *ex ante* supply and demand schedules in a centralized market as determining the basic price and quantity norms for a market, then it is evident that decentralization alone would introduce the strong likelihood of a difference between these norms and the actual volume traded and average of trading prices. No matter how trading partners and transactions prices are determined by decentralized traders, there is no particular reason either to expect prices to average out at the supply-demand intersection, or to expect the actual quantity traded to equal the intersection quantity. Thus, the efficiency of an imperfect, decentralized market in the realization of potential transactions might be measured in at least three dimensions:

a. The relationship of its average transactions price to the intersection level, and also the dispersion of transactions prices (there being no dispersion in a centralized, perfectly competitive market).

b. The relationship of its trading volume to the intersection level. Note that, *a priori,* we should not be surprised if fortuitous pairings re-

---

[4] Sosnick combines the revenue and potential transactions criteria by proposing that "the ratio of actual to potential gains from trade should be maximized [24, p. 114]."

sulted in *larger* quantities being traded in decentralized markets than would have been traded under centralized conditions.

c. The achievement of the potential gains from trade—that is, buyers trading for less and sellers for more than the prices at which they would withdraw from the market. There is also the question of the distribution of these gains among market participants.

In general, potential and actual market results can be compared only through the projection of static questions from cross-section or time-series data, or from experimentation under laboratory conditions. Early and still highly suggestive experiments involving decentralization and market imperfections were reported by Chamberlin [9], and more recent and complex experiments were reported by Vernon Smith [22, 23]. The particular pattern of decentralized trading adopted by Chamberlin appeared to result in larger quantities traded at lower prices than a centralized, full-information market would have achieved. He observed that actual average trading prices were lower than the intersection price of the *ex ante* array of bids and offers in 39 of 46 classroom market experiments; trading volume was greater than intersection quantity in 42 cases and the same in four cases.

Smith's extension of the Chamberlin experiments involved a learning feature and a more elaborate information structure. Adaptive behavior was observed over a series of market periods, and a "remarkably strong tendency for exchange prices to approach the predicted equilibrium" was observed in eight out of 15 experiments [22, p. 116]. If, however, one examines only the first period of each experiment, before any learning had occurred, one gains the impression that decentralized trading tended to produce outcomes different from the *ex ante* intersection norm, but not systematically biased in any particular direction. Compared to the intersection norms, quantities were greater in four cases, smaller in five and equal in six; prices were greater in six cases, smaller in eight and equal in one. Nor did larger quantities and lower prices tend to be associated, as they were in the Chamberlin experiments; prices and quantities varied from intersection levels in opposite directions in only three of Smith's 15 experiments.[5]

In a subsequent group of experiments [23], Smith examined the effect of trading initiative on market outcomes. Specifically, he conducted experiments in which only sellers, only buyers, and both sellers and buyers were permitted to make trading offers. The hypothesis that equilibrium prices would tend to be ordered from the seller-offer case (low) to the buyer-offer case (high) was accepted on the basis of statistical analysis. Both the average buyer-seller-offer price and the overall average price for this

---

[5] Calculated from [22, Table 1, p. 117].

entire group of experiments were within one cent of the intersection price of $2.10.

Taken together, these results suggest that decentralization and the particular conditions under which transactions are carried out may be expected to produce substantial departures from the market outcomes anticipated from underlying supply and demand structures, and that these departures may be significantly affected by the timing and repetitiveness of market activity and the particular patterns of communication and trade-initiation that develop.

It is generally agreed that the failure of a market to accomplish all the potential transactions intra-marginal to the intersection norm determined by the underlying supply and demand conditions is a sign of inefficiency. This argument, however, rests on a conception of supply and demand schedules *net* of information costs; the cost of information may itself be unknown to many market participants. An additional problem is raised by the possibility that markets will result in trading volumes greater than intersection levels, at either lower *or* higher prices. Smith proposes "the ability of . . . markets to ration out submarginal buyers and sellers . . . [as] one measure of [their] effectiveness or competitive performance . . . [22, p. 114]."

On the other hand, the usual aggregate economic criterion that *more* is *better* might justify a preference for imperfect, high-volume markets, particularly if the average price results were fairly close to intersection price levels. The presence of market intermediaries between initial suppliers and final demanders further complicates the picture. These intermediaries affect the cost and information structure of the market and, therefore, have an important impact on the volume of potential transactions and the conditions under which they might take place. Intermediaries not only affect the *achievement* of the potential of the market; they contribute to the determination of the potential itself.

Application of the Criteria: Simulation Results

A group of statistical indicators generated by simulation experiments were selected and analyzed in order to illustrate the several criteria of market efficiency and to examine the possible interrelations among them. Experimental results were obtained from 34 runs of a market simulation model adapted from the original construction of Hoggatt and Balderston [7] and subjected to more detailed analysis in [19].

Although the original version of this model used the West Coast lumber industry as its "empirical referent," the present model is entirely theoretical in conception. It is, in effect, a laboratory within which controlled market experiments can be undertaken with full information on results. Characteristics of firms in the model were synthesized from the current research literature, and the patterns of market contact established are simplifications of those existing in many actual industries.

The model portrays a single hypothetical industry in which there are three vertically related groups of firms—suppliers, wholesaler-brokers, and retailers. Individual firms are simulated at each level. Final demand for the industry's product is an aggregate function, and the decision criteria of final consumer buyers are not portrayed. All firms are single-plant enterprises; the opportunity to buy out or merge with other market units does not exist. There is no forward dealing, no contracting beyond the immediate market period and no preference of one market partner for another. Geographic location and transportation costs do not enter the system. All activities take place instantaneously or with explicitly stated one-period time lags.

Suppliers in the model have no conception of final demand for the industry and no contact with the retail market. Their pricing practices, which are entirely behavioral, may be interpreted as the intention to sell "a maximum quantity at a good price." Each firm bases its offer price on a forecast of the direction of price change for the entire market (common to all firms) and an analysis of its own past profit, price, and sales experience. It then offers its entire stock of merchandise for sale at this price.

The essential activity of wholesalers is to inquire among firms on either side of the market in search of profitable (to them) supplier-offer and retailer-bid prices. When they locate a profitable transaction, they send order messages to the two firms involved. If both firms confirm that they are able to make the transaction as indicated in their initial responses, the wholesaler executes the transaction. He then continues the contracting process until his working capital is exhausted or his search activity is otherwise constrained.

The retail firms in this model are profit maximizers in the textbook tradition. From an assumed price-quantity demand function, the retailer computes marginal revenue and determines the sales volume that will equate marginal revenue with marginal cost (purchase cost of merchandise). However, retailers do not necessarily sell their expected quantities at the set price. Retail demands are interrelated in such a way that retailers with above average prices will sell somewhat less than they anticipate and retailers with below average prices, somewhat more. The total sales volume in the retail market depends on the particular pattern of retail prices established. Retailers base their buying prices on past purchasing experience, with respect to price and quantity. Purchase and selling price decisions are linked because sales quantity determines desired purchase quantity after a time lag.

The simulation model is continuously interlinked and, once started, self-contained. At the beginning of a market period each wholesaler sends "search" messages to a retailer and a supplier, and each firm contacted sends back a "reply" stating its bid or offer price and quantity. After all wholesalers have had the opportunity to search one pair, each examines the replies to determine whether a profitable transaction has been discovered. If so, he sends an "order" message to the retailer and supplier involved. If not, he awaits the beginning of a new cycle with the opportunity to search again. A particular retailer or supplier may receive no, one, or several orders during any one cycle, but only one may be accepted. If several orders are received, a random procedure is used to determine which is accepted. If either party rejects an order, the transaction is void and the wholesaler awaits the next cycle. If both parties accept the order, the wholesaler executes the transaction and draws down his working capital by paying the supplier firm. The wholesaler does not receive his payment from the retailer until the end of the entire period; thus, working capital is a constraint on the wholesaler's activities. When every wholesaler has had the opportunity to complete or otherwise terminate the potential transaction discovered during the initial search period, the market cycle is ended.

Each firm in the system then has the opportunity to determine whether it will stay in the market for another cycle. Wholesalers leave the market when they have insufficient working capital to execute at least a one-unit transaction at prevailing prices or when their search experience has been disappointing for several periods. Retailers and suppliers leave the market when their requirements have been filled or stocks exhausted.

The next cycle begins with the wholesaler proceeding to another retailer-supplier pair and repeating the search process. Trading cycles continue as long as any wholesaler remains in the market. When there is no wholesaler remaining and wishing to trade, the market period is over. At this point the retailers pay the wholesalers for their purchases. Retailers then set their final prices, offer quantities and sell in the final market. All firms then compute their incomes and costs for the period and calculate profits. Firms with negative working capital go out of business while other firms readjust capacity as indicated by their individual decision rules and capabilities. New entrants appear if the aggregate profitability of the firms at any level of the market permits.

Each run of the model lasts for 60 market periods, and 34 experimental runs were made for purposes of this analysis. Each run differs from the others in one or more of the following respects: number and size of firms, condition of entry, stability of final demand, operating costs, and internal decision criteria. The output series include the two prices (retailer-bid and supplier-offer) in the intermediate market, the intermediate market trading quantity, retail selling prices, and retail sales quantities. These data are obtained on an individual firm basis, and parameters of the data distributions are computed as are average and aggregate values for periods 10–60 of each simulation run. The first nine periods of each run were arbitrarily excluded to eliminate large, one-time fluctuations caused by changes in initial conditions. From the entire collection of output data one or more indicators have been selected as representative of the performance of the market system model with respect to each of the efficiency criteria. The indicators have been selected for illustrative purposes, and we have chosen a minimum number necessary to suggest the diversity of the results and their implications for study of actual markets. The particular series selected for each criterion are described in the following paragraphs.

Viability—Stability

Neither costs nor final demand conditions vary within the simulation runs in such a way as to produce marked differences in the patterns of variability observed in the output variables. Therefore, the measurement of overall variability serves as a reasonable proxy for measurement of the random component. The variability of four output series measured over periods of 10–60 of each simulation run have been selected as indicators of stability in the market:

1. Standard deviation of average period supplier prices;
2. Standard deviation of average period retail prices;
3. Standard deviation of period wholesale market quantity;
4. Standard deviation of period retail market quantity.

Trading Volume and Marketing Effort

Selected as a measure of real cost of the transactions activity itself is:

5. Number of trading messages sent per unit traded in the wholesale market, average for periods 10–60 of each run.

Revenues of Market Participants

The simulated market grew in total size and profitability over most of the experimental runs as a result of the entry of retailers, and total capital in the system accumulated over time. Variations in profits per firm and in the number of firms at each level making losses, although suggestive for some analytical purposes, were strongly affected by the initial number of firms and entry conditions in the various runs. One indicator of differential revenue experience of firms at several market levels appeared appropriate for present purposes. It was the change in the percentage distribution of total system capital among firms at each level over each of the runs. Given the initial capital distribution, a tendency of firms at one market level (*e.g.,* wholesalers) to gain capital relative to firms at another level (*e.g.,* suppliers) indicated differences in their sharing of profits resulting from market expansion. This tendency was measured as the difference between initial percentage shares of capital and average shares for periods 10–60 of each run. Three indicators are identified as follows:

6. Change in share of total capital accounted for by suppliers;
7. Change in share of total capital accounted for by wholesalers;
8. Change in share of total capital accounted for by retailers.

Realization of Potential Transactions

The effectiveness of the market in realizing potential transactions was measured by:

9. Difference between supply-demand intersection quantity in the intermediate market (identified from the arrays of *ex ante* supplier offer and customer bid prices) and the actual wholesale trading quantities, expressed as a percentage of the intersection quantity, average for periods 10–60 of each run.

Correlation Matrix

Relationships among the values of the nine indicators of market efficiency were examined by computing a matrix of simple correlation coefficients between each pair of values for the 34 experimental simulation runs (Table). A simple correlation coefficient computed from 34 observations must be at least as great as .34 to be significantly different from zero at the 5 per cent level; 14 of the 36 computed coefficients meet this test, and these are indicated in the table.[6]

Three significant coefficients are obtained from pairings of the four stability measures (Indicators 1–4). *A priori,* one would expect positive correlations among these four indicators. The variability of prices would be expected to be associated with the variability of quantities at any single market, and instability at the wholesale level with instability at the retail level of vertically related markets. Results show an association between the variability of retail and supplier prices. However, no significant associations are revealed between the variability of supplier prices and quantities, or between the variability of the quantities traded at the two market

---

[6] It should be noted that in a correlation matrix of this size, approximately two of the coefficients may appear significant at the five percent level when they are not so in fact.

Correlation Matrix for Market Efficiency Indicators

	Indicator Number								
	1	2	3	4	5	6	7	8	9
Viability-Stability									
1. Variability of Supplier Prices	1.0	.522[a]	.193	.363[a]	.412[a]	–.474[a]	.641[a]	–.529[a]	–.231
2. Variability of Retail Prices		1.0	.163	.740[a]	.238	–.224	.335	–.311	–.313
3. Variability of Wholesale Quantity			1.0	.169	–.310	.340[a]	.166	–.291	.359[a]
4. Variability of Retail Quantity				1.0	.033	–.025	.184	–.362[a]	–.321
Trading Volume and Effort									
5. Message per Unit Traded					1.0	–.887[a]	.761[a]	.055	.005
Revenues									
6. Change in Capital Share, Suppliers						1.0	–.910[a]	.070	.227
7. Change in Capital Share, Wholesalers							1.0	–.475[a]	–.316
8. Change in Capital Share, Retailers								1.0	.264
Realization of Potential Transactions									
9. Difference Between Actual and Potential Wholesale Quantity Traded, Percent of Potential									1.0

[a] Significant at 5 percent level.

levels. Thus it may be said that the correlation among the stability measures is only partially in accord with *a priori* expectations.

Two significant correlation results involve pairing of the revenue measures (Indicators 6–8). If changes in the shares of total system capital for any one group of market participants varied only randomly among the experimental runs, one would expect no significant correlations among these indicators. Results, however, show a strong negative correlation between changes in the capital shares of wholesalers and suppliers, and a weaker association—also negative—between changes in the shares of wholesalers and retailers. The strong association between wholesaler gains and supplier losses is confirmed from a more detailed examination of the simulation results.

The remaining nine significant correlations coefficients involve indicators reflecting different dimensions of market efficiency, as previously described. *A priori,* we might except *positive* correlations among the indicators of stability, effort/volume, and the accomplishment of potential transactions (Indicators 1–4, 5, and 9). The rationale for this expectation is, *ceteris paribus,* that markets characterized by relatively unstable prices and trading quantities would give rise to high communication expenses associated with uncertainty (instability) and, at the same time, would allow the occurrence of large discrepancies between potential and realized transactions. High *negative* correlations between any of these indicators and the revenue measures (Indicators 6–8) would reveal a tendency for the profit position of one group of market participants to improve as the indicated measure of market efficiency improves, and vice versa. Causal relationships are not inferred from these results; rather, it is simply asked whether there is any tendency for changes in other efficiency measures to be associated with changes in the position of any particular group of market participants *vis-a-vis* the others.

Examining these relationships in detail, one observes that there is a positive association between the variability of supplier prices (Indicator 1) and the effort/volume ratio (Indicator 5), although this ratio does not show a significant correlation with any other stability measure. Supplier price variability is also associated with relative declines in the suppliers' share of system capital (Indicator 6), and corresponding increases for wholesalers (Indicator 7). The capital share of retailers (Indicator 8) also declines as supplier price variability increases.

The variability of quantity in the wholesale market (Indicator 3) is weakly associated with *increases* in the suppliers' share of system capital (Indicator 6), and the variability of retail quantity (Indicator 4) with *decreases* in the retailers' share (Indicator 8). Although these coefficients are on the margin of significance, the difference in sign between them suggests the complexity of market performance relationships. The positive association between the variability of wholesale market quantity and the discrepancy between actual and potential transactions, although weak, is in accord with the *a priori* expectations.

The positive association between the effort/volume ratio (Indicator 5) and the capital share of wholesalers (Indicator 7) may appear paradoxical. That is, one might expect that the greater the number of messages per unit traded, the lower the profits of wholesalers would be. However, increases in communication requirements in this model were generally associated with other market developments (*e.g.,* declines in total trading volume) which affected wholesalers less unfavorably than other market participants, particularly suppliers. Hence, increased message requirements are correlated with declines in the relative share of capital held by suppliers, with corresponding gains for the wholesalers.

It seems particularly significant that no association is revealed between the effort/volume ratio and the discrepancy between actual and potential transactions. This lack of association may be due to more complex relationships involving the numbers of firms, total trading quantity, *etc.,* in the market. It may be explained more directly by two potentially offsetting tendencies—(a) a tendency for a larger percentage of transactions to be accomplished when message requirements are low, for whatever reason, and (b) a tendency for communications efforts per unit traded to rise, as a result of messages leading to no or small volume transactions, when the total volume of transactions approaches the potential level. These two possibilities come from two different causal relationships —low message requirements leading to higher trading volume, and high trading volume leading to high message effort. If both relationships are at work, then the absence of significant association between the two variables is not surprising.

Conclusion

These results are, of course, specific to the model under analysis and to the very few experimental variations attempted. They do not imply that the relationships revealed would be systematically observed over other experimental runs of this model, still less over any sample of actual markets. However, they do suggest that the several indicators of market efficiency identified here are not associated in any uniform or simple way. The only clear network of relationships revealed in the simulated market is that among the variability of prices, a high effort/volume ratio, and relative wholesaler gains (and supplier and retailer losses) in system capital. The absence of other relationships, that might be either expected or desired as evidence of the level of market efficiency, may be explained in terms of the specific properties of this model, including its strong element of random fluctuation.

The more important point is that the attempt to analyze the efficiency of complex market systems or distribution networks requires specification of multiple criteria, and results of this simulation analysis suggest that indicators of these criteria may be imperfectly correlated. Single criteria or indicators of market efficiency thus appear unacceptable, and the task of appraising proposed efficiency increasing changes in marketing organization or practices is more complicated than may have been supposed. It is urged that careful specification of criteria for appraising performance in marketing systems and trading networks be a primary task for marketing theory, and the measurement or estimation of indicators of efficiency criteria in specific contexts be a major challenge for marketing research.

REFERENCES

1. M. A. Adelman, "Pricing by Manufacturers," *Proceedings: Conference of Marketing Teachers from the Far Western States,* Berkeley, Calif.: University of California, 1958, 147.

2. Wroe Alderson, *Marketing Behavior and Executive Action,* Homewood, Ill.: Richard D. Irwin, Inc., 1957.

3. ———— and Miles W. Martin, "Toward a Formal Theory of Transactions and Transvections," *Journal of Marketing Research,* 2, (May 1965), 117–27.

4. Harry Allison, "Framework for Marketing Strategy," *California Management Review,* 4, (Fall 1961), 75–95.

5. F. E. Balderston, "Design of Marketing Channels," in Reavis Cox *et al.,* eds., *Theory in Marketing: Second series,* Homewood, Ill.: Richard D. Irwin, Inc., 1964, 176–89.

6. ————, "Communication Networks in Intermediate Markets," *Management Science,* 4, (January 1958), 154-71.

7. ———— and Austin C. Hoggatt, *Simulation of Market Processes,* Berkeley, Calif.: Institute of Business and Economic Research, University of California, 1962.

8. H. Barger, *Distribution's Place in the American Economy,* N. Y.: National Bureau of Economic Research, Inc., 1955.

9. E. H. Chamberlin, "An Experimental Imperfect Market," *Journal of Political Economy,* 56, (April 1958), 95–108.

10. Reavis Cox, in association with Charles S. Goodman and Thomas C. Fichandler, *Distribution in a High-Level Economy,* Englewood Cliffs, N. J.: Prentice-Hall, Inc., 1965.

11. ———— and Charles Goodman, "Marketing of Housebuilding Materials," *Journal of Marketing,* 21, (July 1956), 36–61.

12. James W. Culliton, *The Management of Marketing Costs,* Boston, Mass.: Harvard University, Graduate School of Business Administration, 1948.

13. Margaret Hall, John Knapp, and Christopher Winstein, *Distribution in Great Britain and North America,* London: Oxford University Press, 1961.

14. Stanley C. Hollander, "Measuring the Cost and Value of Marketing," in Perry Bliss, ed., *Marketing and the Behavioral Sciences,* Boston, Mass.: Allyn and Bacon, Inc., 1963, 529–43.

15. John A. Howard, *Marketing Management,* rev. edition, Homewood, Ill.: Richard D. Irwin, Inc., 1963.
16. James B. Jeffreys, Simon Hausberger, and Göran Lindbold, *Productivity in the Distributive Trades in Europe,* Paris: Organization for European Economic Co-operation, 1954.
17. Peter Newman, *The Theory of Exchange,* Englewood Cliffs, N. J.: Prentice-Hall, Inc., 1956.
18. Almarin Phillips, *Market Structure, Organization and Performance,* Cambridge, Mass.: Harvard University Press, 1962.
19. Lee E. Preston, and Norman R. Collins, *Studies in a Simulated Market,* Berkeley: University of California, Institute of Business and Economic Research, forthcoming.
20. Charles H. Sevin, "Analytical Approach to Channel Policies—Marketing Cost Analysis," *Marketing Channels,* Richard Clewett, ed., Homewood, Ill.: Richard D. Irwin, Inc., 1954, 433–69.
21. ———, *How Manufacturers Reduce Their Distribution Costs,* U. S. Department of Commerce, Washington, D. C.: U. S. Government Printing Office, 1948, Chapter iii.
22. V. L. Smith, "An Experimental Study of Competitive Market Behavior," *Journal of Political Economy,* 70 (April 1962), 111–37.
23. ———, "Effect of Market Organization on Competitive Equilibrium," *Quarterly Journal of Economics,* 78 (May 1964), 181-202.
24. S. H. Sosnick, "Operational Criteria for Evaluating Market Performance," in P. L. Farris, ed., *Market Structure Research,* Ames, Iowa: Iowa State University Press, 1964, 81–125.
25. G. J. Stigler, "The Economics of Information," *Journal of Political Economy,* 69 (June 1961), 213–25.
26. ———, "Public Regulation of the Securities Markets." *Journal of Business,* 37 (April 1964), 117-42, and subsequent comments, *Ibid.,* (October 1964).
27. P. J. Verdoorn, "Marketing from the Producer's Point of View," *Journal of Marketing,* 20 (January 1956), 221–35.

19

Symbolism and Life Style

SIDNEY J. LEVY

The author probes the symbolism which pervades our daily lives. Each of us has a life style of some kind, expressed to assert who we think we are. The view is taken that an individual's life style is a large complex symbol in motion, composed of sub-symbols. Objects and events are processed within these values. Examples are given of consumer life styles and how these affect perceptions of products and services.

The symbolic nature of consumer objects has received much attention in recent years. At least it has been fashionable to designate various outstanding objects as symbolic, thereby giving lip service to this idea. We comfortably note that language is symbolic, as are visual materials in modern art, and television commercials. Having noted this, or used the term to accuse someone of striving for status symbols, the matter is commonly dropped. This usually occurs because it is hard to keep thinking about the symbolic meanings of objects and behavior. To do so requires practice in adopting a view of actions that is sufficiently detached to permit analysis and interpretation, and sufficiently empathetic to produce insights. It is usually simpler to deal with the objects and behaviors themselves.[1]

It is easier to take for granted that people do what they do because, being themselves, they must, with no more need for explanation than we

Reprinted with permission from *Toward Scientific Marketing,* Stephen A. Greyser, ed. (Chicago: American Marketing Association, 1964), pp. 140-150.

[1] David McK. Rioch has a relevant discussion in distinguishing between two separate problems in communication which face the physician—"that of commitment to the patient as a person and that of analyzing the mechanisms involved and their disorders." See: David McK. Rioch, "Communication in the Laboratory and Communication in the Clinic," *Psychiatry,* (1963) Vol. 26, #3, pp. 209-221.

must offer to explain our own actions. It is easier to explain behavior by categorizing it as the result of the person's being between the ages of 40 and 45, upper middle class, and in the over $15,000 income bracket. If we are daring, we may go so far as to hint that these consumers are sociable or introverted or discriminating in personality. These are all legitimate rubrics, and provide convenient and useful ways of dividing up data in order to compare frequency distributions.

But we are challenged to try to analyze *meaning*—and thus become engaged with the study of symbolism and the role of symbols in the daily life of average citizens. Here I must emphasize that in speaking of symbols and symbolizing, I am not referring shyly and euphemistically to the study of phallic objects on cars or to dreams of nudity in the streets— although I would not, of course, exclude such curious phenomena from consideration. As Langer points out:

Obvious only in man, is the *need of symbolization*. The symbol-making function is one of man's primary activities, like eating, looking, or moving about. It is the fundamental process of his mind, and goes on all the time. Sometimes we are aware of it, sometimes we merely find its results, and realize that certain experiences have passed through our brains and have been digested there.[2]

If this is so, there are several implications. First, as I have mentioned, it is hard to notice people's symbolizing any more than we notice their breathing or blood circulating, unless something goes wrong with these functions. Similarly, we notice symbolizing when it becomes dramatic, blatant, or so alien to our understanding that we are struck by the discrepancy between someone else's meanings and our own. Moreover, since symbolizing is so implicit, asking people about it may elicit no simple answers since the symbolizer may not be self-conscious about what he is doing.

Nevertheless, the pervasive and inescapable nature of symbolizing means that analyzing it is what we are really doing whenever we study human behavior. This then applies to the ordinary actions that constitute consumer behavior as well as the extraordinary. Now, how can we examine symbolizing as a life style force? I would like to start by offering the view that an individual's life style is a large complex symbol in motion. It is composed of sub-symbols; it utilizes a characteristic pattern of life space; and it acts systematically to process objects and events in accordance with these values.

---

[2] Susanne K. Langer, *Philosophy in a New Key,* Harvard University Press, 1951, Cambridge, Mass., p. 41.

A Large Complex Symbol in Motion

Everyone's life has a cycle of some kind. As a total entity moving through time, a person builds a characteristic assertion of who he is and how he regards his own being, and he expresses it in the specific manner of his actions. To realize this is merely to note that people have recognizable personalities that remain familiar to us—they do not appear as strangers each time we meet them. But this also means that there is more to them than that they eat when hungry, sleep when tired, and love when stimulated. They develop the wish to do these things in particular ways regarded as suitable for themselves. And *what is thought suitable rests in who they are, how they grew up, their nationality, the groups they participate in or seek, and ultimately in all of this, the individual person they aim to be.*

In a sense, everyone seeks to prove something, and this—or some central set of recurring motifs—is identifiable as the summary fashion of his wrestling with existence. To observe this takes some largeness of view; perhaps it can never be fully observed until a man is dead, and then the one person who experienced it all and might know most about it is gone. Still, we do observe other people's life styles, even if we capture only fragments and part-motifs.

We can think of people in categorical terms derived from their customary behavior, emotional tone, expressed wishes; by being donors and recipients to their special forms of taking and giving. So the persons oriented to display may take attention and admiration from us, the ambitious leader wants us to obey, the careless driver may want to share an accident with us. As they show us themselves, order us about, or collide with us, they bring their life styles to our attention. We discover something about the content of their personalities and the special fashion or form they give to it. So perhaps this driver apologizes profusely—as perhaps he always does when he hurts others; this leader keeps insisting it is all for the good of others; and this exhibitionist does it by putting on striking clothes rather than removing them.

As we sense the meaningful currents in people's behavior and emotional expression, we become aware of what they are trying to do and the means they employ. We decide they are generous, moral, corrupt, subtle, bitter, active, sweet; and when we pronounce such as judgments we are usually referring to the ongoing symbolic quality of the person rather than to a specific action. We mean the deeper attributes that go on despite the times he is not generous, subtle, or active.

Contrasting Styles of Life

In expressing their values, in describing the kinds of roles they play in life and how they think those roles should be fulfilled, people reveal both real and ideal life styles. In one marketing study in Montana, life was described as slow-paced, with the people geared to the rigors and virtues of frontier life where it is cold and demanding; where the skills and rewards of hunting and fishing looms large; where men are rugged, touched with the nobility of the natural man and superior to the wan and tender Eastern city man. A man's life style was generally conceived as one of good fellowship, whether with a gun, a rod, or a drink. This may sound like parody; to show the reality of these views, I quote the comments of some of the men describing the people and life style of Montana.

The men here are real good, you can trust them. Most of them are outdoor men; they have to be or else they wouldn't live here. Most of them are honest.

The men here are true Westerners; big, tough and rugged.

Men are men here, and they are manly. Somewhat more honest and less sharp dealing than in the more civilized parts of the country.

It's wonderful here. It's God's country. I like the frontier atmosphere. Life is casual and leisurely here, no frantic big city pace.

This contrasts with the kinds of life style men in metropolitan environments offer to sum up who they are. Here we find the familiar tunes of urban-suburban people, where men are first husbands and fathers, and run to the ragged rather than the rugged.

The men here are very nice, a well-educated group of men who have many outside interests and are very congenial. They're home-loving and conscientious.

Most of my neighbors are young families and pretty well child-oriented. The men are typical suburbanites, very much concerned with crab grass and PTA. They all work hard and bring home brief cases.

To grasp these life styles and how they are exemplified in individual lives requires an orientation to configurations, to patterns of ideas, feelings, and actions. We need to sense the man at work, to feel with him the peculiar flavor with which he invests his work or draws from it joy, irritation, monotony, impatience, anticipation, anxiety about today or tomorrow, comfort, competence, pride, a restless urge to succeed visibly, or a restless urge to reach five o'clock. We can think about what kind of motivation is useful in distinguishing the achieving executive from the adequate one, the upward striving white collar worker from the man who just wants to make a living. *To explore this large, complex symbol in motion that is a man's grand life style is to seek to define his self-concept,* to describe the central set of beliefs about himself and what he aspires to, that provide consistency (or unpredictability) to what he does. Information about such self-concepts may come from various directions. Two students writing class autobiographies conveyed the contrasting sense of focus each felt about what he sought to achieve in life—one summing up that he wanted to live in accordance with "intelligence, truth, and justice," while the other said his aims boiled down to "thrift, security, and cleanliness." Presumably, the former young man represents a better potential market for books, the latter is possibly more geared to soap.

Such self-definitions can help us perceive the coherence of behavior in housewives who relentlessly pursue antiseptic cleanliness, in children accomplishing characteristically in school, as well as in doting or dismal fathers. This idea of one's self as "naturally" following its bent, accompanied by the feeling "doesn't everyone?" is the core personal symbol. When we understand this about a person, we can start to trace out the intricate pattern of his actions, to see how it affects the handling of money, choice of clothes, food preferences, interest in shopping, cooking, giving gifts, home workshopping. We can see how the persisting needs of one man to bend people to his will can make him a topnotch salesman, or where the urge to resist produces an obdurate purchasing agent.

In anthropological analogue to this thought, Redfield noted the significance of maize as a vital symbol to the Mayan villagers of Chan Kom in the Yucatan.

"So I began to form another way of conceiving parts as related to one another in a system of activity and thought. This third system is neither chainlike or maplike. It is radial: maize is a center and other things are grouped around it, connected to it in different ways, some by a series of useful activities, some by connections of symbolic significance. The mind goes out from maize to agriculture, from maize to social life, from maize to religion. Maize is always the center of things."[3]

Life Style Is Made of Sub-Symbols

If we can thus think of the life style of a person or a group as having a general symbolic character, one that refers to and expresses a certain central emphasis in motivation and action, we can describe as sub-symbols the things—objects, activities—that are used to play out this general symbolic meaning and to embody it. The clotheshorse needs clothes, the bookworm needs books, the cliffdweller needs cliffs. For example, *housing has a meaning that varies with who is to live in it.*

Back noted that in Puerto Rico a public housing project could be regarded as a custodial institution or as a technique for upward mobility, mak-

---

[3] Robert Redfield, *The Little Community,* The University of Chicago Press, 1955, p. 22.

ing the most progressive and the most dependent families inclined toward the project. Families falling between these extremes tend to prefer to stay in private housing, even though it may be objectively inferior.[4]

Apartment living versus living in a house provides a contrast in the meanings of sub-symbols. Apartment dwellers who are not familially oriented and who use housing that exemplifies the exciting values of urban life, like the freer kind of life it represents.

I like living in apartments . . . The thing I like best about it is the convenience of having everything taken care of.

Apartment life is very relaxing—no fires to tend to, sidewalks to shovel, and no painting. More time for enjoyment.

Those with a greater yearning to belong and to share in a feeling of some social responsibility see apartments as a stopgap that falls short of true participation in life.

The only advantage to apartment living is that it is a stopgap until you can buy a house.

There is very little opportunity for a sense of community life in an apartment.

Multiple Meanings

As these contrasting views of apartment living so aptly illustrate, a complication for understanding marketing problems is caused by the multiple meanings of objects and communications. The same person may see several meanings and different people may see different meanings. A picture of a skier shows a man standing on two sticks: this may signify a pleasant sport, a dangerous sport, an expensive pastime, new ways of leisure in America, superior social status at an elegant resort, the competitiveness of the Olympics, even a cause of perspiration in a deodorant advertisment.

Examples could be multiplied to show how people behave in accordance with their own view of themselves and how they want to do things that fit this view. This extends into interesting realms of action and nonaction. A study of why women do not visit physicians for examination as often as they should to detect cancer showed that one reason was a reluctance to change one's underwear habits—for example, to iron a brassiere in order to seem like the kind of women the doctor is presumably accustomed to examining. It was also clear that some women did not want to explore the possibility of having cancer because they believe it is a venereal disease and would reveal their sexual practices. Such anxieties

---

[4] Kurt W. Back, *Slums, Projects, and People,* Duke University Press, 1962.

are similarly related to skin problems among young people, where ideas about self-indulgence, sex, and hostility become interwoven with the sense of self, producing feelings of shame and guilt. For example:

I saw an ad—it was either for pimples or athlete's foot—that was pretty gruesome. It was like some of the awful pictures shown in the windows of the cheap low class drug stores for skin diseases, and everyone knows what they are trying to show without coming right out and saying venereal disease.

The utilization of sub-symbols affects all customers, not merely buyers of consumers' goods looking for "status symbols." A study of institutional food buyers showed the pervasive effects of how the buyers defined themselves, their institutions, and their customers, to give their food purchasing its special flavor and meaning. Dietitians and home economists, pursuing their professional roles, tended to emphasize nutritional values and balanced menus; buyers oriented to cooking or the clientele of an establishment devoted to the arts thought in terms of the palate and visual esthetics; more business-oriented managers made money a foremost consideration in the style of planning they showed. These were occupational life styles, each reflecting the typical symbolic configuration that had developed as suitable. The sub-symbols of place, titles, preferred suppliers, utensils, foods, all played roles in sustaining the larger significance these people sought to convey.

It is easiest to see objects being employed symbolically where the goal is to display, where visibility is high; and it is in these situations where they probably do reach their fullest flowering and elaboration. In dress furniture, when "company is coming," and so on, the importance of audiences intensifies the presentation of life style. Nevertheless, one's life style is always going on, even if privately at a different level. It is hard for us to believe that there is ever a time when no one is looking—there is always God. And even if we relax our standards with Him and scratch our behinds, wear our socks a second day, or read faster than comprehension can keep up, our lapses are also part of ourselves. They support the purchase of sub-symbolic products that make up the covert life styles that let one sneak a secret drink, consume pornography, or watch more television than one likes to admit.

A Characteristic Pattern of Life Space

An interesting aspect of symbolism is the significance of life space. As a person expresses his life style, he moves through his environment, perceiving it and using it in his own special ways. Probably we can observe a typical continuum ranging from expansive to constricted use of the environment. Higher status people have a larger world view, they look toward and move toward more distant horizons. They are among that classic 20% of the population who do 80% of the living, using airplanes and long distance telephones in sharply disproportionate degree. Lower status people are apt to use even their own city in narrower fashion, some never going downtown or leaving the home neighborhood. This is not merely a matter of economics, although money (and its relative availability) is a related parameter.

Individuals vary in their yearnings for space, some loving roomy old houses, others preferring restricted, efficient space. Michael Balint[5] has devoted a book to exploring the psychological consequences of basic interest in things versus basic interest in the spaces between things. He believes that people have fundamental orientations that lead them either to emphasize clinging to objects or to emphasize moving between objects. The latter orientation is characteristic in the thrill-seeking of skiing and roller-coastering, whereas clinging to objects turns ocnophils (as Balint calls them) toward stability and security. A study of mobile home dwellers highlighted this contrast with cases of women who bewept the fact that their less root-minded husbands did not provide homes with entrenched foundations and space to accumulate more objects.

Such concerns can be extended into assessments of how people organize objects in the space available. Are they orderly and precise or do they want things to "look lived in?" We may judge people and companies for their life style by how they use space, ranging from Japanese austerity to Victorian clutter, understanding perhaps that a clear desk means efficiency, high status, or a figurehead who lets others do the work. A desk piled high may be interpreted as sloppy; comfortable; the home of a drudge, a procrastinator, or a hard worker. Modern architectural design struggles with whether to "waste space" by leaving open areas or allot everyone a tight cubicle; should an office building be like a hospital or like an atrium, will the public think better of the corporation if the street level is built like an expensive garden plaza instead of having convenient and profitable shops flush to the sidewalk?

Processing Objects and Events

What are the practical implications of this view of life style that stresses its symbolic character? It emphasizes the fact that buyers see objects and events in the real world as having certain potentialities. These potentialities are scanned, screened, and processed for their symbolic

---

[5] Michael Balint, *Thrills and Regressions.* International University Press, 1959.

suitability, not only because the products can provide some specific results, but because they become incorporated into the life style of the person. This does not mean all product choices are razor's edge decisions between the real-me and the not-me, with a nod to the fake-me. But still, what do they all add up to?

From a marketing point of view—one that might startle traditional academicians (other than anthropologists, perhaps)—*a consumer's personality can be seen as the peculiar total of the products he consumes.* Shown a picture of a young man in an advertisement, one female respondent deduced the following:

He's a bachelor, his left hand is showing and it has no ring on it. He lives in one of those modern high-rise apartments and the rooms are brightly colored. He has modern, expensive furniture, but not Danish modern. He buys his clothes at Brooks Brothers. He owns a good Hi-fi. He skis. He has a sailboat. He eats Limburger or any other prestige cheese with his beer. He likes and cooks a lot of steak and he would have filet mignon for company. His liquor cabinet has Jack Daniel's bourbon, Beefeater gin, and a good Scotch.

Through his life style does she know him.

If we think of a housewife who uses Crosse and Blackwell soups, subscribes to *Gourmet* magazine, flies live lobster in from Maine to Chicago to serve guests, drives a Renault, and doesn't shave under her arms, we sense a value system engaged in choosing things from the marketplace that add up to a life style quite different from that of the woman who uses Campbell's, reads *Family Circle* for ideas on how to furnish a playroom, makes meat loaf twice a week (stretching it with oatmeal), rides in her husband's Bel Air, and scrubs the kitchen floor three times a week.

By studying these configurations of life style, by observing how people put together those ways of living they think appropriate for a 40 year old surgeon on the make, a prosperous factory foreman in a working class suburb, a woman who feels she leads a dog's life and likes to "go out and eat," or "a woman who feels she is not a raving beauty, but is attractive to men," we can find out how they use products most meaningfully for themselves. Close analysis of consumption systems of different kinds of people is revealing,[6] as is accumulating life history information which does not focus so closely on products that it loses the larger ongoing symbolic aims I have been discussing.

---

[6] See Harper W. Boyd, Jr., and Sidney J. Levy, "New Dimension in Consumer Analysis," *Harvard Business Review,* November-December, 1963, pp. 129-140.

Conclusion

The descriptions I have made here to capture or convey some of these life style issues seem awkward and inadequate. Much work is needed to study consumer life styles, to create a taxonomy of life styles that helps us to think more systematically about different kinds of people, to build a theory that illuminates the dynamic process by which people turn their primitive needs into nuanced and elaborated sets of discriminations among the objects in the market place. We each know that such a process is true of ourselves, but so often when studied, it seems to fall between the meshes of the research net. It laughs at the grossness of personality inventories or the stodginess of questionnaires that fail to take account of the ludicrous, shy, quicksilver, or perverse elements of life style, the felt absurdity of caring about invisible differences in unessential products.

Earlier work has suggested the importance of symbols in the marketing world, particularly in regard to age, sex, and social class.[7] My present purpose is to reaffirm this importance. It is also to point attention to the fact that *marketers do not just sell isolated items that can be interpreted as symbols; rather, they sell pieces of a larger symbol—the consumer's life style.* Marketing is then a process of providing customers with parts of a potential mosaic from which they, as artists of their own life styles, can pick and choose to develop the composition that for the time may seem the best. The marketer who thinks about his products in this way will seek to understand their potential settings and relationships to other parts of consumer life styles, thereby to increase the number of ways he fits meaningfully into them.

---

[7] Sidney J. Levy, "Symbols for Sale," *Harvard Business Review,* July-August 1959, pp. 117-124.

20

Product Characteristics and Marketing Strategy

GORDON E. MIRACLE

According to Webster, a science is "any branch or department of systematized knowledge considered as a distinct field of investigation or object of study." By this definition, marketing certainly may be designated as a science, albeit a science in the early stages of development. Scholars and students of marketing are concerned with the collection, analysis, and interpretation of marketing knowledge; and some progress has been made in systematizing and classifying marketing phenomena.

In recent years social scientists have begun to employ a method known in the physical sciences as *systems analysis*. As one social theorist has observed:

As judged by history of the physical, biological, and social sciences, study in any field is apt to begin with a none-too-ordered description of phenomena in the field, followed by a cataloguing of them on bases that seem to make sense. As understanding grows, the systems of classification become more closely related to the functioning of interacting elements. Gradually, generalizations about functioning are reached which are useful in predicting future events. As the generalizations gain in rigor, they take the form of analytical models of the behavior of the elements being studied. They take the form, that is, of systems.[1]

The development of marketing knowledge seems to be going through similar stages.

Reprinted with permission from the *Journal of Marketing,* national quarterly publication of the American Marketing Association, Vol. 29 (January, 1965), pp. 18-24.

[1] Everett E. Hagen, *On the Theory of Social Change* (Homewood, Illinois: The Dorsey Press, Inc., Inc., 1962), p. 4.

A system is a set of interdependent or interacting elements. The investigation of the factors that determine the state of the system is called systems analysis. This type of analysis may be applied to a business firm as well as to a society or other organization. Exogenous and endogenous factors may be examined to determine their influences on the firm in its movement toward an equilibrium.

Exogenous factors influencing the business firm include a profusion of economic, sociological, political, and cultural circumstances and trends. Endogenous factors influencing the movement of a firm toward equilibrium include the several elements in a firm's marketing program, usually described as the firm's marketing mix. The marketing mix, in its general form, includes decisions and activities of business firms in the areas of product policy, channel policy, promotional policy, and pricing policy.[2]

The term "marketing mix" suggests a relationship between interacting elements. The development of the term constituted a step forward in the classification of interrelated marketing efforts. Although more is becoming known about the relationships among elements of the marketing mix, it is still common practice to think of it as a blend of marketing efforts, essentially nonquantifiable, the development of which often depends on experience, judgment, and perhaps a measure of good fortune.

The concept of a system provides a means of improving further the framework within which we think about the interrelationships between and among marketing activities. After all, a business firm engages in marketing activities (endogenous factors in the system) in order to adapt to its environment (exogenous factors). This adaptation is intended to move the firm toward an equilibrium in which the level of operation is such that the goals of the firm are being achieved.

The Characteristics of Goods Theory

An observable relationship exists between the characteristics of a product and the approximate marketing mix for that product. This is by no means a startling assertion. However, up to the present, there appears to be no systematic statement of the relationships between product characteristics and *each* of the elements in the marketing mix.

Historically, one of the most widely accepted classification of goods has been that of convenience, shopping, and specialty goods. The definitions of these goods are based on consumer buying habits.[3] They focus

---

[2] Neil H. Borden, "A Note on the Concept of the Marketing Mix," in Eugene J. Kelley and William Lazer, Editors, *Managerial Marketing: Perspectives and Viewpoints* (Homewood, Illinois: Richard D. Irwin, Inc., 1958), pp. 272-275.

[3] Melvin T. Copeland, "Relation of Consumers' Buying Habits to Marketing Methods," *Harvard Business Review,* Vol. 1 (April, 1923), pp. 282-289.

on consumer behavior and assist in answering questions as to why the consumer "shops" for some goods but not for others. Although the classification is helpful in guiding marketing policies, it is not altogether satisfactory.[4] If a businessman classifies his product in the traditional manner, the relationships between product classification and marketing policies still may be quite uncertain.

The theory presented here is a revision and an extension of "The Characteristics of Goods Theory" proposed by Leo V. Aspinwall.[5] But whereas Aspinwall discusses the characteristics of goods theory only in respect to channels of distribution and promotional policy, the theory presented here is broadened to include the areas of product and pricing policy.

Definition of Product Characteristics

If product characteristics are to be utilized to explain marketing policies and methods, each distinguishing characteristic must be reasonably stable during the period of time the explanation is to be valid. Also, each characteristic must be universal in the sense that it is to some degree a feature of all products.

A product is defined by most modern marketers as the sum of the physical and psychological satisfactions the buyer receives when he makes a purchase.[6] For example, when he makes a purchase the consumer receives an article with certain physical characteristics, or a service with certain features; he receives the item at a convenient location; he is able to purchase at a convenient time: he receives an item about which he has some knowledge (from the salesperson or from consumer advertising).

While the product may not be absolutely perfect from the point of view of each consumer, producers and sellers usually attempt to offer a "total product" that suits a large number of consumers reasonably well. The "bundle of utilities" purchased by the consumer is "collected" by incurring product development costs, channel costs, promotional costs, and other marketing costs. The "total product," in a broad sense, includes all of the features and conveniences for which the consumer pays in the retail selling price of the item.

Considerable ambiguity often exists in the definitions of product characteristics, consumer characteristics, and market characteristics. The

---

[4] Richard M. Holton, "The Distinction Between Convenience Goods, Shopping Goods, and Specialty Goods," JOURNAL OF MARKETING, Vol. 23 (July, 1958), pp. 53-56.

[5] Leo V. Aspinwall, "The Characteristics of Goods Theory," in William Lazer and Eugene J. Kelley, Editors, *Managerial Marketing; Perspectives and Viewpoints* (Homewood, Illinois: Richard D. Irwin, Inc., 1962), pp. 633-643.

[6] Harry L. Hansen, *Marketing: Text, Cases, and Readings* (Homewood, Illinois: Richard D. Irwin, 1961), p. 312.

amount of time and effort spent in purchasing a product may *seem* to be a consumer characteristic. But if convenience of location is part of the "bundle of utilities" and hence part of the "total product" for which the consumer pays, it seems reasonable that the "short" length of time the consumer spends searching for a place to buy a pack of cigarettes is a characteristic of the product. The "convenience" is provided as one feature in the "bundle of utilities." Another way of stating this point is that the nature of the product determines how much time (or what kinds of effort) consumers will wish to spend in buying the product. Thus, "consumer" and "market" characteristics may be described in terms of product characteristics.

Redefining consumer and market characteristics in terms of product characteristics permits development of a single list of characteristics instead of several.

Classification of Products

Observation of a large number of "products" indicates certain "product characteristics":

1. Unit value
2. Significance of *each* individual purchase to the consumer
3. Time and effort spent purchasing by consumers
4. Rate of technological change (including fashion changes)
5. Technical complexity
6. Consumer need for service (before, during, or after the sale)
7. Frequency of purchase
8. Rapidity of consumption
9. Extent of usage (number and variety of consumers and variety of ways in which the product provides utility)

By reviewing a list of products (for example, candy bars, hardware, radios, automobiles, and electronic computers) the variations in product characteristics can be observed in detail. Unit value ranges from low to high; the significance of each individual purchase to the consumer ranges from low to high; and so on down the list.

Products such as candy bars would be rated low for the first six characteristics, and high for the last three. For electronic data processing equipment, the opposite would tend to be true for each product characteristic. Hardware items or radios would be rated somewhere between. Thus, if products are arrayed on a continuum, they might range from such items as cigarettes and razor blades at one extreme, to steam turbines or large specialized machine tools at the other.

For convenience in exposition, it was decided to "break up" the array of products into five arbitrarily chosen groups, ranging from one extreme to the other, and including in each group some examples of items with similar product characteristics. The following groups were chosen:

Group I: Examples are cigarettes, candy bars, razor blades, soft drinks.

Group II: Examples are dry groceries, proprietary pharmaceuticals, small hardware items, industrial operating supplies.

Group III: Examples are radio and television sets, major household appliances, women's suits, tires and inner tubes, major sporting and athletic equipment.

Group IV: Examples are high quality cameras, heavy farm machinery, passenger automobiles, high quality household furniture.

Group V: Examples are electronic office equipment, electric generators, steam turbines, specialized machine tools.

Table 1 shows the variation in product characteristics for each group.

Table 1. Product Characteristics of Five Groups

Product Characteristic (see list)	Group				
	I	*II*	*III*	*IV*	*V*
1	Very Low	Low	Medium to High	High	Very High
2	Very Low	Low	Medium	High	Very High
3	Very Low	Low	Medium	High	Very High
4	Very Low	Low	Medium	High	Very High
5	Very Low	Low	Medium to High	High	Very High
6	Very Low	Low	Medium	High	Very High
7	Very High	Medium to High	Low	Low	Very Low
8	Very High	Medium to High	Low	Low	Very Low
9	Very High	High	Medium to High	Low to Medium	Very Low

It is, of course, an artificiality to classify products by groups; and it would be more accurate to place products on a continuum, or within a spectrum ranging from one extreme to another. Leo Aspinwall utilizes the "color classification" to express the idea of gradation of products on the basis of their characteristics. He utilizes red and yellow as the extremes of the spectrum, indicating that the blend of these colors produces orange

—in fact, various shades of orange. Products in Group I would be classified as "red" goods. Products in Groups II, III, IV, and V range from
orange to yellow.

A product might not always remain in the same classification. It
might fall initially into Group III or IV; then, as larger numbers of consumers gradually accept it, as time and effort spent in purchasing is
reduced, as consumer needs for service decline, and as other characteristics
change, the product may move into Group II, or even Group I. At a
later time marketers may succeed in improving or differentiating a product
so that it is again in Group III or IV.

Product Policy

An important aspect of marketing is the determination of the number of
variations in products that are to be offered: the degree of product homogeneity or heterogeneity.

The problem for the businessman is to determine the effective demand
for various product features—for example, style, color, model, quality
level, and durability. The marketer must communicate this knowledge
effectively to designers and production personnel, so that a product line
can be developed that is consistent with the desires of consumers, the state
of technology, the firm's capabilities, and other uncontrollable factors.

If the *unit value* or size of purchase is low, frequently the product
will be highly standardized; perhaps only one variety within a brand category will be offered for sale—for example, Baby Ruth candy bars or
Lucky Strike cigarettes. Likewise, if the *significance of each individual
purchase* is low, and if the *time and effort spent in the purchasing process*
is low, product variety offered by each manufacturer tends to be low.
Also, when the *rate of technical change* is low, few varieties tend to be
offered; manufacturers are able to develop a product that remains suitable
to consumers for an extended period of time.

Also, *technically simple* products often tend to be standardized to few
varieties or a single variety. Likewise, a lack of *consumer need for service*
often is associated with a standardized product. These characteristics
with a rating of low or very low are typical of products in Group I.

On the other hand, *very high frequency of purchase, rapidity of
consumption,* and *broad usage of the product* by a large number of consumers of diverse types, typically are associated with products in this
group. Therefore, as indicated in Table 2, *a suitable product policy for
products in Group I is to keep very low the varieties of products offered
for sale.*

Table 2. Product Policy

Product Group	Degree to Which a Manufacturer Offers Product Varieties *(for example: style, color, model, flavor, price) to Consumers*				
	Only One, or Very Few Varieties	Few Varieties	Several Varieties	Many Varieties	Different Variety for Every Sale
I	X				
II		X			
III			X		
IV				X	
V					X

For products in Groups II, III, and IV, with successively higher values of charactertistics 1 through 6 and successively lower values of characteristics 7, 8, and 9, the number of varieties offered tends to increase. At the other extreme, for products with a very high value for characteristics 1 through 6, and a very low value for characteristics 7, 8, and 9, the other extreme is reached in respect to the number of varieties offered.

Usually each product is "custom built" or "custom installed" according to the needs of each customer; every product sold is different from that sold to another customer.

Marketing Channel Policy

Channel policies include selection of the types of distributors and number of each type. Intensity of distribution usually refers to the number of distributors utilized, from among those which might be suitable. A policy of intensive distribution means utilization of all available outlets regardless of their characteristics.

The selection of distributors according to their capability and suitability is called selective distribution. A policy of highly selective distribution is understood to mean the utilization of only a few (selected) outlets. The extreme case would be for a manufacturer to utilize no middlemen at all, that is, to sell directly to consumers or users, and either assume the wholesale and retail functions or pass them on to the consumer or user.

Intermediate policies, between the extremes of intensive and selective distribution, are indicated in Table 3. Moderately intensive distribution refers to the situation in which products are sold in a wide variety of outlets, but somewhat limited to certain classes. Some selectivity in dis-

Table 3. Marketing Channel Policy

	Intensity of Distribution				
Product Group	Intensive	Moderately Intensive	Some Selectivity	Considerable Selectivity	Highly Selective, or Direct Sale to Customers
I	X				
II		X			
III			X		
IV				X	
V					X

tribution refers to the policy of selling products through a large number of outlets but limited somewhat to those with desired characteristics. Considerable selectivity means that the number and types of outlets are limited to those with specifically desirable characteristics.

When the unit value is very low; when the significance of each individual purchase is low; when little time and effort are spent in the purchasing process; when the rate of technological change is low; when the product is not complex technically; when consumers need little service; and when the frequency of purchase, rapidity of consumption, and extent of usage are high, highly intensive distribution usually is preferred over selective distribution. At the other extreme, when the values of characteristics are just the opposite, highly selective distribution is the rule. Various intermediate values of characteristics for products in Groups II, III, and IV suggest a range of policies between the extremes.

Note also that products in Group I typically are sold through a relatively long channel of distribution, while products in Group V often are sold through the shortest of channels—direct to user or consumer.[7] In fact, in Table 3 the phrase "length of channel" could be used with some validity instead of "intensity of distribution."

Promotional Policy

A major aspect of promotional strategy is to decide how much effort is to be placed on mass media consumer advertising vis-a-vis the amount of effort on personal selling.

For products in Group I, observation suggests that the emphasis usually is on consumer advertising. In the extreme case a firm may have

---

[7] Aspinwall, same reference as footnote 5, at page 635.

no sales force at all. On the other hand, products in Group V depend almost entirely upon personal selling effort, although advertising in trade magazines may play a supplementary role. Products in Groups II, III, and IV require a combination of consumer advertising and personal selling, as illustrated in Table 4.

Table 4. Promotional Policy

Product Group	Relative Emphasis on Mass Media Consumer Advertising and Personal Selling				
	Sold Almost Entirely by Consumer Advertising	*Sold Primarily by Consumer Advertising*	*Consumer Advertising and Personal Selling Both Needed; Neither of Predominant Importance*	*Sold Primarily by Personal Selling*	*Sold Almost Entirely by Personal Selling*
I	X				
II		X			
III			X		
IV				X	
V					X

Pricing Policy

The pricing policy of a firm depends upon the degree to which a firm has control over price. If the firm has no control, if prices are set "in the market place" by custom or by any other means beyond the control of the firm, there is no need for the firm to have any pricing policy at all (except to sell or not to sell at the going price).

Thus, a starting point in establishing a firm's pricing policy is to specify the degree of control which the firm has over price. It is only after this has been ascertained that the businessman can turn to the specific tasks of price determination and price administration.

The degree of control that a firm has over price of its products seems to vary according to the enumerated product characteristics. As shown in Table 5, firms have little control over prices of items in Group I, relatively more control in the middle groups, and the highest degree of control in Group V.

Pricing policies are established with regard to (1) the degree of variation from customer to customer, and (2) the degree of adherence to list prices versus dependence on negotiating the price for each sale. As can

Table 5.   Pricing Policy

| Product Group | Degree to Which Seller Controls Price | | | | |
	Very Little	*Slightly*	*Moderately*	*Significantly*	*Substantially*
I	X				
II		X			
III			X		
IV				X	
V					X

be observed in Table 6, products in Group I usually show little variation in price, whereas prices of products in Group V change relatively more frequently and often are substantially different for different customers purchasing similar products. Concomitantly, the prices of products in Group V are likely to be established independently for each sale. The prices of products in Group I are not often negotiated in this manner.

Table 6.   Pricing Policy

| Product Group | Variations in Prices Over Time, Short Term, Seasonally, Cyclically, or by Customer Categories | | | | |
	Stable	*Slight Variation*	*Moderate Variation*	*Significant Variation*	*Substantial Variation*
I	X				
II		X			
III			X		
IV				X	
V					X

The Marketing Mix

By way of summary, the marketing mix for products in Group I should be substantially as follows:

1. Relatively little effort and money spent on product development. Since a standard variety of the product is suitable for a broad group of customers, there is relatively less need for frequent change than for products in other groups.

2. Considerable effort spent in achieving intensive distribution. Products must be available quickly and conveniently.

3. Heavy consumer advertising—little or no personal selling. Consumers typically are presold by advertising.

4. Relatively little effort and time spent on pricing. Firms have little control over price; variations in price are relatively infrequent; prices are not negotiated between seller and consumer.

At the other extreme, we would expect to find that products in Group V usually are:

1. Custom built.
2. Sold directly from manufacturer to user.
3. Sold primarily by salesmen, rather than advertising.
4. Sold on the basis of an individually negotiated price.

The marketing mix of products in Group V would involve relatively heavy efforts in the area of product policy; the marketing channel would be short, perhaps direct; personal selling is relatively more important than mass media; and considerable time and effort are spent on the determination and negotiation of price.

The marketing mix of products in Groups II, III, and IV can be characterized as modifications of the two extremes.

Conclusions

Knowledge of the product characteristics can be utilized to predict the nature of the marketing mix which is suitable for a given product. The prediction is, of course, an approximate *ideal* for a product with given characteristics. As a practical matter, the ability of a firm to engage in the indicated marketing methods may be limited in a number of ways, such as financial capabilities, or availability of personnel with the requisite skills, or management talent.

The primary contribution of the present theory is a modest increase in the analytical character of the marketing mix. Hopefully the next steps will be to develop more precise measures of the functional relationships among the elements in the marketing mix.

Businessmen may find the present theory handy as a shorthand method of ascertaining an appropriate marketing mix for a new product. Or if policies not in accordance with the theory are being followed, a businessman may be well advised to review carefully the reasons for his policies. It may even happen that the characteristics-of-goods theory will point the way to profitable policy changes.

As another example, a firm faced with the need to justify in a court of law its past marketing methods might use the theory as a broad framework to illustrate the reasons for its past decisions. Or the model might serve to direct the attention of researchers into relevant channels, or provide assistance to executives in the tasks of organizing marketing facts as a basis for making marketing decisions.

21

Price Policies and Theory

EDWARD R. HAWKINS

Although the theory of monopolistic competition is now almost twenty years old it remains virtually unused by marketing students, even those who are attempting to develop theory in marketing. In particular, "marketing price policies" are still treated as though they have no relation to economic theory of any sort. In the leading marketing text books there are sections describing such pricing policies as "odd prices," customary prices," "price lining," "psychological prices," etc.[1] These are presented as descriptions of market behavior, presumably discovered by marketing specialists and unknown to economists. Even the one marketing text that explains the basic pricing formula under conditions of monopolistic competition fails to use it in the discussion of price policies.[2] Since text book writers treat the subject in this way it is not surprising that prac-

Reprinted with permission from the *Journal of Marketing,* national quarterly publication of the American Marketing Association, Vol. 18 (January, 1954), pp. 233-240.

[1] R. S. Vaile, E. T. Grether, and Reavis Cox, *Marketing in the American Economy* (New York: Ronald Press, 1952), ch. 22; E. A. Duddy and D. A. Revzan, *Marketing* (New York: McGraw-Hill, 2nd ed. 1953), ch. 29; P. D. Converse, H. W. Huegy, and R. V. Mitchell, *Elements of Marketing* (New York: Prentice-Hall, 5th ed. 1952) ch. 10; H. H. Maynard and T. N. Beckman, *Principles of Marketing* (New York: Ronald Press, 5th ed. 1952) ch. 35, 36; R. S. Alexander, F. M. Surface, R. E. Elder, and Wroe Alderson, *Marketing* (Boston: Ginn & Co., 1940) ch. 16. Since these policies are fully described in marketing texts the explanation of them in this article will be brief. The attempt, rather, is to express the policies in terms of demand curves in order that the relationship to the theory of monopolistic competition may be seen.

[2] Charles F. Phillips and Delbert J. Duncan, *Marketing, Principles and Methods* (Chicago: Richard D. Irwin, Inc., rev. ed. 1952), ch. 29, 30, 31.

titioners writing on pricing do not attempt to relate their policies to economic theory.[3]

It is the purpose of this article to show that these price policies are special cases of the general theory of monopolistic competition. Perhaps clarification of this point will serve to narrow the gap between the economic and marketing conceptions of pricing, and to systematize the discussions of price policies in marketing literature.

The thesis is that each of the familiar price policies represents an estimate of the nature of the demand curve facing the seller. It is not possible, on the basis of available evidence, to generalize on the validity of these estimates in various situations. The point merely is that a seller using one of these policies is implicitly assuming a particular demand curve. In the following sections various price policies are discussed in these terms, after a brief review of the general theory of pricing which is basic to all of the policies discussed.

The General Theory of Pricing

The theory of correct pricing under conditions of monopolistic competition, as developed by Chamberlin and Robinson is illustrated in Figure 1. Each seller with some degree of monopoly created by product differentia-

Figure 1.

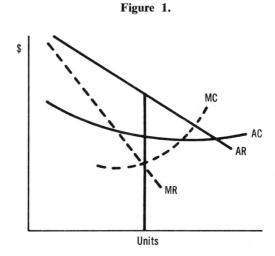

[3] For example, Oswald Knauth, "Considerations in the Setting of Retail Prices," *Journal of Marketing,* v. XIV, no. 1, July 1949, pp. 1-12; Q. Forrest Walker, "Some Principles of Department Store Pricing," *Journal of Marketing,* vol. XIV no. 4, April 1950, pp. 529-537.

tion has his own negatively-inclined average revenue curve, AR. From this he derives the marginal revenue curve, MR, and determines his price by the intersection of MR and MC, his marginal cost. Marginal cost can be derived from either average cost, AC, or average variable cost, AVC, since it would be the same in either case. In practical terms this means that for correct pricing the seller does not need to allocate overhead cost to individual items. For that matter, he does not even need to compute MR and MC, for the same correct price can be derived from AR and AVC by maximizing the total of the spread between them multiplied by the volume.

An alternative solution which may be more understandable to business men can be obtained from break-even charts. The customary break-even chart is deficient for pricing purposes because it is based on only one price and reveals nothing but the quantity that would have to be sold at that price in order to break even. A modification can be devised that remedies this shortcoming of the break-even chart, and even has some advantages over the MC-MR formula. Figure 2 shows such a chart, in

Figure 2.

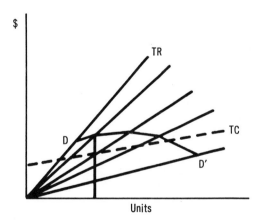

which a number of different total revenue (TR) curves are drawn, indicating the total revenue that would result at various volumes at different prices. On each such TR curve a point can be estimated showing the sales volume that would actually be obtained at that price. If these points are connected a type of demand curve results (DD'), indicating total revenue rather than average revenue as in the usual demand curve.[4] The

---

[4] Cf. Joel Dean, *Managerial Economics* (New York: Prentice-Hall, Inc., 1951), p. 405. Dean shows a total revenue curve without, however, indicating its relationship to break-even charts.

objective of correct pricing is to maximize the vertical distance between DD' and the TC (total cost) curve. This formulation has an advantage over the MC-MR one in that in addition to indicating the correct price and volume it also shows total cost, total revenue, and total net profit. It may also be more acceptable to business men and engineers who are accustomed to break-even charts.

In the following discussion of marketing price policies, however, the AR curve will be used because it more clearly illustrates the points made.

Marketing Price Policies

Odd Prices

The term "odd prices" is used in two ways in marketing literature; one refers to a price ending in an odd number, while the other means a price just under a round number. If a seller sets his prices according to the first concept it means that he believes his AR curve is like the one shown in Figure 3.[5] In this case each price ending in an odd number will produce

Figure 3.

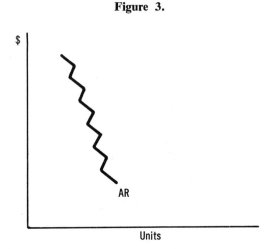

---

[5] This curve might be regarded as discontinuous, especially since the difference between points is only one cent. But it is customary to draw demand curves as continuous even though, as Chamberlin has said, *any* demand curve could be split into segments. E. H. Chamberlin. "Comments," *Quarterly Journal of Economics,* v. XLIX, November, 1934, p. 135; and A. J. Nichol, although drawing important conclusions from the supposed discontinuity of certain demand curves, states that the curves would be continuous if it were feasible to change prices by small amounts. A. J. Nichol, "The Influence of Marginal Buyers on Monopolistic Competition,"

a greater volume of sales than the next lower even-numbered price. Many sellers appear to believe this is true, although the only large-scale test ever reported was inconclusive.[6]

The second concept of odd-pricing implies an AR curve like the one shown in Figure 4, with critical points at prices such as $1, $5, and $10.[7] The presumption is that sales will be substantially greater at prices just under these critical points, whether ending in an odd or even number.

Psychological Prices

Some of the marketing text books give the name of "psychological pricing" to policies quite similar to the one just discussed. It has been found in some pricing experiments that a change of price over a certain range has little effect until some critical point is reached. If there are a number of such critical points for a given commodity the AR curve would look like the one in Figure 5, resembling a series of steps. This differs from

---

Quarterly Journal of Economics, v. XLIX, November, 1934, footnote 7, p. 126. Henry Smith believes that discontinuous demand curves might result from such heavy advertising of a certain price that the product would be unsalable at any other price. *Cf.* "Discontinuous Demand Curves and Monopolistic Competition: A Special Case," *Quarterly Journal of Economics,* v. XLIX, May, 1935, pp. 542-550. This would not seem to be a very common case, however, since marketing literature reveals heavily advertised products selling at various prices.

[6] Eli Ginsberg, "Customary Prices," *American Economic Review,* v. XXVI, no. 2, 1936, p. 296. Some economists doubt the validity of positively-inclined segments of demand curves, believing either (a) that the case could happen only if consumers regard price as one of the qualities of the product, thus making it improper to show these "different" products on one demand curve, or (b) that it simply does not happen that consumers will buy more of a product at a higher price than they will at a lower one. In regard to the first view, the important thing for purposes of the seller's pricing policy is the shape of the AR curve for what *he* knows is the same product. And while he may be interested in the psychology lying behind the consumer's demand curve he is not committed to the belief that it must be capable of explanation in terms of indifference curves. In regard to the second point, many marketing writers have commented on the view that a higher price will sometimes sell more than a lower one. For example, Phillips and Duncan say it may be possible to sell a greater number of a 15-cent item at 19 cents than at 15 cents (*op. cit.,* p. 656). Q. Forrest Walker, *loc. cit.,* suggests that 98 cents may sell better than 89 cents. Maynard and Beckman state "It is said that more articles can be sold at 17 cents than at 14 cents." (*op. cit.,* p. 656). Converse and Huegy say "Some sellers feel that odd prices are better than even prices; others, that it makes little difference" (*op. cit.,* p. 209). A New England supermarket chain reports that their meat prices never end in the figure "1," because their price tests show they can sell more at a price ending in "3." And a U. S. Department of Commerce study reports a price of 79 cents selling more than a price of 75 cents, and a case where silk underwear sold more readily at $2 or $5 than at $1.95 or $4.95 or $4.95 respectively. *Cf.* F. M. Bernfield, "Time for Businessmen to Check Pricing Policies," *Domestic Commerce, XXXV* (March, 1947), p. 20.

[7] This idea is applied even to very high prices. Thus, an automobile may be sold at $1995 rather than at $2,000.

Figure 4.

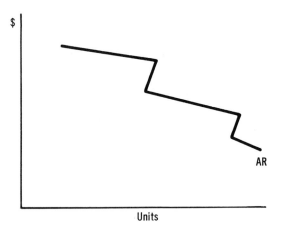

Figure 5.

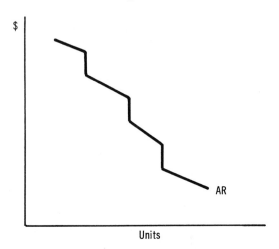

the concept of odd pricing in that the curve does not necessarily have any segments positively inclined, and the critical points are not located at each round number but only at the prices psychologically important to buyers. Pricing tests at Macy's have disclosed such step-shaped AR curves.[8]

---

[8] Oswald Knauth, "Some Reflections on Retail Prices," in *Economic Essays in Honor of Wesley Clair Mitchell* (New York: Columbia University Press, 1935), pp. 203-4. Although these tests involved *changes* in price, the important thing is that changes that reduced price below the critical points produced much greater increases in sales than changes that did not. In other words, the demand curve had very different elasticities at different points.

Customary Prices

Another pricing policy usually described as though it has no relationship to theory is the one using "customary prices." This is most frequently associated with the five-cent candy bar, chewing gum, soft drink, or subway fare. The chain stores have experimented, apparently successfully, with combination cut prices on some such items, and inflation has brought about upward changes in others. In the main, however, the five-cent price on items for which it has been customary has persisted. To the extent that the policy is correct it merely means that the AR curve is like the one shown in Figure 6, with a kink at the customary price.[9]

Figure 6.

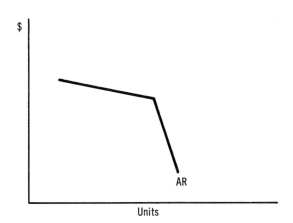

Pricing at the Market

Figure 6 also illustrates the estimate of the AR curve which results in a policy of "pricing at the market." A firm that adopts this policy believes that a price above those of competitors would curtail sales sharply, while a lower price would not significantly increase them. This pricing policy is one of the most common, possibly because ignorance of the true shape of the AR curve suggests that the safest policy is to imitate competitors.

The policy of pricing at the market is also designed to avoid price competition and price wars. But a rule-of-thumb policy is not the correct solution to this problem, for the theory of monopolistic competition pro-

---

[9] Of course where the policy of customary pricing is not correct, as may be true in some of the chainstore cases mentioned, the demand curve would be quite elastic below the customary price.

vides the basis for the proper calculation. What is required is an estimate
of the AR curve after competitors have made whatever response they
would make to the firm's pricing moves. In Figure 7 this is indicated by

Figure 7.

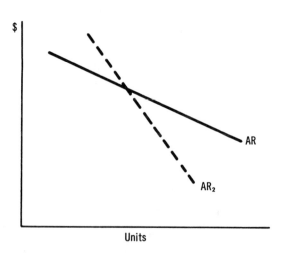

AR₂, while AR is the customary curve based on an assumption of "all
other things remaining the same." While it is very difficult for a seller to
guess what competitors will do, the theory of correct oligopoly pricing
along the AR₂ curve is quite clear, and does not necessarily call for
"pricing at the market."

Prestige Pricing

It has often been pointed out in marketing literature that many customers
judge quality by price. In such cases sales would be less at low prices than
at high ones. This idea was the original legal basis for Fair Trade laws.
While most manufacturers appear to be less impressed by this possibility
than retailers are, there have been cases reported in which low prices led
to reduced sales. The shape of the AR curve illustrating this situation has
already been indicated in economic literature.[10] See Figure 8.

---

[10] F. R. Fairchild, E. S. Furniss, and N. S. Buck, *Elementary Economics* (New
York: Macmillan Co., 1939), 4th ed., v. 1, p. 166. Converse and Huegy cite an
instance of aspirin being tried out at different prices, 19¢, 29¢, 39¢, and 49¢, with
the highest sales resulting at 49¢ (*op. cit.,* p. 207). And they comment on this reason for positively inclined demand curves, "Thus merchandise can be priced too low
as well as too high. Customers may fear that at the low price it cannot be of good
quality, and will actually buy more at a somewhat higher price than they would
at a lower price" (p. 206).

Figure 8.

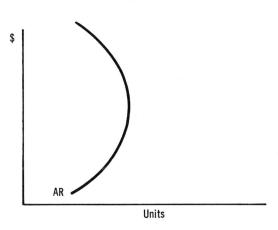

Price Lining

Many retailers when questioned about their pricing policies seem to feel they have avoided the problem entirely by adopting customary price "lines." Once the lines are decided upon, prices may be held constant over long periods of time; changes in market conditions are met by adjustments in the quality of the merchandise.

While this policy does not require pricing decisions, except initially and in case of special sales, it does present the seller with exactly the same choice as a variable price policy does in respect to the question of whether to equate marginal cost and marginal revenue, or to use a customary per cent of markup. This decision is made with reference to the prices paid for merchandise rather than the prices at which it will be sold. Although manufacturers and wholesalers dealing in types of merchandise which is customarily price-lined at retail usually tailor their own prices to fit the retail prices, the retailer does have some choice in regard to the quality of goods he buys. Presumably, the more he pays the more he can sell, at any given price line. That is, the lower his per cent of markup the higher his sales volume should be. Figure 9 illustrates this situation, where P is the established price at retail, and CG shows the various quantities that could be sold at different costs of goods to the retailer. The retailer should equate his marginal cost with marginal revenue (the price), paying NM for the goods and selling quantity OM. If instead he buys at a price that provides a customary or arbitrary per cent of markup it would be purely accidental if he would obtain the maximum gross margin.

Since there are few variable costs associated with the sale of most items at retail, except the cost of goods, the retailer's aim in general

Figure 9.

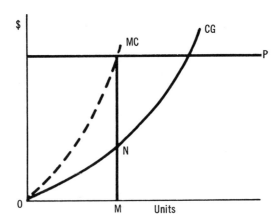

should be simply to maximize his gross margin dollars. If, however, other variable costs are significant they can be added to the cost of goods and a calculation made of the average variable costs, from which marginal cost can be computed. In Figure 9 the curve CG would merely be replaced by an AVC curve.

Resale Price Maintenance

Another situation in which the retailer feels he has no pricing problem is when the manufacturer maintains resale prices by means of Fair Trade contracts. Even here, however, the retailer may find it advantageous to sell above the Fair Trade price in some cases, in states where the Fair Trade laws call for minimum rather than specified prices. In any case the retailer must decide whether to equate marginal cost and marginal revenue or to insist upon a customary per cent of markup. If he selects the latter he may refuse to handle, or to push, many low markup items which would actually be very profitable to him.

The price policy appropriate for a manufacturer using resale price maintenance is illustrated in Figure 10. At any given retail price, P, which he may set, he will have an AR curve determined by the retailers' attitudes towards the amount of markup resulting from the price at which he sells to them. At low markups some dealers will refuse to handle the item, and others will hide it under the counter. At relatively high markups dealers will push the item and will be able to sell more than consumers would otherwise take at the given retail price. The manufacturer should calculate his optimum price by computing MR from this AR curve and equating this with his MC. He should do this with the AR curve associated with

Figure 10.

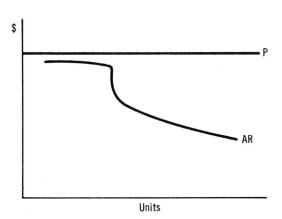

each retail price and then select the combination of retail and wholesale prices that will result in maximum profit for him.[11]

Quantity Discounts

Quantity discounts are usually described in marketing texts, and explained in terms of the lower unit cost of handling large orders, or simply the desire to increase sales volume. Economic analysis of the quantity discount policy would focus on the theory of price discrimination. With reference to this theory, a quantity discount schedule, open to all buyers, is a very rough device for price discrimination, and should not be used if the laws allowed freedom of discrimination. Instead, the seller should estimate the demand curve of each buyer, and offer each the price (or prices) that would maximize the seller's revenue in respect to that buyer.[12] This might well mean lower prices for some small buyers than for some large ones, depending on the elasticity of their demand curves.

Figure 11 illustrates a case in which the large buyer's demand curve is inelastic in this significant range, while the small buyer's curve is quite elastic. It would therefore be foolish to offer them a quantity discount schedule that would give the large buyer lower prices than the small one. The large buyer would take almost as large a quantity at high prices as at low ones, while the small buyer will not. This may not be a usual situa-

---

[11] For a fuller discussion see E. R. Hawkins, "Vertical Price Relationships," ch. 11 in Reavis Cox and Wroe Alderson (ed.), *Theory in Marketing* (Chicago: Richard D. Irwin, Inc., 1950).

[12] If the buyer is in a monopsonistic position he does not have a demand curve in the Marshallian sense, but it is possible to estimate how he will respond to various price offers.

Figure 11.

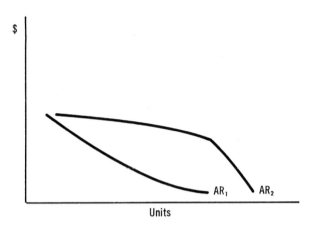

tion, but it is a possible one, and indicates that the seller should consider the elasticities of demand rather than adopt an arbitrary discount schedule.

The correct theory of price discrimination, where each buyer is to be offered a different price, has been outlined by Mrs. Robinson.[13] It indicates that the seller should equate the marginal revenue from each buyer with the marginal cost of the entire output.

Different costs of selling to different buyers can be taken into account by computing the AR curves as *net* average revenue curves, after deduction of the variable costs associated with the particular sales. And it would still be possible that the large buyer should be charged a higher price than the small one.

Some economists have used the term "quantity discount" to refer to a situation, unusual in marketing practice, in which each buyer is offered a quantity discount scale tailored to his own demand curve.[14] Of course a "quantity discount" of this kind would usually produce more net profit for the seller than a single price to each buyer, since it is an approach toward the maximum profit situation of perfect price discrimination, in which each buyer would be charged the highest price he would be willing to pay for each successive unit he bought. A seller may be attempting to gain some of the advantages of this type of pricing when he constructs a general quantity discount schedule with an eye to its effects on certain large buyers. In so doing, he would have to take care that the gain would not

---

[13] Joan Robinson, *The Economics of Imperfect Competition* (London: Macmillan Co., 1933), p. 182.

[14] James M. Buchanan, "The Theory of Monopolistic Quantity Discounts," *Review of Economic Studies*, v. XX, no. 3, 1952-3.

be cancelled by the adverse effect of the schedule on his net profits from other buyers.

Geographic Pricing

While some economists have long been concerned with the geographic aspects of pricing, and this interest has recently been spreading, on the whole marketing specialists and economic geographers have regarded the spatial aspects of economics as their own province. Unfortunately they have developed theories which do not include the essential economic aspects of the problem. Figure 11 may be used to illustrate some of the problems of geographic pricing. If the AR curve of each buyer is taken as a *net* average revenue curve, after deduction of transportation costs, then it is clear that the nearer buyer should not necessarily be given the lower delivered price. The elasticity of each buyer's demand curve is the important factor which should be considerd. As has been indicated by Mrs. Robinson, the correct net price to each buyer would equate the seller's marginal revenue with the marginal cost of his entire output.[15]

While the Robinson-Patman Act does not permit the free price discrimination that would maximize the seller's profit, it does allow some discretion in pricing. The seller is not permitted to employ price differentials greater than his cost differentials, but he is free to give discounts less than the amount of cost saving to him. Moreover, he is allowed some discretion to employ price differentials when the buyers are not in competition with each other, or where he himself is "meeting competition." He may also, of course, discriminate by selling slightly different products, under different brand names.

Conclusion

The discrepancy between economic theory and actual pricing policies, as observed by marketing specialists, is more apparent than real. Most of the pricing behavior reported by marketing students is quite consistent with the general theory of monopolistic competition, and can be integrated with that theory. A considerable gain can be made on both sides if this integration is accomplished. Economists need to know more about the pricing policies actually used by businessmen. On the other hand, marketing students can understand these policies better if they appreciate the theoretical basis for them. Most of the "price policies" described by

---

[15] Joan Robinson, *loc. cit.*

marketing specialists are merely special cases of the general theory of monopolistic competition. If so regarded, not only would clarification result, but perhaps additional insight would be gained regarding the advantages and disadvantages of each policy, and the situations to which they are appropriate.

22

A Note on Some Experimental Findings About the Meanings of Price

HAROLD J. LEAVITT

Conventional price analysis takes the generalized view that demand curves are negatively sloped. The purchase of a product is expected to decline as its price increases and to increase as its price declines—other factors being equal. The exceptions to this rule are usually attributed to the inequality of these other factors. Rare exceptions at the extreme necessity end of the product range have been accounted for by the "income-effect" concept. But the general rule is an inverse price-volume relationship, both for generic classes of products and for brands within classes.

This note questions one part of this prevalent conception of the price-volume relationship. It questions especially the applicability of conventional analysis to brands within product classes; and it further questions the assumption of "rational" consumer attitudes toward price implicit in such analysis. More positively, this paper is concerned with the idea that the price of a product may be given more than one interpretation by a potential buyer. It is concerned also with the hypothesis that several interpretations may coexist and conflict, often making choice difficult and often, too, leading the consumer finally to select a higher- rather than a lower-priced brand.

Unfortunately, this note cannot survey the research that has already been carried out in this area. So far as the writer knows, there has been no published[1] research *directly* concerned with the consumer's interpretation of price. In general, we seem implicitly to have assumed that money,

Reprinted from the *Journal of Business,* Vol. 27 (July, 1954), pp. 205-210, by Harold J. Leavitt by permission of The University of Chicago Press. Copyright 1954 by the University of Chicago.

[1] I suspect that a good deal of relevant marketing research has been done, but the results are usually locked up by their owners.

for the consumer, means something-not-to-be-given-up. However, some indirectly related published material does exist. There is, for example, a good deal of observational material by retailing people pointing to "oddities" in which consumers will choose a higher-priced item in preference to a lower-priced one of equal quality.[2] Some psychologists have also worked at the general problems of decision-making and predicting choice behavior.[3] Although all these materials are indirectly relevant, a big untapped area seems to remain—the area concerned specifically with the influence of price on consumer choice.

Each of us needs only to refer to his own experience as a consumer to agree that a price difference may have more than one meaning. Most often, perhaps, we think of high prices negatively, in terms of the sacrifice we must make to get what we want. In other cases, however—and in enough cases to be worth counting—we think of a higher price positively, as a symbol of extra quality or extra value or extra prestige. In some cases, perhaps, we buy a higher-priced brand just because it is higher.

It seems important here to distinguish between price differences and price changes. Our concern is only with differences between already established prices of competing brands or the prices of new products. When an established price of one brand is *changed,* we have quite a different psychological phenomenon, for now the consumer has three pieces of information to interpret—the old price of the brand, the new one, and the prices of the competing brands. This is a different and more complicated situation than the one we have been talking about—the simple difference between established prices of competing brands (or between the prices of new products).

Stated this way, there is nothing very startling about the idea that, other things being equal, the various meanings of price may sometimes resolve themselves into a decision to buy a higher-priced item, sometimes a lower-priced one.

But if we approach the same idea from the perspective of the price-maker rather than of the consumer, the problem begins to look a little different. When we view the world as price-makers, we tend to shift over toward the notion that price has but one meaning and that the meaning is always a kind of negative, economic meaning that drives the consumer invariably toward the lower-priced brand. For example, this "elasticity" question is often raised in one form or another: "How many more unit sales will we gain if we price our brand X cents under com-

---

[2] See, e.g., Eli Ginsberg, "Customary Prices" in Jules Backman, *Price Practices and Price Policies* (New York: Ronald Press Co., 1953); also Q. Forrest Walker, "Some Principles of Department Store Pricing," in Backman, *op. cit.*

[3] See, e.g., D. Cartwright and L. Festinger, "A Quantitative Theory of Decision," *Psychological Review,* L (1953), 595-621.

petition?" Or, conversely, "How many unit sales will we lose if our price is *X* cents higher than competition?" The assumption built into these questions is the widely accepted one that the consumer just naturally will be more ready to buy lower-priced than higher-priced brands in a competitive market. In effect, this is the view that the demand curve is always negatively sloped. Therefore, one need be concerned only about a unidirectional price-volume relationship.

Might not these questions be legitimately restated this way: "How many unit sales will we lose *or* gain by setting our prices above those of competitors? Or by setting them below those of competitors?" This revised version may look especially silly to price-markers who do not work with consumer products. Perhaps it looks a bit more sensible to people selling consumer products—especially to retailers who have observed the phenomenon of the dormant shirt that comes to life when the price is marked *up*.

Some Experimental Possibilities

If there is room for debate about problems like these, there is also room for experiment and analysis. One way to go about systematizing these problems is to think about choice situations in which one might hold constant all variables other than price and then vary price and observe choice behavior.

To do this would require us to set up situations in which the consumer must choose among two or more brands, when all he has to go on is price information. We can give him other information about the brands, but not other *differential* information. We can ask him to choose, for example, between two unknown (to him) brands of canned peas. Both cans will be the same size, with covered labels; he can be told that both are "large" size, "select" peas, etc. But their prices differ. If price has only one meaning—an economic "sacrifice" meaning—then obviously our consumer will simply choose the lower-priced brand. If price sometimes has more than an economic meaning, if it also carries with it some implications about quality or good value or social propriety, then we would expect (1) that the consumer would feel some "conflict" in making a choice and (2) that he would in some cases make the higher-priced choice. The pressures toward the lower price, in other words, deriving from his concern about spending his money, might be balanced, or even overbalanced, by his concern about getting good quality or the "right" product. The questions now become: "When might we expect maximum 'conflict' in making such a choice?" And "When might we expect a significant number of high choices?"

Some armchair analysis may be useful at this point. Clearly, a whole host of variables may be relevant here. For example, the price level of the product we are talking about may certainly be related to the difficulty and direction of choice. A consumer may feel quite differently about purchasing a higher-priced television set. The frequency with which he purchases the product may influence his thinking. A loaf of bread may be treated quite differently from a can of spice, for example. The consumer himself and his role is society may be relevant. Evidence is already available that indicates differences in price consciousness within different social strata of our society. Some groups may, for example, be expected to choose higher prices more frequently because they are more concerned with doing the socially "right" things—things that will guarantee acceptance either by their peers or by the members of the next higher stratum. Finally, the products themselves may, for many reasons, carry with them some stereotyped notions about their own quality. It is possible, for example, that consumers may feel that certain products are all alike from brand to brand, while other products are really different from one another.

An Experimental Method

Over the past few months we have conducted some small-scale experiments in this area, with hypothetical choice situations. For these experiments we selected only products in the 50-cent to $1.00 price range. We concerned ourselves only with two variables: the size of the price difference and consumers' stereotypes about similarities or differences among different brands of each of the products.

To get some products with different stereotypes we used a list of fifteen household products in the price range—products like aspirin tablets, bacon, hand towels, ice cream, bobby pins, deodorants, floor wax, etc. Unsystematically and nonrandomly we simply asked a number of friends and acquaintances to place five of the products in each of these three categories: (1) all brands pretty much alike, (2) big quality differences from brand to brand, (3) in between.

The results were consistent enough to give us four products to work with. Cooking sherry and moth flakes were placed in the "all-alike" category by most of our subjects. Razor blades and floor wax took top honors in the "considerable-difference" category.

We then took these four products—the two in which quality differences were seen as minimal and the two in which quality differences were seen as maximal—and set up some hypothetical choice situations for a new population of sixty (plus) subjects. Thirty of them were Air

Force officers, majors and lieutenant colonels; the remainder were male and female graduate students, most of them in their thirties or forties.

Here are the major methodological steps in these experiments:[4] Subjects were asked to imagine themselves in a situation in which they had to choose between two brands of each of our four products. Their only differential information was price. For example, male subjects were told:

Your wife sends you out to the local supermarket to buy a pint of floor wax. She specifies a brand, but when you get to the store you find that they are all out of that brand. You know your wife needs the wax quickly, and there is no other convenient store in which to buy it, so you must choose between the brands that are carried. The store does have two brands. You have heard of both brands, but you know nothing about either one.

When I give you the signal, will you please turn the page where you will find the prices of the two brands. Circle the choice that you would make.

Roughly equal numbers of subjects were presented with these pairs of prices to choose from:

Brand A at $0.68 versus brand B at $0.72
Brand A at $0.66 versus brand B at $0.74
Brand A at $0.62 versus brand B at $0.78
Brand A at $0.52 versus brand B at $0.88

Subjects were also asked, after they had made their choices, to check one of these two statements:

(   ) I am satisfied with the choice I made.
(   ) I feel doubtful about the choice I made.

A kind of aborted Latin-square design was used in these experiments. We used four products; four sets of prices for each product. Each group of subjects was subdivided into four groups. Each member of each subgroup was given four choice situations, one for each product, one pair of prices per product. Thus a subject in group A might have received razor blades at 68 versus 72 cents; then floor wax at 62 versus 78 cents; then cooking sherry at 52 versus 88 cents; and moth flakes at 68 versus 74 cents. Subjects in other subgroups received the same four products, but with prices shifted. Thus we ended up with about equal numbers of subjects for each product at each pair of prices. After all choices had been made, the subjects were asked to rank the four products—cooking sherry, floor wax, moth flakes, and razor blades—in terms of the quality differences they believe to exist among brands.

---

[4] We have omitted several methodological details from this discussion. They are available to those who may be interested.

Some Preliminary Results

Here is a brief summary of our results:

1. These sixty subjects differentiated among these four products in the same order as our preliminary subjects had done. They ranked floor wax and razor blades as large "quality-difference" products, in that order; cooking sherry ranked a very poor third, and moth flakes a definite fourth.

2. When faced with choices between two brands of floor wax, 57 per cent of our subjects selected the higher-priced brand (all pairs of prices are pooled here); 30 per cent of the subjects chose the higher-priced razor blades; 24 per cent the higher-priced moth flakes; and 21 per cent the higher-priced cooking sherry. The difference between the extremes is significant at better than the 1 per cent level.

Let's shift gears a little and consider for each subject the product which he ranked No. 1, no matter what particular product it may be, and the product he ranked No. 2, and so on. For products ranked No. 1, 57 per cent of the subjects chose the higher-priced item; for products ranked No. 2, 46 per cent chose the higher-priced item; for products ranked No. 3, 15 per cent; and for products ranked No. 4, 2 per cent.

3. The idea that "psychological conflict" increases with the subject's belief in quality difference is also supported, if the "doubt" item can be taken as an indication of conflict. For cooking sherry, 10 per cent of the subjects indicated doubt about the choice they had made; moth flakes, 12 per cent; but for the large quality-difference items the frequency of doubtful choices rises: 20 per cent of the subjects were doubtful about their razor-blade choices, and 38 per cent were doubtful about their floor-wax decisions. Incidentally, subjects tend, if anything, to be more doubtful about their low choices than about their high choices; that is, the percentage of doubtfuls which end up as low choices is *greater* than the percentage of doubtfuls which end up high.

4. Another finding may be worth mentioning. Some relationship *may* exist between the tendency to choose high or low and the *size* of the price differential. At first guess, one might think that the direction of such a relationship would be inverse—that is, as the price difference increased, subjects would tend more and more to choose the lower-priced product. On the other hand, an analysis of the situation in psychological-conflict terms would probably lead to a more complicated conclusion. Unfortunately, neither the common-sense direction nor the conflict-analysis direction seems at this point to hold much water. What actually happened at each price difference is shown in Table 1.

"Product rank for quality" in Table 1 is each subject's own rank.

Table 1. Percentage of Subjects Choosing Higher-Priced Brand

Product Rank for Quality	Price Differences (cents)			
	68–72	*66–74*	*62–78*	*52–88*
1 (Big Difference)	64	50	61	50
2	47	44	54	41
3	6	6	10	35
4 (All Alike)	0	0	7	0

So, for example, when choosing between a 68- and a 72-cent brand for their No. 1 product, 64 per cent of our subjects indicated they would select the 72-cent brand.

The vertical differences in Table 1 are clear. However, the only statistically significant horizontal difference is that between the extremes for product rank 3. In that case, one might interpret the results to mean that as the price differences increase, subjects feel that the probability of quality differences also increases.

Summary and Some Implications

The results of our experiments are not startling. Our particular subjects, in these particular hypothetical choice situations, simply indicated that they would often choose the higher-priced of two alternative brands when their only differential information was price. They are consistent in their beliefs that different brands of certain products are "all alike," while different brands of certain other products are "different." They are more ready to make the higher-priced choice for products among which they believe brands are different than for products that they believe are all alike. They *may*, in fact, be more frequently ready to choose the *higher-*priced brand for some products when the price difference is large than when it is small.

These findings suggest that demand curves may not invariably be negatively sloped, that price itself may have more than one meaning to a consumer, and that a higher price may sometimes increase, rather than decrease, his readiness to buy. Such behavior may be odd and "uneconomic," but perhaps not unrealistic.

Several interesting possibilities seem to arise out of these tentative findings. It may be, for example, that the economists' traditional "inferior good" (diamonds are the usual textbook example) is not so rare as we may believe. One might guess that a high price may be an attracting in-stead of a repelling force for particular brands of many different kinds of items. If the revelant characteristics of the items or of consumer groups can be systematically identified and interrelated, then perhaps one might have the beginnings of a framework from which to set and predict the effects of a particular pricing policy. Moreover, if the kinds of behavior found in these experiments occur with any frequency in "real" life, then any satisfactory predictive theory of pricing would have to account for them. In any case, the area seems deserving of further exploration.

23

Postponement, Speculation and the Structure of Distribution Channels

LOUIS P. BUCKLIN

While the study of marketing has long been concerned with the creation of time, space, and possession utilities, much of the literature of the field has dealt with the problems of ownership. Issues involving space and time, in particular, have been scarcely touched. The role of time with respect to the character of the structure of distribution channels, for example, has just begun to be charted. The purpose of this article is to derive a principle describing the effect of temporal factors upon distribution systems.

The Concept of Substitutability

Underlying the logic of the principle to be developed is the hypothesis that economic interaction among basic marketing functions, and between these functions and production, provides much of the force that shapes the structure of the distribution channel. These interactions occur because of the capability of the various functions to be used as substitutes for each other within certain broad limitations. This capability is comparable to the opportunities available to the entrepreneur to use varying ratios of land, labor, and capital in the production of his firm's output. The substitutability of marketing functions may occur both within the firm and among the various institutions of the channel, *e.g.,* producers, middlemen, and consumers. This substitutability permits the work load of one function to be shrunk and shifted to another without affecting the output of the channel. These functional relationships may also be seen to be at the root of the

Reprinted from Louis P. Bucklin, "Postponement, Speculation and the Structure of Distribution Channels," the *Journal of Marketing Research,* a publication of the American Marketing Association, Vol. II (February, 1965), pp. 26-31.

"total cost" concept employed in the growing literature of the management of the physical distribution system [3, 9].

A familiar example of one type of substitution that may appear in the channel is the use of inventories to reduce the costs of production stemming from cyclical demand. Without the inventory, production could only occur during the time of consumption. Use of the inventory permits production to be spread over a longer period of time. If some institution of the channel senses that the costs of creating a seasonal inventory would be less than the savings accruing from a constant rate of production, it would seek to create such a stock and to retain the resulting profits. The consequence of this action is the formation of a new and alternate channel for the product.

The momentum of change, however, is not halted at this point. Unless there is protection against the full brunt of competitive forces, the institutions remaining in the original, and now high-cost channel, will either be driven out of business or forced to convert to the new system as well. With continued competitive pressure the excess profits, initially earned by the institutions which innovated the new channel, will eventually be eliminated and total channel costs will fall.

In essense, the concept of substitutability states that under competitive conditions institutions of the channel will interchange the work load among functions, not to minimize the cost of some individual function, but the total costs of the channel. It provides, thereby, a basis for the study of distribution channels. By understanding the various types of interactions among the marketing functions and production that could occur, one may determine the type of distribution structure that should appear to minimize the total channel costs including those of the consumer. The principle of postponement-speculation, to be developed below, evaluates the conditions under which one type of substitution may occur.

Postponement

In 1950, Wroe Alderson proposed a concept which uniquely related certain aspects of uncertainty and risk to time. He labelled this concept the "principle of postponement," and argued that it could be used to reduce various marketing costs [2]. Risk and uncertainty costs were tied to the differentiation of goods. Differentiation could occur in the product itself and/or the geographical dispersion of inventories. Alderson held that "the most general method which can be applied in promoting the efficiency of a marketing system is the postponement of differentiation . . . postpone changes in form and identity to the latest possible point in the marketing flow; postpone change in inventory location to the latest possible point in time" [1]. Savings in costs related to uncertainty would be achieved "by moving the differentiation nearer to the time of purchase," where demand, presumably, would be more predictable. Savings in the physical movement of the goods could be achieved by sorting products in "large lots," and "in relatively undifferentiated states."

Despite its potential importance, the principle has received relatively little attention since it was first published. Reavis Cox and Charles Goodman [4] have made some use of the concept in their study of channels for house building materials. The Vaile, Grether, and Cox marketing text [10] also makes mention of it. As far as can be determined, this is the totality of its further development.

As a result, the principle still constitutes only a somewhat loose, and possibly misleading, guide to the study of the distribution channel structure. The major defect is a failure to specify the character of the limits which prevent it from being applied. The principle, which states that changes in form and inventory location are to be delayed to the latest possible moment, must also explain why in many channels these changes appear at the earliest. As it stands, the principle of postponement requires modification if it is to be applied effectively to the study of channels.

Postponement and the Shifting of Risk

If one views postponement from the point of view of the distribution channel as a whole, it may be seen as a device for individual institutions to shift the risk of owning goods to another. The manufacturer who postpones by refusing to produce except to order is shifting the risk forward to the buyer. The middleman postpones by either refusing to buy except from a seller who provides next day delivery (backward postponement), or by purchasing only when he has made a sale (forward postponement). The consumer postpones by buying from those retail facilities which permit him to take immediate possession directly from the store shelf. Further, where the consumer first contacts a number of stores before buying, the shopping process itself may be seen as a process of postponement—a process which advertising seeks to eliminate.

From this perspective it becomes obvious that every institution in the channel, including the consumer, cannot postpone to the latest possible moment. The channel, in its totality, cannot avoid ownership responsibilties. Some institution, or group of institutions, must continually bear this uncertainty from the time the goods start through production until they are consumed.

Since most manufacturers do produce for stock, and the ownership of intermediate inventories by middlemen is characteristic of a large proportion of channels, it is clear that the principle of postponement can reach its limit very quickly. As a result, it provides no rationale for the forces which create these inventories. Hence, postponement is really only half a principle. It must have a converse, a converse equally significant to channel structure.

Speculation

This converse may be labelled the principle of speculation. It represents a shift of risk to the institution, rather than away from it. The principle of speculation holds that changes in form, and the movement of goods to forward inventories, should be made at the earliest possible time in the marketing flow in order to reduce the costs of the marketing system.

As in the case of postponement, application of the principle of speculation can lead to the reduction of various types of costs. By changing form at the earliest point, one makes possible the use of plants with large-scale economies. Speculation permits goods to be ordered in large quantities rather than in small frequent orders. This reduces the costs of sorting and transportation. Speculation limits the loss of consumer good will due to stock outs. Finally, it permits the reduction of uncertainty in a variety of ways.

This last point has already been well developed in the literature. It received early and effective treatment from Frank H. Knight [6]. He held that speculators, by shifting uncertainty to themselves, used the principle of grouping, as insurance, to transform it into the more manageable form of a relatively predictable risk. Further, through better knowledge of the risks to be handled, and more informed opinion as to the course of future events, risk could be further reduced.

The Combined Principle

From the point of view of the distribution channel, the creation of inventories for holding goods before they are sold is the physical activity which shifts risk and uncertainty. Such inventories serve to move risk away from those institutions which supply, or are supplied by, the inventory. Such inventories, however, will not be created in the channel if the increased costs attending their operation outweigh potential savings in risk. Risk costs, according to the substitutability hypothesis, cannot be minimized if other costs increase beyond the savings in risk.

This discussion shows the principle of speculation to be the limit to the principle of postponement, and vice versa. Together they form a basis for determining whether speculative inventories, those that hold goods prior to their sale, will appear in distribution channels subject to competitive conditions. Operationally, postponement may be measured by the notion of delivery time. Delivery time is the number of days (or hours) elapsing between the placing of an order and the physical receipt of the goods by the buyer [9, p. 93]. For the seller, postponement increases, and costs decline, as delivery time lengthens. For the buyer, postponement increases, and costs decline, as delivery time shortens. The combined principle of postponement-speculation may be stated as follows: A speculative inventory will appear at each point in a distribution channel whenever its costs are less than the net savings to both buyer and seller from postponement.

Operation of the Principle

The following hypothetical example illustrates how the postponement-speculation principle can be applied to the study of distribution channels. The specific problem to be considered is whether an inventory, located between the manufacturer and the consumer, will appear in the channel. This inventory may be managed by the manufacturer, a consumer cooperative or an independent middleman.

Assume that trade for some commodity occurs between a set of manufacturers and a set of customers, both sets being large enough to insure active price competition. The manufacturers are located close to each other in a city some significant distance from the community in which the customers are situated. All of the customers buy in quantities sufficiently large to eliminate the possibility of savings from sorting. Manufacturing and consumption are not affected by seasonal variations. Assume, further, that production costs will not be affected by the presence of such an intermediate inventory.

To determine whether the intermediate inventory will appear, one must first ascertain the shape of the various relevant cost functions with respect to time. In any empirical evaluation of channel structure this is likely to be the most difficult part of the task. For present purposes, however, it will be sufficient to generalize about their character.

The costs incurred by the relevant functions are divided into two broad categories. The first includes those costs originating from activities associated with the potential inventory, such as handling, storage, interest, uncertainty, and costs of selling and buying if the inventory is operated by a middleman. It also includes those costs emanating from transportation, whether the transportation is direct from producer to consumer or routed through the inventory. All of these costs will, in turn, be affected by the particular location of the inventory between the producer and the consumer. In the present instance, it is assumed that the inventory will be located in the consumer city.

In general, this first category includes all the relevant costs incurred by the producer and intermediary, if any. These are aggregated on Diagram 1. In this diagram, the ordinate represents the average cost for moving one unit of the commodity from the producer to the consumer.

Diagram 1.   Average Cost of Distributing One Unit of a Commodity to a Customer With Respect to Delivery Time in Days

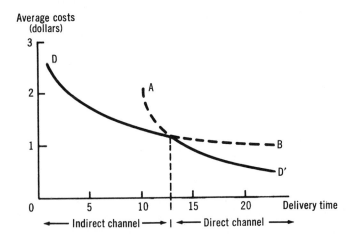

The abscissa measures the time in days for delivery of an order to the consumer after it has been placed. The curve DB measures the cost of using the speculative inventory to supply the consumer for the various possible delivery times. Curve AD' shows the cost of supplying the consumer direct without use of such an inventory. DD' is the minimum average cost achievable by either direct or indirect distribution of the commodity.

The diagram shows that DD' declines as the delivery time is allowed to increase [7]. With very short delivery times the intermediate inventory is absolutely necessary because only in this way can goods be rushed quickly to the consumer. Further, when virtually immediate delivery is required, the safety stock of the inventory must be kept high in order to prevent temporary stockouts from delaying shipment. Also, delivery trucks must always be available for short notice. These factors create high costs.

As the delivery time to be allowed increases, it becomes possible to reduce the safety stocks, increase the turnover and reduce the size of the facilities and interest cost. Further increases permit continued savings. Eventually, a point will be reached, I in Diagram 1, where the delivery time will be sufficiently long to make it cheaper to ship goods directly from the factory to the consumer than to move them indirectly through the inventory. This creates the discontinuity at I as the costs of maintaining the inventory and the handling of goods are eliminated.

In part, the steepness of the slope of DD′ will be affected by the uncertainties of holding the inventory. Where prices fluctuate rapidly, or goods are subject to obsolescence, these costs will be high. The extension of delivery time, in permitting the intermediate inventory to be reduced in size, and eventually eliminated, should bring significant relief.

The second category of costs involves those emanating from the relevant marketing functions performed by the customer. Essentially, these costs will be those of bearing the risk and costs of operating any inventory on the customer's premises. These costs are shown as C on Diagram 2, with the ordinate and abscissa labelled as in Diagram 1.

Diagram 2. Average Inventory Cost for One Unit of a Commodity to a Customer With Respect to Delivery Time in Days

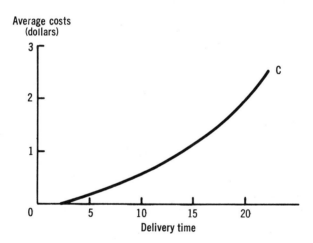

The shape of C is one that increases with delivery time. The longer the delivery time allowed by the customer, the greater the safety stock he will have to carry. Such stock is necessary to protect against failures in transport and unpredictable surges in requirements. Hence, his costs will increase. The greater the uncertainty cost of inventory holding, the steeper will the slope of this function be.

Determination of the character of the distribution channel is made from the joint consideration of these two cost categories, C and DD′. Whether an intermediate inventory will appear in the channel depends upon the relationship of the costs for operating the two sets of functions and how their sum may be minimized. Function DD′ + C on Diagram 3 represents the sum of functions DD′ and C. The diagram reveals, in this

Diagram 3.   Total of Average Distributing and Customer Inventory Costs With Respect to Delivery Time in Days

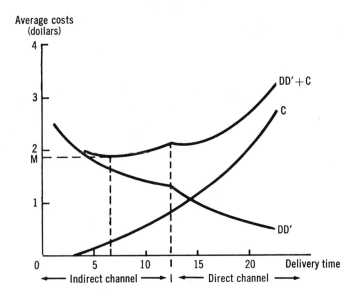

instance, that costs of postponement are minimized by use of a speculative inventory as the minimal cost point, M, falls to the left of I. If, however, the risk costs to the customer had been less, or the general cost of holding inventories at the customer's home (or plant site, as the case may be) had been lower, then C would be farther to the right. M would also shift to the right. With a sufficient reduction in consumer cost, M would appear to the right of the discontinuity, indicating that direct shipment in the channel would be the means to minimize postponement cost.

Significance of the Principle

As developed, the principle of postponement-speculation provides a basis for expecting inventories to be present in channels because of production and distribution time requirements. In particular, it treats the role of speculative inventories in the channel. The concept, as a consequence, extends beyond the physical flow of the goods themselves to the flow of their title. Speculative inventories create the opportunity for new institutions to hold title in the channel. Wthout such inventories, there may be little economic justification for a title holding intermediary to enter the channel. The economic need to have such an inventory in the physical flow opens the door to a middleman to show whether he is capable of reducing the risk cost of that inventory below the level attainable by either the producer or some consumer cooperative.

The presence of an inventory in the channel for either collecting, sorting, or dispersing does not create the same type of opportunity for a title-taking intermediary to appear in the channel. Such inventories are not speculative in character. They do not need to hold uncommitted stocks of goods available for general sale in order to fulfill their purpose. For example, the REA Express, the parcel post system, freight forwarders, and even the Greyhound Bus Corporation's freight system sort a substantial volume of goods through many nonspeculative type inventories each day. Milk producers establish handling depots where bottled milk is transferred from large, long-distance vehicles to city delivery trucks. Catalogue sellers discharge full truck shipments upon the post offices of distant cities where customers reside. None of these inventories involves the risk of unsolds goods. None of these inventories provides the basis for the emergence of a title-holding middleman.

From this perspective, the principle of postponement-speculation may be regarded as a concept which broadens the channel analyst's understanding of the intimate relationship between title and physical flows. The intertwining of the roles of ownership and the holding of speculative stocks provides a fundamental rationale for the position of the merchant middleman. The principle of postponement-speculation, as a consequence, can be employed to provide at least part of the explanation for the number of ownership stages in the channel. This, of course, is one of the basic questions toward which traditional distribution analysis is directed [5].

In this light, for example, the principle may be of use in explaining the emergence of an "orthodox channel of distribution." This concept, developed by Shaw [8], was used to characterize the nature of the distribution channel through which a large proportion of products traveled, to wit: the manufacturer-wholesaler-retailer route. That such a concept should emerge to characterize products, whose sorting needs are different because of diverse physical characteristics and market research, is of extreme interest. Similarities among channels for different products implies that forces, which may not vary significantly among many types of goods, should be sought as explanatory variables of channel structure. Since many groups of consumer goods generate similar temporal types of risk, the principle of postponement-speculation may provide a major explanation for this phenomenon.

Testing the Principle

The principle of postponement-speculation will not be easy to test for a number of reasons. First of all, it is normative. It is derived from assumptions of profit maximization and predictions are based upon what firms should do. Second, it approximates the real world only when the channel environment is sufficiently competitive to produce a variety of price-product-delivery time offers. Finally, it cannot predict the necessary time delays that occur in the channel for new facilities to be built or old ones abandoned.

Despite these problems, a number of hypotheses may be generated from the model and subjectd to evaluation by surveys of existing channels. These surveys would locate any intermediate, speculative inventory in the channel and measure the time elapsing between the placing of an order by, and its delivery to, the customer. Use of industrial or commodity channels would undoubtedly be the best initial subjects for the surveys. The confounding effects of collecting, sorting, and dispersing in consumer channels will make the impact of the principle of postponement-speculation more difficult to isolate.

Six hypotheses which could be tested in this manner follow:

1. The shorter the delivery time, the greater the probability the channel will include an intermediate, speculative inventory.
2. The shorter the delivery time, the closer any speculative stock will be to the consumer.
3. The shorter the distance between a customer and a speculative stock, the greater the probability of a second such inventory in the channel.
4. Products which are heavy, bulky, and inexpensive are likely to flow through channels with more intermediate, speculative inventories than products with the opposite characteristics.
5. Products which consumers find expensive to store on their premises, but whose use is both urgent and difficult to forecast, have a greater probability of passing through an intermediate, speculative inventory than products with the opposite characteristics.
6. The greater the inelasticity of consumer and/or producer cost with respect to changes in delivery time, the greater the stability of the most efficient channel type over time.

All of these hypotheses are subject to the *ceteris paribus* limitation. Tests, as a result, should include only those channels operating under reasonably similar economic conditions. This is particularly important with respect to the distance between the producer and the consumer, Variations in this factor will affect the cost of providing any given delivery time. Channels which traverse longer distances, in other words, are likely to require more speculative inventories than those which move goods less extensively.

The *ceteris paribus* limitation also contains an important implication beyond that of the problems of testing. Consideration of this limitation provides the rationale for the presence of several different types of channels supplying the same type of product to a given group of customers. Producers, for example, provisioning some market from a distance, may be forced to use channels distinct from their competitors located adjacent to the customers. This diversity of channels may also be produced by imperfections in competition as well as variations in the urgency of demand among consumers in the market. Those who can easily tolerate delays in delivery are likely to use a different channel from those patronized by customers with dissimilar personalities or capabilities.

Implications of the Principle

The principle of postponement-speculation, in addition to providing a basis for developing hypotheses for empirical testing, makes it possible to do some *a priori* generalizing concerning the type of channel structure changes one may expect to see in the future. Any force, or set of forces, which affects the types of costs discussed may be sufficient to move the balance from speculation to postponement, or vice versa.

One type of change, already occurring and which may be expected to spread in the future, rests upon the relationship between the cost of transportation and speed. Rapidly evolving methods of using air transport economically and efficiently are serving to narrow the spread between the cost of high-speed transportation and low-speed transportation. This has the effect of reducing the relative advantage of speculation over postponement. Hence, intermediate inventories will tend to disappear and be replaced by distribution channels which have a direct flow.

The increasing proliferation of brands, styles, colors, and price lines is another type of force which will affect the balance. This proliferation increases the risk of inventory holding throughout the entire channel, but particularly at those points closest to the consumer. Retailers will attempt to minimize this risk by reducing the safety stock level of their inventories and relying more upon speedy delivery from their suppliers. The role of the merchant wholesaler, or the chain store warhouse, will become increasingly important in this channel. Indeed, there will probably be increasing efforts on the part of retailers to carry only sample stock in those items where it is not absolutely necessary for customers to take immediate delivery. General Electric, for example, is experimenting with wholesaler-to-consumer delivery of large appliances. Drugstores, where the role of the pharmacist appears to be slowly changing from one of compounding prescriptions to inventorying branded specialities, will become further dependent upon ultra-fast delivery from wholesalers.

Those stores, such as discount houses, which are successfully able to resist the pressure toward carrying wide assortments of competing brands are likely to utilize channels of distribution which differ significantly from their full-line competitors. Large bulk purchases from single manufacturers can be economically delivered directly to the discount house's retail facilities. Where warehouses are used in discount house channels they can serve stores spread out over a far greater geographical area than would be normally served by a wholesaler. Such stores are also apt to find their market segments not only in middle income range families, but also among those consumers who tend to be heavily presold by manufacturer advertising, or who simply are less finicky about the specific type of item they buy.

A final possible trend may spring from consumers who find that their own shopping costs represent too great an expenditure of effort with respect to the value received from postponement. As a result, such consumers are likely to turn more and more to catalogue and telephone shopping. Improved quality control procedures by manufacturers and better means of description in catalogues could hasten this movement. The acceptance of Sears telephone order services in large cities testifies that many individuals are prone to feel this way. If the movement were to become significantly enlarged, it could have a drastic effect upon the existing structure of distribution.

Summary

The study of distribution channels, and why they take various forms, is one of the most neglected areas of marketing today. Part of the neglect may be due to the absence of effective tools for analysis. The principle of postponement-speculation is offered in the hope that it may prove useful in this regard and stimulate work in the area.

The principle directly treats the role of time in distribution and, indirectly, the role of distance as it affects time. The starting point for the development of the constructs of the principle may be found in the work of Alderson and Knight [2, 3, 7]. Postponement is measured by the change of delivery time in the shipping of a product. Increasing the delivery time decreases postponement costs for the seller, increases them for the buyer and vice versa. Justification and support for the relationships suggested between the costs of marketing functions and delivery time may be found in the recent literature of physical distribution.

The principle reveals the effect upon channel structure of the interaction between the risk of owning a product and the physical functions employed to move the product through time. It holds that, in a competitive environment, the costs of these functions be minimized over the entire channel, not by individual function. The minimum cost and type of channel are determined by balancing the costs of alternative delivery times against the cost of using an intermediate, speculative inventory. The apperance of such an inventory in the channel occurs whenever its additional costs are more than offset by net savings in postponement to the buyer and seller.

REFERENCES

1. Wroe Alderson, *Marketing Behavior and Executive Action,* Homewood, Illinois: Richard D. Irwin, Inc., 1957, 424.
2. ————, "Marketing Efficiency and the Principle of Postponement," *Cost and Profit Outlook,* 3 (September 1950).
3. Stanley H. Brewer and James Rosenweig, "Rhochematics," *California Management Review,* 3 (Spring 1961), 52-71.
4. Reavis Cox and Charles S. Goodman, "Marketing of Housebuilding Materials," *The Journal of Marketing,* 21 (July 1956), 55-56.
5. William R. Davidson, "Channels of Distribution—One Aspect of Marketing Strategy," *Business Horizons,* Special Issue—First International Seminar on Marketing Management, February, 1961, 85-86.
6. Frank H. Knight, *Risk, Uncertainty and Profit,* Boston: Houghton Mifflin Company, 1921, 238-39, 255-58.
7. John F. Magee, "The Logistics of Distribution," *Harvard Business Review,* 38 (July-August 1960), 97-99.
8. Arch W. Shaw, "Some Problems in Market Distribution," *The Quarterly Journal of Economics,* (August 1912), 727.
9. See Edward W. Smykay, Donald J. Bowersox, and Frank J. Mossman, *Physical Distribution Management,* New York: Macmillan Company, 1961, Ch. IV.
10. Roland S. Vaile, Edward T. Grether, and Reavis Cox, *Marketing in the American Economy,* New York: Ronald Press Company, 1952, 149-50.

24

Toward a Formal Theory of
Transactions and Transvections

WROE ALDERSON
MILES W. MARTIN

This article presents the initial steps in the formalization of a partial theory of marketing. The partial theory pertains to the movement of goods and information through marketing channels, and the theory utilizes two basic concepts of marketing system behavior, namely, transactions and transvections. Current approaches to the problem of constructing formal theories are compared and reasons are given for choosing the "molar" approach.

This article has both a special and a general objective. The special objective is to advance a particular area of theory which seems promising for practical applications, particularly in planning. The general objective is to exemplify some aspects of the technical procedure for generating formal theory in marketing.[1]

There would appear to be two main routes to be followed in the construction of formal theory. The first is to build the theory step by step from very simple elements offering proof for each step in turn. Most readers will be familiar with this process from a study of elementary geometry or other areas in mathematics. The process starts out with some terms

Reprinted from Wroe Alderson and Miles W. Martin, "Toward a Formal Theory of Transactions and Transvection," the *Journal of Marketing Research,* a publication of the American Marketing Association, Vol. II (May, 1965), pp. 117-127.

[1] For one view of theory construction, see Martin, R. M., "On Atomic Sentential Forms and Theory Construction [4]"; pertinent writings by the same author include "Toward A Systematic Pragmatics," Amsterdam, North Holland Publishing Company, 1964.

that are called primitives because they are regarded as rudimentary building blocks and are not defined within the logical structure. Among the primitives of elementary logic are the words "and," "or" and "not." These words are replaced by convenient symbols in mathematical logic.

There are other terms known as subject matter primitives which must be introduced in developing a particular field of theory. Thus, J. H. Woodger, in developing an axiomatic theory of biology, introduced three subject matter terms, namely, the relation of one entity being a part of another, the relation of one entity being prior to another in time, and the relation of an entity being a member of the class of entities known as cells. The step-by-step creation of a logical system requires that all notions other than the primitives be defined in terms of the primitives or other notions previously developed from the primitives.

To indicate the link to marketing theory as quickly as possible, we believe that the primitive concepts needed for marketing theory are sets, behavior and expectations. A set is a mathematical concept which can apply to any collection of elements, whether the elements are points in a plane, goods or people. A number of ideas that are more obviously relevant for marketing can then be defined in terms of sets. A system, for example, is a set consisting of people and the supporting facilities. An organized behavior system is defined as a particular type of system. Similarly, a collection is a special type of set and an assortment of goods is a special type of collection.

A formal theory must have a formal language. This language is constituted by setting up primitive terms and definitions relating back to these terms. A formal theory must also have rules of inference and a series of propositions which are linked together by a sequence of logical proofs. Here gain we can divide propositions into two classes. One class must be taken as given and the other class of propositions must be developed on the basis of the first class. The propositions that are taken as given are called axioms. The propositions which cannot be accepted until proven are called theorems.

M. H. Halbert, in his forthcoming book, *The Meaning and Sources of Marketing Theory,* takes a strong position favoring formal theory in marketing [3]. He believes that we have a great need in marketing to make our language more precise, to be sure we know what we are talking about. He also contends that marketing must have a body of self-consistent propositions all derived deductively from simpler propositions as a basis for guiding empirical research. He does not believe that many assertions exist in marketing which can be called theoretical propositions because the proper deductive apparatus is almost completely lacking. Mr. Halbert's general position implies the kind of step-by-step procedure represented by the work of Martin and Woodger, although he does not undertake to set up such a deductive apparatus himself.

Let us now return to the contrasting route to theory which was alluded to earlier. This would consist in setting up meaningful equations or other relationships arrived at intuitively and then going as far back in the chain of reasoning as seemed necessary to validate these propositions. No doubt both methods will be employed by different writers according to their temperaments and special competence. The method of starting with the desired results and working backward is especially recommended here because of the urgent need for marketing theory as seen by Mr. Halbert and other authorities.

This article will follow the molar approach insofar as possible, rather than the atomistic approach illustrated by Dr. Martin in his recent essay in *Theory in Marketing.* One justification for the molar approach which starts with the end result and works backward is in the procedures followed by physicists. We recently talked to a leading physicist at the University of Pennsylvania, describing the deductive apparatus which Mr. Halbert sets up as a prerequisite for marketing theory. This informant hastened to say that physicists did not possess any such deductive apparatus, however logical it might appear to economists and marketing men. He indicated that physics was kept in such a constant state of flux through one empirical discovery after another that only a few theorists are concerned about the ultimate logical foundations of physics. The proper retort might be that economists and marketing men need this kind of deductive apparatus much more than physicists because of the elusive nature of their subject matter.

We were further influenced by an article by Phillipp Frank on the foundations of physics [2]. Dr. Frank is concerned to develop a self-consistent set of propositions for physics, and he adopts a molar rather than an atomistic strategy in the pursuit of his aim. Dr. Frank says, "We are not going to set up a complete system of symbols and operational definitions from which one could derive all facts of physics. Such a systematic presentation would be a very hard job and at that I suspect that only a very few scientists would read it. . . . The scientist is interested in logical analysis if and only if this analysis is not trivial or commonplace."

With these preliminary comments on the strategies of theory construction, we can turn to a sketch of the theory of transactions and transvections, both for its direct value as a branch of marketing theory and as an illustration of the molar approach. Following the lead of John R. Commons, an attempt was made to present the first rough sketch of a theory of transactions in 1957 [1]. Soon after this book was published, the senior author of this article developed the notion of a transvection[2] which was first presented at a graduate seminar at Ohio State University in 1958.

A transvection is in a sense the outcome of a series of transactions, but a transvection is obviously more than that. The transactions as such are limited only to the successive negotiations of exchange agreements. A transvection includes the complete sequence of exchanges, but it also includes the various transformations which take place along the way. The pair of shoes in the hands of the consumer is obviously a very different thing from the raw materials in the state of nature. The student of transvections is interested in every step by which this flow through the marketing system was accomplished.

Other contrasts can be drawn between a transaction and a transvection with respect to their use in planning and decision-making. Transactions involve a transfer in ownership of use privileges covering not only sales but all forms of short-term rent and lease agreements. It is assumed that further transformations will take place under the new ownership, but ordinarily this is not required under the terms of the exchange agreement. In market planning there is necessarily substantial emphasis on means of motivating these further transformations following a transfer of ownership.

If planning is approached from the transvection standpoint, on the other hand, it is often convenient to consider first what might take place if the product remained under a single ownership throughout. This provides a way of specifying the transformations which are really essential in order to complete the transvection and the sorts or assignments which must intervene to link any pair of successive transformations. While the transaction concept is valuable for market planning, the transvection concept is more fundamental. Beginning from the perspective of the transvection, for example, will be useful in shaping the character of the transactions which need to occur at successive stages.

Derivation of Definitions

Returning to the problem of sketching a formal theory for some segment of marketing, it has been pointed out previously that this problem has two aspects. One is to develop a precise language, using primitive terms and

---

[2] The word comes from the Latin roots "trans" and "vehere." By its etymology the word was meant to convey the meaning of "flowing through," with special reference to something which flows through a marketing system in one end and out the other. A transvection is the unit of action for the system by which a single end product, such as a pair of shoes, is placed in the hands of the consumer after moving through all the intermediate sorts and transformations from the original raw materials in the state of nature. The choice of a word which would sound something like "transaction" was deliberate since the two ideas were obviously closely related.

definitions. The other is to develop a consistent set of theorems based on a limited number of axioms. With respect to the first problem of clarifying the language of marketing, the initial task is to develop a terminology which depends on as few primitive terms as possible, is consistent, and exhaustive in the sense of being capable of describing every kind of system relevant to marketing analysis, and which is complete in the sense of allowing for the formulation of theorems concerning transactions and transvections.

Chart I.   Definitions Derived From the Primitive Term—Sets

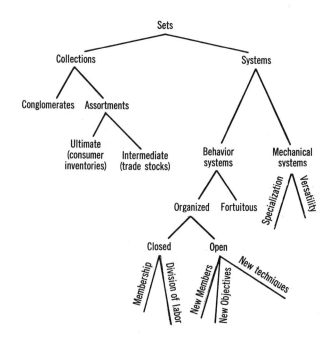

The three primitive terms adopted here are sets, behavior and expectations. These may be taken as three fundamentally different ways of looking at the same marketing system or, for purposes of analysis, three kinds of systems which interact in the same industrial process. The terms[3] which are appropriate to each system and their relationships are given in the form of three tree diagrams which are to be read in the following manner:

1. Each possible path down a branch stemming from the primitive descriptive terms constitutes a set of logically possible descriptors for that type of system. The test for determining whether a term belongs in the

---

[3] A complete list of the terms used and definitions appears in the Appendix.

Chart II. Definitions Derived From the Primitive Term—Behavior

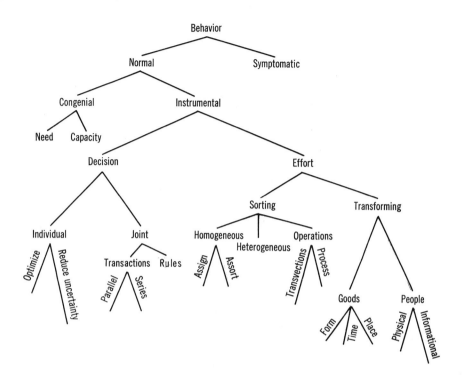

branch to which it has been assigned is that of *consistency* with the other terms in that branch. For example, if we look at the tree stemming from "sets" we can see that it would be a mistake to consider "systems" on the same branch with "collections" since systems are sets with interactions, whereas collections are sets with no interactions. If these two terms were on the same branch we would be holding that it was possible to describe some industrial process as being at the same time and in the same way both interacting and noninteracting. Since this is self-contradictory or inconsistent, systems and collections must be on separate branches of the "set" tree.

2. Each set of terms on the same level, in the sense of constituting all the nodes directly connected with the same high node, are to be read as jointly constituting an exhaustive description of the possible kinds of items encompassed by the higher node from which they originate, with no overlap, *i.e.*, with no item described twice. The test of whether a term is on the right level is therefore whether, in conjunction with the other terms on that level, an exhaustive nonoverlapping description exists. Perhaps an example will make the point clearer.

Chart III.   Definitions Derived From the Primitive Term—Expectations

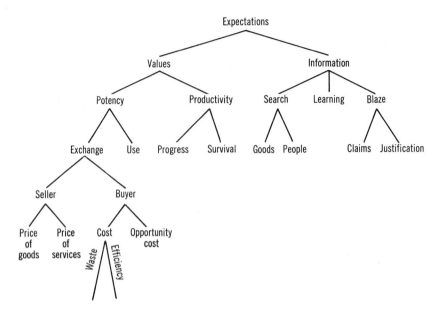

If we turn to the tree under "expectations" and ask whether "survival" and "progress" belong on the same level, we see from the definitions that productivity is the capacity to generate outputs, that progress is the capacity to generate new outputs, and survival is the capacity to retain potency, *i.e.,* ability to generate outputs. The kinds of productivity are either new or old—they exhaust the possibilities and no productive output can be considered both new and old in the same way at the same time. We conclude, therefore, that progress and survival belong on the same level—under productivity.

The advantages of exhibiting terms in this form is that problems regarding consistency and exhaustiveness are readily pinpointed. The question of completeness of the terms can only be answered after the development of an acceptable list of theorems. We will know then whether more or fewer terms are needed and there will necessarily be further refinements in their definitions as the work proceeds.

The other and more difficult problem is that of developing a consistent and meaningful set of theorems based on a small number of axioms. Following the molar approach, which has been described, propositions will be stated in the form of conjecture, followed by an attempt to give them logical substantiation. This means working back upstream far enough to provide some initial confidence in the validity of these propositions. So far as this article is concerned, the results will necessarily remain largely conjectural since the objective is to sketch a program and an approach, rather than to produce a full realized version of formal marketing theory.

Only a part of the definitions of the terms shown in the three charts are directly involved in the development of the concepts of transactions and transvections. The propositions stated will be limited to some basic propositions about transactions and transvections. Propositions will be stated both in English and in formal symbols. A method of proof will be indicated rather than attempting a full logical development.

Transactions

The discussion of transactions will begin with a statement which might be called the Law of Exchange. This law states the conditions under which an exchange can take place, but it does not assert that the exchange actually occurred, since there are fortuitous factors which could interfere with the exchange in a given case. In the expression $x \rightleftharpoons y$, it is merely asserted that x is exchanged for y, the sign for Libra, or the balance, being adopted to represent exchangeability. The Law of Exchange, stated verbally, would be:

Given that x is an element of the assortment A_1 and y is an element of the assortment A_2, x is exchangeable for y if and only if these three conditions hold:

a. x is different from y

b. The potency of the assortment A_1 is increased by dropping x and adding y

c. The potency of the assortment A_2 is increased by adding x and dropping y

In symbols the Law of Exchange would be stated as follows:

$$x \rightleftharpoons y$$

if, and only if,

$$x \neq y \, (xeA_1 \text{ and } yeA_2),$$
$$P(A_1 - x + y) > P(A_1),$$

and

$$P(A_2 + x - y) > P(A_2);$$

where

$x \rightleftharpoons y$ means x is exchangeable for y,
$x \neq y$ means x is different from y,
xeA_1 means x is an element of A_1,
$P(A_1)$ means the potency of A_1.

This formulation makes no explicit reference to the cost of executing an exchange transaction. For a complete statement of the Law of Exchange, it should be stated explicitly that the increase in the potency of the assortment A_1, brought about by the transaction, should be greater than the cost of the transaction assignable to A_1, and that the same thing should be true for the assortment A_2. This corollary of the Law of Exchange might be stated symbolically as follows:
$x \rightleftharpoons y$ implies that

$$C[P(A_1 - x + y) - P(A_1)] > C_{A1}(Tr),$$
$$C[P(A_2 + x - y) - P(A_2)] > C_{A2}(Tr);$$

where the increase in potency is assumed to be measurable in dollars, C, and where $C_{A1}(Tr)$ is the cost of the transaction to the owner of assortment i.

At a first level of consideration, x and y might be regarded as two different products in a primitive economy, such as a basket and a hat, with exchange taking place on a barter basis. Given a medium of exchange, y might be regarded as an amount of money paid by the buyer to obtain the article. The definitions of buyer and seller need not detain us except to note a very general distinction. The buyer in a transaction is adding a less liquid item to his assortment, while the seller is adding a more liquid asset, very likely with the intent of exchanging this in turn for more specialized assets later on.

We are now in position to state three propositions with more obvious relevance to the problem of planning a marketing system. The first is concerned with the optimality of exchange in a particular exchange situation. Viewing exchange from the standpoint of one of the decision makers, we can say that exchange is optimal if he prefers it to any available alternative. Similarly, for the decision maker on the other side of the transaction, it will be optimal for him if he prefers it to any available alternative. It is assumed that if a concrete situation offers an exchange opportunity, the number of alternatives realistically available to either side is not infinite in number but limited to only a few. Faced with a decision, an individual must be guided by his present knowledge of alternatives and the ordering according to his preferences within that set.

Subject to these constraints, it may be said that exchange is optimal if the individual decision maker I_1 prefers x to any of the available alternatives V_1 to V_n and if the decision maker I_2 prefers y to any of the available alternatives W_1 to W_n. It is scarcely necessary to go through the procedure of stating this proposition symbolically since it would follow the pattern previously illustrated. The principle of optimality rests on the Law of Exchange and its corollary. The principle would hold only where the conditions were consistent with the previously stated propositions. The exchange of x for y is preferred by each decision maker precisely because it offers the greatest increase in the potency of his assortment.

The next proposition to be asserted is that a set of transactions in series can replace direct sales by the supplier to the ultimate consumer if the transactions are optimal at each step. Let us assume initially that a sale is made directly by the supplier to the ultimate consumer. Now let us assume that a single intermediary intervenes between these two. If the exchange between the supplier and the intermediary is optimal, it means that the supplier prefers this exchange to dealing directly with the consumer. Similarly, if the exchange between the consumer and the intermediary is optimal, it means that the consumer prefers this transaction to a direct exchange with the supplier. This sequence of two transactions would therefore be eligible to replace the direct exchange between supplier and consumer.

If one intermediary can intervene between the supplier and the consumer, it follows that a second intermediary can intervene between the supplier and the first intermediary or between the first intermediary and the consumer, provided that the principle of optimality still obtains. Similarly, other intermediaries could be added to the chain as long as the principle of optimality was not violated.

Two major problems in planning the flow of transactions pertain to the case of transactions in series, which has just been discussed, and the case of parallel transactions occurring at the same level of distribution as, for example, between the supplier and the first intermediary. One of the aims of planning is to reduce the cost of individual transactions, particularly the cost of negotiation. The choices are to negotiate each of the parallel transactions separately or to negotiate a rule under which all transactions of a given type can be routinized. This can be reduced to a clear-cut decision based on the relative costs of negotiating individual transactions as compared to the cost of negotiating a rule, plus the cost of negotiating the routinized transactions to be controlled by the rule. A formula for this calculation might be stated in words as follows:

Routinize if the cost of rule negotiation plus the cost of negotiating the routinized transactions while the rule holds is less than the total cost of negotiating the individual transactions without the rule.

The calculation would start by estimating the number of transactions which will probably occur while the rule is in force, and multiplying this number by the average cost of a routinized transaction. If this cost is less than the cost of negotiating the same number of individual transactions, it would be worthwhile to negotiate the adoption of a rule. This, of course, assumes that the difference is greater than the cost of negotiating the rule. Generally, the saving would have to be substantial to force the decision-maker on either side to initiate the process of negotiating a rule. There are, of course, many practical cases in which literally thousands of transactions are to be covered by the rule, so that the condition of overall cost-saving would be fully satisfied.

Transvections

The marketing process is the continuous operation of transforming conglomerate resources as they occur in nature into meaningful assortments in the hands of consumers. As is seen from Chart I, provision is made for defining conglomerates and assortments as types of collections, and a collection, in turn, as a type of set. Symbolically, the marketing process or operation might be shown as follows:

$$O(C) = \sum_{t_0 \to t_1}^{n} \underset{t_0 \to t_1}{\Delta} (A_1, A_2, \cdots, A_n, W).$$

where

C means conglomerate,
$O(C)$ means the marketing operation performed $t_0 \to t_1$ on C during time period t_0 to t_1,
$\Delta(A_i)$ means the increment in assortment A_i $t_0 \to t_1$ during time period t_0 to t_1,
W means waste.

In words, this proposition states that applying the operation O to the conglomerate C over the period from t_0 to t_1 results in increments to the assortments held by consumers, plus an allowance for waste.

A transvection by contrast with the continuing market process refers to a single unit of action of the marketing system. This unit of action is consummated when an end product is placed in the hands of the ultimate consumer, but the transvection comprises all prior action necessary to produce this final result, going all the way back to conglomerate resources.

The definition of a transvection can be shown symbolically as $T_v = STSTS—TS$ where S is a sort and T is a transformation.

The statements so far about transvections indicate a need for two simple but fundamental proofs. The first is a proof that the sum of all transvections would correspond to an exhaustive description of the marketing process. The only difficulty here is in the selection of a long enough time period. By definition every sale of an end product has a transvection behind it. Thus, all the end products sold during a given year with their corresponding transvections would be approximately the same as the total marketing process for that year. Even if a four- or five-year period was considered, there would always be transvections beginning in the period which would terminate in a subsequent period. This is not so much a problem of proof as a problem of defining the marketing process and a transvection in such a way that they can be reconciled with each other.

The other problem is more clearly a problem of logical proof. That grows out of the definition of a transvection as shown in symbolic form. As shown in the formula, there is a continuous alternation between sorts and transformations. It will now be asserted that this alternation is inherent in the nature of a transvection. Before attempting to prove this assertion, it will be necessary to define and discuss both sorts and transformations.

Sorts and Transformations

First let us consider sorts or sorting, a concept with which the senior author has been identified for some time. Sorting is reclassification resulting in the creation of subsets from a set or of a set from subsets. Earlier treaments have identified four aspects of sorting, one of which is allocation, possibly the most fundamental concept for economics. It now seems possible to compress these types of sorting from four to two to achieve greater simplicity. Most characteristically, sorting suggests sorting out, which means breaking down a heterogeneous set into homogeneous subsets. Sorting out can also be called assignment, since it means assigning each member of a set to the appropriate subset. Assignment is the more general term, while allocation can still be employed to designate the special case in which the original set is regarded as homogeneous.

The other basic type of sorting is assorting. This means drawing members from subsets to form a heterogeneous set or assortment. Again the formation of a homogeneous set can be recognized as a special case designated as "assembly" or "accumulation." Assignment is the sorting perspective of the supplier or purveyor of goods. The broader term purveyor, rather than supplier, is adopted to avoid the implication that there is a supplier who necessarily disposes of the goods through a sales transaction. Assorting is the sorting perspective of the buyer or procurement agent. For the sake of simplicity, the notion of assignment will be generally adopted in the discussions of transvections as if the process was under the management of purveyors throughout.

The proposition that there is an alternation of sorts and transformations throughout the course of a transvection implies that an action of assignment always intervenes between a transformation just completed and the one which is to follow. That this is necessarily true will become clear when the term transformation is more fully explained. A transformation is a change in the physical form of a product or in its location in time and space which is calculated to increase its value for the ultimate consumer who adds it to his assortment. In other words, transformations add form, space, and time utility. Marketing theory is not concerned with the techniques of creating form utility but only in their marketing implications. For example, marketing theory might need to distinguish between very broad categories of production such as refining and combining.

With respect to time and place utility, marketing is concerned with detailed techniques as well as broad perspective. Sorting might assign some goods to transportation by vehicles suitable for long hauls and others to vehicles designed for short hauls. Similarly, in the creation of time utility, some goods might be stored in one way while other similar or dissimilar goods could be stored more appropriately in a different type of facility. Credit is another way of creating time utility and again there is always an assignment problem prior to the selection of a mode of transformation.

Against this background, the formal proof of the alternating sequence might take the following form: Two sorts cannot follow each other in sequence in any significant sense since sorting out is the act of placing the members of a set in relevant subsets. If members are sorted into subsets and then moved from one subset to another, it is to be regarded as inefficient or exploratory sorting and not two successive sorts in a sequence. Similarly, two transformations cannot appear successively without an intervening sort. Different facilities are required for fabrication, shipment, storage and credit. Thus, there has to be an intervening assignment to the appropriate facilites. In very rare cases facilities might be combined, as in further aging or agitation of a product while in transit. The point, however, is that assignment always precedes the use of a facility and that typically separate facilities are required for each transformation. There are, of course, possibilities for breaking down the sequence of transformation still further with additional intervening sorts, and this topic will now be treated briefly.

A distribution network quickly becomes too complicated for complete evaluation of marketing effectiveness. The concept of the transvection offers a means of piecemeal analysis for planning purposes without violating the principle of the total systems approach. Looking at a transvection in relation to a given end product, it can be bounded or marked off from other related transvections. A network may consist largely of divergent paths, particularly if the basic production process is one of refining, with the end product distributed to thousands of consumers. A network may consist largely of convergent paths, particularly if the basic production process is one of combining materials and components and the ultimate consumer is government or a few large industrial buyers. In either case, there are a number of branching points on the main path along which the product flows through the network.

The bounding of the transvection means evaluation of additions or subtractions at each branching point along the way. Take the relatively simple case of a pair of shoes in which the principle component is leather. At each branching point at which lines converge, the costs of other components such as shoe findings must be added in. At each branching point where lines diverge, there may be waste or by-products to be evaluated. Waste may carry a cost penalty for disposal while by-products may contribute revenue to the main stream.

Optimal Number of Steps in a Transvection

Against this background a basic principle for the evaluation of transvections may be stated. A transvection has the optimal number of steps if costs cannot be decreased, either by increasing or decreasing the number of steps. First, let us take a hypothetical case in which the only types of transformation pertain to spatial location. Assume that a natural product is being distributed and that it is snapped up immediately by consumers available at the terminal points. Even in this illustration, in which the creation of form and time utility are ruled out, there is still a problem of optimality for the number of steps in a transvection. Suppose an item is to be moved a distance of twenty-five miles. Obviously it would be a very poor solution to send a truck from Point x to Point y for direct delivery if the item was a small parcel making up a very tiny fraction of a truck load. The cost of direct delivery might easily exceed the value of the product at the point of origin.

Suppose now that two trucks are available for a delivery system. One truck picks up parcels from an area regarded as a collection area. The parcels are brought into a center where they are sorted into a sequence for most efficient delivery and then go onto another truck for this purpose. It could easily have required ten trucks previously to handle direct delivery for all origin and destination points for what can now be handled by two trucks.

Some existing parcel delivery networks are far more complex. A pickup truck collects parcels and brings them into a minor sorting center. Here most of the packages may be assigned to a large over-the-road vehicle which carries them to a major sorting center or hub. At this point they are assigned to other large trucks and carried to minor sorting centers. Here they will once more be assigned to small trucks for delivery to their final destination.

For any given system it is possible to compare two network plans. Suppose the following relationship holds: daily cost of transportation facilities, plus daily cost of sorting, under Plan A (4 sorts) > Plan B (5 sorts). It is clear that cost figures should be marshalled to test the possibility that Plan C (6 sorts) would cost still less. The number of possibilities is quite limited so that it would usually suffice to test only two plans against the network already in force, namely, those with one less sort and one more sort.

Actually the situation is not static but dynamic, because of changing technologies both of transportation and sorting. Mechanical sorting equipment has made great strides recently, thus creating the possibility that more sorts would lead to greater efficiency. There are practical limits to the length of a transvectional chain. At some point the cost of delay in the system would out-weigh any further savings to be made through additional sorts. When transformations are considered more generally rather than dealing with transportation only, the same kind of reasoning still holds in principle. A detailed analysis might be required for the given network, since the possible patterns may now be large though finite. For example, fabrication may involve both refining and combining. It may be efficient to separate these two by hundreds of miles even though additional sorts and transformations are introduced. An improvement in storage facilities may make it possible to store the product closer to the consumer or even to move it into the consumer's assortment more promptly. It is this last step in the forwarding of goods which may be accomplished through various forms of consumer credit.

Some networks and choices of technologies may involve hundreds of possibilities as to the design of the transvection. While a computer may be needed to test all the possibilities, including differences in number of warehouses and spatial dispersion of production, the test of optimality is in principle the same for all types of transvections. There are considerations as to movement of information and movement of people which lie beyond the scope of this article. Suffice it to say tht there is a large segment of marketing in which it is more efficient to bring the people to the goods rather than the goods to the people. There are also many opportunities for reducing the cost of moving goods or people by moving information instead. Mr. Halbert has drawn some interesting parallels between the movement of goods and the flows and stocks of information. We are primarily concerned here with delineating a transvection which represents the shortest path to market, taking account of the several possible types of movement.

The concept of the transvection as a planning tool has continued to evolve. Even in some of its earlier versions it has had fruitful applications in planning distribution systems for Douglas fir plywood, Irish linen, leather, and dry, edible beans. The results obtained can be illustrated by a study of the latter commodity made for the United States Department of Agriculture. It was observed that beans were bagged and rebagged at several places along the way. Analysis from the transvection viewpoint led to recommendations for eliminating bagging entirely. It was also recommended that sorting into grades be postponed until the terminal market was reached, since earlier sorting increased the number of less than carlot shipments required. Similar recommendations could be obtained more readily today with a more fully developed theory of transvections.

Conclusion

This article can well terminate with a final reminder to the reader of what it has attempted to accomplish: to illustrate the molar approach to the development of formal theory in marketing and, in a few cases, to present something resembling proof as a means of relating propositions to each other and showing that they are consistent. It has also attempted to contribute more specifically to a theoretical treatment of transactions and transvections. In the case of transvections in particular, the effort has been to show both the extent of the difficulties and the promise of useful results in the development of formal theory.

APPENDIX

Definitions

Sets

1. Sets are aggregates containing some class of components, such as points in a plane, physical objects or human beings.
2. Collections are sets which can be taken as inert with no interaction among the components.

3. Systems are sets in which interactions occur which serve to define the boundaries of the set.

4. Conglomerates are collections as they occur in a state of nature and which may be regarded as random or neutral from the standpoint of human expectations.

5. Assortments are collections which have been assembled by taking account of human expectations concerning future action.

6. Ultimate assortments (consumer inventories) have been collected by the consumer in the hope and expectation of being prepared to meet future contingencies (probable patterns of behavior).

7. Intermediate assortments (trade stocks) have been collected to provide a choice of alternatives for (a) the consumer, (b) others in the trade.

8. A behavior system is a system in which persons are the interacting components. Broadly defined, a behavior system includes the assortment of assets which the members control and its point of contact with the environment which enable it to accept inputs and generate outputs.

9. An organized behavior system is one with these minimum characteristics:

    a. A criterion for membership

    b. A rule or set of rules assigning duties

    c. A preference scale for outputs.

10. A fortuitous behavior system is one in which interactions are taking place, resulting in outputs with some positive or negative value, but without the degree of coordination suggested by the requirements for an organized behavior system.

11. An organized behavior system is closed in terms of current operations (all finite sets are closed).

12. An organized behavior system is open in terms of plans for future operation. (Plans involve the possibility of new goals, new techniques, new inputs, new members.)

13. Rules of membership state rules of eligibility or exclude from membership specified classes in the general population.

14. Division of labor is specified by formal rules, or a process is specified for choosing a leader who will assign duties to other members.

15. A behavior system is open if it is considering new objectives which generally offer many variations as to the direction in which the system is to move and the amount of effort to be expended.

16. A behavior system is open if it is currently engaged in revising its techniques or even if it is generating techniques which are almost certain to require changes.

17. A behavior system may be regarded as open if it is seeking new members. This is particularly true of members higher up in the scale of

responsibility who are likely to have an impact both on goals and techniques.

18. Mechanical systems are listed for the sake of completeness and contrast with behavior systems. Interactions occur among nonhuman components.

19. Some mechanical systems have highly specialized outputs and are structured with a view to maximum efficiency in producing these outputs.

20. Other mechanical systems have greater versatility with respect to potential outputs and are structured with a view to maintaining flexibility in meeting the demands of the market.

Behavior

21. Behavior is activity occupying time.

22. Normal behavior is that which is an end in itself, or a means to an end.

23. Symptomatic behavior is that which is not functional in that it is neither an end or a means to an end.

24. Congenial—also called consummatory—behavior is that which is chosen because it is presumed to be an end in itself and is directly satisfying.

25. Instrumental behavior is that which is regarded as a means to an end. There may be a sequence of instrumental acts culminating in a desired state of affairs, one of which is the opportunity to engage in congenial behavior.

26. Some congenial behavior is satisfying because it reduces need—tension.

27. The same behavior can be both. It is directed toward gaining an end but also satisfying a basic need directly—that of manifesting skills or capacity.

28. Instrumental behavior consists of decision and the application of effort. It is convenient to think of decision as occurring instantaneously.

29. Effort occupies an interval of time.

30. Decision is choice among alternative ways of applying effort.

31. Individual decision involves allocation by an individual of the resources he controls.

32. An individual decision under certainty undertakes to optimize certain values.

33. An individual decision under uncertainty can be interpreted in terms of expected values.

34. Joint decision involves agreement between two or more individuals.

35. A decision can apply to a single event such as a transaction.

36. Transactions can be parallel involving problems of coordination.

37. Transactions can be in series involving problems of optimal sequence.

38. A decision can mean the adoption of a rule governing many transactions.

39. Effort in marketing takes two primary forms—either sorting or transformation.

40. Sorting is recallification, and involves the creation of subsets from a set or a set from subsets.

41. Homogeneity lies at the zero end of the sortability scale. That is to say, no further division into classes is possible at the level of discrimination applied.

42. Heterogeneity lies at the other end of the sortability scale. That is to say, the classes discriminated are as numerous as the units of the set.

43. The seller assigns products from heterogeneity sets to subjects. The assignment from homogeneous sets is taken as a special case.

44. The buyer assorts products into heterogeneity sets or assortments. The selection in homogeneous sets is taken as a special case.

45. Transformation in marketing applies to goods or people.

46. Transforming changes the physical form of goods or their location in time and space.

47. Transforming changes the awareness or attitudes of people (their informational and motivational states) or their physical location.

48. Marketing operations can be defined as an alternating sequence of sorts and transformations.

49. A transvection is a unit of action of the marketing system resulting in placing a final product in the hands of the consumer but reaching all the way back to the raw materials entering into the product.

50. The marketing process is the marketing operation regarded as a total and continuous flow of marketing activities rather than the sum of all transvections.

Expectations

51. Expectations are attached to what the individual thinks may happen and the favorable or unfavorable results of these future events.

52. Values are based on the favorable or unfavorable consequences of an event or condition which the individual expects.

53. Information is expected in the three directions of probability of an event occurring, instructions on reaction to the event, and whether the consequences will or will not be favorable.

54. Search is the sorting of information which precedes the sorting of goods or people.

55. Learning in marketing is the acquisition of information with particular reference to the impact on future searching and sorting.

56. Blaze is the obverse of search. It is the imparting of information by one party intended to influence search by the other party.

57. The consumer searches for goods and trade intermediaries engage in vicarious search on his behalf.

58. The seller searches for people who will buy his goods or intermediaries who will sell them to consumers.

59. One aspect of blaze is the information incorporated in claims.

60. The second aspect of blaze is the justification for accepting these claims.

61. Potency is the expected value of an assortment or its anticipated effectiveness in meeting contingencies.

62. Exchange value is the anticipated potency relative to what is given in exchange.

63. Use value is the realized potency expressed as the product of the incidence of use and the conditional value if used, that value depending on the intensity of satisfaction with the product when used.

64. The seller of goods is generally giving them up for a more liquid or intangible asset.

65. The buyer of goods is generally accepting them in exchange for a more liquid or intangible asset.

66. The price of a good is measured by the asset the buyer gives up in exchange.

67. The price of a service such as that of a retailer is the difference between his purchase price and his selling price (gross profit).

68. The cost of a good to one person is the price he paid for it to another person.

69. Opportunity cost is measured by the alternative which was rejected in order to buy or sell the particular good.

70. Productivity is the capacity of a system to generate outputs.

71. Progress is the capacity to generate new techniques.

72. Survival is the capacity to retain potency over time.

REFERENCES

1. Wroe Alderson, *Marketing Behavior and Executive Action,* Homewood, Ill.: Richard D. Irwin, Inc., 1957.
2. Phillipp Frank, "Foundations of Physics," in *International Encyclopedia of Unified Science,* Vol. 1, Part 2, University of Chicago Press, 1955.

3. Michael H. Halbert, *The Meaning and Sources of Marketing Theory,* forthcoming publication by McGraw-Hill Book Company. [Published, 1965.—Editors]

4. R. M. Martin, "On Atomic Sentential Forms and Theory Construction," *Theory in Marketing: Second Series,* Homewood, Ill.: Richard D. Irwin, Inc., 1964.

25

How Communication Works

WILBUR SCHRAMM

The Process

It will be easier to see how mass communication works if we first look at the communication process in general.

Communication comes from the Latin *communis,* common. When we communicate we are trying to establish a "commonness" with someone. That is, we are trying to share information, an idea, or an attitude. At this moment I am trying to communicate to you the idea that the essence of communication is getting the receiver and the sender "tuned" together for a particular message. At this same moment, someone somewhere is excitedly phoning the fire department that the house is on fire. Somewhere else a young man in a parked automobile is trying to convey the understanding that he is moon-eyed because he loves the young lady. Somewhere else a newspaper is trying to persuade its readers to believe as it does about the Republican Party. All these are forms of communication, and the process in each case is essentially the same.

Communication always requires at least three elements — the source, the message, and the destination. A *source* may be an individual (speaking, writing, drawing, gesturing) or a communication organization (like a newspaper, publishing house, television station or motion picture studio). The *message* may be in the form of ink on paper, sound waves in the air, impulses in an electric current, a wave of the hand, a flag in the air, or any other signal capable of being interpreted meaningfully. The *destination* may be an *individual* listening, watching, or reading; or a member of a *group,* such as a discussion group, a lecture audience, a football crowd, or

Reprinted with permission from *The Process and Effects of Mass Communication,* Wilbur Schramm, ed. (Urbana: The University of Illinois Press, 1955), pp. 3-26.

a mob; or an individual member of the particular group we call the *mass audience,* such as the reader of a newspaper or a viewer of television.

Now what happens when the source tries to build up this "commonness" with his intended receiver? First, the source encodes his message. That is, he takes the information or feeling he wants to share and puts it into a form that can be transmitted. The "pictures in our heads" can't be transmitted until they are coded. When they are coded into spoken words, they can be transmitted easily and effectively, but they can't travel very far unless radio carries them. If they are coded into written words, they go more slowly than spoken words, but they go farther and last longer. Indeed, some messages long outlive their senders — the *Iliad,* for instance; the Gettysburg address; Chartres cathedral. Once coded and sent, a message is quite free of its sender, and what it does is beyond the power of the sender to change. Every writer feels a sense of helplessness when he finally commits his story or his poem to print; you doubtless feel the same way when you mail an important letter. Will it reach the right person? Will he understand it as you intend him to? Will he respond as you want him to? For in order to complete the act of communication the message must be decoded. And there is good reason, as we shall see, for the sender to wonder whether his receiver will really be in tune with him, whether the message will be interpreted without distortion, whether the "picture in the head" of the receiver will bear any resemblance to that in the head of the sender.

We are talking about something very like a radio or telephone circuit. In fact, it is perfectly possible to draw a picture of the human communication system that way:

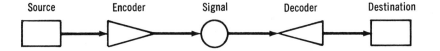

Substitute "microphone" for encoder, and "earphone" for decoder and you are talking about electronic communication. Consider that the "source" and "encoder" are one person, "decoder" and "destination" are another, and the signal is language, and you are talking about human communication.

Now it is perfectly possible by looking at those diagrams to predict how such a system will work. For one thing, such a system can be no stronger than its weakest link. In engineering terms, there may be filtering or distortion at any stage. In human terms, if the source does not have adequate or clear information; if the message is not encoded fully, accurately, effectively in transmittible signs; if these are not transmitted fast enough and accurately enough, despite interference and competition, to the desired receiver; if the message is not decoded in a pattern that corresponds to the encoding; and finally, if the destination is unable to handle the decoded message so as to produce the desired response — then, obviously, the system is working at less than top efficiency. When we realize that *all* these steps must be accomplished with relatively high efficiency if any communication is to be successful, the everyday act of explaining something to a stranger, or writing a letter, seems a minor miracle.

A system like this will have a maximum capacity for handling information and this will depend on the separate capacities of each unit on the chain — for example, the capacity of the channel (how fast can one talk?) or the capacity of the encoder (can your student understand something explained quickly?). If the coding is good (for example, no unnecessary words) the capacity of the channel can be approached, but it can never be exceeded. You can readily see that one of the great skills of communication will lie in knowing how near capacity to operate a channel.

This is partly determined for us by the nature of the language. English, like every other language, has its sequences of words and sounds governed by certain probabilities. If it were organized so that no set of probabilities governed the likelihood that certain words would follow certain other words (for example, that a noun would follow an adjective, or that "States" or "Nations" would follow "United") then we would have nonsense. As a matter of fact, we can calculate the relative amount of freedom open to us in writing any language. For English, the freedom is about 50 per cent. (Incidentally, this is about the required amount of freedom to enable us to construct interesting crossword puzzles. Shannon has estimated that if we had about 70 per cent freedom, we could construct three-dimensional crossword puzzles. If we had only 20 per cent, crossword puzzle making would not be worth while).

So much for language *redundancy*, as communication theorists call it, meaning the percentage of the message which is not open to free choice. But there is also the communicator's redundancy, and this is an important aspect of constructing a message. For if we think our audience may have a hard time understanding the message, we can deliberately introduce more redundancy; we can repeat (just as the radio operator on a ship may send "SOS" over and over again to make sure it is heard and decoded), or we can give examples and analogies. In other words, we always have to choose between transmitting more information in a given time, or transmitting less and repeating more in the hope of being better understood. And as you know, it is often a delicate choice, because too slow a rate will bore an audience, whereas too fast a rate may confuse them.

Perhaps the most important thing about such a system is one we have been talking about all too glibly — the fact that receiver and sender must be in tune. This is clear enough in the case of a radio transmitter and receiver, but somewhat more complicated when it means that a human receiver must be able to understand a human sender.

Let us redraw our diagram in very simple form, like this:

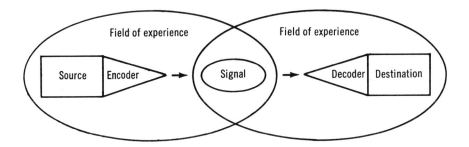

Think of those circles as the accumulated experience of the two individuals trying to communicate. The source can encode, and the destination can decode, only in terms of the experience each has had. If we have never learned any Russian, we can neither code nor decode in that language. If an African tribesman has never seen or heard of an airplane, he can only decode the sight of a plane in terms of whatever experience he has had. The plane may seem to him to be a bird, and the aviator a god borne on wings. If the circles have a large area in common, then communication is easy. If the circles do not meet — if there has been no common experience — then communiction is impossible. If the circles have only a small area in common — that is, if the experiences of source and destination have been strikingly unlike — then it is going to be very difficult to get an intended meaning across from one to the other. This is the difficulty we face when a non-science-trained person tries to read Einstein, or when we try to communicate with another culture much different from ours.

The source, then, tries to encode in such a way as to make it easy for the destination to tune in the message — to relate it to parts of his experience which are much like those of the source. What does he have to work with?

Messages are made up of signs. A sign is a signal that stands for something in experience. The word "dog" is a sign that stands for our generalized experience with dogs. The word would be meaningless to a person who came from a dog-less island and had never read of or heard of a dog. But most of us have learned that word by association, just as we learn most signs. Someone called our attention to an animal, and said "dog." When we learned the word, it produced in us much the same response as the object it stood for. That is, when we heard "dog" we could recall the appearance of dogs, their sound, their feel, perhaps their smell.

But there is an important difference between the sign and the object: the sign always represents the object at a reduced level of cues. By this we mean simply that the sign will not call forth all the responses that the object itself will call forth. The sign "dog," for example, will probably not call forth in us the same wariness or attention a strange dog might attract if it wandered into our presence. This is the price we pay for portability in language. We have a sign system that we can use in place of the less portable originals (for example, Margaret Mitchell could re-create the burning of Atlanta in a novel, and a photograph could transport world-wide the appearance of a bursting atomic bomb), but our sign system is merely a kind of shorthand. The coder has to be able to write the shorthand, the decoder to read it. And no two persons have learned exactly the same system. For example, a person who has known only Arctic huskies will not have learned exactly the same meaning for the shorthand sign "dog" as will a person who comes from a city where he has known only pekes and poms.

We have come now to a point where we need to tinker a little more with our diagram of the communication process. It is obvious that each person in the communication process is both an encoder and a decoder. He receives and transmits. He must be able to write readable shorthand, and to read other people's shorthand. Therefore, it is possible to describe either sender or receiver in a human communication system thus:

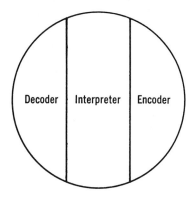

Decoder | Interpreter | Encoder

What happens when a signal comes to you? Remember that it comes in the form of a sign. If you have learned the sign, you have learned certain responses with it. We can call these mediatory responses, because they mediate what happens to the message in your nervous system. These responses are the *meaning* the sign has for you. They are learned from experience, as we said, but they are affected by the state of your organism at the moment. For example, if you are hungry, a picture of a steak may not arouse exactly the same response in you as when you are overfed.

But subject to these effects, the mediatory responses will then determine what you do about the sign. For you have learned other sets of reactions connected to the mediatory responses. A sign that means a certain thing to you will start certain other processes in your nerves and muscles. A sign that means "fire," for example, will certainly trigger off some activity in you. A sign that means you are in danger may start the process in your nerves and muscles that makes you say "help!" In other words, the meaning that results from your decoding of a sign will start you *en*coding. Exactly *what* you encode will depend on your choice of the responses available in the situation and connected with the meaning.

Whether this encoding actually results in some overt communication or action depends partly on the barriers in the way. You may think it better to keep silent. And if an action does occur, the nature of the action will also depend on the avenues for action available to you and the barriers in your way. The code of your group may not sanction the action you want to take. The meaning of a sign may make you want to hit the person who has said it, but he may be too big, or you may be in the wrong social situation. You may merely ignore him, or "look murder at him," or say something nasty about him to someone else.

But whatever the exact result, this is the process in which you are constantly engaged. You are constantly decoding signs from your environment, interpreting these signs, and encoding something as a result. In fact, it is misleading to think of the communication process as starting somewhere and ending somewhere. It is really endless. We are little switchboard centers handling and rerouting the great endless current of communication. We can accurately think of communication as passing through us — changed, to be sure, by our interpretations, our habits, our abilities and capabilities, but the input still being reflected in the output.

We need now to add another element to our description of the communication process. Consider what happens in a conversation between two people. One is constantly communicating back to the other, thus:

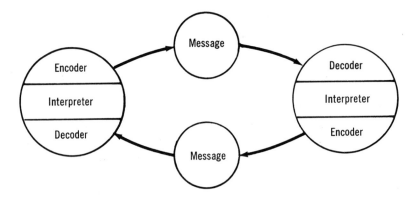

The return process is called *feedback,* and plays a very important part in communication because it tells us how our messages are being interpreted. Does the hearer say, "Yes, yes, that's right," as we try to persuade him? Does he nod his head in agreement? Does a puzzled frown appear on his forehead? Does he look away as though he were losing interest? All these are feedback. So is a letter to the editor of a newspaper, protesting an editorial. So is an answer to a letter. So is the applause of a lecture audience. An experienced communicator is attentive to feedback, and constantly modifies his messages in light of what he observes in or hears from his audience.

At least one other example of feedback, also, is familiar to all of us. We get feedback from our own messages. That is, we hear our own voices and can correct mispronunciations. We see the words we have written on paper, and can correct misspellings or change the style. When we do that, here is what is happening:

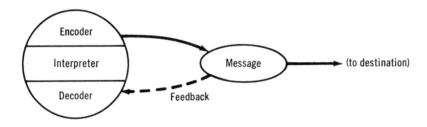

It is clear that in any kind of communication we rarely send out messages in a single channel, and this is the final element we must add to our account of the communication process. When you speak to me, the sound waves from your voice are the primary message. But there are others: the expression on your face, your gestures, the relation of a given message to past messages. Even the primary message conveys information on several levels. It gives me words to decode. It emphasizes certain words above others. It presents the words in a pattern of intonation and timing which contribute to the total meaning. The quality of your voice (deep, high, shrill, rasping, rich, thin, loud, soft) itself carries information about you and what you are saying.

This multiple channel situation exists even in printed mass communication, where the channels are perhaps most restricted. Meaning is conveyed, not only by the words in a news item, but also by the size of the headline, the position on the page and the page in the paper, the association with pictures, the use of boldface and other typographical devices. All these tell us something about the item. Thus we can visualize the typical channel of communication, not as a simple telegraph circuit, in which current does or does not flow, but rather as a sort of coaxial cable in which many signals flow in parallel from source toward the destination.

These parallel relationships are complex, but you can see their general pattern. A communicator can emphasize a point by adding as many parallel messages as he feels are deserved. If he is communicating by speaking, he can stress a word, pause just before it, say it with a rising inflection, gesture while he says it, look earnestly at his audience. Or he can keep all the signals parallel — except *one*. He can speak solemnly, but wink, as Lowell Thomas sometimes does. He can stress a word in a way that makes it mean something else — for example, "That's a *fine* job you did!" And by so doing he conveys secondary meanings of sarcasm or humor or doubt.

The same thing can be done with printed prose, with broadcast, with television or films. The secondary channels of the sight-sound media are especially rich. I am reminded of a skillful but deadly job done entirely with secondary channels on a certain political candidate. A sidewalk interview program was filmed to run in local theaters. Ostensibly it was a completely impartial program. An equal number of followers of each candidate were interviewed — first, one who favored Candidate A, then one who favored Candidate B, and so on. They were asked exactly the same question, and said about the same things, although on opposite sides of the political fence, of course. But there was one interesting difference. Whereas the supporters of Candidate A were ordinary folks, not outstandingly attractive or impressive, the followers of Candidate B who were chosen to be interviewed invariably had something slightly wrong with them. They looked wild-eyed, or they stuttered, or they wore unpressed suits. The extra meaning was communicated. Need I say which candidate won?

But this is the process by which communication works, whether it is mass communication, or communication in a group, or communication between individuals.

Communication in Terms of Learning Theory

So far we have avoided talking about this complicated process in what may seem to you to be the obvious way to talk about it — in the terminology and symbols of learning theory.[1] We have done so for the sake of simplicity. Now in order to fill in the picture it seems desirable to sketch the diagram

---

[1] For the model in the following pages the author is indebted to his colleague, Dr. Charles E. Osgood. Dr. Osgood will soon publish the model in a more advanced form.

of how communication looks to a psychlogist of learning. If psychological diagrams bother you, you can skip to section 3.

Let's start with the diagram, then explain it.

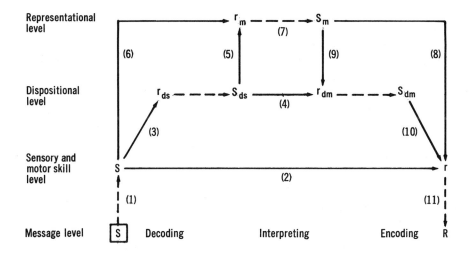

The diagram isn't as complicated as it looks. Remember that time in the diagram moves from left to right, and then follow the numbers and you won't get far off the road.

Begin with (1). This is the input. At the message level we have a collection of objectively measurable signs Ⓢ. These come to your sense organs, where they constitute a stimulus for action. This stimulus we call s. When the process gets as far as s, you are paying attention. The message has been accepted. It may not have been accepted as intended; Ⓢ may not equal Ⓢ; the sensory mechanism may have seen or heard it incompletely. But everything else that happens as a result of the message in that particular destination will now necessarily be the result of the stimulus accepted by your sense organs.

Now look at number (2). The message may not have to go to any other level in order to bring about a response. If a man waves his fist near your nose, you may dodge. If he squeezes your hand, you may say "ouch!" These are learned, almost automatic, responses on the sensory and motor skill level.

But the stimulus may also bring about other kinds of activity within your nervous system. Look at number (3). The stimulus s may be translated into a grammatical response on your dispositional level—by which we mean the level of learned integrations (attitudes, values, sets, etc.) which make it so easy for you to dispose of the variety of stimuli that come to you in the course of a day. These are what we call the intervening variables. Suppose the stimulus stirs up activity in this area of intervening variables. Two things may happen. Look at number (4). The response may be so well learned that it doesn't even have to go to the level of thinking. You hear a line of a poem, and almost automatically say the second line. In that case the activity is through numbers (4) and (10).

More often, however, the activity goes through number (5). Here the original stimulus has been decoded into grammar, fed through the intervening variables, and sent up to the representational level of the central nervous system, where meanings are assigned and ideas considered. Occasionally a stimulus comes to that level without going through the intervening variables—as is number (6). These stimuli create activity in the central nervous system (r_m) which is the terminus of the decoding part of the process. This is equivalent to the meaning or significance of the signs $\boxed{S}$. What happens in number (7), then, is what we have been referring to as interpretation. The response r_m which we call meaning becomes in turn a stimulus which sets the encoding process in action, so that (7) is both the terminus of decoding and the start of encoding. We learn to associate meanings with desired responses. And so the encoding process moves through (8) or (9). That is, we give certain orders which either pass directly to the neuro-muscular sytem (through 8) or are passed through the intervening variables (through 9 and 10). In any case, all this activity of the nervous system finally results in a response on the motor skill level (r), which results in output (number 11). If the output is an overt response (R), then we have another message, which may offer itself as a collection of signs $\boxed{S}$ and be accepted by still another person as a stimulus (s).

This is what we believe happens when someone says to you, "cigarette?" and you answer "yes, please," or "no, thanks." If you are interested in doing so, you can translate all that is said about the communication process in this paper into the psychological symbols we have just been using. But to make the account simpler, we are going to shift gears at this point and talk about communication effects and mass communication in the terms we used in section 1.

How Communication Has an Effect

The chief reason we study this process is to learn something about how it achieves effects. We want to know what a given kind of communication does to people. Given a certain message content, we should like to be able to predict what effect that content will have on its receivers.

Every time we insert an advertisement in a newspaper, put up a sign, explain something to a class, scold a child, write a letter, or put our political candidate on radio or television, we are making a prediction about the effect communication will have. I am predicting now that what I am writing will help you understand the common everyday miracle of communication. Perhaps I am wrong. Certainly many political parties have been proved wrong in their predictions about the effects of their candidates' radio speeches. Some ads sell goods; others don't. Some class teaching "goes over"; some does not. For it is apparent to you, from what you have read so far, that there is no such thing as a simple and easily predictable relationship between message content and effect.

Neverthless, it is possible to describe simply what might be called the conditions of success in communication—by which we mean the conditions that must be fulfilled if the message is to arouse its intended response. Let us set them down here briefly, and then talk about them:

1. *The message must be so designed and delivered as to gain the attention of the intended destination.*

2. *The message must employ signs which refer to experience common to source and destination, so as to "get the meaning across."*

3. *The message must arouse personality needs in the destination and suggest some ways to meet those needs.*

4. *The message must suggest a way to meet those needs which is appropriate to the group situation in which the destination finds himself at the time when he is moved to make the desired response.*

You can see, by looking at these requirements, why the expert communicator usually begins by finding out as much as he can about his intended destination, and why "know your audience" is the first rule of practical mass communication. For it is important to know the right timing for a message, the kind of language one must use to be understood, the attitudes and values one must appeal to in order to be effective, and the group standards in which the desired action will have to take place. This is relatively easy in face-to-face communication, more difficult in mass communication. In either case, it is necessary.

Let us talk about these four requirements.

1. *The message must be so designed and delivered as to gain the attention of the intended destination.* This is not so easy as it sounds. For one thing, the message must be made available. There will be no communication if we don't talk loud enough to be heard, or if our letter is not delivered, or if we smile at the right person when she isn't looking. And even if the message is available, it may not be selected. Each of us has available far more communication than we can possibly accept or decode. We therefore scan our environment in much the same way as we scan newspaper headlines or read a table of contents. We choose messages according to our impression of their general characteristics—whether they fit our needs and interests. We choose usually on the basis of an impres-

sion we get from one cue in the message, which may be a headline, a name in a radio news story, a picture, a patch of color, or a sound. If that cue does not appeal to us, we may never open our senses to the message. In different situations, of course, we choose differently among these cues. For example, if you are speaking to me at a time when I am relaxed and un-busy, or when I am waiting for the kind of message you have (for instance, that my friends have come to take me fishing), then you are more likely to get good attention than if you address me when noise blots out what you say, or when all my attention is given to some competing message, or when I am too sleepy to pay attention, or when I am thinking about something else and have simply "tuned out." (How many times have you finished speaking and realized that your intended receiver had simply not heard a word you said?) The designing of a message for attention, then, involves timing, and placing, and equipping it with cues which will appeal to the receiver's interests.

2. *The message must employ signs which refer to experience common to both source and destination, in order to "get the meaning across."* We have already talked about this problem of getting the receiver in tune with the sender. Let us add now that as our experience with environment grows, we tend to classify and catalog experience in terms of how it relates to other experience and to our needs and interests. As we grow older that catalog system grows harder and firmer. It tends to reject messages that do not fit its structure, or distort them so that they do fit. It will reject Einstein, perhaps, because it feels it can't understand him. If an airplane is a completely new experience, but a bird is not, it may, as we have said, interpret the plane as a large, noisy bird. If it is Republican it will tend to reject Democratic radio speeches or to recall only the parts that can be made into pro-Republican arguments; this is one of the things we have found out about voting behavior. Therefore, in designing a message we have to be sure not only that we speak the "same language" as the receiver, and that we don't "write over his head," but also that we don't conflict too directly with the way he sees and catalogs the world. There are some circumstances, true, in which it works well to conflict directly, but for the most part these are the circumstances in which our understandings and attitudes are not yet firm or fixed, and they are relatively few and far between. In communicating, as in flying an airplane, the rule is that when a stiff wind is blowing, one doesn't land across-wind unless he has to.

3. *The message must arouse personality needs in the destination and suggest some way to meet those needs.* We take action because of need and toward goals. In certain simple situations, the action response is quite automatic. When our nerves signal "pain-heat-finger" we jerk our fingers back from the hot pan. When our optic nerve signals "red traffic light"

we stop the car. In more complicated situations we usually have more freedom of choice, and we choose the action which, in the given situation, will come closest to meeting our needs or goals. The first requisite of an effective message, therefore (as every advertising man knows), it that it relate itself to one of our personality needs—the needs for security, status, belongingness, understanding, freedom from constraint, love, freedom from anxiety, and so forth. It must arouse a drive. It must make the individual feel a need or a tension which he can satisfy by action. Then the message can try to control the resulting action by suggesting what action to take. Thus an advertisement usually tells you to buy, what, and where. Propaganda to enemy troops usually suggests a specific action, such as surrender, subversion, or malingering. The suggested action, of course, is not always the one taken. If an easier, cheaper, or otherwise more acceptable action leading to the same goal is seen, that will probably be selected instead. For instance, it may be that the receiver is not the kind of person to take vigorous action, even though that seems called for. The person's values may inhibit him from doing what is suggested. Or his group role and membership may control what action he takes, and it is this control we must talk about now.

4. *The message must suggest a way to meet those needs which is appropriate to the group situation in which the destination finds himself at the time when he is moved to make the desired response.* We live in groups. We get our first education in the primary group of our family. We learn most of our standards and values from groups. We learn roles in groups, because those roles give us the most orderly and satisfying routine of life. We make most of our communication responses in groups. And if communication is going to bring about change in our behavior, the first place we look for approval of this new behavior is to the group. We are scarcely aware of the great importance our group involvements have for us, or of the loyalties we develop toward our several groups and institutions, until our place in the group or the group itself is threatened. But yet if our groups do not sanction the response we are inclined to make to communication, then we are very unlikely to make it. On the other hand, if our group strongly approves of a certain kind of action, that is the one we are likely to select out of several otherwise even choices.

You can see how this works in practical situations. The Jewish culture does not approve the eating of pork; the Indian culture does not approve the slaughter of cows, and the eating of beef. Therefore, it is highly unlikely that even the most eloquent advertisement will persuade an orthodox Jewish family to go contrary to their group sanctions, and buy pork; or an orthodox Hindu family, to buy beef. Or take the very simple communication situation of a young man and a young woman in a parked automobile. The young man communicates the idea that he wants a kiss. There isn't much likelihood of his not gaining attention for that communication or of its not being understood. But how the young woman responds will depend on a number of factors, partly individual, partly group. Does she want to be kissed at that moment? Does she want to be kissed by that young man? Is the situation at the moment—a moon, soft music from the radio, a convertible?—conducive to the response the young man wants? But then, how about the group customs under which the girl lives? If this is a first date, is it "done" to kiss a boy on a first date? Is petting condoned in the case of a girl her age? What has she learned from her parents and her friends about these things? Of course, she won't knowingly have a little debate with herself such as we have suggested here, but all these elements and more will enter into the decision as to whether she tilts up her chin or says, "No, Jerry. Let's go home."

There are two things we can say with confidence about predicting communication effects. One is that a message is much more likely to succeed if it fits the patterns of understandings, attitudes, values and goals that a receiver has; or at least if it starts with this pattern and tries to reshape it slightly. Communication research men call this latter process "canalizing," meaning that the sender provides a channel to direct the already existing motives in the receiver. Advertising men and propagandists say it more bluntly; they say that a communicator must "start where the audience is." You can see why this is. Our personalities—our patterns of habits, attitudes, drives, and so forth—grow very slowly but firmly. I have elsewhere compared the process to the slow, sure, ponderous growth of a stalagmite on a cave floor. The stalagmite builds up from the calcareous residue of the water dripping on it from the cave roof. Each drop leaves only a tiny residue, and it is very seldom that we can detect the residue of any single drop, or that any single drop will make a fundamental change in the shape or appearance of the stalagmite. Yet together all these drops do build the stalagmite, and over the years it changes considerably in size and somewhat in shape. This is the way our environment drips into us, drop by drop, each drop leaving a little residue, each tending to follow the existing pattern. This personality pattern we are talking about is, of course, an active thing—not passive, like the stalagmite—but still the similarity is there. When we introduce one drop of communication into a person where millions of drops have already fallen and left their residue, we can hardly expect to reshape the personality fundamentally by that one drop. If we are communicating to a child, it is easier, because the situation is not so firmly fixed. If we are communicating in an area where ideas and values are not yet determined—if our drop of communication falls where not many have fallen before—then we may be able to see a change as a result of our communication.

But in general we must admit that the best thing we can do is to build on what already exists. If we take advantage of the existing pattern of understanding, drives, and attitudes to gain acceptance for our message, then we may hope to divert the pattern slightly in the direction we want to move it. Let's go back to elections again for an example. It is very hard to change the minds of convinced Republicans or Democrats through communication, or even to get them to listen to the arguments of the opposing party. On the other hand, it is possible to start with a Republican or Democratic viewpoint and slightly modify the existing party viewpoints in one way or other. If this process goes on for long enough, if may even be possible to get confirmed party-men to reverse their voting pattern. This is what the Republicans were trying to do in the 1952 election by stressing "the mess in Washington," "time for a change," "the mistakes in Korea," and "the threat of Communism," and apparently they were successful in getting some ordinarily Democratic votes. But in 1952, as in every campaign, the real objectives of the campaigning were the new voters and the undecided voters.

The second thing we can say with confidence about communication effects is that they are resultants of a number of forces, of which the communicator can really control only one. The sender, that is, can shape his message and can decide when and where to introduce it. But the message is only one of at least four important elements that determine what response occurs. The other three are the situation in which the communication is received and in which the response, if any, must occur; the personality state of the receiver; and his group relationships and standards. This is why it is so dangerous to try to predict exactly what will be the effect of any message except the simplest one in the simplest situation.

Let us take an example. In Korea, in the first year of the war there, I was interviewing a North Korean prisoner of war who had recently surrendered with one of our surrender leaflets on his person. It looked like an open and shut case: the man had picked up the leaflet, thought it over, and decided to surrender. But I was interviewing him anyway, trying to see just how the leaflet had its effect. This is what he told me.

He said that when he picked up the leaflet, it actually made him fight harder. It rather irritated him, and he didn't like the idea of having to surrender. He wasn't exactly a warlike man; he had been a clerk, and was quiet and rather slow; but the message actually aroused a lot of aggression in him. Then the situation deteriorated. His division was hit hard and thrown back, and he lost contact with the command post. He had no food, except what he could find in the fields, and little ammunition. What was left of his company was isolated by itself in a rocky valley. Even then, he said, the morale was good, and there was no talk of surrendering. As a matter of fact, he said, the others would have shot him if he had tried to surrender. But then a couple of our planes spotted them, shot up their hideout, and dropped some napalm. When it was over, he found himself alone, a half mile from where he had been, with half his jacket burned off, and no sign of any of his company. A couple of hours later some of our tanks came along. And only then did the leaflet have an effect. He remembered it had told him to surrender with his hands up, and he did so.

In other words, the communication had no effect (even had an opposite effect from the one intended) so long as the situation, the personality, and the group norms were not favorable. When the situation deteriorated, the group influence was removed, and the personality aggression was burned up, then finally the message had an effect. I tell you this story hoping it will teach you what it taught me: that it is dangerous to assume any simple and direct relationship between a message and its effect without knowing all the other elements in process.

The Nature of Mass Communication

Now let us look at mass communication in the light of what we have already said about communication in general.

The process is exactly what we have described, but the elements in the process are not the same.

The chief source, in mass communication, is a communication organization or an institutionalized person. By a communication organization we mean a newspaper, a broadcasting network or station, a film studio, a book or magazine publishing house. By an institutionalized person we mean such a person as the editor of a newspaper, who speaks in his editorial columns through the facilities of the institution and with more voice and prestige than he would have if he were speaking without the institution.

The organization works exactly as the individual communicator does. It operates as decoder, interpreter, and encoder. On a newspaper, for example, the input to be decoded flows in through the news wires and the reporters. It is evaluated, checked, amplified where necessary, written into a story, assigned headline and position, printed, distributed. This is the same process as goes on within an individual communicator, but it is carried out by a group of persons rather than by one individual. The quality of organization required to get a group of reporters, editors, and printers working together as a smooth communication unit, decoding, interpreting, and encoding so that the whole operation and product has an individual quality, is a quite remarkable thing. We have become so used to this performance that we have forgotten how remarkable it is.

Another difference between the communication organization and the individual communicator is that the organization has a very high ratio of output to input. Individuals vary, of course, in their output-input ratios. Persons who are in the business of communicating (preachers or teachers, for example) ordinarily have higher ratios than others, and so do naturally talkative persons who are not professional communicators. Very quiet persons have relatively higher input. But the communication institution is so designed as to be able to encode thousands—sometimes millions—of identical messages at the same time. To carry these, intricate and efficient channels must be provided. There have to be provisions for printing and delivering thousands of newspapers, magazines, or books, for making prints of a film and showing them in hundreds or thousands of theaters, for translating sound waves into electricity and distributing it through wires and through the air to millions of receiving sets.

The *destinations* of mass communication are individuals at the ends of these channels—individuals reading the evening paper, looking through the new magazine, reading the new book, sitting in the motion picture theater, turning the dial on the radio set. This receiving situation is much different from that which pertains in face-to-face communication, for one thing, because there is very little direct *feedback* from the receivers to the sender. The destination who, in a face-to-face situation, will nod his head and smile or frown while the sender is speaking, and then encode a reply himself, will very seldom talk back to the radio network or write a letter to the editor. Indeed, the kind of feedback that comes to a mass communication organization in a kind of inferential expression—receivers stop buying the publication, or no longer listen to the program, or cease to buy the product advertised. Only in rare instances do these organizations have an opportunity to see, more directly than that, how their messages are going over. That is one reason why mass communication conducts so much audience research, to find out what programs are being listened to, what stories are being read, what ads attended to. It is one of their few substitutes for the feedback which makes interpersonal communication so relatively easy to plan and control.

The following chapters will have something to say about the audiences of the different media, and we need not discuss them in any detail here. These audiences cluster, not only around a newspaper, magazine, or television station, but also around certain stories in the paper, certain parts of the magazine, certain television or radio programs. For example, Station A will not have the same audience at 8:00 as it had at 7:00, because some of these listeners will have moved to Stations B or C, and some of the listeners from B and C will have moved to A. Newspaper D will not have the same audience on its sports pages as on its society pages, although there will be some overlap. What determines which offering of mass communication will be selected by any given individual? Perhaps the easiest way to put it is to say that choice is determined by the Fraction of Selection—

$$\frac{\text{Expectation of reward}}{\text{Effort required}}$$

You can increase the value of that fraction either by increasing the numerator or decreasing the denominator, which is to say that an individual is more likely to select a certain communication if it promises him more reward or requires less effort than comparable commnuications. You can see how this works in your own experience. You are much more likely to read the newspaper or magazine at hand than to walk six blocks to the news stand to buy a bigger newspaper or magazine. You are more likely to listen to a station which has a loud clear signal than to one which is faint and fading and requires constant effort from you to hear at all. But if the big game of the week is on that faint station, or if your favorite author is in the magazine at the news stand, then there is more likelihood that you will make the additional effort. If you were a member of the underground in occupied France during World War II, you probably risked your life to hear news from the forbidden Allied radio. You aren't likely to stay up until 2 a.m. simply to hear a radio program, but if by staying up that long you can find out how the Normandy invasion is coming or who has won the Presidential election—then you will probably make the extra effort just as most of the rest of us did. It is hardly necessary to point out that no two receivers may have exactly the same fraction of selection. One of them may expect more reward from Milton Berle than will the other. One of them may consider it less effort to walk six blocks to the news stand than does the other. But according to how this fraction looks to individuals in any given situation, the audience of mass communication is determined.

Unlike lecture audiences and small groups, mass communication audiences (with the exception of the people in a motion picture theater at the same time) have very little contact with each other. People in one house listening to Jack Benny don't know whether anybody in the next house is listening to him or not. A person reading an editorial in the New York *Times* has little group feeling for the other people in this country who read editorials in the New York *Times*. These audiences are individuals, rather than groups. But each individual is connected with a group or groups—his family, his close friends, his occupational or school group— and this is a very important thing to remember about mass communication. The more we study it, the more we are coming to think that the great effects of mass communication are gained by feeding ideas and information into small groups through individual receivers. In some groups, as you well know, it is a sign of status to be familiar with some part of mass communication (for example, in the teen-age group to hear the currently screamable crooner, or in some business groups to read the *Wall Street Journal*). In many a group, it is a news story from the radio, or an editorial from the *Tribune*, or an article from the *Times*, or an article from one of the big magazines, that furnishes the subject of conversation on a given day. The story, or article, or editorial, is then re-interpreted by the group, and the result is encoded in group opinion and perhaps in group action. Thus it may well be that the chief influence of mass communication on individuals is really a kind of secondary influence, reflected to the group and back again.

We are ready now to draw a diagram of mass communication, and to talk about the kinds of messages this sort of system requires and what we know about predicting their effects. This is the way mass communication seems to work:

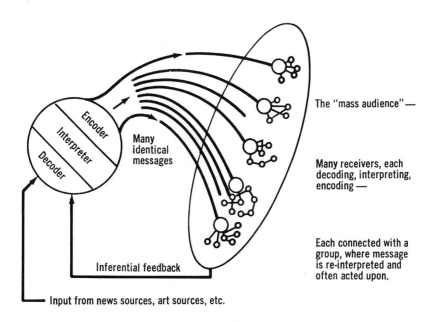

The "mass audience" —

Many receivers, each decoding, interpreting, encoding —

Each connected with a group, where message is re-interpreted and often acted upon.

Organization

Now it is easy to see that there will be certain restrictions on the kinds of program which can be carried over these identical circuits to these little-known and changing audiences. The communication organization knows it is dealing with individuals, yet does not know them as individuals. Its audience research classifies, rather than individualizes, the audience. Audience research, that is, says that so many people are listening at a given time, or that so many men and so many women are likely to read a given kind of article, or that the readers of a given magazine are in the upper economic bracket and have had on the average 12 years of schooling. Whereas the individual communicator is dealing with individuals and able to watch the way his message is received and modify it if necessary, the organization is dealing only with averages and classes. It must pitch its reading level somewhere below the estimated average of its audience, in order not to cut off too many of the lower half of the audience. It must choose its content according to the best estimate it can make of what the broadest classes of receivers want and need. Whereas the individual communicator is free to experiment because he can instantly correct any mistake, the organization is loathe to experiment. When it finds an apparently successful formula, it keeps on that way. Or it changes the details but not the essentials. If one organization makes a great success with a given kind of message, others tend to copy it—not because of any lack of originality, but because this is one of the few kinds of feedback available from the mass audience. That is why we have so much sameness on the radio, why one successful comic strip tends to be followed by others of the same kind, one successful news or digest magazine by others, one kind of comedy program by others of the samed kind, and so forth.

What can we say about the effects of these mass communication messages? For one thing, mass communication has pervasive effect because in many respects it has taken over the function of *society communicating.* Our society, like any other communication unit, functions as decoder, interpreter, and encoder. It decodes our environment for us,

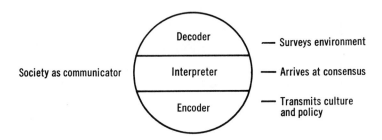

watches the horizon for danger and promise and entertainment. It then operates to interpret what it has decoded, arrives at a consensus so that it can put policy into effect, keep the ordinary interactions of communal life going, and helps its members enjoy life. It also encodes—messages to maintain our relations with other societies in the world, and messages to transmit our culture to its new members. Mass communication, which has the power to extend our eyes and ears almost indefinite distances, and to multiply our voices and written words as far as we can find listeners or readers, has taken over a large share of the responsibility for this social communication. Newspapers, radio, television watch the horizon for us. By telling us what our leaders and experts think, by conducting a discussion on public issues, these media, and magazines and films as well, help us to interpret what is seen on the horizon and decided what to do about it. The textbook and educational films have led all the other media in encoding our culture so that the young persons coming into our society may learn as quickly and easily as possible the history, standards, roles, and skills they must know in order to be good members of society. This is not to say that all the media do not contribute in some degree to all these functions. For example, a book like *1984* may be as much a report of the horizon as the most current news story. And on the other hand, it is certainly true that a great deal of our culture is transmitted currently through television, radio, newspapers, and magazines. But the faster media are better equipped to be watchmen, and are more often so used. The slower, longer lasting media are better equipped to be teaching aids and are so used. The important thing is that *all* the mass media have important uses in providing the network of understandings without which the modern large community could not exist.

So much for the basic effect, which we see every day in the kind of customs around us, the people and problems talked about, and the language we speak. This is the slow, imperceptible effect. This is like building the stalagmite. But how about the specific effect of a given message transmitted by mass communication? How can we predict what the effect will be on the mass audience?

We can't predict the effect on the mass audience. We can only predict the effect on individuals. Communication organizations have developed group encoding, but there is only individual decoding. Therefore, we can predict the effect of mass communication only in the way we try to predict the effect of other communication—that is, in terms of the interaction of message, situation, personality, and group.

The first thing which becomes obvious, therefore, is that inasmuch as there are many different combinations of personality, situation, and group in any mass audience, there are likely to be many different kinds of effects. It is equally obvious that since mass communication doesn't know much about the individuals in its audience, predicting effects is going to be extremely difficult.

Nevertheless, there are certain things to be said. The problem of attention constantly faces mass communication. The average American (whoever he is) probably gives four or five hours a day to mass communication. If he lives in a big city, he gets a paper that would itself take half that time to read. (He doesn't read all of it.) He is offered the equivalent of two weeks of radio and television every day from which he can choose. He is offered a bewildering array of magazines and books and films. From these also he must choose. Other attractive ways to spend leisure compete with communication. He sometimes combines them—listening to music while he reads, playing cards or eating while he hears a newscast, playing with the baby while he watches television. Therefore, we can predict at least that any individual will have a fairly small chance of selecting any given item in mass communication, and that if he does select it, his level of attention may be rather low. This is responsible for many cases of "mis-hearing" radio. We know also that readership of the average newspaper story falls off sharply after the first few paragraphs, so that a member of the mass audience is likely not to see at all the latter part of a long newspaper story.

There are of course many cases in which markedly high attention is aroused by mass communication, and plentiful instances of listeners identifying closely with radio characters and adopting the mannerisms and language of movie heroes. It has been said that the mass media have brought Hollywood, Broadway, and Washington nearer than the next town, and there is a great deal of truth in this. There are also some cases in which very spectacular overt results have been accomplished by mass communication.

Let us recall one of them. Can you remember when CBS broadcast Orson Welles' performance of H. G. Wells' "War of the Worlds"? The script featured the invasion of the United States by armies from outer space. Perhaps you were one of the people who ran screaming for the hills, or armed yourself to wait for the invaders, or tried to call your loved ones long distance for a farewell talk. Or perhaps you were not. Perhaps you were one of those who heard the CBS announcers explain carefully that it was a play made from a book of fiction. Those who didn't hear those announcements were engaged in proving what we have just said about the low level of attention to some parts of mass communication.

But that doesn't entirely explain why people became hysterical and did things they were rather ashamed of the next day. And in truth, this is one of the really spectacular examples of mass communication effect. This happened without any specific reference to groups; it happened spontaneously in thousands of homes near the supposed scene of invasion. Why did it happen? Research men have studied the incident, and think they have put together the puzzle. For one thing, it was a tense time. People were full of anxiety, which could have been triggered off in many ways. In the second place, people trusted—still trust—radio news; the play was in the form of newscasts and commentaries. Therefore, the communication as it was interpreted really represented a spectacular change in the situation: the Martians were invading! Apparently the group element played no large part in this event, but the other three did. The message was accepted (minus the important identification as fiction). The listeners had a good deal of anxiety ready to be used. The message convinced them that the situation had indeed changed for the worse. Each according to his own personality and situation then took action.

As we have said, that was, fortunately, one of the few really spectacular examples of mass behavior. Another one was the Gold Rush that resulted in the 1890's when the newspapers brought word of gold in Alaska. Some people might say that what the Communists have been able to accomplish is a spectacular advertisment for the power of mass communication, and that subject is worth looking at because it shows us not only some of the differences between the ways we use the mass media and the way dictators use them, but also some of the principles of communication effect.

It is true that one of the first acts of the Communists, when they take over a country, is to seize the mass communication system. (That was also one of Hilter's first acts.) They also seize the police power and the control of productive resources, and they organize an intricate system of Party groups and meetings. I don't know of any case in which the Communists have put the whole burden of convincing people and gaining members on mass communications alone. They always provide a group structure where a convert can get reinforcement, and meetings to which a potential convert can be drawn. They use mass communication almost as an adjunct to these groups. In Korea and China, the mass media actually become texts for the groups. And the Communists do one thing more. If at all possible, they secure a monopoly on the mass communication reaching the people whom they are taking over. When they took Seoul, Korea, in 1950, they confiscated radio receivers wherever they found receivers despite the fact that they had captured Radio Seoul, intact, the most powerful transmitter in that part of Asia. They were willing to give up the use of Radio Seoul, if by so doing they could keep their subjects from foreign radio.

Now obviously, a state monopoly on communication, as well as control of resources and organization of a police state, is a long way from our system. And as long as our mass media are permitted free criticism and reporting, and as long as they represent more than one political point of view, we have little to worry about in a political way from them. But even though we may look with revulsion at the Communist way of using mass communication, still we can study it. And let us refer back to the four elements which we said were instrumental in bring about communication effects—message, situation, personality, and group. The Communists control the messages. By their police power, control of resources (and hence of food and pay), they can structure the situation as they see fit. Their group organization is most careful, and offers a place—in fact compels a place—for every person. Thus they control three of the four elements, and can use those three to work on the fourth—the personalities of their receivers.

The Communists, who have now had 35 years practice in the intensive use of mass communication for accomplishing specified effects, are apparently unwilling to predict the results of their communication unless they can control three of the four chief elements which enter into the effect.

Let us take one final example. There is a great deal of violence in mass communication content today. Violence is interesting to children. Yet only a few childen actually engage in acts of criminal violence. Most children do no such things. They sample the violent material, and decide they would rather play football. Or they attend faithfully to the violent material, use it to clear out vicariously some of the aggressions they have been building up, and emerge none the worse for the experience. Or they adopt some of the patterns in a mild and inoffensive way when they play cops and robbers. Only a few children learn, from the mass media, techniques of crime and violence which they and their pals actually try out. Now what is it that determines which of those children will be affected harmfully by those messages of violence, and which will not?

We can attempt to answer this question from cases we have studied. And the answer is simply that the other three elements—personality, situation, and group influence—will probably determine the use made of the message. If the child is busy with athletics, Scouts, church, or other wholesome activities, he is not likely to feel the need of violent and antisocial actions. On the other hand, if he is bored and frustrated, he may experiment with dangerous excitement. If he has a healthy personality, if he has learned a desirable set of values from his family group, he is less likely to give in to motivation toward violence. On the other hand, if his value standards are less certain, if he has lost some of his sense of belonging and being loved (possibly because of a broken home), he may entertain more hospitably the invitation to violence. If the group he admires has a wholesome set of standards, he is not likely to try an undesirable response, because the group will not reinforce it. On the other hand, if he belongs to a "gang" there is every reason to expect that he will try some of the violence, because in so doing he will win admiration and status in the group. Therefore, what he does will depend on the delicate balancing of these influences at a given time. Certainly no one could predict—except possibly on an actuarial basis—from merely seeing such a message exactly what the response to it would be. And it is entirely probable in the case we have mentioned that the community, the home, and the school—

because they influence so greatly the other three elements—would have much more to do with the young person's response than would the message itself.

The all-pervasive effect of mass communication, the ground swell of learning that derives from mass communication acting as *society communicating*—this we can be sure of, and over a long period we can identify its results in our lives and beliefs. The more specific effects, however, we must predict only with caution, and never from the message alone without knowing a great deal about the situation, the personality, and the group relationship where the message is to be acted upon.

26

Meaning, Value, and the Theory of Promotion

JEROME B. KERNAN
MONTROSE S. SOMMERS

There are conceptualizations of human behavior that posit it as a series of choices among alternatives.[1] Whether and whom one marries, whether and how one votes, and whether and what one buys, for example, may be construed as reflections of choosing between "this and that." The manifest consequences of choices—the vote cast, the spouse married, and product purchased—readily command attention. The elusive elements of behavior —the determinants which prompt choices—however, are perhaps of greater import. If behavior is to be understood, predicted, or controlled, attention must inevitably be focused on those cognitive processes that precede it. *Why* is "this" and not "that" done?

An Interactionist Approach to Behavior

It is generally agreed that people make choices—behave—on the strength of what they know or think they know.[2] This is to assert that information, whatever specific processes govern its acquisition, interpretation, and disposition, is central to behavior. In a behavioral context, information implies communication.

The emerging theory of signs affords one means of explicating the ambiguities encountered in the study of human communication.[3] It recog-

Reprinted with permission fro n the *Journal of Communication*, Vol. 17 (June, 1967), pp. 109-135.

[1] In particular, see [23].

[2] These notions are developed in [11].

[3] For a concise treatment, from the standpoint of consumer behavior, see [10], especially pp. 119-124.

nizes three levels of analysis: pragmatics, semantics, and syntactics.[4] A *sign* is any event by means of which one organism affects the behavior of another. *Pragmatics* concerns signs as they relate to their users. *Semantics* concerns signs as they relate to significates (what signs stand for). *Syntactics* concerns the calculus of signs, that is, signs as they relate to one another.

To be interested in how communication affects behavior is, ultimately, to be interested in pragmatics. As yet, however, this is such a loosely structured field that one must repair to semantics and syntactics. Syntactical approaches to communication, commonly called information theory, are reflected in the likes of the Shannon-Weaver model [19]. Such approaches, in the nature of quantitative analogs, focus on the *amount* of information communicated. Only nominal deference is accorded the "meaning" of the information. Semantic approaches to communication, on the other hand, focus on the *qualitative* aspects of information, on what it "means," with less emphasis on measuring it.[5] Semanticists—Hayakawa [9] is an example—are concerned more with how people react to communication. Paradigms of the "communication process," of course, are not in short supply.[6] To locate the notions developed in this paper in a sign-theoretic context, it would be reasonable to say that the approach is essentially semantic, but with a concomitant (albeit modest) attempt at syntactics. The particular tack taken, of course, is prompted by the function envisaged for the model—to explicate the communicative antecedents of a certain category of behavior.

A basic position taken in the present formulation is what might be called an interactionist approach to behavior. This approach is reflected in the comments of one of its leading advocates, Shibutani:[7]

What characterizes the interactionist approach is the contention that *human nature and the social order are products of communication.* From this standpoint, behavior is not regarded merely as a response to environmental stimuli, an expression of inner organic needs, nor a manifestation of cultural patterns. The importance of sensory cues, organic drives, and culture is certainly recognized, but the *direction taken by a person's conduct is seen as something that is constructed in the reciprocal give and take of interdependent men who are adjusting to one another.* Furthermore, *a man's personality,* those distinctive behavior patterns that characterize a given individual—*is regarded as developing and being reaffirmed from day to day in his interaction with his associates.* Finally, *the culture of a group* is not viewed as something external that is imposed upon people, but as consisting of *models of*

---

[4] For a full development, see [4].

[5] For a discussion of attempts to measure semantic information, however, see [8] and [1].

[6] For example, see [3].

[7] See [20], pp. 22-23.

appropriate conduct that emerge in communication and are continually rein-
forced as people jointly come to terms with life conditions. If the motivation
of behavior, the formation of personality, and the evolution of group structure
all occur in social interaction, it follows logically that attention should be
focussed upon the interchanges that go on among human beings as they come
into contact with one another.

This position is, of course, to assert that communication is central to
interpersonal behavior—a position hardly novel to communication theorists
[2, 5]. The notion is that communication links people with their environment and, depending on what environmental configuration this link portrays, some adaptive behavior may be expected to follow.

Consumer Behavior

The particular manifestation of interpersonal behavior to which present
attention is directed is that of consumer behavior. Given that whenever
interest is so localized some facets of behavior are emphasized to the ex-
clusion of others, it is well to note that, basically, the concern remains
with interpersonal behavior. The following discussion, then, has application beyond the consumer context. The only question is how much adaptation is required to fit it to each particular form of nonconsumer activity.

The more obvious aspect of consumer behavior is the purchase, or,
technically, the economic exchange of money (or a substitute) for a product or service. Since exchange activity regulates the success (or lack of
it) of economic enterprises, it has been and remains the focus of businessmen's attention. Such concern is reflected in the trite admonition: "Nothing happens until a sale is made." In broader perspective, however, it is
obvious that exchange is only an overt aspect of a large activity pattern,
the transaction. This basic unit of business activity comprises, in addition
to exchange, the necessary activity, *negotiation.* That negotiation is a
necessary but not sufficient condition to exchange explains why there is
often a discrepency between people's measured "intentions to buy" and
their actual purchase behavior. The former gauges only—and often
crudely—their announced disposition to enter into an implicit or explicit
dialogue with sellers of products. Any number of factors might intervene
as their intentions are brought to fruition.

This paper is concerned with a generalized explanation of the
cognitive processes *antecedent to explicit negotiation.* The model developed does not seek nor does it pretend to explain "who buys what."
Computer simulations notwithstanding, pretentions at predicting who will
buy what are just that—pretentions. The model is limited to explicating
the role of sellers' communication in prompting (on a probabilistic basis)
would-be buyers to enter into an overt form of negotiation. Further, with-

out in any way denying the reality of interchanges of communication in the broad scheme of interpersonal behavior, the present focus is on the unilateral communication that flows from sellers to would-be buyers. In the present scheme, "sellers" are roughly equivalent to the Westley-Mac-Lean [25] notion of "advocacy roles."

Promotion as a Case of Communication

As previously noted, exchange is what commercial entities seek. It is on negotiation, however, where they expend vast resources. From the perspective of would-be buyers—receivers of communication, or "behavioral system roles" in the Westley-MacLean sense—some negotiation activities may be recognized as explicit (behavioral) while others are implicit or cognitive in nature.

Explicit negotiation activity would be exemplified by a compilation of product specifications and a discussion of these and their terms of sale with a seller. If both seller and buyer can agree on the terms of the proposed exchange, the negotiation can be successfully concluded, exchange can take place, the transaction can be consummated. Implicit negotiation activity, of which there probably is a great deal more, begins when prospective buyers become aware of advertisements and other promotional efforts or observe or hear about products or services in use. This activity continues when would-be buyers engage themselves in a dialogue (intrapersonal communication), often because the seller is not immediately available. Moreover, this implicit, internal negotiation occurs before as well as during the explicit activity of negotiating.[8]

Prospective buyers seek information and it is expected that sellers (but not *only* sellers) will supply it. In a communication context, then, their situation is not substantially different from voters contemplating political candidates or men seeking women to marry. Such characteristics of promotional communication, if any, which render it peculiar stem from its obviously persuasive intent, its somewhat specialized content, and its ultimate goal—to encourage negotiation and exchange. By promotion is meant any identifiable effort on the part of a seller to persuade prospective buyers to accept the seller's information and store it in retrievable form. Such effort is commonly manifested in product and package design, advertising, personal selling, sales promotion, publicity, and public relations. The collective intent of these activities is to imbue a seller's product with appropriate meanings—that is, ideations about the product that will encourage favorable evaluations of it and increase the likelihood of explicit negotiation for its purchase.

---

[8] Advocates of cognitive dissonance [6] would argue that intrapersonal dialogue occurs *after* explicit negotiation—indeed, after exchange—as well.

Theoretical Foundations of Promotion

Before attempting to explicate the cognitive processes that precede consumer behavior, it is useful to consider the nature of that behavior. To appreciate the object to be explained is to facilitate its explanation.

Behavioral Structures and Processes

Expanding the interactionist approach to behavior previously asserted, it is useful to characterize human activity in the context of role behavior. A role may be construed as a functional characterization in a social setting. In the sense of role behavior, then, an individual does what he does in response to (or certainly at least tempered by) what he perceives his role(s) to be. This suggests that human activity is very much an orderly phenomenon, people doing what their roles call for. Such "random behavior" as might be observed is, in this perspective, not random at all—only misperceived. That is, if seen in the appropriate role context, all behavior can be associated with some role. And it is only when behavior is mismatched with roles that it appears anomalous.

Role theory[9] immediately recognizes two aspects of behavior, structure and process. *Structure* refers to the social configuration within which behavior takes place. To speak of structure is to speak of the pattern of interacting, intrapersonal and interpersonal roles operating in a given behavioral setting.[10] *Process* refers to the playing of roles—i.e., to behavior, per se. It includes not only activity, but also its genesis, namely, how role behavior is learned. Both process and structure are central to an understanding of behavior; the former, because it treats what activities people perform and the latter because, as it specifies the environmental context, suggests behavioral typologies and thus mutations.

Role behavior may be considered first in terms of the concept role type. By *role type* is meant a societally imposed cluster of activities. Thus, for each role type, such as mother, father, soldier, student, and much more particular designations, there exist social expectations as regards behavior. These expectations, both culturally and group derived, range from the highly codified (job specifications in the civil service) to the vaguely specified (female behavior on the first date). Also, they change with time and circumstance, which is to say that behavioral structure (context) affects behavioral processes.

The role-type notion characterizes behavior in terms of activities. Accountants and bricklayers differ because what they *do* is different. This is not to imply that all role players of a given type behave similarly, however

---

[9] An explicit treatment is given in [18], pp. 3-19.
[10] The interacting effects of roles are treated in [15], pp. 6-14.

[13]. Obviously, since accountant A and accountant B likely differ in the non-accountant roles they play, a different set of *role interactions*—and thus different activity patterns—is involved for each.

The role-type notion is particularly useful in the analysis of *consumer* behavior because it specifies not only activities but also the kinds of products sanctioned for use in their performance. This is to assert the fundamental behavioral proposition that human activity patterns and product clusters are functionally related. A product or cluster of products symbolizes or is symbolized by an activity or pattern of activities. Thus, for each role type, some combination of cultural and group influences sanction or prescribe both an activity pattern *and* a product cluster. The extent to which one violates this social propriety—whether in sanctioned activities or appropriate products or both—is in large measure determined by one's commitment to role.

By *role commitment* is meant an individual's intrapersonal disposition to perform the activities and use the products (services) sanctioned for a particular role type. Role commitment operates on a continuum, ranging from very weak (little or no disposition to behave as the role type specifies), through moderate, to strong (a commitment to play the role "by the book").

Within a given role type—for example, housewife—variations in behavior (activities performed and products used) are determined by two factors. First, role interactions will affect behavior in the housewife role. The housewife who is also a mother, PTA member, and Junior League activist may be expected to behave differently than the housewife who plays none of these other roles. Second, role commitment will affect behavior. The housewife who is heritage bound, who does things "the way mother always did," may be expected to behave differently than her counterpart who perceives the same role in dilettante fashion. Both these factors, role interaction and role commitment, must be considered simultaneously with the concept of role type. Together, all three serve as the basis upon which commercial promotion can be formulated.

The Nature and Function of Promotion

The consumer behavior in which sellers have an ultimate interest is purchase behavior. What is purchased, however, is closely intertwined with the notions of (interacting) role type and commitment to role. The exchange manifesting purchase behavior, therefore, is necessarily approached with considerable deference to these notions. More particularly, the negotiation necessary to exchange represents a consideration by would-be buyers of sellers' information in the light of role type and commitment. This is true of both explicit negotiation, wherein interpersonal dialogue between seller and would-be buyer is manifested, and implicit negotiation, that is, intrapersonal dialogue on the would-be buyer's part.

Implicit negotiation is the focus of this paper. It is a cognitive process that at once commands the attention of a variety of behavioral science disciplines. In a marketing context, implicit negotiation is usually located in some sort of "hierarchy of effects" of promotion, such as attention—interest—desire—action or, in behavioral jargon, cognitive—affective—conative [17]. In this paper, implicit negotiation refers to the intrapersonal dialogue experienced by a would-be buyer in response to sellers' promotional information. It occurs both before and during explicit negotiation but serves primarily to induce the latter. Although it is essentially a cognitive (thinking) process, it manifests affective (emotional) and conative (motivational) elements. From the standpoint of a seller, the function of promotion is to create and transmit such information as promises to result in at least implicit negotiation on the part of would-be buyers. This is an intentionally guarded view of promotion and differs considerably from the assertion that promotion functions "to sell." Perhaps the latter is a laudable aspiration; it is hardly a realistic conceptualization, however.

Realistically, marketing strategists must consider promotion as a problem in supplying consumers with information. The "appropriate" information may well lead to implicit negotiation, explicit negotiation and, finally, exchange. But the propriety of information varies with circumstances, hence the low predictive ability of stimulus-response models purporting to explain sales behavior as a function of specific promotional input [12].

Promotional activities result in the creation and transmission of two broad categories of symbols: (1) products or services; and (2) information about products or services. A product (service) is not only an object of exchange, it is a symbol with action potential. Its physical presence or depiction communicates information. Its shape, size, color, texture, price, brand name, label, etc. comprise a complex of promotional information. In this sense, a product is both promotional and promotable for its speaks for itself and is spoken for as it becomes the object of other promotional efforts. These other efforts are reflected in the information carried by salesmen, catalogues, price lists, and advertisements in the various trade and consumer media.

Both the product and the promotional efforts that communicate information about it operate as symbols which convey the meaning of the product. Philosophical labyrinths on the "meaning of meaning" notwithstanding, it is useful to consider the meaning of a product symbol to be a combination of what the symbol *is* in physical terms and what it *does* in functional terms. To contemplate the meaning of a product, then, is at once to consider its physical makeup and what uses that makeup suggests.

Any given promotional symbol—a product, service, advertisement, publicity stunt, or whatever—can and does have different meanings for different individuals. People are prompted to act toward symbols on the basis of what is perceived—the meaning one ascribes to the symbol. To be sure, ascribing meaning is a complex phenomenon and the meanings attributable to a given symbol are many indeed. The dictionary meaning of lipstick, for example, is that it is a kind of pomade, a perfumed ointment or rouge, put in a stick form and used to adorn the lips. Very obviously the meaning of lipstick varies among a movie starlet, a middle-aged spinster, a teenage girl, her five-year-old sister, and a man, however [24]. Each perceives differently, both what the lipstick "is" and what it "does." The commercial significance of how consumers ascribe meaning to products and services hardly need be stressed.

Toward a Theory of Promotion

A systematic treatment of promotion demands more explicit consideration of the term, meaning. In this paper, *meaning refers to a receiver's aggregate perception of a communicated symbol.* Meaning is derived from two dimensions of perception, herein designated as attribute and performance. *Attribute, the physical dimension of meaning, refers to a receiver's perception of the role propriety of a communicated symbol's characteristics.* A receiver judging the attributes of a symbol asks: "Does this have physical characteristics appropriate to my role type or not, and to what extent?" *Performance, the functional dimension of meaning, refers to a receiver's perception of the role propriety of a communicated symbol's action potential.* A receiver judging the performance of a symbol asks: "Does this do appropriate things or not, and to what extent?"

Since both attribute and performance are relatively defined, they have an arbitrary zero point and both positive and negative domains. In the positive sector, characteristics or action potential are appropriate to the receiver's role type while in the negative sector, they are inappropriate. The zero point on either scale reflects the receiver's inability to ascertain propriety. Meaning, unlike its component dimensions, however, exists only in the positive range. One either has ideations about a symbol or not. Negative meaning does not exist in the present formulation.

What is sometimes confused with "negative meaning" is one's evaluation of a symbol. In this paper, the term value is used to designate reaction to communicated symbols. *Value refers to a receiver's net reaction to meaning.* A receiver judging the value of a symbol asks: "Given the attribute and performance perceptions I experience with regard to this symbol, in balance, is the symbol's meaning attractive or repulsive to me, and to what extent?" Value, then, is a function of meaning (that is, of attribute and performance) and has both positive (attraction) and negative (repulsion) dimensions.

As noted above, promotional information functions to encourage at least implicit negotiation on the part of consumers. Assuming this occurs at all (the promotion might be ignored, of course), it is in terms of the meaning (attributes and performance) and value (attraction or repulsion) experienced by receivers. And although a host of arrangements of attribute and performance dimensions may be at play, whether would-be buyers are prompted to move to the stage of explicit negotiation depends on whether their reactions to symbolic meanings are positive.

Propositions Underlying the Formulation

The foregoing notions may now be stated in more succinct, propositional form.

1. *The purpose of promotion is to create information and transmit it to an information market.*

This proposition asserts that sellers ultimately seek the buyer's willingness to conclude negotiation activity and commence the exchange process. For this to happen, however, it is first necessary that buyers obtain both the quality and quantity of information to support a reasonable exchange. For the individual buyer, all information is made up of symbols which convey meaning and which can be evaluated. If the meaning of the information, the attribute and performance dimensions of symbols, becomes clear to an individual, then value, positive or negative, can be attributed to that perceived meaning. If the attribute and performance dimensions of symbols are not clear—cannot be understood—then attributing any kind of value to them becomes an impossible task. When a buyer perceives meaning in promotional symbols and attributes to this meaning what for him is sufficiently positive value, he is then and only then prepared to undertake explicit negotiation activity with the view to concluding it through exchange. Where meaning is clear but not enough positive value is associated with it, or when meaning is clear but negative value is associated with it, or when meaning is not apparent at all, a deficiency of information exists. This information gap or deficiency is, in effect, a market for sellers' information —a market for promotional symbols.

2. *Information, in a promotional context, consist of clusters of symbols which are perceived as having meaning. The meaning of a symbol derives from its attribute and performance dimensions.*

Engaging the notions of role theory, it becomes apparent that the perception of a symbol's meaning is a highly individualistic phenomenon. Role propriety, whether on a physical characteristic (attribute) or functional (performance) basis, can and does vary to the extent that innumerable role typologies might be injected into the perceptual process. Also, the relative contribution of the attribute and performance dimensions to a symbol's meaning varies considerably among individuals, groups, and cultures [14].

It is possible to envision various combinations of a symbol's attribute and performance dimensions which result in a receiver attaching meaning to it. Again, take the case of lipstick. When a little girl has her first encounter with this symbol it is probably in terms of its attribute dimension. Lipstick has a set of physical characteristics which, for her exploratory purposes, may be appropriate (the tube may be shiny and therefore engaging) or inappropriate (the cap may resist her best efforts at removal). As the child observes her mother using lipstick, she begins to associate the symbol with an action pattern. Again, this may be appropriate (it makes Mommy pretty) or inappropriate (it means Mommy is going out again). In either event the meaning of lipstick is becoming more complete—is being learned—and, as this occurs, the child is increasingly able to judge the symbol, to assess its attributes and performance. That she has been able to do this is apparent in her use of lipstick when she dresses up to play house. In her simulated mother role lipstick has the meaning she has learned.

By the time our little girl has reached age twelve or thirteen, she has learned much more about the meaning of lipstick. The attribute dimension has become more clear in that she has more information on colors, fragrances, containers, prices, etc., any one of which characteristics may, for her role type, be appropriate or inappropriate. Similarly, the performance dimension has become more clear in that she is now very much aware of the uses (some appropriate, some not) to which lipstick can be put. Our teenager has substantially greater sources of information and ability to process it than does the child, and the social parameters appropriate to her behavior are significantly more numerous than those imposed on the child. The meanings attached to the lipstick symbol perforce are different.

The learning of attributes and performance, the ascription of meaning to symbols, is a continuous process. An individual plays many different roles in his life span and, as these change, so also do the meanings attached to symbols by the individual. Thus, although it is conceptually sound to segment mass audiences according to role type, communicators tend to find little operational comfort in such a strategy. Mass audiences reflect too many different role types (to say nothing of commitment) to be considered clusters of homogeneous receivers in any practical sense. The "typical" reaction to communication by a mass audience is just that; it is a modal result whose cognitive antecedents vary substantially among the individuals comprising the mass.

    3. The value of a symbol is that net degree of attraction or repulsion ascribed to the symobls meaning. The greater the meaning of a symbol—the more apparent the attribute and performance dimensions—the greater the value (positive or negative) that is attributed to it.[11]

It is in terms of a symbol's meaning that an individual reckons like or dislike. Value, that is, the net attractiveness or repulsiveness engendered, is a function of meaning—that is, of the dimensions attribute and performance. Meaning and value are directly related; the more meaning, the more value—positive or negative. Generally, value derives from accumulated meaning, which is to say that, when meaning is slight, the ratio of value response to it is less than proportional. As meaning increases in magnitude, however, the ratio of value response to it becomes more than proportional.[12]

    Value reflects a receiver's *net* reaction to a symbol's meaning. Reaction to meaning is hardly ever singularly "like" or "dislike"—attraction or repulsion. Rather, it is typically a combination, an ambivalence which, *in balance,* is either favorable or unfavorable.

    Dissonant perceptions of the meaning of a symbol usually lead to ambivalence in its evaluation. Often, this is in the nature of sensing what seems to be a mixture of appropriate and inappropriate meaning elements. Some products, for example, seem a mixed blessing: a fountain pen writes nicely but may leak; a ball-point pen may not leak but often skips when writing; wire wheels on a sports car afford "the classic look" but are a nuisance to clean; natural wood may be genuine but it lacks the durability of plastic laminates. On the basis of either consonant or dissonant meaning elements, however, individuals attach value to communicated symbols. In the process of doing so, they inject the variables, role commitment and role interaction. The general cases of the process are depicted in Table 1.

---

    [11] The dimensions of information specified in this paper (attribute, performance, value) are not to be confused with those empirically derived by Osgood *et al.* [16]. Although their measures: potency, activity, and evaluative are similar, respectively, to attribute, performance, and value, fundamental differences exist between semantic differentiation and the present formulation. In the former, potency, activity, and evaluative are the results of factor analyses; *each* is a dimension of meaning; and no functional relationship among the three is implied. In the present formulation, meaning has only two dimensions—attribute and performance—and these two are functionally related to value. Value is not a dimension of meaning but a bivariate function of its two dimensions.

    [12] In the sense of the mathematical notion of elasticity:

$$\text{in low meaning ranges,} \quad \frac{\Delta \% \text{ Value}}{\Delta \% \text{ Meaning}} < 1;$$

$$\text{in high meaning ranges,} \quad \frac{\Delta \% \text{ Value}}{\Delta \% \text{ Meaning}} > 1.$$

Table 1. Role, and the Meaning and Value of Information

Attribute Propriety	Performance Propriety	Dominant Meaning	Role Commitment	Intervening Effect of Role Interaction	Resultant Value
Yes	Yes	Attribute & Performance	Strong[1]	Insignificant[1]	Attraction
Yes	No	Attribute (Performance)	Moderate[2]	Conformity (Deviance)[2]	Attraction
No	Yes	(Attribute) Performance	Moderate[3]	(Deviance) Conformity[3]	Attraction
No	No	Attribute & Performance	Weak[4]	Insignificant[4]	Attraction
No	No	Attribute & Performance	Strong[1]	Insignificant[1]	Repulsion
No	Yes	(Attribute) Performance	Moderate[2]	Deviance (Conformity)[2]	Repulsion
Yes	No	Attribute (Performance)	Moderate[3]	(Conformity) Deviance[3]	Repulsion
Yes	Yes	Attribute & Performance	Weak[4]	Insignificant[4]	Repulsion

[1] If role commitment should be moderate, intervening effect of role interaction would be in the nature of conformity.

[2] If role commitment should be strong, intervening effect of role interaction would be in the nature of conformity, attribute dominating performance. If commitment should be weak, intervening effect would be toward deviance, performance dominating attribute.

[3] If role commitment should be strong, intervening effect of role interaction would be in the nature of conformity, performance dominating attribute. If commitment is weak, intervening effect would be toward deviance, attribute dominating performance.

[4] If role commitment should be moderate, intervening effect of role interaction would be in the nature of deviance.

As illustrated in this table, the symbol's meaning is perceived as some combination of attribute (appropriate to role or not) and performance (appropriate to role or not). Where the symbol's meaning (attribute *and* performance) is role appropriate, a strong role commitment operates to render the symbol attractive (positive value). In the same case, however, when the receiver manifests a weak role commitment, the symbol is rendered repulsive (negative value). In this latter case, where the symbol is exactly what the role type calls for, it is "rejected" by virtue of the fact that the receiver is *not* committed to role-sanctioned symbols—indeed, he may be committed to their antithesis. Such a receiver (weak commitment) ascribes attraction to symbols whose meaning (attribute *and* performance) is role-inappropriate. Contrariwise, a receiver with a strong role commitment sees role-inappropriate symbols as repulsive.

Where the meaning of symbols is not uniform, that is, where role propriety exists for the symbol's attributes *or* performance (but not both), another variable enters into a receiver's evaluative processes, that of role interaction. In these cases, the receiver's role commitment *typically* is moderate (see footnotes 2 and 3 in Table 1, however), which suggests that, in the face of meaning ambivalence, evaluation would be moot. This question is resolved and value is assigned, however, as the intervening effects of role interaction come into play.[13] Focusing on the dominant dimension of the symbol's meaning—either its attributes or performance, either but not both of which are appropriate or inappropriate—the receiver finds himself in a quandry. The symbol, on the strength of role commitment (which is moderate) alone, may be either attractive—have positive value—or repulsive—have negative value. The dilemma is resolved as role interaction is considered. Thus, although the symbol's value is ambiguous in the context of the role for which it is primarily considered, its attraction or repulsion becomes more evident as a broader context of additional, interacting roles played by the receiver is taken into account. There is, then, an intervening variable—role interaction—which operates in the receiver's evaluative processes when either an extreme commitment (strong or weak) is absent in the primary role for which the symbol is being assessed or where the meaning of the symbol is not uniform (where role propriety exists for attributes or performance, but not both).

---

[13] The case of uniform meaning (both attribute and performance being either appropriate or inappropriate) with moderate role commitment is not considered a special case (see footnotes 1 and 2 in Table 1, however) since such highly crystallized meaning is likely to be associated with either strong or weak role commitments. Highly crystallized meaning tends to be (in balance) either attractive or repulsive. Thus, even if moderate role commitments were involved, role-interaction intervening effects would operate to a far less significant extent than when meaning was not so highly crystallized.

4. *Positive evaluation of meaning leads to explicit negotiation; negative evaluation of meaning is associated with distortion of sellers' information.*

This proposition asserts that attractive and repulsive symbols engender different responses on the part of receivers. The differences, it should be noted, are not merely a matter of degree; they differ in nature.

When the meaning of a promotional symbol is such that a receiver assigns positive value to it, evaluates the meaning as attractive, he recognizes the symbol as useful in playing his role in the fashion he chooses(his commitment). It is reasonable, therefore, that the more (thus) useful a symbol is recognized to be, the more interested a receiver would be in making an overt effort to acquire it. He would be interested, to put it another way, in engaging in explicit negotiation with a seller with the ultimate purpose (but not necessary result) of concluding the process of exchange, consummating a transaction. Since attraction and acquisition cannot be causally isolated, one must be content with a probabilistic statement on this count. To that end, it is asserted that increases in positive value are accompanied by an increase in the probability that a receiver of promotional information will explicitly negotiate with a seller for the acquisition of whatever the information symbolizes.

When the meaning of a promotional symbol is such that a receiver assigns negative value to it, evaluates the meaning as repulsive, he recognizes the symbol as at variance with his notion of role playing. This means, first, that he will not be moved to explicitly negotiate for the purchase of whatever the symbol stands for. Second, this disposes the receiver to distort sellers' additional information (the intended, encoded ideas) so as to insure that it conforms to his initial assessment of the symbol. Once having categorized a symbol negatively, in other words, it is to the receiver's advantage in maintaining his role playing image to categorize *all* symbols reflecting the same product as negative. Not to do so implies dissonance [7]. And since at least some sellers' information would otherwise be attractive, distortion is the receiver's only recourse in maintaining confidence in his judgments.[14]

The relationship between negative value and distortion is likewise asserted probabilistically: Increases in negative value are accompanied by an increase in the probability that a receiver of promotional information will distort the seller's additional information. The cases of distortion and explicit negotiation are separate. Before a receiver has *any* probability of explicit negotiation, he must first have *no* probability of distortion, or vice versa.

---

[14] The reader should not infer from this that distortion is assumed to exist only as presently highlighted. Obviously, many factors, well enumerated in the literature of communication, can operate to "distort" messages.

An A Priori Model

The four preceding propositions may be formalized in a model. This a priori formulation is offered as suggestive, not proposed as definitive. Empirical validation, noted below, is necessary before any absolute parameters can be asserted.

In this model of promotional information three characteristics bear emphasis. First, value is posited to be a function of meaning (which itself is bivariate). Since it has been argued that value responds to cumulative meaning, in some ranges less than, and in other ranges more than proportionately, a parabolic function of value on meaning seems reasonable. Second, since meaning has been posited as a bivariate function of attribute and performance, which dimensions can combine in many, many ways, it is useful to construe meaning as a circular area. This renders the information model a function of meaning—that is, attribute and performance—and value, a circular paraboloid. Further, by considering the accumulation of meaning (areas) contained in the paraboloid surface, the probabilities of explicit negotiation and distortion may be thought of as analogous to volume. This raises the third characteristic of the model, which is that explicit negotiation—a function of positive evaluation, and distortion—a function of negative evaluation, are treated as distinct functions. As may be observed by reference to Figures 1 and 2, "positive value" is one distinct case; "negative value" is another. They are not just polar opposites of the same thing.

The following variable dictionary will aid in interpreting the model.

I: *Promotional Information.* This is a quadric surface, a circular paraboloid.

M: *Meaning.* This is a circular area, horizontally positioned.

m: *The Radius of (M).* Its square is the variable measure of (M) and (V).

a: *Attribute.* Its square is one of the determinants of (m^2) and (V).

p: *Performance.* Its square is one of the determinants of (m^2) and (V).

V: *Value.* The net attraction or repulsion associated with a given amount of meaning.

Pr[Φ]: *Probability of Explicit Negotiation.* This is the likelihood that a would-be buyer will exert overt effort to negotiate for the purchase of the product or service which is the subject of promotional information. It is a function of *accumulated* meaning associated with *positive* value.

Pr[Δ]: *Probability of Distortion.* This is the likelihood that a receiver of promotional information will distort (refuse to store) what meaning(s) have been intended in messages by sellers. It is a function of *accumulated* meaning associated with *negative* value.

As shown in Figures 1 and 2, promotional information (I) can be represented by three variables, attribute (a), performance (p), and value (V). That is,

(1) $$I = f(a, p, V).$$

First consider Figure 1. This depicts the case where meaning (M) is evaluated positively—that is, where value (V) is positive. The information surface in Figure 1 can be expressed by the equation

(2) $$V_j = a_i^2 + p_i^2; \quad 0 \leq V_j \leq \omega.$$

This says simply that the height of the parabolic surface is the sum of the squares of the two components of meaning and the value (the height) can be no less than zero and no more (in an operational sense) than omega.

Since (I) is a *circular* paraboloid any of its horizontal cross sections represents a circle. Any such cross section, then, can be expressed by the equation

(3) $$m_i^2 = a_i^2 + p_i^2; \quad 0 \leq m_i \leq n.$$

In other words, the square of the radius of any horizontal cross section of (I) equals the sum of the squares of the two components of meaning.

Figure 1. Promotional Information (Positive Value)

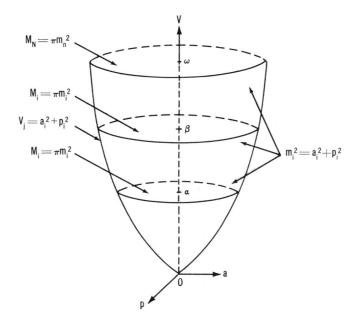

The radius of (M) can be as small as zero and as large as "n."

From equations (2) and (3) it can be observed that the sum of the squares of attribute and performance $(a_i^2 + p_i^2)$ equals both value (V_j) and the radius of meaning (m_i^2). By transitivity, then,

$$(4) \qquad\qquad V_j = m_i^2.$$

This statement says that, for any given amount of meaning (M_i), the square of its radius equals the associated value.

Since meaning has been defined as a circular area it may be represented by the equation

$$(5) \qquad\qquad M_i = \pi m_i^2; \; 0 \leq M_i \leq N,$$

where (m_i) is the radius of the circular area. Meaning (M_i) can be as small as zero or as large as "N."

Since, from equation (4), the relationship between (V) and (m^2) is known, equation (5) can be rewritten substituting (V) for (m^2). That is

$$(6) \qquad\qquad M_i = \pi V_j.$$

This is to say that any given meaning area (M_i), divided by pi, yields the value (V_j) level associated with that meaning.

It remains to relate the foregoing to the probability of negotiation $(Pr[\Phi])$. For those versed in integral calculus this involves a routine procedure. Intuitively, the rationale is as follows. Meaning (M_i) has been defined as a circular, cross-sectional, area. The quadric surface (I) may be construed as an infinite number of circles, of increasing radius, placed one atop another. Now the sum of the *areas* of this infinite number of circles is the *volume* contained in (I). In the model, volume is analogous to the probability of negotiation, since it represents *accumulated* meaning.

The total volume contained in (I), by the nature of probability, must equal one. This total probability of negotiation, using equation (6) and the foregoing rationale, may be expressed as

$$(7) \qquad\qquad Pr[\Phi] = \pi[\int_0^\omega (V) \, dV] = 1.$$

Now consider the case where meaning is associated with negative value. This case is displayed in Figure 2.

Only a few minor adjustments are required to express this case. Equation (1) still holds since all that has been done is to "flip" the surface shown in Figure 1. Equation (2) must now read

$$(8) \qquad\qquad -V_j = a_i^2 + p_i^2; \; 0 \geq V_j \geq -\omega.$$

This says simply that attribute and performance result in negative value.

Equation (3) holds for this case also, except that "d" is prescribed as the larger limit for (m_i) rather than "n."

One need add only a minus sign to equation (4) so that it reads, for this case

$$(9) \qquad -V_j = m_i^2.$$

Equation (5) requires adjustment only in the larger limit constraining (M_i). For this case this is (D) instead of (N).

Equation (6) must now read

$$(10) \qquad M_i = \pi(-V_j).$$

Finally, the limits of integration in equation (7) must be changed to accommodate negative value. The total probability of distortion is expressed by

$$(11) \qquad Pr[\Delta] = \pi[\int_0^{-\infty}(V) \, dV] = 1.$$

The probability of distortion can be no less than zero and no more than one.

The reader will recognize the great similarity in Figure 1 (positive value) and Figure 2 (negative value). In spite of their mathematical similarity, however, they reflect two very different situations.

The case where meaning generates positive value is intuitively plausible. The obverse case, however, is not so clear. When the attribute and performance dimensions of meaning are, in balance, evaluated negatively, information receivers are repulsed. Negative value obtains. The significance of this is that it precludes receivers from storing the information *intended* by the seller—the sender of the message. It causes receivers to distort or reject seller's information. The more repulsive the meaning (the more negative the value ascribed to it) the greater is the likelihood that information decoded will differ from information encoded.

Now before a would-be buyer can be persuaded to negotiate—that is, before positive value can come into effect—he must first be dissuaded of his negative value; purged, as it were, of all the meaning giving rise to repulsion. The optimal result, *in this situation,* is to effect the case where meaning (M_i) = 0 and thus where ($-V_j$) = 0. At this point the probability that the receiver will store the seller's informtion is certain; i.e., $Pr[\Delta]$ = 0. This point should not be confused with one's probability of negotiating for, where (M_i) = 0, $Pr[\Phi]$ = 0. It says simply that before persuasion ($+V_j$) must come (if necessary) dissuasion away from ($-V_j$).

Figure 2.   Promotional Information (Negative Value)

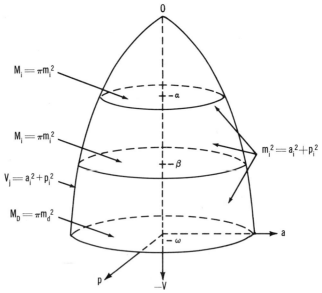

In sum, it may be observed that the cases of positive and negative values are *not* continuous. One does not "move" a would-be buyer from $(-\omega$ to $+\omega)$ on the value scale in one continuous sweep because, in the range $0 \leq V_j \leq \omega$, the model reflects the probability that a person will *negotiate* $(\Pr[\Phi])$; whereas, in the range $0 \geq V_j \geq -\omega$, the model reflects the probability that a person will *distort*, or fail, or refuse to store seller's information $(\Pr[\Delta])$. Clearly, these are two different things being measured.

Intensely practical problems might be approached through the model. For example, in the case where positive value is involved, the additional meaning required to raise value from one level, say, (α), to a higher level, (β), can be approximated by computing

(12) $\pi[\int_\alpha^\beta (V)\ dV]$.

By the nature of the model (see Figure 1), increasing value from (α) to (β) is equivalent to increasing the probability of negotiation.

An analogous situation obtains where negative value is involved (Figure 2). The amount of meaning that must be dispelled in order for negative value to be reduced from a level $(-\beta)$ to another level $(-\alpha)$ is given by

(13) $\pi[\int_{-\alpha}^{-\beta} (V)\ dV]$.

This reduction in meaning brings about a reduction in the probability of distortion of promotional information.

The nature of the model—particularly equations (4) and (9)—is such that value responds to meaning far greater in the higher ranges than in the lower. This is to say that it is relatively easier to generate positive value with a certain increment of meaning *given* that an accumulation of meaning already obtains; similarly with the case of negative value. The "purging" of a given amount of meaning will reduce repulsion far more when there is a great deal of it present than when there is not. The last vestige of repulsion is difficult to remove.

These relationships are anything but novel. The model merely quantifies them. It also accommodates the fact that a given level of meaning—and hence of value and likelihood of negotiation or distortion—can be the result of a great many combinations of attribute and performance. Indeed, each horizontal cross section of the information surface is an iso-value curve—a locus of points satisfying the condition ($m_i^2 = a_i^2 + p_i^2$). Since any product or service may be more susceptible to persuasion along one of these dimensions of meaning than the other, this relationship is very useful. It affords clues to product design, packaging, pricing, selling methods, and content analysis of promotional messages—both for a seller's product or service and its competition—to cite just a few examples.

Toward Validation

An a priori model is useful for purposes of discussion and explanation, but to qualify as a predictive device, it must pass the difficult test of empirical validation. Toward this end, some issues should be noted.

The model posited requires independent measures of several variables, which may be grouped into three classes: criterion variables, predictor variables, and classification variables. The first category, criterion variables, are those to be explained—the dependent variables, as it were. They consist of positive or negative value and the probability of a receiver explicitly negotiating with or distorting sellers' information. The second class, predictor variables, are those that explain—the independent variables, so to speak. They comprise the dimensions of meaning, attribute and performance. The third category, classification variables, are in the nature of typological—those which locate an information receiver in the broad spectrum of all possible information receivers. These variables are role type, role commitment, and role interaction.

Although the model presented is fairly simple in structure, a moment's reflection on the variables incorporated into it suggests a massive array of testing problems.

With regard to the first category of variables, for example, how might attraction or repulsion be measured? To say nothing of the morass of problems associated with scaling such notions, do behavioral scientists have adequate concepts of "attraction" and "repulsion"?[15] Are they simply like-dislike notions or are more complex ideations involved? Also, to speak of the probability of a receiver explicitly negotiating or distorting is *not* to speak of the certainty of these events in any deterministic sense. In terms of measurement, this raises the thorny issue of how such probabilities should be reckoned. Should a receiver's intentions (subjective probabilities) or his behavior (objective probabilities) be considered more appropriate? It would seem that reasonable arguments could be made in behalf of either. Perhaps this suggests a prudent application of Bayesian principles [21], whereby a receiver's prior probabilities could be revised on the strength of additional information.

As regards the predictor variables, attribute and performance, substantial scaling problems exist. Not only does the posited model assume these to be measured on an interval scale (itself a heroic assumption), but it also assumes that the zero point on each scale can be readily specified. Given that zero on these scales is a function of the receiver's perception of role, however, it likely varies among receivers. Because perceptions of role vary among individuals, what is appropriate (and to what extent) for one in terms of attributes and/or performance may not be appropriate for another. Although meaning (M) is measured in the model by the sum of the squares of attribute and performance ($M = \pi m^2$ where $m^2 = a^2 + p^2$), it is important from the promoter's standpoint to know whether on either or both dimensions of meaning the symbol is perceived as appropriate or inappropriate.

The classification variables, which "type" the individual receiver, present empirical problems simply because of the infinite number of role types potentially at play. In terms of which role does the receiver "see" the communicated symbol? To what extent is role interaction involved and what is its nature? Is the interaction complementary or conflicting? How does the individual's commitment to *each* of the operant roles affect his perception of the symbol communicated? How should one measure role type, role commitment, and role interaction? To what extent does the distance between realized and ideal role perception affect one's reaction to a communicated symbol?

If the reader is impressed that this section offers questions and not answers his comprehension of the authors' intention is correct. The foregoing reflects the kinds of questions with which we are wrestling in working with the model. To imply that we have no such questions would be sophomoric and dishonest. The model presented in this paper is an attempt to apply workable structure to the terribly complex process of marketing communication—nothing more or less. If it does this, the nature of empirical research in this and related areas is somewhat more clearly prescribed. If it does not, one more false door may be ignored.

---

[15] A very direct discussion of scaling may be found in [22], pp. 21-30.

REFERENCES

1. Bar-Hillel, Y., and R. Carnap, "Semantic Information," in W. Jackson, ed., *Communication Theory*. Butterworths Scientific Publications, London, 1953, pp. 503-512.
2. Berlo, D. K., *The Process of Communication*. Holt, Rinehart and Winston, Inc., New York, 1960.
3. Bryson, L., ed., *The Communication of Ideas*. Harper & Brothers, New York, 1948.
4. Cherry, C., *On Human Communication*. John Wiley & Sons, Inc., New York, 1957.
5. Davison, W. P., "On the Effects of Communication," *Public Opinion Quarterly,* Vol. XXIV (1960), pp. 344-360.
6. Engel, J. F., "Are Automobile Purchasers Dissonant Consumers?" *Journal of Marketing,* Vol. 27, No. 2, pp. 55-58.
7. Festinger, L., *A Theory of Cognitive Dissonance*. Row, Peterson and Company, Evanston, Illinois, 1957.
8. Harrah, D., "A Model of Semantic Information and Message Evaluation," in F. Massarik and P. Ratoosh, eds., *Mathematical Explorations in Behavioral Science*. Irwin-Dorsey Press, Homewood, Illinois, 1965, pp. 56-65.
9. Hayakawa, S. I., *Language in Thought and Action,* Second Edition. Harcourt, Brace & World, Inc., New York, 1964.
10. Howard, J. A., *Marketing: Executive and Buyer Behavior*. Columbia University Press, New York, 1963.
11. Kernan, J. B., W. P. Dommermuth, and M. S. Sommers, *Promotion: An Introductory Analysis*. McGraw-Hill Book Company, New York, forthcoming.
12. Kernan, J. B. and J. U. McNeal, "The Closest Thing to Measuring Advertising Effectiveness," *Business Horizons,* Vol. 7, No. 4, pp. 73-80.
13. Kernan, J. B. and M. S. Sommers, "The Behavioral Matrix: A Closer Look at the Industrial Buyer," *Business Horizons,* Vol. 9, No. 2, pp. 59-72.
14. Lipset, S., "The Value Patterns of Democracy: A Case Study in Comparative Values," *American Sociological Review,* Vol. 28 (1963), pp. 515-531.
15. McNeal, J. U., ed., *Dimensions of Consumer Behavior*. Appleton-Century-Crofts, New York, 1965.
16. Osgood, C. E., G. J. Suci, and P. H. Tannenbaum, *The Measurement of Meaning*. University of Illinois Press, Urbana, 1957.
17. Palda, K. S., "The Hypothesis of a Hierarchy of Effects: A Partial Evaluation," *Journal of Marketing Research,* Vol. III, No. 1, pp. 13-24.
18. Rose, A. M., ed., *Human Behavior and Social Processes*. Houghton Mifflin Company, Boston, 1962.
19. Shannon, C. E. and W. Weaver, *The Mathematical Theory of Communication*. University of Illinois Press, Urbana, 1949.

20. Shibutani, T., *Society and Personality: An Interactionist Approach to Social Psychology*. Prentice-Hall, Inc., Englewood Cliffs, New Jersey, 1961.

21. Schlaifer, R., *Probability and Statistics for Business Decisions*. McGraw-Hill Book Company, New York. 1959.

22. Siegel, S., *Nonparametric Statistics for the Behavioral Sciences*. McGraw-Hill Book Company, New York, 1958.

23. Siegel, S. (in collaboration with A. E. Siegel and J. M. Andrews), *Choice, Strategy, and Utility*. McGraw-Hill Book Company, New York, 1964.

24. Sommers, M. S., *The Use of Product Symbolism to Differentiate Social Strata*. University of Houston Center for Research in Business & Economics, 1964.

25. Westley, B. H. and M. S. MacLean, Jr., "A Conceptual Model for Communications Research," *Journalism Quarterly*, Winter, 1957, pp. 31-38.

V

MODEL BUILDING AND MARKETING THEORY

27

Formal Reasoning and Marketing Strategy

HARRY A. LIPSON

The past 15 years have seen the glorification of formal systems and their imposition where they have not been used before. The newer writings concerning decision-making processes should make marketers conscious of using formal systems to solve marketing problems. Several recent books have been specifically concerned with the application of formal systems to marketing.[1]

The search for formal models or conceptual structures of marketing stems from those who desire orderly, systematic, formal reasoning from which inferences can be applied to single instances. These persons believe that every investigation requires a model or theory to develop an optimal decision. The basic tool is not mathematics—it is formalizing.

It may seem that mathematics is the basic tool, but this is not the case. A theory is a set of mathematical formulas based upon a system of axioms, postulates, and definitions plus procedural rules from logic (formal reasoning).

Marketing men have been essentially empiricists rather than rationalists. They often start with data (from activities that are working reasonably well) and work through a series of intuitive leaps to generalizations. They sense that choice is not a mechanical but a creative act. They feel that

Reprinted with permission from the *Journal of Marketing,* national quarterly publication of the American Marketing Association, Vol. 26 (October, 1962), pp. 1-5.

[1] Frank M. Bass, Robert D. Buzzell, Mark R. Greene, William Lazer, Edgar A. Pessemier, Donald L. Shawver, Abraham Shuchman, Chris A. Theodore, and George W. Wilson, *Mathematical Models and Methods in Marketing* (Homewood, Illinois: Richard D. Irwin, Inc., 1961); Harold Bierman, Jr., Lawrence E. Fouraker, and Robert K. Jaedicke, *Quantitative Analysis for Business Decisions* (Homewood, Illinois: Richard D. Irwin, Inc., 1961); and Robert Schlaifer, *Probability and Statistics for Business Decisions* (New York: McGraw-Hill Book Company, Inc., 1960).

skilled executives may make many nonrational and/or unconscious decisions which are good decisions.

In the current formulation of marketing strategy, there are those who use formal models and those who do not. Those who build and/or use these formal models believe they have constructed a theoretical approach (or foundation) by means of which to make better marketing decisions. They believe that production has been rationalized; they suggest that distribution likewise may be rationalized.

The present article is a survey of the contribution of the formalists to the development of marketing strategy. The annotated footnotes provide a reference source for those persons wishing to investigate the application of formal thinking to marketing strategy.

The Formulation of Marketing Strategy

In the context of formal thinking, strategy may be considered a sequence of decision rules which give a complete description of the marketing practices of a company, their order, and their timing.[2] These rules are formulated so as to provide for the best action in the event of any one of all possible happenings. The essence of strategy defined in this manner is that, in planning, the future is never known, so that the decision maker should provide in his plan for all eventualities.

Strategy implies that all dimensions of the marketing plan have been consciously integrated. The term "marketing mix" is frequently used to describe the state of these dimensions at any given point in time. Some believe that a marketing strategy consists of two parts: (1) operating objectives (called targets or goals), and (2) combination of instruments (called marketing mix or means).[3]

A great deal has been written and said about the sequence of steps involved in the development of recurrent and continuous market plans. There is some question as to the order of the first three steps because of their interdependence. Usually the steps are given in this order: (1) determination of goals or objectives, (2) market position audit, (3) generation of strategies, (4) design of the program, and (5) acceptance and installation.[4]

---

[2] John A. Howard, *Marketing Management* (Homewood, Illinois: Richard D. Irwin, Inc., 1957), pp. 36-40.

[3] Alfred R. Oxenfeldt, "The Formulation Of A Market Strategy," in *Managerial Marketing,* edited by Edward J. Kelley and William Lazer (Homewood, Illinois: Richard D. Irwin, Inc., 1958), pp. 264-272, at p. 267.

[4] Edward S. McKay, "How To Plan And Set Up Your Marketing Program," Blueprint for an Effective Marketing Program, Marketing Series Number 91 (New York: American Management Association, 1954), pp. 14f; and "Theory And Practice of Market Planning," *Cost and Profit Outlook,* Vol. II (July-August, 1958), pp. 1-4.

It is difficult to set up company objectives without knowledge of the situation of the company in its industry. Often the market-position audit must be taken before the goals or objectives can be identified and stated. Those experienced in market planning tend to regard alternative goals as hypotheses to be tested. They select the appropriate objective, and the action program designed to achieve the goal, by reviewing the alternative action plans or sequence of steps necessary for achievement of the goal. It is during these initial explorations in the planning process that strategy is significant.

It must be stressed that the initial phases of creating plans for marketing activities may be a circular process. The selection of the optimum alternatives is based upon the information fed back to the preceding phases. Feasibility, then, becomes the decision criterion by which the desired goal and the approach to achieve the goal are rationally selected.

The Goals of Marketing Strategy

There is a considerable division of opinion as to the role and goals of business enterprise in our economy. Survival, growth, profits, market position, size, degree of horizontal and vertical integration—and other goals of marketers—arouse vigorous debate. It must be recognized that there has been a shifting focus of objectives which characterize "the evolution of modern business—first, from a focus on profit for the owner to striving for market position and success against competition, and more recently to a focus on growth in which there is a continuing planned effort to enlarge the size of the market." [5]

As Joel Dean says, a business firm is designed to make profits.[6] John A. Howard hedges by saying that "strategy is designed to maximize long-term profits within the limits determined by top management's view of the company's basic objectives." [7] In his view this is the ideal toward which a firm strives.

The argument can be raised about maximum profits over what period of time and for whom? Herbert A. Simon argues that the notion of "satisficing" rather than maximization is significant.[8] Satisficing has long been of more interest to the psychologist than to the economist. In many psycho-

---

[5] J. B. McKitterick, "What Is The Marketing Management Concept?" *The Frontiers of Marketing Thought and Science,* edited by Frank .M. Bass (Chicago, Illinois: American Marketing Association, 1957), pp. 71-82, at p. 77.

[6] Joel Dean, *Managerial Economics* (New York: Prentice-Hall, Inc., 1951), p. 3.

[7] John A. Howard, same reference as footnote 2, p. 36.

[8] Herbert A. Simon, "Theories of Decision-Making In Economics and Behavioral Science," *American Economic Review,* Vol. 49 (June, 1959), pp. 255-283, at p. 262f.

logical theories a motive to act is based upon a drive, and action ends when the drive is satisfied. Simon believes, like many others, that these models of satisficing are richer than models of maximizing behavior.

Economists have given us the assumptions of perfect knowledge and costless transactions. A real question for marketing men is the optimal method and cost of reducing the uncertainty from inadequate information. This is the aim of much research. The strategy to be followed by a marketer must come from a study of the firm itself, from study and analysis of competition, and from investigation of the market. How the marketer will solve his basic problems will depend upon the goals set for the business.

The Conceptualizing of Marketing Decisions

The use of models in decision making should be familiar to those making marketing decisions and marketing plans. Models are used to show how the variables or factors in the particular operation will interact in the proposed solutions. These models, whether verbal, mathematical, mechanical, or physical, are a simplified framework of an operation, representing only those aspects which are of primary importance to the problem under study.

The empiricist tends to follow this sequence of steps in his research program: (1) probe, (2) look, (3) form the problem, (4) obtain data, and (5) develop a model. Using this method for developing marketing strategy involves less risk, but it is time-consuming. So much effort is spent in looking and relooking and reworking the material.

The rationalist notion of the scientific method of research is to: (1) formulate the problem, (2) develop the model, (3) obtain data, (4) draw the inferences—deductive conclusion from findings, and (5) recycle and rework the model.

Another way of looking at this sequence is to: (1) focus on one or more goals, (2) isolate the more obvious variables, (3) state the problem in its simplest terms, that is, by formulas using symbolic logic, (4) work out the solution using the formulas developed to have a *first approximation* to the answer, and (5) rework the problem after being alerted to the errors or variables found in reality which determine changes in the answer.

Those trained in the newer approaches to decision making are using the rationalist sequence of steps. Many disciplines converge on decision making. These include anthropology, business administration, economics, engineering, logic, mathematics, philosophy, political science, psychology, sociology, and statistics. All are interested in control processes.

The social scientist and the marketing planner have been criticized for never knowing when they have solved a problem in the optimal manner.

Proponents of the rigorous models believe better and precise answers may be forthcoming in the future if marketers are informed in some of these areas—decision theory, organization theory, game theory, operations research, and linear programing.

Decisions and Uncertainty

Consumers and business managers must make many decisions or choices for many purposes. Decision theory (mathematical or physical models) concerns expressed preferences. The empirical study of individuals' choices has been relatively undeveloped and is only coming into prominence as a field of investigation.[9]

The books giving attention to analytical economic relationships between multiple markets, multiple plants, and multiple products are welcome additions to the literature.[10] Marketing managers looking for help in making decisions about market allocation and segmentation, price and product discrimination in buying and selling, and the problems of disequilibrium and dynamics in market behavior should be familiar with these tools.

There is a need for businessmen to recognize that marginal analysis may be used to make decisions under conditions of uncertainty based on anticipation of the future. The marginal productivity of inputs in relation to outputs may sharpen the thinking of executives about location, sales force, channels, promotion, and pricing problems. By focusing attention on incremental costs, improved decisions may be obtained in seeking the proper "marketing mix." These tools, pertinent to marketing, require further sharpening to reduce uncertainty. But such sharpening is not a job only for the pure theorists; they and marketing men must work together.

Quantitative analysis, including mathematics and statistics and parts of accounting, is receiving increasing recognition. A significant aspect of quantitative analysis, as it applies to marketing men, is statistical decision theory and hypotheses testing. Such tools of quantitative analysis are es-

---

[9] An account covering the psychological and economic theories of riskless and risky decision-making is found in Ward Edwards, "Behavioral Decision Theory" (unpublished paper, Engineering Psychology Group, Willow Run Laboratories, University of Michigan). For a review article covering 1930-1954, see Ward Edwards, "The Theory of Decision-Making," *Psychological Bulletin,* Vol. 51 (September, 1954), pp. 380-417. A nonmathematical review is found in Kenneth J. Arrow, "Utilities, Attitudes, Choices: A Review Note," *Econometrica,* Vol. 26 (January, 1958), pp. 1-23.

[10] Dean, same reference as footnote 6; and for general numerical prediction techniques under uncertainty, see Milton H. Spencer and Louis Siegelman, *Managerial Economics* (Homewood, Illinois: Richard D. Irwin, Inc., 1959). A contribution to business management concerning marketing strategy is found in Robert A. Schlaifer, *Probability and Statistics For Business Decisions* (New York: McGraw-Hill Book Co., Inc., 1959).

sential to a critical understanding and evaluation of many marketing problems, and constitute the analytical equipment necessary to measure the effects of alternative decisions in marketing.

Marketing men need to be familiar with the literature concerning decision processes and decision criteria.[11] They need to understand that the decision criterion under certainty (game against nature) is an extremely special case. There is only a one-column matrix, for the decision maker knows the payout of each strategy. It is just necessary to scan the column for the highest payoff to make a choice. Under uncertainty, the decision criteria may be that of pessimism, optimism, minimax, least regret, or the rational approach of the highest payout.

Organization Theory

The individual decision premise becomes the smallest unit of description in the rational model approach to decision making. It is recognized that individuals live in an environment which limits choices. Here the economist and the social psychologist have a common ground for studying rational behavior and intuitive choice.[12]

Alderson emphasizes that consumer-buyers are essentially problem solvers in the face of uncertainty. He emphasizes that marketing behavior is primarily group behavior. It is his thesis that each individual acts as a member of an organized behavior system whose formation and persistence is explained by expectations. He goes on to say that a behavior system may be observed as a: (1) power system, (2) system of communications, (3) system of inputs and outputs, and (4) system of internal and external adjustments.

To develop good strategy, marketing men need to be familiar with the classical organization theories of Taylor, Gilbreth, Bernard, Mooney, Gulick, and Urwick, as well as recent literature. Marketers will not understand the Aldersonian notions without familiarity and understanding of the lit-

[11] A number of books have been written in recent years about decision theory. For a simple introduction see Irwin D. F. Bross, *Design For Decision* (New York: The Macmillan Company, 1953). For a good annotated bibliography, see Paul Wasserman and Fred S. Silander, *Decision-Making: An Annotated Bibliography* (Ithaca, New York: Graduate School of Business and Public Administration, Cornell University, 1958).

[12] See Wroe Alderson, *Marketing Behavior and Executive Action* (Homewood, Illinois: Richard D. Irwin, Inc., 1957); C. Joseph Clawson, "Quantifying Motivation Research To Predict Consumer Behavior," *Advancing Marketing Efficiency,* edited by Lynn H. Stockman (Chicago, Illinois: American Marketing Association, 1959), pp. 54-70, at pp. 55ff; and Robert A. Dahl, Mason Haire, and Paul F. Lazarsfeld, *Social Science Research on Business: Product and Potential* (New York: Columbia University Press, 1959).

erature on administration.[13] Here they will come to grips with the fact that the model of the economic man and the model of the administrative man are not the same. Here they will find that the theory of the firm and the theory of organization are not the same. The decision researcher considers this area of investigation an important influence upon strategy.

Game Theory and Simulation

Game theory deals with competitive situations in which two or more rivals have a common goal, such as that of obtaining a larger share of the market, and also have various strategies with attendant rewards in terms of increased or decreased share of the market.[14] By means of matrix algebra, an optimal strategy can be computed for each set of rivals. This optimal strategy has the unique property that it cannot be defeated even if it is known to the other contestant. Only a limited class of problems can be solved by this method, but one important type of problem than can often be solved by this method is that of plant investment.

Game theory is a formulation of optimal strategy. In the business world each of two or more rivals is trying to achieve maximum payoff for certain actions. A good strategy presumes that each firm wants to leave itself in the best possible position if the worst happens. This is similar to Alderson's "power principle," that each firm acts in such a way as to improve its position to act the next time.[15]

Strategic games are becoming increasingly popular as a method of training executives to make complex sets of decisions under pressure. While they may be overly simplified, not fully realistic, and controlled by rules not found in the business world, the person participating in the game has an opportunity to analyze the complex relationships, use accounting data, appreciate the fast computation of information, and discover the high cost of information acquired by experience. Attempts to solve the problems by rules of thumb based on experience or intuition may lead to costly decisions

---

[13] See James G. March and Herbert A. Simon, *Organizations* (New York: John Wiley & Sons, Inc., 1958). An unusually good analysis of decision-making processes in administrative organizations is found in Herbert A. Simon, *Administrative Behavior,* 2d ed. (New York: The Macmillan Company, 1957). Simon's essays from early journal articles are found in Herbert A. Simon, *Models of Man* (New York: John Wiley & Sons, Inc., 1957). A general book is Mason Haire, editor, *Modern Organization Theory* (New York: John Wiley & Sons, 1959).

[14] See Martin Shubik, *Strategy and Market Structure* (New York: John Wiley & Sons, 1959); R. Duncan Luce and Howard Raiffa, *Games and Decisions* (New York: John Wiley & Sons, Inc., 1957); and John McDonald, "Applications of Game Theory In Business and Industry" (paper read at Games Symposium of the American Association for the Advancement of Science, St. Louis, December 29, 1952). A simple book on game theory is John D. Williams, *The Compleat Strategist* (New York: McGraw-Hill Book Co., Inc., 1954).

[15] Alderson, same reference as footnote 12, p. 56.

which do not bring about optimal achievement of the goals of the firm as stated by the participants before they begin to make decisions.

Business simulation is being used with a considerable degree of success to work out the next sequence of moves by a company in a particular situation. In this type of analysis the essential characteristics of a system are stated in a set of mathematical equations. The variables in the set of equations represent the various internal and external factors affecting the operation of the system. Once it is constructed, the model is tested by inserting historical data as values in the variables, in order to determine how closely the answers agree with past performance of the system. A number of major firms are now working on simulators to look at policy choices. By means of these models, different operating conditions (such as change in price) can be simulated and the results determined without costly experimentation within the industry itself.

Operations Research and Linear Programing

Operations research endeavors to provide managers of organizations with a scientific basis for solving problems involving the interaction of components of the total organization or operating system.[16] The emphasis is on the word *research*. Operations research attempts to prescribe the best decisions for as large a portion of the total organization as possible.

In the narrow sense, operations research may be considered a formal, really mechanistic, quantitative model stating the situation. Some of the important models used by operations researchers in solving problems are the linear programing model, information theory, general systems analysis, inventory models, waiting-line models, and sequencing or programing of resource allocation. The objective of the operations research group is to predict informed decisions. Both operations research and marketing research try to give all the information they can to the executive so he can make conscious choices. Operations research contributes to marketing strategy the systems concept, the model concept, and emphasis on experimentation.

Applications of linear programing, a computational procedure that will maximize a linear equation subject to linear restraints, may be used wherever there is a product-mix or input-mix problem with linear relation-

---

[16] See C. West Churchman, Russell L. Ackoff, E. Leonard Arnoff, *Introduction to Operations Research* (New York: John Wiley & Sons, 1957); Charles D. Flagle, William H. Huggins, and Robert H. Roy, *Operations Research and Systems Engineering* (Baltimore: Johns Hopkins Press, 1960); Martin Kenneth Starr and David W. Miller, *Executive Decisions and Operations Research* (Englewood Cliffs, New Jersey: Prentice-Hall, 1960); and Maurice Sasieni, Arthur Yaspan, and Lawrence Friedman, *Operations Research Methods and Problems* (New York: John Wiley & Sons, 1959).

ships among the variables.[17] Such problems can be solved to yield minimum expense or maximum profits by programing. Problems involving make or buy decisions, transportation movement or warehousing shipments, machine allocation, and problems requiring adjustment of production to a seasonal sales pattern are among those which have been solved by this technique. Nonlinear programing and dynamic programing involve mathematical concepts of a very esoteric nature.

One of the significant arguments occurring between those engaged in operations research is whether the scientist is obliged to study nonrational behavior or to include social morality within the scope of his activities. In the interest of prescribing the optimal (most efficient) decision, many scientists do not feel it necessary to consider the impact upon the people and society involved. Some leaders of the operations research movement argue that it will be possible to measure these important considerations.[18]

Implications

Marketing men can ignore the formal reasoning approach, or let others develop it, or learn the formal symbolic language so they can use it.

Those who are using these new techniques believe they may be able to develop improved marketing strategy, provided all of the variables are included and correctly stated in the new models. If the formal method is used, the marketing strategist may be able to make relatively better decisions, provided he has placed the proper values in his model.

---

[17] For discussion of linear programming, see Harvey C. Bunke, *Linear Programming: A Primer,* Study No. 7 (Ames, Iowa: State University of Iowa, 1960); case on advertising strategy in John G. Kemeny, J. Laurie Snell, and Gerald L. Thompson, *Introduction to Finite Mathematics* (New York: Prentice-Hall, Inc., 1957); Robert Dorfman, Paul A. Samuelson, and Robert M. Solow, *Linear Programming and Economic Analysis* (New York: McGraw-Hill Book Co., Inc., 1958).

[18] C. West Churchman, *Prediction and Optimal Decisions* (New York: Prentice-Hall, Inc., 1960); Thomas A. Cowan, "Experience And Experiment," *Philosophy of Science,* Vol. 26 (April, 1959), pp. 74-84.

28

The Role of Models in Marketing

WILLIAM LAZER

Behavioral sciences and quantitative methods are both in the forefront in the current development and extension of marketing knowledge. It is no mere coincidence that both make frequent reference to two concepts: *models* and *systems*. Certainly models and systems have become powerful interpretive tools.[1]

Models and systems have relevance to such significant marketing problems as: (1) developing marketing concepts and enriching the marketing language by introducing terms that reflect an operational viewpoint and orientation; (2) providing new methods and perspectives for problem-solving; (3) conducting marketing research and designing experiments; (4) developing marketing theories; (5) measuring the effectiveness of marketing programs.

Although they may not be recognized as such, marketing models are fairly widely applied by both practitioners and academicians. The use of analogies, constructs, verbal descriptions of systems, "idealizations," and graphic representations are quite widespread in marketing. For example, pricing models, physical distribution models, models of marketing institutions, and advertising models are useful marketing tools.

Definition of Marketing Models

A model is simply the perception or diagramming of a complex or a system. In marketing, it involves translating perceived marketing relation-

Reprinted with permission from the *Journal of Marketing,* national quarterly publication of the American Marketing Association, Vol. 26 (April, 1962), pp. 9-14.

[1] Paul Meadows, "Models, Systems and Science," *American Sociological Review*. Vol. 22 (February, 1957) pp. 3-9, at p. 3.

ships into constructs, symbols, and perhaps mathematical terms. For example, an internally consistent set of statements concerning wholesaling, advertising, merchandising, or pricing comprises a model. It relates in a logical manner certain constructs or axioms that are envisaged.

Models are really the bases for marketing theories, since they are the axioms or assumptions on which marketing theories are founded. They furnish the underlying realities for theory construction. Where the perceived relationships are expressed in mathematical terms, we have a mathematical model. In this sense, any consistent set of mathematical statements about some aspect of marketing can be regarded as a model.

All marketing models are based on suppositions or assumptions. These assumptions do not correspond exactly with the real marketing world. Usually they are employed to simplify an existing marketing situation. Therefore, models cannot depict marketing activities exactly. Moreover, no matter how precise mathematical models may be, they do not correct themselves for false assumptions.

Model Building

There are two approaches to the construction of marketing models: *abstraction* and *realization*.[2]

In abstraction, a real world situation is perceived and it is mapped into a model. If it is mapped into a mathematical system, a mathematical model results. This is illustrated by Figure 1.

In abstraction, the model builder must perceive of a marketing situation in a way that permits him to recognize the relationships between a

Figure 1. Model Building by Abstraction

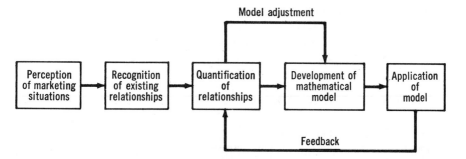

[2] See C. H. Coombs, H. Raiffa, and R. M. Thrall, "Some Views On Mathematical Models and Measurement Theory," in R. M. Thrall, C. H. Coombs, and R. L. Davis, editors, *Decision Processes* (New York: John Wiley and Sons, Inc., 1954), pp. 20-21.

number of variables. For example, he may perceive of relationships between transportation costs, customer satisfaction, and the location of distribution centers; the number of sales calls and resulting sales and profits; the allocation of advertising expenditures and the achievement of favorable consumer response.

Based on this, the model builder will become aware of logical conceptual relationships which he is able to state fairly succinctly and clearly. These relationships may then be quantified through the use of available records and data, experiments, or simulations. The basis for the establishment of a mathematical model is obtained.

Once the mathematical model is determined, it may be applied in "the real world." Feedback will result which will provide the basis for a further alteration of the quantification of the conceptual relationships perceived. It will lead to a refinement and improvement in the mathematical model.

As an example of model building by abstraction, consider the construction of a model representing consumer response to company advertising expenditures.[3] Through observation, analysis of relevant data, and experience, the model builder may recognize that with little or no advertising expenditures consumer purchases of a product are very small. Then it may appear that, as expenditures increase over a certain range purchase responses increase quite sharply. While response increases even further with additional advertising expenditures, it is noted that eventually it tapers off and tends toward some limit.

The resulting model may be depicted graphically as in Figure 2. Through research these relationships may be quantified and expressed in terms of mathematical formulas. A model is thus developed which represents the relationships existing between advertising expenditures and consumer response. Such a model has been constructed, and with further mathematical refinements was used to determine the optimum allocation of advertising expenditures.[4] The model also proved to be useful in developing advertising-response curves, analyzing the impact of time lags in advertising effect, evaluating the interaction of competing promotional effort and estimating the impact of varying promotional resources.

Model Building by Realization

In realization, the process of modeling is reversed. The model builder starts with a consideration of a logically consistent conceptual system. Then some

---

[3] A. P. Zentler and Dorothy Ryde, "An Optimal Geographical Distribution of Publicity Expenditure In A Private Organization," *Management Science,* Vol. 2 (July, 1956), pp. 337-352.

[4] Same reference as footnote 3.

Figure 2. Relationship of Consumer Response to Advertising Expenditures

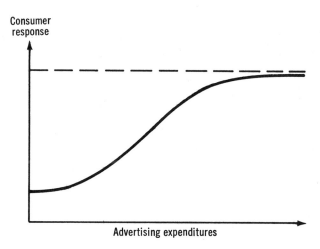

aspect of the real world can be viewed as the model of the system. It is a process of going from the logical system to the real world.[5] This is portrayed in Figure 3.

Model building by realization may be illustrated by considering the mathematical model known as Markov process. This process is a model that is useful in the study of complex business systems. It studies the present state of a marketing system and what has happened through some transition time. For example, it can be of help in studying the users and nonusers of a product (the present state of the system), and what has happened as advertising is applied over a period (the state transitions). It is a theoretical, logically consistent, and abstract model.

Figure 3. Model Building by Realization

Model
adjustment

| Theoretical and abstract statements about marketing | → | Internally consistent set of statements | → | Abstract model | → | Perception of real marketing situations | → | Congruency of model with a particular marketing situation | → | Application of model |

Feedback

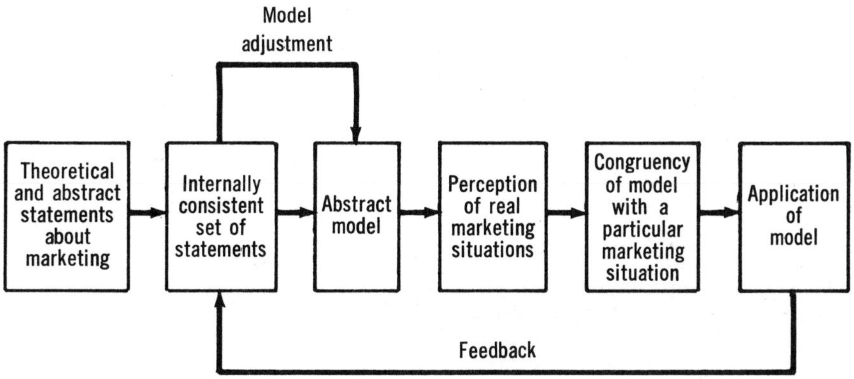

[5] Same reference as footnote 2, p. 21.

Starting with this model, the model builder may perceive that such marketing situations as the use of advertising to switch brand loyalties of consumers, or to change consumers from the state of nonusers to users, deal with the current state of a system and the transition of the system through time. Therefore, he may use the Markov process to study the effects of advertising impact. As experience from application of the model is developed, feedback will result and the model can be adjusted. In using this procedure, the model builder has gone from a logical mathematical system to the world of marketing.

Herniter and Magee and also Maffei have discussed the application of Markov process models.[6] Their research indicates that such models are extremely useful in determining the choice of promotional policy for maximizing profits in the long run; in specifying the kinds of experimentation required to measure the impact of promotional effort; and in calculating cost and revenue changes resulting from the use of alternative marketing strategies over time.

Kinds of Marketing Models

It is difficult to classify marketing models, since there are many dimensions and distinguishing characteristics that may be used as criteria for classification.

Mathematicians, for instance, might classify marketing models according to the type of equations used. They could distinguish among algebraic, difference-equation, differential-equation, and mixed-difference and differential equation models.[7] Physical models can be distinguished from abstract models. Loose verbal models may be contrasted with precise mathematical models. Models that take into consideration changes in factors through time are referred to as dynamic models and are distinguished from static models. Deterministic models are differentiated from stochastic models (models in which some of the variables are random factors and cannot be completely determined). Micro-marketing and macro-marketing models exist, as do linear and nonlinear models. Perhaps one of the most meaningful distinctions from a marketing point of view is that of goal models and systems models.

---

[6] Jerome Herniter and John F. Magee, "Customer Behavior As A Markov Process," *Operations Research,* Vol. 9 (January-February, 1961), pp. 105-122; Richard B. Maffei, "Brand Preferences and Simple Markov Processes," *Operations Research,* Vol. 8 (March-April, 1960), pp. 210-218.

[7] This breakdown is taken from an unpublished paper prepared by Dr. Paul Craig, at the Institute of Basic Mathematics for application to business, sponsored by the Ford Foundation at Harvard University during 1959-1960. The actual classification of models was suggested by Dr. Samuel Goldberg.

Systems Models and Goal Models

A distinction has been made in the behavioral-science literature between *systems models* and *goal models*.[8]

In marketing, a goal model or end-means model starts with a marketing task to be achieved. For instance, it focuses on the marketing objectives and the uses of company resources to achieve them as efficiently as possible. It is the achievement of marketing goals, and not necessarily corporate goals, that becomes important.

The goal model does not lend itself readily to a representation of a multifunctional unit. The marketing department is not viewed as being comprised of a number of different departments with possible conflicting goals, but rather as one over-all unit with a major goal. The implication here is that if we increase the marketing means, we thereby increase our effectiveness in achieving marketing goals. In this model, moreover, the effectiveness of the marketing department is measured by the devotion to the achievement of marketing goals. Although the goal model is useful, it is Utopian and unrealistic.

In the systems model, the starting point is not a goal. The starting point is the model of a total functioning system, for example, the marketing department. It is the model of a marketing unit capable of achieving goals. The systems model recognizes that there can be many conflicting objectives within an organization and that concessions must be made. In this model, the multifunctional units involved in achieving marketing goals are recognized. This model also considers that some means must be allocated to non-goal directed effort, such as the resources necessary to maintain the marketing organization. Given certain marketing conditions and resources, the main consideration is—how can they be programed to achieve the optimum position for the total business system?

The systems model is the superior model for marketing management. It is the model that the operations researcher uses when he perceives of a business as an over-all system of action when he plans the optimal use of resources. The systems approach to the study of marketing is appearing in the literature and should result in a better understanding of the existing interrelationships among marketing elements, a clearer grasp of marketing behavior, and a more effective allocation of marketing resources.[9]

---

[8] Amitai Etzioni, "Two Approaches to Organizational Analysis: A Critique and A Suggestion," *Administrative Science Quarterly,* Vol. 5 (September, 1960), pp. 257-278, at p. 258.

[9] See Wroe Alderson, *Marketing Behavior and Executive Action* (Homewood, Illinois: Richard D. Irwin, Inc., 1957); William Lazer and Eugene J. Kelley, "Interdisciplinary Contributions to Marketing Management," (Bureau of Business and Economic Research, Michigan State University 1959); William Lazer, "Transportation Management: A Systems Approach," *Distribution Age,* Vol. 59 (September, 1960), pp. 33-35; John F. Magee, "Operations Research in Making Marketing Decisions," *Journal of Marketing,* Vol. 25 (October, 1960), pp. 18-24.

Models and Marketing Theory

The terms "models" and "theories" are often used interchangeably. An interesting and useful distinction for marketing can be drawn from an idea expressed by Coombs, Raiffa, and Thrall: "A model is not itself a theory; it is only an available or possible or potential theory until a segment of the real world has been mapped into it. Then the model becomes a theory about the real world." [10]

As a theory, a marketing model can be accepted or rejected on the basis of how well it actually works. The actual model itself, however, is "right or wrong" (internally consistent) on logical grounds only.

One can distinguish between models and theories by considering marketing research techniques. A stipulated technique for marketing measurement may be called a model. For example, the forecasting technique known as exponential smoothing, or forecasting by exponentially weighted moving averages, has proved to be a useful forecasting model.[11] As a model, it need only be internally consistent. It is a potential marketing theory.

When data are actually measured by the exponential smoothing technique and are mapped into the model, then the model becomes a theory about the marketing data. The resulting theory may be a good one or a poor one.

The relationship among marketing models, theories, and hypotheses now follows directly. Within a theoretical framework, we are able to test certain hypotheses. The assumptions of a marketing model itself, however, need not be subjected to tests, whereas hypotheses should be tested. It should be noted that assumptions in one model may be hypotheses in another.

Use of Models in Marketing

Five major uses for models in marketing can be suggested.

1. *Marketing models provide a frame of reference for solving marketing problems.* They suggest fruitful lines of inquiry and existing information gaps. Marketing models do this by playing a descriptive role. The descriptive model does not go beyond presenting a representation or picture of some aspect of marketing activity. However, it serves an extremely important function in the extension of marketing thought. The use of flow diagrams in depicting existing relationships or in developing a logical computer program is an example of the use of descriptive models.

---

[10] Same reference as footnote 2, pp. 25-26.
[11] Peter R. Winters, "Forecasting Sales by Exponentially Weighted Moving Averages," *Management Science,* Vol. 6 (April, 1960), pp. 324-342.

2. *Marketing models may play an explicative role, and as such they are suggestive and flexible.* Such models are more than simple metaphors; they attempt to explain relationships and reactions. The marketing scientist not only is interested in describing marketing phenomena and examining them, but he desires to explain existing relationships and frames of references. For example, "switching models" often attempt to explain the relationships between advertising and brand loyalty.[12]

3. *Marketing models are useful aids in making predictions.* For instance, in answer to the question why models should be used, Bross explains that the real answer to this question is that the procedure has been followed in the development of the most successful predicting systems so far produced, the predicting systems used in science.[13] Marketing practitioners and scientists wish to predict and consequently employ various types of forecasting models and inventory models. These models become more than just an explanation and a representation of an existing situation. They become means of presenting future reality.

4. *Marketing models can be useful in theory construction.* Formulators of marketing models may hypothesize about various aspects of marketing as they might exist. Thereby, we have "reality" as it is hypothesized. Simulation, for example, which really involves experimentation on models, can lead to valuable insights into marketing theory. In the same vein, an ideal may be developed as a model. Although the ideal may not be achieved, it provides a useful vehicle for extending knowledge.

5. *Marketing models may stimulate the generation of hypotheses which can be verified and tested.* Thereby, it furthers the application of the scientific method in marketing research and the extension of marketing knowledge.

Benefits of Mathematical Models

Why should marketing scientists and practitioners utilize mathematical models rather than other kinds of models.[14] Perhaps the most important reasons are four:

1. *The translation of a model from a verbal to a mathematical form makes for greater clarification of existing relationships and interactions.* It is a rigorous and demanding task; and conceptual clarity and operational definitions are often achieved. The models developed may also become more generally applicable.

2. *Mathematical models promote greater ease of communication.* Within business administration and related subject-matter areas, there is

---

[12] Same reference as in footnote 9.

[13] Irwin D. J. Bross, *Design for Decisions* (New York: The Macmillan Company, 1953), p. 169.

[14] Paul Craig, same reference as footnote 7.

the difficulty of cross-communication because of the terminology used by specialized disciplines. Through the use of mathematical models, all of the disciplines may be reduced to a common mathematical language which may reveal inter-relationships and pertinence of research findings not previously known.

3. *Mathematical models tend to be more objective, while verbal constructs lean heavily on intuition and rationalizations.* Scientific marketing can be advanced through the application of objective mathematical analysis.

4. *Analyses that are not feasible through verbal models may be advanced through mathematical models.* Mathematics provides powerful tools for marketing academicians and practitioners. Mathematical models lend themselves to analysis and manipulation. In the manipulation of verbal models, the inter-relationships and logic are easily lost.

Concluding Observations

The usefulness of a marketing model is a function of the level of generalization the model achieves, and the degree of reality it portrays. Symbolization is used in model building to achieve greater internal consistency and more correspondence with reality. The greater the level of symbolization, and the fewer the restrictions, the more adequate and more generally applicable is the model.

For example, it is true that linear-programing models are more abstract, more general, and more valuable than are mere descriptive models representing a factory and warehousing complex. However, it may well be that the linear-programing model is by no means more widely used.

All marketing models are based on simplifications and abstractions. Only by making assumptions is a model molded to fit reality. Sometimes the reality beyond the boundaries of the model, however, is much greater than the reality within the boundaries. The model then becomes severely limited by the assumptions on which it is based.

To be effective, marketing models should be plausible, solvable, and based on realistic assumptions. The current level of model building in marketing is not yet a sophisticated one. It cannot compare favorably with the level of model building in the physical or biological sciences. As the disciplines of marketing matures, however, it will use an increasing number of models and will develop more complex models that have broader application.

29

Mathematical Models and Marketing Theory

ALFRED A. KUEHN

In the last few years we have witnessed rapid growth in the use of mathematical models in the solution of complex problems in production scheduling, inventory control, routing of product shipments, and equipment replacement. The impact that model building is having upon theory and practice in these areas of business is widely recognized.

In contrast, the use of mathematical models has gained only a limited degree of acceptance within marketing. Relatively few individuals and groups are actively attempting to employ this approach to the analysis of marketing problems. Furthermore, the subject of model building has taken on emotional overtones. At one extreme, mathematically oriented theorists often speak quite glibly of solving a variety of problems that have defied market analysts. In defense, conventional market theorists generally point to the unique character of the consumer and the temporal nature of market conditions as factors which distinguish marketing from those subjects which have been successfully treated with mathematical models; these theorists go on to express serious doubts as to whether the really important marketing problems are amenable to quantification and mathematical analysis. This controversy is as yet unresolved to the satisfaction of most students of marketing since only a limited number of mathematical models relevant to marketing theory and practice have been reported in the literature and most of these have been exploratory in nature; very few models have been subject to empirical test.

In this paper we will (1) review briefly the concept of a model and the development of mathematical model building, (2) examine the types of models which can be applied to marketing problems, pointing out their

Reprinted with permission from *Proceedings: Conference of Marketing Teachers from Far Western States,* Delbert J. Duncan, ed. (Berkeley: Schools of Business Administration, University of California, 1958), pp. 45-56.

characteristics, strengths, and limitations, and (3) speculate as to the role that model building will play in the future development of marketing theory. To illustrate points 2 and 3 I will refer to models outlined in the literature and to the models which have been constructed during the course of my research into the dynamics of consumer purchasing behavior.

The Concept of a Model

Webster defines the term "Model" as a pattern of something to be made, a style of structure, an archetype, a representation of a thing. We are all familiar with the use of models in the design of architecture, aircraft and automobiles, furniture and clothing. Many of us have also seen working models used by engineers to provide estimates of the performance of the devices the models represent. In each instance the model gives new perspective to its creator and enables him to communicate his thoughts to others more effectively. The problems with which the designer is attempting to cope in the above examples are too complex for solution without the perspective gained from the use of models. In most cases the concepts developed are also of such a nature that they cannot be communicated adequately by resorting to verbal description.

Models are useful only insofar as they represent adequately the essence of the problem studied. A model should be as simple as possible, yet incorporate all of the important aspects of a problem. Models can be very misleading—the results provided are no better than the model from which they are derived. Thus model building is not a simple art but rather requires that painstaking attention be given to developing an understanding of the process or system being represented. The ultimate test of the model's adequacy is whether the model provides the perspective needed to reach improved decisions or new understanding.

It is not always convenient or even possible to build physical models of the processes we seek to study. In the case of advertising, for example, we have no physical analogy with which to build a working model to describe the influence of advertising upon the subsequent purchasing behavior of the consumer. It may, however, be possible to construct mathematical models to describe such influence processes. To the extent that existing mathematical techniques enable us to incorporate the essence of the advertising problem into a mathematical model we have a powerful tool with which to test and extend advertising theory. Model building can in such an application be a means by which we may pull ourselves up by our bootstraps. First we build as realistic a model as possible, then we study its performance and seek to understand the factors leading to its deviation from reality, and finally we repeat the cycle in an attempt to correct for the deficiencies observed. This process forces us to give explicit definition to hypothesized relationships, places already recognized facts in perspective, and points out unforeseen implications of the theory (model) being constructed.

Development of Mathematical Model Building

A mathematical model is a simplified representation of a concept, system or process usually expressed as a quantitative relationship. The first models developed in physics employed nothing more complex than algebraic equations. The laws of levers expounded by Archimedes, the law of the pendulum discovered by Galileo, and the law of gravitation formulated by Isaac Newton are examples of the early use of such models. More recently, the development of the calculus and statistical theory and the advent of electronic computers have broadened the horizon for mathematical application. In the analysis of nuclear reactions, for example, it is now possible to study in probabilistic terms the movement, collision, scattering, and disintegration of individual particles of matter. Insofar as these models adequately simulate the behavior of the reactor system, design engineers may use the results obtained therefrom to reduce or eliminate the risks and costs associated with the development of physical "working models."

Economics was the first of the social sciences to resort to mathematical model building in pursuing the construction and communication of theory. As in the case of physics, the development of model building in economics was closely related to the availability and recognition of mathematical techniques that are useful in representing processes and systems of theoretical interest. As a result of advances in probability theory, decision rules based upon perfect forecasts of the outcome of events have been replaced or supplemented by decision rules which outline optimal behavior in the face of uncertainty. The availability of electronic computers has also opened new doors by enabling economists to work with models which were previously too complex to evaluate. Simulation of complex decision processes and economic systems is now being attempted at a number of universities and research centers; one such simulation model depicts quite well the growth of American Can Company and Continental Can Company in the years following their separation.

It seems likely that mathematical models will also play a growing role in the development of marketing theory as researchers and theorists working in this field become more adept at the use of existing mathematical techniques and as new techniques are developed. This is not to say that all marketing problems are subject to quantification—it is not necessary to defend model building on these grounds. It is sufficient that the use of models holds great promise in the analysis of a number of such problems. We should not expect such model building to be easy—the problems are complex indeed, perhaps more complex than those which have been studied in the natural sciences. We can expect numerous models to be constructed, temporarily accepted and subsequently replaced as more satisfactory representations are developed. On the other face of the coin, however, is opportunity; since the problems to be solved are of such complexity, the prospects of improvement in marketing practice and theory through the use of models are correspondingly great.

In the next section we will distinguish between several types of models that can be applied to marketing problems, pointing out the strengths and limitations of each. Subsequently we will examine the use of such models by following the development of a theory of consumer brand shifting behavior.

Mathematical Models for Use in Marketing

Mathematical models have been categorized in several ways: static or dynamic, exact or probabilistic, and in some instances, empirically derived, or theoretical. Virtually all of the models that have been constructed in marketing have been static and exact. Some of these models have been primarily theoretical in character, other are largely empirical; very few have foundation in both theory and empirical evidence.

Static models differ from dynamic models in that the former do not explicitly take the passing of time into account as a variable. The static model is of primary interest in the analysis of equilibrium conditions, that is, the state of the market that would eventually be attained if all relevant market variables were to remain constant over time. In marketing application, such models are of most interest when there is a very short period of adjustment on the part of consumers, distributors, and/or manufacturers to a change in market conditions.

Dynamic models are designed so as to describe conditions at equilibrium and during the preceding period of market adjustment (transition periods). Useful models of this type are therefore more difficult to construct; not only must the model correctly depict the relationship between market variables at equilibrium, but it must also be capable of representing the process of adjustment. The dynamic model has numerous advantages with respect to its static counterpart. For example, let us assume that a change in shelf display is made for a single brand of product in a super market. If the effect of this alteration in shelf display is an immediate and lasting change in the brand's share of market within the store, a static model provides a satisfactory description of the situation. If, on the other hand, customers adjust slowly to the new display, the static model is at best an incomplete representation of the consumer's reaction to the new set of market variables. At worst, the use of a static model in such a situation leads to erroneous results; researchers using static models of the "before-after" type must be very careful not to accept empirical data obtained during the transition period as being a measure of equilibrium conditions. The availability of a sound dynamic model to describe the process of consumer adjustment would avoid this source of error, enable researchers to evaluate the overall effect of the display change more quickly, and provide better information to management for decision making purposes.

Exact models represent a direct relationship between sets of variables whereas *probabilistic* or stochastic models couch relationships in probability terms. The exact model is less demanding computationally and has, as a result, been used almost exclusively. It seems likely that the bulk of model building in marketing in the foreseeable future will continue to rely upon such models. Probabilistic models do, however, appear to offer definite advantages in some areas of research and application. The use of a model to be described later in this paper has, for example, enabled me to simulate quite accurately the sequence of brand purchases by consumers. This development shows promise of leading to an improved understanding of consumer behavior and, in conjunction with consumer panel data (and perhaps survey data), to improved techniques of market analysis including forecasting, evaluation of couponing and dealing, and the appraisal of a brand's competitive position with respect to specific other brands in the market.

Models have been classified as *empirical* or *theoretical* on the basis of the evidence that supports their use in business application or as a starting point for subsequent research. It is of course desirable that a model have foundation in both theory and experimental evidence.[1] Most of the marketing models reported in the literature are weak on one of these scores. For example, the model on the effect of promotional effort on sales reported by John F. Magee is based upon the partially tested assumption that the sales of a manufacturer to individual customers are distributed over time according to the Poisson distribution. This is an interesting em-

---

[1] An interesting example of the faulty use of an empirical model was contained in a recent news commentary. It was reported that a man had been found who had voted "correctly" (that is, voted for the winning candidate) in each of the last 13 presidential elections. The opinion of this man was being solicited as a basis for predicting the outcome of the next presidential election. At first impression one might be inclined to take seriously the opinion of a man with such a voting record. It should be noted, however, that if voters cast their ballots by chance alone we should expect to find one such voter in every 10,000 having cast a ballot in the last 13 elections. The fact that we can find a voter with such a record is therefore little assurance that his prediction is better than that of other voters.

pirical observation. If such a relationship holds for a variety of products and customer groups, some theoretical explanation should be available. To make maximum use of mathematical model building in the development of marketing, it is necessary that theoretical and empirical research be coordinated.

Development of a Mathematical Model of Consumer Brand Shifting

To illustrate the use of mathematical model building in the development of marketing theory, I will outline the procedure that was followed in my research into the dynamics of consumer behavior. Mathematical model building has played a central and continuing role in this research directed at the development and testing of theory. Use of this example will permit me, later in this paper, to add substance to the general expectations that I hold regarding the future role of model building in the development of marketing theory and practice.

The study of consumer brand shifting was initiated as an attempt to develop a better understanding of the dynamic effects of advertising, distribution, price and product characteristics upon consumer behavior. For simplicity the study was initially limited to advertising, an area in which it was thought that a theory might be most readily tested. Detailed data on advertising expenditures and sales for individual brands of a product were not, however, available to help direct the development of a model (theory). Consequently, the form taken by the model was guided largely by the following four requirements:

1. Hypotheses about consumer behavior to be incorporated into the model should be reasonable in the light of psychological and economic theory.

2. Mathematical techniques capable of expressing the above hypotheses must be available and be recognized.

3. It must be possible to draw some implications from the mathematical structure employed, perhaps in the form of a decision rule, so as to provide new perspective to the problem.

4. The implications or decision rule drawn from the model must be consistent with *what is known to be true* about the effects of advertising and good business practice.

The approach used in the development of the model was to begin with a very simple set of behavioral relationships (after earlier attempts with more complex systems proved unwieldy) in which each consumer was assumed to make one purchase per time period and to have a certain *basic* probability r of repurchasing the brand last bought. As a consequence of the second assumption, each consumer was assigned a probability of $1-r$ of being a potential brand shifter in any given time period, in which event it was further assumed that his probability of buying any given brand (including the brand last purchased) would be proportional to the influence of the advertising in behalf of each brand. This model, extended by the addition of a "birth and death" process to permit the entry and exit of consumers with respect to the market, proved to satisfy the four requirements listed above. Aggregated across all consumers, the model of consumer brand shifting behavior described above provided the following relationship between the sales volume obtained by a specific brand and its advertising.

$$S_{i,\,t} = re\,S_{i,\,t-1} + I_{t-1}\,[g + (1 - r)e] \cdot A_{i,\,T}$$

where

$S_{i,t}$ = Sales of brand (i) during time period t,

r = Basic probability of brand repeat, assumed to be equal and constant for all brands,

e = Probability of "survival" of past customers of this product, i.e., (1-probability of "exit"),

I_{t-1} = Sales of all brands of the product during the time period $t-1$,

g = Entry of potential customers into the market for this product, expressed as a fraction of the size of the market in the previous time period, and

$A_{i,T}$ = Probability of "potential brand shifter" or new customer of the product being drawn to brand (i) in time period t as a result of advertising in time period T. The distinction between t and T takes cognizance of the fact that there may be a time lag between the advertising and its effect upon consumer purchasing behavior.

If we then define the $A_{i,\,T}$'s for all brands as being proportional to the product of the advertising expenditures $(C_{i,\,T})$ for each brand and its effectiveness $(E_{i,\,T})$, where $\Sigma\,A_{i,\,T}=1$, we can compute the optimal advertising expenditure for brand (i),

$$C_{i,\,T} = \left[\frac{C_{c,\,T}E_{c,\,T}}{E_{i,\,T}} \right] \left[\frac{1 - \sqrt{\dfrac{C_{c,\,T}E_{c,\,T}(1 - \rho re)}{m_i I_o E_{i,\,T}(\rho k)^L k^{(T-1)}(k - re)}}}{\sqrt{\dfrac{C_{c,\,T}E_{c,\,T}(1 - \rho re)}{m_i I_o E_{i,\,T}(\rho k)^L k^{(T-1)}(k - re)}}} \right]$$

Where

$C_{i,T}$ = Advertising expenditure by brand (i) at time T; in the above decision rule, it represents the optimal expenditure,

$C_{c,T}$ = Total advertising expenditures by competitors in time period T,

$E_{c,T}$ = Average weighted effectiveness of advertising in behalf of competitive brands at time T, the effectiveness of each brand's advertising being weighted by its dollar expenditures,

ρ = Discount factor applied to future dollar receipts and expenditures = $1/(1 + \text{rate of interest})$,

m_i = Profit margin on sales of brand (i) apart from advertising costs,

I_o = Total industry sales in the base period ($t - o$),

k = $e + g$ = the net growth of industry sales per period, and

L = the lag (number of time periods) between the advertising expenditure and its influence upon new and shifting customers.

The share of market that would be obtained at equilibrium given this rate of expenditure ($C_i, _T$) would be equal to $A_i, _T$, the share of the brand shifters attracted, or

$$A_{i,\,T} = 1 - \sqrt{\frac{C_{c,\,T}E_{c,\,T}(\rho re)}{m_iI_oE_{i,\,T}(\rho k)^L k^{T-1}(k - re)}}$$

This decision rule for the firm can be evaluated in part by comparing it with the advertising rules of thumb reported in the literature. The "optimal behavior" outlined by the above equations is in agreement with the following, generally accepted, propositions:

1. The prospects for advertising are greatest in industries of high growth.

2. The greater the profitability of the industry, the stronger the case for advertising (profitability refers to the product of the sales volume of the industry and the available profit margin apart from advertising expenditures).

3. Advertising designed to stimulate primary demand (consumer "entry" into the market or industry growth) can be more valuable to an individual firm than advertising for selective demand. This is particularly the case for a firm having a larger share of market.

There has been some disagreement in the literature regarding the relationship between brand loyalty and the value of advertising. It has been said that product classes in which high loyalties exist should be advertised most heavily since customers attracted will not soon shift away. Conversely, it has been argued that advertising is more profitable if there is a great deal of shifting among brands since advertising can be more effective in attracting customers under those conditions. The results obtained from an analysis of the decision model suggest that each of these propositions is partially correct but under differing circumstances.

1. If the basic probability of brand repeat r (a measure of brand loyalty) is equal for all brands and constant over time, a high value for r will increase the effectiveness of advertising if $\rho > 1$. If ρk is less than 1, a high value of r will decrease the optimal level of advertising.

2. If r varies cyclically over time for all brands, the firm should increase its advertising expenditures as r decreases, and conversely, spend the least when brand loyalty is at a maximum.

3. Assuming equal attraction for shifting customers, brands with high r should rationally be advertised more heavily than brands with a low basic brand repeat probability.

In general, when a firm in an industry increases its advertising budget, its competitors seem to react with a similar increase. This is inconsistent with the behavior outlined as optimal by the advertising decision rule. If a firm has less than approximately 50% of the market, the decision rule indicates that the firm should decrease its advertising expenditures when competitors increase theirs, and vice versa. If a firm has more than ½ of the market, it should increase its advertising expenditures when competitors increase their budgets but by a smaller percentage.[2] Several factors may account for the difference between observed market behavior and the "optimal" behavior outlined by the decision rule:

1. The model treats any change in a merchandising variable as being completely reversible. This may not always be the case. For example, once shelf position is lost (perhaps as a result of lack of sales promotion), it may be very difficult or even impossible to recover. In such a case, there would be definite lower limits on sales promotion below which management would not care to operate.

2. Management may be guided foremost by share of market rather than by profit considerations.

3. Management may tend to copy the behavior of other firms in the belief that others know (or may know) what they are doing. "Keeping pace with the industry" is, in the absence of adequate information with which to succeed independently, a means by which risk can be reduced.

---

[2] These findings are generally consistent with those obtained from a more advanced model which incorporates the effects of price, product characteristics, and distribution as fixed merchandising influences (in the advertising model presented in this paper, these other merchandising factors were not assumed to have any influence). As is outlined above, the firm should always either decrease its advertising expenditures or increase them by a smaller percentage amount when competitors increase their advertising. The more advanced model does, however, replace the "50% of the market" rule for determining whether to increase or decrease the advertising budget with a rule which is a function of the other merchandising variables (price, product characteristics, and distribution) included in the model.

4. If these results are viewed in the framework of oligopoly or game theory, it may be desirable for a firm to increase its advertising in response to an increase by a competitor. In the short run, this may force the competitor to withdraw from his position; in the long run it will make the prospects of increasing advertising expenditures appear less desirable to one's competitors.

Many firms set their advertising appropriation for a time period at a given percentage of expected sales in that period. An analysis of the decision rule outlined in this paper indicates that, under certain assumptions, such a policy is a sensible approach to overall advertising budgeting. The rule, "set the firm's advertising to sales ratio equal to that of the industry," is near optimal for the individual firm (in the absence of collusion) given that (1) there is no lag in the effects of advertising, (2) the effectiveness of the firm's advertising is equal to that of the weighted industry average, (3) the profit margin available to the firm apart from advertising costs is equal to the weighted industry average, and (4) the industry's overall advertising to sales ratio is near that which would result if at least one firm of moderate size were to use the advertising decision rule.[3] According to the model, each firm could do even better by agreeing with its competitors to reduce advertising expenditures proportionally to a very low level. Such a solution neglects two considerations, however: (1) industry sales and growth may be a function of total industry advertising, and (2) new firms might be expected to be attracted to industries in which there is little competition (low advertising and high profits).

Empirical Testing of the Model of Consumer Brand Shifting

The advertising implications of the model of consumer brand shifting outlined in the previous section appear to be quite reasonable. An empirical study is needed, however, to test more directly some of the assumptions upon which the model is based. In this section I will outline some of the major findings obtained in an analysis of the purchase patterns of more than 600 Chicago families (Chicago Tribune consumer panel records of frozen orange juice concentrate purchases, 1950-52).

It was assumed in the previous section that the consumer has a fixed basic probability of repeating the purchase of the brand last bought. This implies that only the most recent purchase of the consumer influences

---

[3] There appear to be substantial pressures leading to optimal advertising to sales ratios. If the ratio is too low, it is profitable for either a new firm or an existing competitor to increase total industry advertising. If the ratio is too high, its effect on industry profitability will tend to result either in increased prices (at which point the ratio may be optimal) or to decreased advertising, depending upon the relative influence of price and advertising upon consumer choice.

his future choice of a brand. The empirical study initiated to test this assumption indicated:

1. Use of the past two and four purchases of the consumer as a basis for forecasting his future choice of a brand decreases the forecast error (standard deviation) by only 4.8% and 7.0%, respectively, relative to the use of only the most recent purchase.

2. When studying long sequences of past purchases by consumers, the effects of past purchases upon the probability of repurchase *decline exponentially* as one goes back in the purchase history.

A second factor of major importance upon the consumer's probability of continuing to purchase a brand is the time elapsed between purchases. It was discovered that the probability of a consumer repurchasing the same brand on successive purchases decays to the share of the market of the brand with the passing of time. In other words, given a sufficiently long period of time elapsed, the probability of continued purchase of the brand is just equal to chance. A brand therefore cannot rely exclusively upon its "brand loyal" customers since loyalty decays with the passing of time. When analyzing the sequential purchases of customers buying the product with different frequencies it was discovered that

1. customers purchasing the commodity with high frequency have a higher probability of choosing the brand again if a purchase is made D days after an earlier purchase than do consumers who purchase the commodity less frequently during the interim, and

2. the time rate of decay of purchase probability is a *constant* independent of the consumer's frequency of purchase. These findings are of interest since they imply that the probability of repurchase is a function of frequency of purchase. In the advertising model outlined in the last section no provision has been made for differences in frequency of purchase. Fortunately, however, the model need not be changed; since the decay rates are constant, independent of frequency of purchase, all that is required is that 1) the variable "*r*" be redefined as 1 minus the decay rate per unit time, and 2) each consumer be weighted according to the product of his purchase frequency and the intercept value of his characteristic decay curve (i.e., the repurchase probability of the appropriate frequency at $t = 0$).

One final check on the acceptability of distributing the "potential brand shifters" as is done in the model was provided by an analysis of within-store repurchase probability as a function of the brand's share of market within the store. This was considered reasonable since the share of market obtained by a brand can be considered to be the combined effect of all merchandising influences within the store. In this analysis, the probability of a consumer shifting to Brand A ($P_{s,A}$) from another brand is approximately equal to a constant of proportionality (K_1) times the share of market of Brand A. In contrast, the probability of repeat purchase of Brand A ($P_{r,A}$) is approximately equal to the constant K_o (where $K_o = 1 - K_1$) plus $P_{s,A}$, the probability of a customer of another brand shifting to Brand A. These findings are consistent with the brand shifting behavior postulated in the model.

The Future Role of Model Building in Marketing

Earlier in this paper I predicted that model building will play a growing role in the advancement of marketing theory and practice as we become more adept in the use of mathematics and as new analytical techniques are developed. It seems quite possible that the use of this approach will develop to the point where it will be of major importance in the formulation and testing of marketing theory.

The behavior of consumers and the processes by which such behavior is influenced by market variables seem to be so complex that it is difficult to envision approaching these problems without the analytic power provided by model building. Model building forces the theorist to set forth his hypotheses in explicit form and generally provides insight with respect to unforeseen implications of these assumed relationships. It provides a basis for quantifying relationships previously discussed only in qualitative terms.

The details of the direction that the future development of model building will take are of course open to speculation. It seems likely, however, that the use of dynamic models and simulation techniques will open a number of areas previously thought to be unapproachable. The research I have reported here, for example, has been extended to the point where I feel quite confident that, within the next year we will have:

1. A means of evaluating consumer panel data so as to provide a very short term measure of a brand's market position, thereby making possible the evaluation of a manufacturer's program for regional sales promotion.

2. A much improved method of evaluating the effect of couponing and dealing.

3. A means of evaluating the nature of competition between specific brands of a product.

4. Greater insight into the effects of shelf space and location within the super market upon the sales of a brand of product.

Ten years ago most of these programs would have been difficult or impossible to undertake. Computer technology and experience in model building have advanced rapidly since that time until now such analyses are definitely feasible.

30

The Requirements for Theory in Marketing[*]

MICHAEL H. HALBERT

In any examination of the organized behavior system we called civilizations, we can observe some people devoted to reflection on the nature and operation of various activities of such systems. These people are often distinguished from those more active in the conduct of affairs by calling the first group, thinkers, and the second group, doers. It is abundantly clear, however, that in many areas of human activity, developments occur without any serious attempt to be reflective about their origins, their current activities, and their possible future. The greatest periods of culture growth have not necessarily coincided with the periods of greatest reflection. If we look at the current state of marketing activity and marketing thought, two apparently incongruous pictures appear. In the world as a whole and in the United States particularly, marketing is flourishing. It is growing and changing more quickly than perhaps any other institution of the society and rapidly increasing its impact on the total economic system. As an activity, then, marketing is both dynamic and progressive.

But when we look at the development and the present state of marketing theory the picture is just the reverse. From the point of view of the aid that theory can furnish to the practitioner, marketing has very little to offer. From the viewpoint of the established sciences, marketing has no theory that is defensible on the grounds of its logical consistency,

Reprinted from *Theory in Marketing: Second Series,* Reavis Cox, Wroe Alderson, and Stanley J. Shapiro, eds. (Homewood, Illinois: Richard D. Irwin, Inc., 1964), pp. 17-36, by permission of the American Marketing Association. Copyright © 1964 by American Marketing Association.

* This chapter is based on part of the material to be published in a book entitled *The Theoretical Basis for Marketing Science,* developed by the Marketing Science Institute. It is reproduced with the permission of the Institute. [EDITORS' NOTE: The book referred to is Michael H. Halbert, *The Meaning and Sources of Marketing Theory* (New York: McGraw-Hill Book Company, 1965).]

philosophic adequacy, or experimental foundation. Why is it that we have and can have a marketing practice that is highly successful without an equally successful development of marketing theory? Before we can develop the requirements for theory in marketing we must look at the way the grounds differ for developing a practice as opposed to developing a theory adequate to explain that practice.

In every culture studied by anthropologists or historians, some form of exchange has existed. That exchange should develop is predetermined by two factors that are to be found in any organized human society—specialization and motivation. Not only are productive skills an objective of specialization within a culture, so also is specialization in resources and specialization in wants and desires. When specialization is coupled with motivation, exchange naturally occurs. Anything so vital a part of a society tends to become institutionalized, acculturated, and ritualized. This is borne out by anthropological studies in which every culture examined shows some ritualistic aspects associated with the problems and practices of exchange. In fact, in early societies most of the exchange structure was integrated with the religious and other ritualistic aspects of the system. There is also good reason to believe that exchange of goods between tribes had its origin in a practice designed as a symbolic guarantee that the tribes were at peace rather than as a method of trading surpluses for mutual satisfaction and use. As man increased his ability to produce more finely differentiated means for the satisfaction of his wants and desires, the importance of the exchange function in culture increased until at the present time we have in many parts of the world cultures that could be described as marketing societies rather than as agricultural or manufacturing societies.

But to do a thing well it is not necessary to have an adequate theory of how it is done. Many people eat well without being nutritionists; men learned to see long before they learned the theory of optics; women had babies before they had obstetricians. The two necessary conditions for the development of a theory are the need for it (either for practical reasons or for intellectual satisfaction) and the availability of the techniques to develop the theory. The practice of marketing has attracted many able, competent, and highly motivated men who serve as marketing executives and marketing managers. These men realize that their marketing activities are growing more and more difficult as the complexity of the marketing environment increases and as the commitment to marketing alternatives becomes more binding for longer periods of time and involves larger and larger proportions of the total corporate assets. Thus, each of these men begins to develop marketing theory for himself.

In general the marketing executive or manager does not call it marketing theory. While he is concerned with gaining a practical understanding of how his system works, this concern is manifested in finding rules of thumb and immediate guides to action; his "theory" is implicit rather than explicit. His motivation is intensely practical and directed towards the performance of an almost impossible task. He needs ways of thinking about this task that tend to make it manageable and that enable him to relate his experience in past situations to his current problems. It is this kind of theory development that supports the notion that experience is the best teacher. Yet to learn from experience one must have a framework of concepts within which to interpret past events; otherwise experience cannot be relevant and nothing can be learned from it.

At the same time that the pressure for more adequate theory in marketing develops from the people who operate the marketing system, a parallel pressure for the development of theory is generated by the force of intellectual curiosity. Every large segment of human activity has been subjected to an attempt to organize it on the part of people with theoretical interests. The extent to which this attempt is successful usually depends upon the availability of appropriate analytic and conceptual techniques, upon the total amount of manpower and intelligence devoted to the effort, and upon the cooperation of the operating system being studied. In the current case of marketing theory it appears that the conditions are more favorable than they have ever been in the past for the emergence of a more definitive science in marketing. More and more, intellectually curious people are studying the business system and the marketing part of that system. More and more, they are given adequate opportunities, adequate cooperation, and adequate support.

The purpose of the theorizer is to understand the phenomenon he investigates. Since understanding is a communicative process, especially so in science, the theorist would like to develop concepts about which he can talk in such a way that a great deal can be explained with a few concepts and that the confusing world of appearances can be reduced to an orderly world of understandable relationships among definable entities. Thus, the conventional theorist is motivated more by his dislike of confusion than by his desire to improve the operation of the system while the practical operating marketing man is motivated by his need for improved practice rather than by his intellectual desire to order his world. But each needs the other, and it often turns out that the theorist is an intensely practical, down-to-earth researcher, while the pragmatically oriented practitioner is concerned with concepts, theories, definitions, and relationships as much as his more theoretical counterpart. The theoretician needs data from operating systems. He needs a laboratory from the real world to experiment in, to check his hypotheses, and to validate his theories.

The main concern of this essay, then, is with the requirements for theory in marketing. This task presupposes some description of what is meant by theory (in marketing or other disciplines) and a statement of where marketing theory currently stands. Accordingly, one finds discussed in the remaining sections of this essay—

1. The meaning of theory as used in this chapter, including the place of observation and measurement in theory.

2. The contributions which marketing and other fields (e.g., business, law, economics, the behavorial and methodological sciences) have made to what currently exists as marketing theory.

3. The requirements which continued developments in marketing theory will have to meet.

The Meaning of Theory

Like all abstractions, the word "theory" has been used in many different ways, in many different contexts, at times so broadly so as to include almost all descriptive statements about a class of phenomena, and at other times so narrowly as to exclude everything but a series of terms and their relationships that satisfy certain logical requirements. We shall want to take a somewhat middle position here and say that at the very least a theoretical statement within the domain or framework of marketing must do more than merely describe the phenomena being observed. Even here, though, we must be careful, for to describe implies to have observed, and to have observed implies a choice as to which aspects of the marketing world should be chosen for observations.

Also implied in any description are choices of what the measurements or classifications used in the descriptions were. All of these are decisions which are based ultimately on a theory or a set of theories that explain what it is important to observe and report about marketing phenomena. Thus, the process of observation or recording or description cannot be divorced from the process of theory construction.

Perhaps more important to our present viewpoint, however, is the notion that we cannot accent the somewhat arbitrary, slightly naive descriptions of scientific method that lay out a sequence including observation, the construction of hypotheses, and theory development, as though theory were the end product of this process rather than an integral and necessary part of each phase of it. This is all by way of emphasizing the distinction between implicit and explicit theory.

Even in the simple recording of a sale of any company's product, there is implicit not only a theory that describes what a sale is, who the parties to the sale are, and what the price is, but the much more pervasive background theory that tells us why it is worth using up company resources to record the sale at all. If it should be recorded, then *how* it should be recorded implies what future operations are to be performed on the data, and this in turn implies knowing the information requirements for managerial decisions and, ultimately, policy decisions. The often heard complaint of analysts or executives that "the data weren't recorded in a way that makes such and such an analysis or decision possible" is an illustration of the awkward results of being implicit instead of explicit about the requirements of the information. Therefore, we shall constrain our discussion of theory at this point to explicit theory.

It is in this sense that a theory must be more than just a recording of observations or the results of an analysis performed upon such data; it must also be more than just a set of definitions and logical operations that can be performed on the definitions. There must be the complete statement of the operational or "semantic" relations between the terms in the definitions and the behaviors in the real world to which the definitions refer.

One of the most common definitions of theory is an explanation of a set of phenomena. But explanation involves people (data don't explain themselves). Why would anyone *want* to explain a set of phenomena? Why, to *use* the explanation, of course—to use it in making decisions, perhaps for the most basic of research needs, perhaps for the most pressing of practical reasons. A theory, then, must include an explanation of its own uses; that is, how one can make decisions with it. Thus (ideally) a theory exists for a set of phenomena when all of the possible decisions to be made involving those phenomena can be explained. These explanations must fit all possible individuals who make these decisions, and the fitting must be satisfactory to the theorist involved.

The inclusion of "must be satisfactory to the theorist" leads to rather interesting consequences. The emphasis on the relation of theory to decision making implies that people are a part of any theory and that the purpose of the development of theory is not to explain and to understand the physical world as separated and apart from human interests and human endeavor, but rather that any adequate notion of theory must include the behavior of people who are operating on the class of phenomena about which the theory is constructed. Thus, if one wishes to find out about the theory of metals, one observes people behaving with metals and asks them to explain the decisions they are making. Those people who can explain most adequately have the best theories of metals, and one usually expects to find them in scientific research laboratories. Following the same line of reasoning, if one wishes to find out about theories of marketing, one observes people making decisions about marketing phenomena, be they buyers or sellers, executives or manufacturers, business or government policy makers. Here we run into what at first looks like an anomaly, for we do not always find the most adequate explanations of the decisions made about marketing in our universities and academic circles.

The more adequately developed the theory of an area is, the more likely we are to find a professional, academic class concerned with this theory. In mathematics, astronomy, chemistry, physics, etc., we expect to find (and do find) the most adequate explanations for the decisions made about these areas in our better universities; yet in most of the business disciplines and in many of the social and behavorial disciplines it is at least as likely that adequate explanations for decision making will be found among the better practitioners (and the more thoughtful and reflective ones) as it is that they will be found in universities or in academic research areas.

This is by no means a criticism of academia; it rather reflects the state of theory development in these areas. If marketing is to develop and proceed as a science in future years, we can confidently expect the development and presence of marketing theory in the university circles to increase very rapidly and to take its expected and respected place among the other scientific disciplines in academic circles. That this is not yet the case merely provides us with a challenge for the future. The interest exists; the practice of marketing goes on and provides the resources wherewith to develop a theory.

The Present State of Marketing Theory

The current state of marketing theory reflects not only the contributions of marketing practitioners and theorists but borrowings from other disciplines as well, e.g., (a) business, law, and economics; (b) the social and behavorial sciences; and (c) the formal or methodological sciences. Marketing, however, has no recognized central theoretical basis such as exists for many other disciplines, notably the physical sciences and, in some cases, the behavorial sciences. This lack of a conceptual foundation for marketing can be seen most clearly in an analysis of the course materials in the marketing curricula of the graduate schools of business in this country. In a survey recently completed by the Marketing Science Institute it is worthwhile noting that out of the 158 curricula surveyed, in which 140 references are used, only 31 of the references can be classified as dealing with marketing theory to any significant degree. This does not reflect a lack of interest in theory on the part of academicians, but rather a lack of available material for the teaching of marketing theory—material that meets the academic and scientific requirements for such an undertaking.

Such a condition is not surprising in light of the point of view developed in the first section of this chapter. Since marketing has been considered by our culture primarily as an art or technique rather than as a science, most of the formal content that current marketing *has* collected has been derived from other areas rather than being original with marketing.

If we are to examine the rest of organized science for the current basis of marketing theory, in which particular directions shall we search? This depends, of course, on the object of the search. Science is a complicated activity, and there are many different ways of classifying its total content. The classification scheme used here is in terms of the different levels of generality of the material.

Content. The *content* material of a science consists of the observations, measurements, and descriptions of the phenomena studied. These are usually called facts or data to distinguish them from theories, although this distinction is not as clear as one might think.

Techniques. The second kind of borrowing that marketing can expect from other areas is the borrowing of *techniques*. Broadly speaking these are the ways of generating the content material just described. Techniques include both the process of measurement and analysis. Moreover, many techniques arising in other fields must be modified and adapted before they are suited to marketing. The questionnaire from psychology and public opinion polls has had extensive development by market researchers, and is more useful than when it was first borrowed. Conversely, many of the early difficulties with motivation research were due to the attempt to use the techniques of clinical psychology without modification or adaptation to the requirements of marketing.

Concepts. The third class of material that comprises a science consists of the concepts, theories, and generalized ideas that form the abstract but essential element which distinguishes a science from an art or practice. Content is concerned with "what"; technique is concerned with "how"; concept is concerned with "why." The borrowing of concepts from another science is extremely dangerous, but can be extremely productive. The literature of marketing, of the other business disciplines, of the social and behavioral sciences, and of the management and methodological sciences was examined to see what it offered in terms of relevant content, technique, and concept. Table 1 puts in perspective the kinds of material we can expect to borrow from the various fields of study. While marketing theory, as currently constituted, does include the concepts of such noted scholars as Alderson, Converse, and Aspinwall, it can be noted from Table 1 that the major contribution of marketing as a discipline to marketing as a science has been in the area of content. We shall wish to examine next the contributions which other fields of study have made (and appear likely to make in the future) to theory in marketing.

**Table 1.   Contributions of Various Sciences and Disciplines to
a Science of Marketing** [1]

Science or Discipline Area	Type of Contribution		
	Content	Technique	Concept
Marketing	Major	Minor	
Business Disciplines	Major	Minor	
Behavioral Sciences	Minor	Major	Minor
Methodological Sciences		Minor	Major

[1] The entries in the table are to suggest the relative importance of the current potential of each scientific area for the content, the techniques, or the concepts of an emerging science of marketing.

The Business Disciplines, Law and Economics

The business disciplines are the first group to be reviewed for potential contributions to marketing theory. It is no surprise that their literature, as well as that of marketing, consists mostly of content and not technique or concept. The relevant books, articles, and speeches are mostly concerned with the operation of various aspects of the business system and not with the theoretical aspects of that operation. Taken as a group, business disciplines supply guidelines on how to recognize a problem when it exists, and what kinds of data are useful in helping to solve the problem. In many cases, the writings also supply a recommended solution. In law and in economics things are a bit different. Both of these areas have a long history, and each has developed its philosophers and theoreticians.

Most of the other areas of business, however, are in no better state than marketing with respect to having a basic conceptual or theoretical framework. If we may distinguish between a discipline and a science on the grounds that a discipline has techniques and a science has theories, then we must go further and say that techniques supply answers to questions and theories supply criteria by which answers are to be judged.

For example, in the area of real estate management there is an extensive literature on how to locate a suburban shopping area and on the evaluation of specific urban sites for specific types of business enterprises. These prescriptions, however, are developed from an analysis of experience and a history of similar situations on which data are available. Few of the writers claim that their advice is deduced from general theories of real estate; rather, it is induced from a careful analysis of experience. There is much practical value in borrowing the techniques and content of the business disciplines, but since these disciplines are themselves lacking established theoretical bases it is not surprising that looking for marketing *theory* in an area that has little enough of its own is unfruitful.

There is a well-developed body of literature concerning the philosophy of law, but its theoretical content is related more to sociology and political science than it is to marketing. Those writings in law which deal with the aspect of legal impingement on marketing do so in general with a rather superficial bow to the notion that the function of law is to enforce the will of society on the recalcitrant few. Thus, there is seen in antitrust discussion some confusion as to what the will of society is. The interpretation of some cases suggests that it is to protect consumers from the evil effects of monopoly power. Other cases and their interpretation suggests that it is to protect some business enterprises from their more successful competitors.

Perhaps the most fundamental idea from legal philosophy that has applicability to marketing theory is that in a society where men are motivated by their own diverse desires, the function of law is to provide a structure that permits maximum attainment of individual desires with minimum infringement on another's ability to attain his desires.

Economics has a longer history than most of the other business disciplines and has a well-developed body of economic theory. Much of this theory has found its way into marketing, and concepts of price elasticity, of market equilibrium, and of economics of scale are familiar to most marketers. The concept of economic man has been of great value to marketing but has also had some unfortunate consequences. But many of the most pressing problems in marketing develop from exactly those aspects of the system that economic theory has chosen to ignore.

This choice on the part of economists was quite conscious and deliberate, for if they did not make these simplifying assumptions, they could not have developed the great wealth of material that has been so useful to date. Economic man is assumed to have full and complete information about the decision under consideration. In classical economics when the problem of price equilibrium is being considered, it is assumed that all customers and all suppliers know the location of all products, and that the information about price, quality, quantity, and availability is instantaneously available and completely correct. Thus, the entire area of negotiation which is so vital to marketing is assumed out of the picture by the economist's emphasis on a single point of equilibrium.

Perhaps the central theoretical concept of economics has been that of rationality. Economic theory holds that people behave in their decision making as though they were trying to achieve the most of some value, often called utility and often measured in money. In his definition of "economic man" the late von Neumann was careful to point out that he had no reason to believe that people behave according to the assumptions that he was making, but that these assumptions were necessary in order to develop the theory advanced in the *Theory of Games and Economic*

Behavior.[1] The concept of rationality so central to economic theory appears on examination to be a very difficult concept indeed. If we define rationality as behavior designed to maximize utility and then define utility as that which behavior tends to maximize, we are not very far ahead. It can easily be shown that for any behavior there is a set of values such that the behavior is rational (maximizing) for those values.

If we pursue this argument to claim that values as well as behavior need to be rational, we are led into the impossible morass of attempting to distinguish rational values from irrational values. The present state of value theory barely enables us to investigate the problem of consistency of values let alone to establish their rationality. The only useful definition of rationality seems to be "your behavior is rational to me if I can explain it." This definition of rationality is a measure of my ability to explain and really tells me nothing about your behavior.

The Social and Behavioral Sciences

The concept of rational and nonrational behavior leads us naturally to a consideration of the social and behavioral sciences as a source for marketing theory. If the economists have done marketing a disservice by over-emphasizing the rational and economic motives of human behavior, the social scientists and, in particular, the psychologists have attempted to swing the pendulum to the opposite extreme by emphasizing irrational and psychodynamic motivations. It is true that a housewife shopping in a supermarket is not solely motivated by the dollars-and-cents consideration and does not have a small computer in her head. It is also true that her marketing behavior cannot be explained adequately by considering only the state of her psyche, the social pressures on her from friends, and the sex symbolism of the various package designs.

Although the "economic man" (or woman) described for us by the classical economists forms only a part of any adequate marketing description of real people, it is an essential part. The complex and perhaps confusing picture of the customer drawn for us by the behavioral sciences seems more like the kind of human beings we meet every day than does the rather pallid utility maximizer of the economists. There is more to behavioral science (and even to psychology) than Freudian psychodynamic personality theory, however, and the overall picture drawn from anthropology, political science, demography, and linguistics, etc., as well as from psychology is extremely useful. Their major contribution is more the open-

---

[1] John von Neumann and Oskar Morgenstern, *Theory of Games and Economic Behavior* (2d ed.; Princeton, N.J.: Princeton University, 1947).

ing up of a whole new area of exploration than the contribution of any specific set of techniques or directly usable ideas.

The behavioral sciences permit, and in fact require, that marketing science take explicit account of the human and social aspects of individuals and of groups engaged in marketing behavior. No longer is the housewife/consumer or the vice president of marketing allowed the refuge of "human nature." If we are to develop an adequate science of marketing we must investigate the people and the social groups that perform the marketing actions with the same scientific care and conceptual honesty with which other scientists investigate the phenomena of interest to them. What the behavioral sciences in total offer is a method of approach and a set of techniques that enable us to design and implement that investigation. These sciences have developed a whole group of techniques that are admirably suited for use in the development of marketing theory. This is not so much because these techniques are useful for measuring marketing behavior per se, but rather that the behavioral sciences have had to deal with the problem of measuring and analyzing systems which to a large extent they cannot control.

The history of successful measurement and experimentation in the physical sciences rests largely on the development of laboratory techniques and the ability to manipulate the environment and the objects of study in very closely controlled and easily repeatable situations. With the social sciences it is almost the reverse. There has been a great deal of laboratory experimentation in psychology, but even in that science and particularly as one moves to personality theory and to clinical psychology, the laboratory becomes less appropriate and the actual world of human behavior is the arena in which the methods of science must be applied in order to develop appropriate data and to test suggested hypotheses. Many of the other social sciences have very little laboratory work behind them, such as sociology, anthropology, linguistics, and political science. Each of these disciplines has some recourse to the laboratory, and so also does marketing.

But each of these disciplines has faced squarely the problem of making measurements and testing hypotheses in the on-going world in which very few of the variables can be controlled, and the particular objects under study, i.e., human beings, have memories and cannot be put through the same procedure twice since they will remember their earlier experiences. They cannot be told to act as if they were trying to maximize their monetary return. Even in the laboratory, values are not so easily manipulated. Since marketing and marketing research are concerned with these same kind of phenomena, it is not surprising that the techniques of social survey research have been so thoroughly borrowed and amalgamated into marketing that now there is as much developmental work in this area being done by market researchers as there is by opinion research specialists.

There are two further specific conceptual notions from the behaviorial sciences that should be incorporated into marketing theory. The first of these has to do with the notion of values as they affect human behavior and especially as they influence the decision-making process. In most of the formal work in statistics and decision theory, values are taken as inputs to the decision-making process. The major notion of decision theory is that the decision maker chooses among alternative courses of action so as to achieve an outcome with the highest value to him, based on the incomplete information that he has at the time of decision making. The extensive and complex developments in decision theory treat primarily the problems that arise because of different kinds and amounts of information and various kinds of available alternatives.

At first glance decision theory appears to be a very satisfactory approach to problems. People certainly do tend to choose those activities which they find rewarding and pleasant, and to avoid those which they find unpleasant and distasteful. Some of the oldest notions in psychology center around this so-called pleasure-pain principle. Yet we frequently see the reverse situation where people tend to like what they do, rather than do only what they like. A taste for avocados must be cultivated, and it is common to be indifferent to chamber music at first and only come to like and appreciate it after several hearings. The extreme proponents of this position claim that the major function and goal of society is to inculcate good taste (values) in the arts, in architecture, food, dress, music, literature, and in ethics and morals. Certainly a person's values are as much conditioned and determined by his behavior as the other way around.

Even if we take the naive position, however, that values are fixed inputs to decision making, we are left with the extremely difficult question of where *do* the values come from and what causes them to change. There is good reason to believe that maturation plays a large part in the development and change of values. Our children look forward with eager anticipation to the time when they are old enough to stay up all night whenever they want to, or to eat as much candy as they want. They refuse to believe their elders when they are told that their values will change, and by the time they can stay up as late as they want, they will be glad to get to bed early, and that they will lose their taste for candy or at least develop tastes for some of the foods they now dislike. The seven ages of man apply no less to his psyche and his values than they do to his physical development. Of all the behavioral sciences it is the sociologists and anthropologists who have the longest history of careful attention to this problem of the generation and modification of value systems.

There are, then, three major ideas or concepts from the social and behavioral sciences that should be incorporated into the development of any science of marketing. The first of these is that there is no simple route to the explanation or understanding of human behavior. The physical and biological sciences are not adequate to explain the kinds of behavior with which marketing men are concerned. The economists have provided an approach to this type of understanding, but it requires the behavioral sciences to broaden that approach so that the human beings described are realistic ones, and behave the way the real humans we know behave.

The second important notion of interest to marketers is that our scientific research methods must be turned inwards as well as outwards. We must study marketing operators and marketing scientists and their behaviors, assumptions, and attitudes as carefully, as rigorously, and as dispassionately as we study any other aspect of the marketing system. It is always easier, as the history of science has shown, to study *things* rather than *people* and to study *other* people rather than *ourselves*. But if we are ever to understand and predict the marketing system and the culture of which it is a part, we must take the final step and study ourselves. Only after we know what we do and how we do it can we begin to do it better.

The third contribution from the behavioral sciences lies in their development of concepts and techniques for the study of on-going real systems involving people in their normal interactive environment. The development of the social sciences in large part is the development of measurement and analytic devices for studying these kinds of systems. While laboratory research has its place, the current limitations on the development of social theory are the limitations imposed by lack of resources and lack of available techniques for field research. The same is true in marketing, but there is much that marketing can learn from the successes and failures of the behavioral scientist in coping with this difficult but crucial problem.

Method vs. Content in Science

When we turn our attention to the formal methodological sciences to see what they have to offer of use in marketing theory, we must first understand the essential difference between the methodological sciences and the content sciences. Any science must have two parts: it must have a philosophy and it must have content. The content refers to the various phenomena to be studied and explained by the particular science. In our case these are clearly the phenomena of marketing. The philosophy of a science refers to the *rules* by which one can *test* statements concerning the phenomena under study. Some sciences are described and named by their content area, such as chemistry, physics, aerodynamics, biology, marketing, etc. Some sciences are described and named by the kind of formalisms with which they deal. Here we have the areas of mathematics, logic, epistemology, theology, etc. To the extent that there is any unified meaning to the notion of "the scientific method" it is derived from these formal sciences rather than from the content sciences.

It is often stated that marketing will never be a science like physics and that unless it is it will not be a "real" science. Remarks of this type indicate confusion between the methodological sciences and the content sciences. Physics is a content science no less than is marketing. It has been able to employ more adequately the techniques of logic and mathematics and it is on *this* ground rather than because physics deals with material objects that it deserves accolade as an exemplary science. This distinction is brought out quite clearly in the following passages:

> As a rule [market researchers] acquire competence in conducting investigations not by mastering principles of scientific inquiry but rather by developing habits of research that are modeled on examples of sound scientific workmanship. Moreover, discussions that are intended to articulate the structure of scientific procedure usually have no direct bearing on the detailed problems with which [marketers] are normally occupied. In consequence broad issues in the logic of science are rarely matters of active concern to practicing [marketers], and most of them devote little serious thought to such "philosophical" questions as the functions a satisfactory theory must perform, how theory is related to the gross objects of familiar experience, and whether the abstract notions of a theory denote things that have some kind of . . . reality.
>
> Nevertheless, questions of this sort may become pressingly relevant to the work of [market researchers], and may require careful attention from them, when new experimental discoveries or radical innovations in theoretical ideas create puzzles that profoundly challenge entrenched scientific doctrines or habitual models of analysis. . . .[2]

The author, Ernest Nagel, is a recognized philosopher and is here distinguishing between the behavior of content scientists and the behavior of philosophers of science. However, as can be seen by the bracketed inserts in the preceding quotation, the item was quoted as though the parties concerned were market researchers and marketers. The original article, however, had the term "physicists" where we have inserted "market researchers." The author was thus talking about physics and physicists and not about marketing. The way in which marketing science *should* be like physics is in the detailed, careful, and extensive use of logic, mathematics, and the rest of the *formal* mechanisms of science. This is the same way in which marketing science should be like astronomy, biology, or any other science. Logic is useful for all sciences, and one cannot have a science without it. One *can* have a science without cyclotrons. In our borrowings from the methodological disciplines, we should not look for concepts that are directly relevant to marketing as a content area, but rather those which are relevant to the development of any science.

---

2 Ernest Nagel, "Review of *Understanding Physics Today*," by W. H. Watson, *Scientific American*, Vol. 209, No. 4 (October, 1963), pp. 145-49.

In summary, current marketing theory has borrowed extensively from the content area of the business disciplines, and the concept and technique area of economic theory (marginalism, opportunity costs, economic rationality). The social and behavioral sciences have provided techniques of measurement and experimentation and concepts useful to the study of people as opposed to things. Finally, it is apparent that we shall have to look increasingly to the methodological sciences to provide concepts and structure in marketing theory.

This brief excursion into the major sources of theory in marketing is but a prelude, however, to a more central question: What are the requirements that theory in marketing should meet? We discuss this question (and the important role that the methodological sciences play in the attempt to answer it) in the concluding section of this essay.

The Requirements of Theory in Marketing

There are many aspects of theory development and testing in marketing for which we shall make increasing demands on the methodological sciences. In this essay, however, we shall discuss only the one notion mentioned earlier— the notion of criteria for the adequacy of theory. The reason for singling out this particular aspect of philosophy for consideration is that much of the confusion in the discussion of possible and proposed theories in marketing (and in business) arises out of a lack of understanding of the *different ways* in which a theory can be inadequate.

These criteria are discussed in logic and philosophy under the names of *syntax, semantics,* and *pragmatics,* although the first two of those terms mean something quite different from their standard common English usage. The discussion treats each in turn. Although our attention is directed to this particular part of the philosophy of science, we should not forget that all of the material that bears on scientific method and adequate theory formulation and testing is of relevance to the design of any science and most especially so to the conscious design of a new science.

One of the earliest concerns of the science of logic has been the exploration of relations among statements. These are called formal properties and depend for their validity on the rules of logic rather than linguistics, semantics, or operational definitions—topics with which we shall deal later. In a formal deductive system there are certain terms or elements called *primitives* which are undefined within that system. It may come as a surprise to some that logic insists on primitives or undefinable terms, yet it was proved in 1931 by the German philosopher and mathematician, Kurt Gödel, that no system can be designed that is completely self-contained; that is, that every term in it can be defined in the language of other terms. This came as a culmination of the fruitless search for a completely defined and probably self-consistent system of arithmetic. After the primitives have been introduced, the next step is to develop postulates and axioms which relate these primitives to each other, thus defining *operators* or terms which serve to interconnect the primitives in the deductive system. For example, in the simple statement "1 + 1 = 2" the "1's" would be primitives of the system and the "+" and "=" would be operators or relational terms.

We are all familiar with the "if . . . then" type of statement such as "if all *A* is *B* and all *B* is *C*, then all *A* is *C*." This is the syllogism, the prototype of all deductive reasoning. A criticism sometimes offered against this type of deduction is that it tells you nothing about the real world; it merely says that *if* certain things are assumed, then certain consequences follow. Admittedly, this type of statement does not tell us anything about the real world. Such statements only tell us things that are logical consequences of what we already know, but this can be a most valuable source of knowledge.

There is a rather famous logical conundrum in which a student is accusing his teacher of wasting his (the student's) time. The student says, "Is what you teach me logical?" To which the teacher replies, "Yes, indeed." The student then says, "Therefore, all of the consequences are contained in that which I already know—the premises." The teacher acknowledges that this is so, and then the student asks, "If there is anything in the consequences that is not contained in the original premises, then the logic is faulty, is it not?" Again the teacher agrees, and the student can now propound the conundrum, "Then everything you teach me is either faulty or that which I already know. Why then should I study with you?"

The fallacy in this particular conundrum is rather obvious; it depends upon the meaning of the term "that which I already know." The conclusion that with only five letters to a license plate I can identify 11,881,376 different automobiles is *contained in* the structure of arithmetic and multiplication but is not *known* to me until I perform the appropriate calculations. In the statement of the conundrum, the student confuses the terms "contained in" and "already known."

Syntactics.   Many of the most fruitful theoretical systems in the history of science have been fruitful because of the richness of the conclusions that could be deduced from a very few original postulates and axioms. We shall deal later with the problem of fruitfulness and richness, but here we are concerned with the formal aspect of theory that is called *syntactics*. Syntactics has to do with the legitimacy of the operations that can be performed on the elements that form the theory. Many of the historical paradoxes in logic derive from using the same term in two different ways or from performing operations on a term that are not appropriate.

In marketing one often tries to solve problems by relating the present problem to other similar cases. This is often what is meant by using experience. Let us suppose we can adequately define "similar," so that we can tell when one situation is similar to another. (This problem will be considered when we discuss *semantics*.) The *syntactical* problem of the legitimate statements we can make about "similar" remains. There is a particular difficulty inherent in this approach that can be used to illustrate the syntactical nature of the problem. If situation *A* is similar to situation *B* and situation *B* is similar to situation *C*, then is situation *A* similar to situation *C*? The answers may be of some importance to us, since we want to know whether we can use our experience gathered, say, in test markets for *A* in assessing the probable outcome of test markets for *C*. The logician would inquire as to whether the relationship of similarity possessed the property of being transitive.[3] If it is defined so that it does, then we can safely conclude that the situation *A* is similar to situation *C*. But the definition of "similarity" that makes it transitive might restrict the term so much that *A* no longer is similar to *B*.

There is an even more powerful question that the logician might raise. Is the relationship of similarity in the *equivalence* class of relationships? This is not the place to explore these particular logical notions,[4] but it is clear that *A* may or may not be similar to *C* depending on the way we define similarity. This brings us to the major point of the illustration. Most of the use of marketing terms such as "similar situation" are not defined well enough so that these logical questions can be answered. Only as a science becomes mature and develops theoretical statements that have been accepted and used for some time does it attract the attention of methodologists and philosophers who then begin to examine the syntax of the theories and often point up extremely fundamental problems in the statement and manipulation of these theories.

The major function of the logician in this situation is to call our attention to the ambiguity in our definitions and in the use of language. This is a formal ambiguity and not the problem of operational definitions. It is the distinction between the use of language to describe relations and the use of language to describe real world phenomena. It is clear that the notion of similar is a relational notion, not an empirical one.

The problems of syntax that we have examined here are mostly trivial and rather easily solved, but many of the most serious problems in logic,

---

[3] Let *R* be any relationship that can hold between two elements of a set (*a*, *b*, *c*, . . .). The relationship is written "*aRb*." This is read, "*a* bears the relationship *R* to *b*." *R* is transitive if and only if, given *aRb* and *bRc*, we can deduce *aRc*.

[4] A relationship is in the equivalence class if it is transitive, reflexive, and symmetrical. Reflexive means that *aRb* implies *aRa*. Symmetrical means that *aRb* implies *bRa*.

whose solutions would affect the fabric of all deductive sciences, are syntactical in nature. In the development of marketing science we will need to pay attention to these problems or, in the most literal sense, we will not know what we are talking about.

Semantics.   A theory may fulfill all of the syntactical requirements with complete adequacy, and still have serious faults. The statement of the primitive notions, the operators, and the permissible manipulation of the symbols in which the theory is stated may all be complete and logically correct. The difficulties may lie with the way in which the theory is related to the real world. We have said previously that science contains two kinds of statements. Some of these statements are to be tested by an analysis of their syntax, i.e., by formal rules, and some of the statements are to be tested by experimentation, i.e., by observations made in the real world. If we are to use a theory to tell us what observations to make, then we must be clear, precise, and complete in our description of what constitutes a relevant observation and how to interpret such observations so as to test the theory. This area of the philosophy of science is called *semantics*. Unfortunately, this term has a substantially different meaning in the branch of linguistics that deals with the human response to the meaningfulness of symbols. In philosophy the notion of semantics is confined to the relationship between the elements and operators in a formal statement of theory and to operations that can be performed on real phenomena either in terms of manipulation or in terms of observation. Most of the pleas in the literature and in private discussions to define terms better are pleas for more rigorous attention to the semantics of the theory being discussed.

Logicians and general system theorists are prone to develop theories in terms of abstract symbols. Thus, some of the rigorous formulations of probability theory define probability as a number between zero and one that can be manipulated in certain ways (i.e., that possesses certain syntactical properties). Some of the proponents of this definition of probability act as if they are unconcerned with the "meaning" of probability as a measurement device or a predictive device or a descriptive term for real occurrences. Theories of this type are at least explicit about their relative unconcern with the semantic problem. A greater difficulty arises when theories use nouns and verbs from common language. Although the terms are in some cases defined syntactically by the theorist so that his manipulations are permissible, they often do not have clear definitions with reference to observations. In almost all cases, common English (or any other natural language) uses words too loosely for direct carry-over to a scientific usage.[5]

---

[5] For further development of this point, see the discussion of explication in R. Carnap, *Introduction to Semantics* (Cambridge, Mass.: Harvard University Press, 1948).

A good example of this is in the use of the term "preference" as it is used in economic utility theory and in consumer analysis. There is much discussion as to whether preferences are transitive or not, i.e., is it logically (syntactically) required that if I prefer lobster to chicken and prefer steak to lobster that I must prefer steak to chicken? Actual investigations of human preferences have revealed that in certain situations preferences are not transitive. In spite of this fact, many theoretical formulations using the concept of preference require that it be transitive. To a logician this is merely a case of using a particular term in two different ways, and if these two separate meanings are kept clearly differentiated, there is nothing but an awkward language problem; there is no logical difficulty. The logical difficulty occurs when the theorist is not specific about which meaning of preference he is using, and thus may try to describe actual consumer data on the basis of a theory that requires (in its formal sense) that preference be a transitive relationship.

As a more basic point in the discussion of the semantic requirements for theory, we can examine the requirements of an operational definition or preference. How do we measure preference? Should a person's preference be defined as the response to a verbal inquiry, or in terms of some actual behavior? If we take either of these positions we must specify the particular form of the verbal inquiry or the particular kind of behavior that we wish to observe. We also must know how to interpret the verbal response or the observation of behavior. If we examine the first possibility and say that we wish to define preference as the response given by a subject to a particularly worded question, we rapidly get into serious difficulty.

Suppose I am asked a particular question and in flippant or recalcitrant mood I answer exactly opposite to my real feelings. Do we wish to accept my response as a measurement of my preferences? If we do, then we need a theory that is useful for prediction even when the responses are from recalcitrant and flip respondents. If we do not, then we need a set of definitions that enables the interviewer to tell when I am being flip and recalcitrant and what to do about it. Since there is so much difficulty in defining preference as a verbal response, it will certainly be no easier to distinguish between a well-intentioned cooperative response and one that is designed to irritate the interviewer. It is this line of reasoning that has occasionally led psychologists to define intelligence as the score achieved on intelligence tests. If one accepts that definition seriously, the predictive power left to the concept of intelligence is the ability to predict scores on intelligence tests—not a very happy state of affairs.

If the operational definition of preferences in verbal terms is so unsatisfactory, let us examine the definition of preference in terms of real behavior. If the researcher wishes to measure my preference for lobster over chicken, and he observes me in a restaurant with a menu on which both lobster and chicken are available, and I choose chicken, is he then justified in saying that I prefer chicken to lobster? Maybe he should observe me in other restaurants at other times. Perhaps I would behave differently if the price for lobster were only half the price for chicken. Perhaps I would behave differently if I were at home rather than in a restaurant. Maybe the person with whom I am dining exerts an influence on my choice. Or perhaps I don't really care, and I pick the item that appears first on the menu. How the researcher handles these questions determines what he *means* by the term "preference." The investigation of preference in its behavioral setting has been one of the most difficult and awkward problems in psychology and in the management sciences.

Certainly a minimum requirement for the measurement of preference seems to be that the preference should be exhibited in more than one situation. If I am given a choice for President of the United States between Roosevelt and Dewey, and if one wishes to measure my preference by my voting behavior, they will have to examine a situation that occurred only once and will never occur again. Is it meaningful therefore to talk about my preference for Roosevelt or Dewey as President? If we say, "Yes, it is," we then have some extremely difficult syntactical problems related to the possibilities in terms of the predictive use of such a measurement. If we say, "No, it isn't," then we must specify how many observations *are* required for an adequate measure of preference. It is in this area of semantics that one can be arbitrary if he wishes, but the meaning of the definition of preference and of theories using it will be greatly affected by the particular result of the arbitrary decision.

Pragmatics. Even if a theory is adequately described in terms of its semantic and syntactic aspects, it still may not be a very good theory. The way in which it fails to be good may be because of a lack of attention to the richness or fruitfulness of the theory in terms of the needs, desires, and problems of the people who may have use for it. The aspect of the analysis of theory concerned with the *use* of theory is call *pragmatics*. We require of our theories that they be rich, fruitful, and useful and apply to important problems as well as that they be formally adequate and definitionally precise.

An investigation of the pragmatic requirements of theory takes us out of the realm of logical formalism and into the more difficult, but perhaps more vigorous, area in which philosophy is concerned with real problems of on-going human systems. If we explore seriously the pragmatic aspects of science, we are led rather directly to a concern with the problem of value. It is not enough for a theory to have a large number of deducible theorems; these theorems should apply to important problems. A theory with but a few deducible theorems that applied to the establishment of universal peace would be considered far more valuable than a theory whose outcome permitted the detailed construction of innumerable TV Westerns. The difficulties of dealing in a philosophically adequate way with the problem of value, though, are far too extensive to be more than indicated in this essay. Probably the central difficulty is the decision as to *whose* values at what time should be the controlling factor. If we adopt the notion that it is always the decision maker's values, then a lawyer should make decisions based on his best interests, not his client's. This approach also makes it difficult to deal with group decision making. It is not always easy to tell whether a theory will be useful and to whom. Many theories have been developed in "pure mathematics" and have later proved to be of high pragmatic value. The intellectual curiosity of one generation is the practical engineering tool of another.

Implications: Marketing Theory and Human Values

When we examine the goal requirements for marketing theory, we can identify at least three groups whose values must be overtly taken into account. These three groups are: the *institutions* engaged in the process of marketing (manufacturers, intermediate sellers, retailers, industrial sales groups, etc.), the *consuming public,* and the *government* policy maker. Even a cursory analysis of the goals for marketing theory and marketing science held by these three groups reveals conflicting as well as cooperative goals. Any major development of marketing science that served the goals of only one group at the expense of either of the other two would pose the same kind of ethical problem that nuclear physicists faced when almost their entire effort was devoted to harnessing the destructive energies of atomic power, rather than to a balanced development including the productive and medical uses of atomic energy.

In fact, one of the most difficult but pressing of all problems facing the development of theory in marketing is the resolution of conflict in goals. This is not only a problem for the eventual science of marketing, it is a problem for all existing sciences and disciplines, and indeed it is a problem for the individual. Every single person has to resolve conflicting demands on his time, on his resources, on his loyalties, on his emotions. That this resolution is not easy nor always satisfactory is shown by the statistics of our mental hospitals and the case records of our psychoanalysts. That it is no less satisfactory on a national and international level is shown by the state of world affairs and of the armaments race. The problem belongs to all of humanity, to philosophy, to mathematics, to politics, and even to marketing science. The requirements for theory in marketing and the problems engendered in meeting these requirements will surely tax the ingenuity and patience of the most resourceful and dogged of marketing theorists for years to come.